"This isn't just another book about how to produce a film; this is THE book about how to produce a film. No other book comes close to the detail, organization, and vast amount of knowledge in this volume. I've assigned Ryan's book as a professor, and I've used it as a resource for myself as a producer. If you want to produce movies, *Producer to Producer* is as essential as a pair of comfortable shoes."
—Jack Lechner, producer, *Blue Valentine, The Fog of War;* professor, Columbia University

"Ryan does for low-budget producing what Julia Child does for French cooking, simplifying the complex art of producing into clear, concise, achievable steps that come together into what looks like magic. With her book in hand, there will be a lot less rookie mistakes to regret. The wisdom of a veteran indie producer distilled into one of the clearest, ego-less guides I have read. She knows how much the details matter and never loses sight of the 'big picture.'"
—Hilary Brougher, writer/director, *The Sticky Fingers of Time, Stephanie Daley*

"I wish I had Ryan's incredible book when making my first three films. It has the answers to all the questions I had—and more. This is an indispensable book for any independent director."
—Ramin Bahrani, director, *99 Homes, Chop Shop*

"Even a few tidbits of hard-earned producing wisdom from Ryan can change your life. Luckily, in *Producer to Producer*, she offers readers several hundred, delivering nugget after priceless nugget of her mammoth expertise to anyone who can read. Follow her advice, and save yourself from the depthless horrors of bad producing!"
—Jeffrey K. Miller, TV producer, *Brew Dog,* and former student

"The information detailed in this book will support you to complete a project with knowledge, integrity and responsibility. Maureen A. Ryan, the author, has your back. If you are an independent filmmaker, live event producer, and/or student, this book is your blueprint to success. *Producer to Producer* is the PhD of Producing and you get a front row seat!"
—Sharon R. Herrick, entrepreneur and film school graduate

"A producer is an integral part of the creative team. *Producer to Producer* reflects Ryan's years of working in the film industry, teaching at a prominent university and mentoring emerging filmmakers. Her writing is both accessible and detailed; providing a stable foundation for those looking to build a producing career. The information is immediately applicable to a production of any size!"
—Veronica Nickel, producer, *First Match;* coproducer, *Moonlight*

"Ryan is a Producer's Producer. This is the manual for flawless producing: on budget, on schedule, and no (added) drama."
—Marilyn Ness, producer, *Cameraperson, Trapped, E-Team, 1971*

"I am very excited that a new edition of Maureen A. Ryan's *Producer to Producer* has been published. It is an invaluable guide, and hands down the best book on hands-on producing yet written. It should be on every producer's desk, kindle, or tablet!"
—Jason Kliot, producer, *Coffee and Cigarettes, Diggers;* professor, Brooklyn College's Feirstein Graduate School of Cinema

"This does what no book on production has done before—you actually can go out and make a movie after you read it. Ryan is one of the best independent producers working today and this book will show you why. Like her, it's thorough, thoughtful, and highly enjoyable. Whether you are a novice or a professional, there is much to learn here."
—Ben Odell, producer, *How to Be a Latin Lover, Spare Parts;* cofounder 3Pas Studios

"This book is essential reading for not just producers; but directors, writers, or anyone who hopes to work in film. Drawn from the author's extensive producing experience in independent film and as the overseer of countless productions at Columbia University, this is the perfect guide for the entire production process. If you can come up with a story, this book will help you make your movie."
—Ben Leonberg, creative director, YouVisit Studios

"*Producer to Producer* is the only book an aspiring producer needs. Ryan has brought her incredible talent and vast experience to the page and given a practical, utterly comprehensive account of independent producing. If you are producing a film and need a guiding hand, this is the book that will be dog-eared and worn at the end of your journey."
—Fritz Staudmyer, filmmaker and professor, Quinnipiac University

"Only Maureen A. Ryan, with her no-nonsense approach to film producing, could produce such a comprehensive and digestible book on such a complex subject. *Producer to Producer* is not only required reading for all of our film students but it is also the most referenced book in our curriculum."
—Justin Liberman, filmmaker and program director, Sacred Heart University, Film and Television Masters Program

"You never will ask 'what does a producer do?' once you read Maureen's brilliant book. She has fully described, in detail, all aspects of production, along with her own personal experiences. I consider it 'The Production Bible' for all producers—it has everything you need to produce your feature, short, or documentary film."
—Carole Dean, author, *The Art of Film Funding*, www.FromTheHeartProductions.com

"Where was this book when I needed it? The table of contents alone would have saved me days and dollars. For the first time ever, no filmmaker can make the excuse, 'I didn't know!'"
—Jeff Pucillo; actor/producer, *Roots in Water, Top of the World, Rich Man's Burden*

"An awesomely clear, detailed, and readable step-by-step guide to everything you ever needed to know about indie film production. And it comes from someone who knows what she's talking about—Maureen Ryan is one of the most effective and accomplished producers on the independent film scene today. This is the book we've all been waiting for! A must-read for everyone making, or even contemplating, an independent film."
—Susanna Styron; writer/director, *Shadrach, 100 Centre Street*

"Finally, a book that lays out, practically, how to get through a shoot. No one ever tells you this stuff—you're expected to learn it the hard way… until now. Written by one of the best producers I've ever worked with."
—Paul Cotter, writer/director, *Bomber, Shameless*

"Ryan's attention to every detail and her veteran outlook provide the assurance, guidance, and clarity for filmmakers to successfully deliver their creative babies. Her straight-shooting tone sets this book apart from 'how to' and theory books—truly marrying experience with the nuts and bolts that bring the process of filmmaking to life."
—Domenica Cameron Scorcese, writer/director, *Roots in Water; Spanish Boots*

"Maureen Ryan shares her extensive, first-hand experience as an independent producer and shepherds aspiring producers, step-by-step, through the entire process, creating a unique road map that will inevitably make both the creative and business journeys easier."
—Sharon Badal, professor, New York University, Tisch School of the Arts; author, *Swimming Upstream—A Lifesaving Guide to Short-Film Distribution*

"The textbook I rely on to support my lectures and reinforce the concepts I am introducing to my class is *Producer to Producer*. It is so well loved by my intermediate and advanced producing students that they no longer refer to as a textbook, but personalize it by saying "Maureen says…." Her templates, examples, resources, even her "crafty" list, are all so appreciated and utilized by my students."
—Laura J. Boyd, professor, Point Park University, Cinema Arts

PRODUCER TO PRODUCER

A Step-By-Step Guide to
LOW-BUDGET INDEPENDENT FILM PRODUCING
2ND EDITION

MAUREEN A. RYAN

MICHAEL WIESE PRODUCTIONS

Published by Michael Wiese Productions
12400 Ventura Blvd. #1111
Studio City, CA 91604
(818) 379-8799, (818) 986-3408 (FAX)
mw@mwp.com
www.mwp.com

Cover design by MWP
Interior design by William Morosi
Copyedited by David Wright

Manufactured in the United States of America
Copyright 2017 by Maureen A. Ryan
All rights reserved. No part of this book may be reproduced in any form or by any means without permission in writing from the author, except for the inclusion of brief quotations in a review.

Library of Congress Cataloging-in-Publication Data

Names: Ryan, Maureen A., author.
Title: Producer to producer / by Maureen A. Ryan.
Description: 2nd edition. | Studio City, CA : Michael Wiese Productions, 2017. | Includes index.
Identifiers: LCCN 2016043935 | ISBN 9781615933570
Subjects: LCSH: Motion pictures--Production and direction. | Low-budget films.
Classification: LCC PN1995.9.P7 R93 2017 | DDC 791.4302/32--dc23
LC record available at https://lccn.loc.gov/2016043935

For Rick

CONTENTS

FOREWORD . . . . *xv*

ACKNOWLEDGMENTS. . . . . *xvi*

INTRODUCTION. . . . . *xviii*

WHAT'S NEW ABOUT THE 2ND EDITION. . . . . *xx*

HOW THIS BOOK WORKS AND WHOM IT IS FOR . . . . *xxii*

1) DEVELOPMENT *1*
    Finding the Idea or Material *1*
    Learning to Say No *2*
    Study Scripts *3*
    Development Process *3*
    Rights Acquisition of Script and/or Underlying Material *4*
    Screenplay Creation and Revision *6*
    Screenwriting Software *15*
    Getting Feedback on the Script *15*
    Script Doctors *16*
    Writers Guild of America *16*
    Log Line—Don't Leave Home Without It *16*
    Log Line Creation *17*
    Creating a Proposal *19*
    Narrative Proposal Example *22*
    Documentary Proposal Example *35*
    IMDb.com *45*
    Creating a Pitch *45*
    Producing a Trailer *46*
    Distribution Plan *47*
    Marketing/Publicity Campaign *48*
    Presales *48*
    Sales Agents *49*
    Deliverables *50*
    Development Wrap Up *50*
    Final Checklist Before Deciding to Produce the Film *50*

2) SCRIPT BREAKDOWN 52
Nuts and Bolts 53
Breakdown Details 54
Filling In the Script Breakdown Sheet 62
Schedule Analysis of *Sundae* 64
Summary 66
Using the Breakdown to Adjust Your Script 66

3) BUDGETING 69
Budgeting Overview 69
When Should You Create a First Budget? 70
Everything but the Kitchen Sink 71
Budgeting Software 71
Budget Breakdown 72
Estimated Budget 74
Spreadsheet Mechanics 74
Geography of the Budget 75
Top Sheet 75
Creating the Estimated Budget 77
Detailed Line Items 77
Sundae Budgeting Case Study 94
Sundae Budget Analysis 103
Cash-Flow Schedule 103
Locked Budget and Working Budget 104
Padding and Contingency 105
Budget Actualization 105
Tax Resale Certificates 105
Tax Incentives/Credits 106

4) FUNDING 108
Presales 108
Sales Agents 109
Equity Investors 110
Deferred Payment Deals 110
Union Signatory Film Agreements 111
Donations and Fiscal Sponsorship 111
Reaching Out to Interested Communities 113
How to Ask for Donations and Discounts 113
Grants 115
Creative Labs 116
Fundraising Trailers 116
Find a Mentor or Executive Producer .116
Crowdfunding 117
Beware of Credit Cards as a Way of Funding Your Project's Budget 118

5) CASTING ... 120
- Hiring a Casting Director ... 120
- Attaching an Actor or "Star" to Your Project ... 122
- Pay-or-Play Deal ... 123
- Attaching Talent and Casting Without a Casting Director ... 123
- The Casting Process ... 124
- Auditions/Casting Sessions ... 124
- Callbacks ... 126
- Labor Rules for Minors ... 126
- Extras/Background Actor Casting ... 126
- Casting Schedule and Backups ... 127
- To Be Union or Not to Be Union ... 127
- SAG-AFTRA Bond/Escrow ... 129
- Union Paperwork/Station 12 ... 129

6) PRE-PRODUCTION ... 131
- Production Triangle ... 131
- Need to Get the Money in the Bank ... 132
- Pre-production Countdown ... 133
- Pre-production Countdown Explanations ... 136

7) LOCATIONS ... 177
- Create Location Lists ... 177
- The Specifics of Location Scouting ... 178
- Location Photo Folders ... 179
- Check with Local Film Commissions for Leads ... 179
- Alternatives to Hiring a Location Scout ... 180
- Finalizing Location Decisions ... 181
- Negotiating the Deal ... 182
- Back-up Locations ... 183
- Paperwork ... 183
- Location Release Form ... 184
- General Liability Insurance Certificate ... 184
- Co-ops and Condos ... 185
- Permits ... 185
- Police/Fire/Sheriff's Departments ... 186
- Tech Scout ... 186
- Shoot-day Protocol ... 186
- Run Through with Owner ... 187
- Leave It Better Than You Found It ... 187
- Green Set Protocols ... 187
- Idiot Check ... 188
- The Day After the Location Shoot ... 188
- Tax Incentive Programs ... 189

8) HIRING CREW 190
Crew Positions: Who Does What 190
Finding Talented Crew 193
Where to Find Crew 193
Hiring Criteria 194
Watch Demo Reels 195
Check References 195
On Hold/Confirm or Book/Release 196
Salary Negotiation/Most Favored Nation 197
Hiring Paperwork 197

9) LEGAL 199
It's All About Rights 200
It's All About Liability 200
Breakdown of a Legal Document 201
Legal Concepts 202
List of Agreements During Each Phase 204
Legal Corporate Entities 206
Never Sign Anything Without Proper Legal Advice 207
Your Lawyer Is an Extension of You 208
Attorney as Financier/Executive Producer/Producer's Rep ... 209

10) INSURANCE 210
Why Do You Need Insurance? 210
Common Insurance Policies 211
Completion Bond/Guaranty 217
How Do You Obtain Insurance? 218
How Insurance Brokers Work 219
Certificate Issuance 220
Insurance Audits 221
What to Do When You Have a Claim 221
Things You Should Know 222
Never Go into Production Without Insurance 222

11) SCHEDULING 224
Overview 224
Script Breakdown 225
Element Sheet Creation 225
Scheduling Principles 239
Scheduling Steps 242
Sundae Shooting Schedule Analysis 243
Shooting Stripboard Creation 245
Day-Out-of-Days Schedule 246

Scheduling each shoot day—how do you know how long
   something will take to shoot?.....................249
Feeding your crew every 6 hours and other union regulations
   that affect the day's schedule....................249
Portrait of a 1st Assistant Director....................251
Locking the Schedule...................................252

12) PRODUCTION..254
The Night Before Your First Day of Principal Photography..........254
First Day of Principal Photography.....................256
Wrap Checklist...260
Second Day Disasters...................................261
Enemy of the Production................................262
Actualized Budget......................................263
Cigars and Fine Chocolates.............................264

13) SAFETY..267
Safety for All...267
Preparing for Safety in Pre-production.................268
Location Permissions and Planning......................270
On-Set Precautions and Protocols.......................272
Speaking Up..275
Security for Post Production and Deliverables..........276
Equipment Monitoring and Protection....................276
Safety Protocols for Equipment and Special Conditions..279
Global Safety Issues...................................284

14) WRAP..287
Wrapping Out...287
Loss & Damaged/Missing & Damaged.......................288
Deposit Checks and Credit Card Authorizations..........288
Actualized Budget......................................288
Petty Cash...289
Budget Analysis..298
Wrap Paperwork...298
Wrap Party...299

15) POST PRODUCTION...................................301
Workflow...301
Picking a Format.......................................302
Camera Test/Workflow Test..............................305
Tech Specs Sheet.......................................305
How to Put Together a Post Production Team.............306

Planning for Post *307*
Digital Workflow Example. *308*
Post Finishing Information (film only) *312*
Film Negative and Match Back (film only) *313*
Deliverables *314*
Work-in-Progress Screenings *317*

16) AUDIO *320*

Sound Recording During Principal Photography. *320*
How to Get the Best Sound on Set. *321*
Tech Scouts *321*
Room Tone *322*
Wild Sound *323*
Audio Post Production *323*
Building Audio Tracks/Sound Design *323*
Adding Sound Effects. *324*
Creating and Recording Foley. *324*
Recording ADR. *324*
Laying in Music Tracks *325*
Sound Mixing *325*
Layback *326*
Dolby Digital, DTS, and THX *326*

17) MUSIC *328*

Obtaining Music Rights. *328*
What Rights Do You Need?. *329*
Putting in the License Request. *331*
Music Rights Request Letter Format *332*
Negotiating for the Music Rights. *333*
Most Favored Nation. *334*
Out-of-Copyright/Public Domain Music. *335*
Fair Use *335*
E&O Insurance *336*
Blanket TV Agreements *336*
Music Cue Sheet. *336*
Cease and Desist. *337*
What Happens if You Can't Find the Copyright Holder?. *337*
Music Rights Clearance Person/Company. *337*
Original Music Compositions for Your Project. *338*
Music Libraries and Royalty-Free Music. *339*
Music Supervisors. *339*

18) ARCHIVE MATERIALS.........................341
- Archive and Research.........................341
- Steps to Acquire and Use Archive Materials in Your Project..........342
- Archive Researcher.........................342
- Archive Libraries.........................343
- National Archives and Records Administration.....................343
- Fair Use.........................344
- Archival Usage and Negotiation.........................344
- License Paperwork.........................345
- Cease and Desist.........................345

19) MARKETING/PUBLICITY.........................347
- Producer of Marketing and Distribution.........................348
- Social Media.........................348
- Website.........................349
- Press Kit.........................350
- Production Stills and Publicity Photos.........................356
- Crowdfunding.........................356
- IMDb.com.........................357
- Screeners.........................357
- Social Action Campaigns (SAC).........................358
- Key Artwork.........................359
- How to Hire a Publicist.........................359

20) FILM FESTIVALS.........................361
- Fee Waivers and Screening Fees.........................362
- Film Festival Strategy—A, B, C and Niche.........................363
- Film Markets.........................364
- Film Festival Premieres.........................365
- Oscar Eligibility.........................365
- Other Awards.........................366
- In or Out of Competition.........................366
- Jury and Audience Awards.........................366
- What to Expect from a Film Festival.........................367
- Posters, Postcards, and Photos.........................367
- Technical Issues at Festivals.........................368
- Tech Test.........................368

21) DISTRIBUTION/SALES................................370
Sales Agents..370
International Sales 372
Theatrical/Television Sales 372
DVD/VOD/Digital Sales................................372
Deliverables 373
Self Distribution 373
Pick of the Week/Contests 373
Future Distribution Models...........................374

22) WHAT'S NEXT?...375

INDEX...377

ABOUT THE AUTHOR 384

FOREWORD

Maureen Ryan has been producing my films from the time of our very first meeting in the spring of 1997. Our first project together was a daunting, ambitious period film with no obvious commercial prospects and a tiny budget provided by the BBC.

You'd have to be crazy to want to produce this film—it involved elaborate historical recreations that needed to be filmed across all four seasons, on location in Wisconsin. There were stunts with horses and steam trains, hangings, shootings, and burnings. The script called for a 19th-century mansion to be burned down. All of this was achieved—and more—across a production that sprawled over two years on a budget that was little more than that of a well-funded music video of the time. It turned out that Maureen wasn't crazy at all—she was just methodical, resourceful, and bold. Looking back now, I still don't know how we did it. Or, rather, how she did it—though some of the answers can now be found in this new edition of her well-regarded book.

The resulting film, *Wisconsin Death Trip*, premiered at the Telluride and Venice Film Festivals and was theatrically released in the United States and the United Kingdom. It even turned a small profit. Our collaborations have grown in budget and scope since then. We've worked together on documentaries and features and have grown together in our experience of production. Like all filmmakers, we've never quite had the resources we wanted. The genius of a great producer is to never let you feel that is a problem.

So, Maureen knows what she is talking about. In this book anyone who's involved—or wants to be involved—in film production, at any level, will find answers to every question and pitfall a production generates. Like her productions, the book is clear, detailed, generous, and inspiring and this edition has been updated to reflect all of the changes to the film industry since the first edition was published.

—*James Marsh, February 2017*

ACKNOWLEDGMENTS

A sincere thanks to all the talented students I've been blessed to work with over the last decades. You constantly remind me of why I love what I do. Especially my students at Columbia University's School of the Arts Graduate Film Program—I've learned more from you than you can imagine.

Thanks to Carole Dean for your constant support and encouragement throughout the writing of this book. Your insights, weekly notes, and intuition have been a steady beacon while I wrote the first edition and this new one.

Thanks to all the contributors for their interviews and expert experience. You took the book to a whole other level with your contributions—Ben Odell, Christine Sadofsky, George Rush, Zach Seivers, Paul Cotter, Dave Anaxagoras, Andrew Hauser, Jennifer Tromski, and Rick Siegel. A special thanks to the filmmakers who shared the case study film materials and proposal examples—Sonya Goddy, Birgit Gernboeck, Tina Braz, Ben Leonberg, Marilyn Ness, Katy Chevigny, and Ross Kauffman.

My thanks to the directors I have had the pleasure of working with and learning from over the last two decades—John Nathan, Michael McNamara, James Marsh, Albert Maysles, Sheila Curran Dennin, Paul Cotter, Alex Gibney, and Johanna Hamilton. You all live the mantra "it's all about the project" and I am grateful to have been able to produce your work.

Thanks to my mentors. This is a tough industry and your example and guidance made all the difference during the forks in the road—Marc Sarazin, Jon Fontana, Lewis Cole, Annette Insdorf, Dan Kleinman, and Jamal Joseph.

A big thank you to my old friend Adam Sexton, this book would not be what it is without your invaluable expertise and guidance. My gratitude to my literary agent Jennifer Unter for all of your help. Thanks to copy editor David Wright—your steady hand and insightful attention to detail made this edition so much better. Thanks to Michael Wiese and Ken Lee at MWP—your support of me and my books has enabled them to get into the world and help so many people. Thank you to research assistant Geoff Quan, designer Bill Morosi and cover artist John Brenner. Gratitude for excellent notes from Assistant Professor Laura J. Boyd and her class at Point Park University. I also want to thank the staff at The Standard Grill in NYC for keeping me hydrated and fed at Table 12 as I worked on this new edition.

I want to thank all the crews I have had the honor to work with. Your dedication and commitment to the work is a moving thing to watch and be a part of. Thanks for making my heart skip a beat every time I walk onto a film set.

Finally, thanks to my partner Rick. Your kind heart, great eye, and constant, unconditional love is a deep source of encouragement and inspiration.

INTRODUCTION

It's a hot August afternoon somewhere in Appleton, Wisconsin. The corset I'm wearing under this Victorian-era peasant dress is digging into my ribs. I and it are filthy because I'm lying in a pit of mud in a chicken coop on some godforsaken farm. Did I mention I'm in rural Wisconsin? As I try to distract myself from the pain and filth, I hear the shout of "Action!" from the film director who sits comfortably behind the video monitor as the key grip and production assistants begin pelting me with potatoes. They actually are trying to hit the wooden slat above my head but they often miss and hit me instead.

Trying not to think about the bruises that are beginning to form on my limbs and back, I concentrate on the very obvious question that I should have asked about an hour ago: "How the hell did I get myself into this?" It's too late now. There's only one answer—I'm producing a low-budget film and we can't afford any more extras.

And the truth is, I wouldn't want to be anywhere else. Why? Because I love what I do—I'm an independent film producer.

Be passionate. Be serious.

Wake up.

—*Susan Sontag*

This book in your hands is about film producing. Every page is filled with all the knowledge I think is essential to produce well. Because that's the goal here—to produce *well*.

Anyone can learn to make a budget, hire a crew, and take all the steps necessary to produce a film and this book will teach you all of those steps. The ultimate goal of this book is to teach you how to produce in a way that gets the project completed on time and under budget, to teach you how to stretch the precious dollar in the right places, but also how to produce with integrity, decency, respect, and wit. I hope that's what makes this book different.

To me, that's the prize. That's what makes all the hard work worthwhile and that's how it should always be. Nothing else will do. If that appeals to you, then please read on.

By the way, my scene never made it to the final cut. But that's OK, that film was the first of six films I would make with that director—one of them won an Academy Award. It's the journey, not the glory, that makes film producing so satisfying. It's about jumping in and doing what it takes. Even if it involves a Victorian dress and a chicken coop on some farm in northern Wisconsin.

—Maureen A. Ryan, April 2017

WHAT'S NEW ABOUT THE 2ND EDITION

A LOT HAS HAPPENED SINCE the first edition of *Producer to Producer* was published in 2010. The book has been more successful than I could have hoped for. Read and used by filmmakers all over the world, that edition was translated into Chinese and Japanese and it's gratifying to hear from filmmakers how the book has helped them produce their many and varied projects. It's become the go-to book for film production classes across the United States and it's satisfying to know that professors have made it required reading for their course syllabi.

A lot has happened in the world of filmmaking, too. The technological advances are coming at a faster rate than ever before, which has changed the way we conceive of and make our projects in big and small ways. Our access to the means of production, distribution channels, and new audiences is evolving constantly. It's a terrific time to be a filmmaker, producer, and content creator. And thus the need for a newly updated and expanded book.

Producer to Producer, 2nd Edition is packed with the most up-to-date

> *Attention is the rarest and purest form of generosity.*
>
> —*Simone Weil*

information about all the steps and ways of making great film projects. It covers the latest innovations and technology that every producer needs to know and understand when making a project. It will help you to connect with everything and everyone you need to support your vision and creation.

In this edition, I added two new chapters that are key to being the best producer you can be: *Hiring Crew* and *Safety*. There's a new case study film titled *Sundae,* new fiction and non-fiction treatments/proposals and the production templates—script breakdown, budget, etc.—at ProducertoProducer.com have all been updated and you can access them anytime at the website. Revising and updating the entire book has enabled me to pack it full with the latest information, best practices, and advice to help you to produce your projects in the best possible way and to realize your full potential.

Those are all the things that have been changed in this revised book. What *has not* changed is the step-by-step, tried-and-true information that allows you to go out and produce well, whether it is your first project or your twentieth. There is something here for everyone, whether you are a film student taking a production course at a university, a first-time producer figuring out how to make a YouTube project, or a professional producer who wants to use the book for its reminders, checklists, case study, and templates. This new edition of *Producer to Producer* will guide and support you in all your creative filmmaking projects.

HOW THIS BOOK WORKS AND WHOM IT IS FOR

I'M ALWAYS ASKED, "WHAT does a producer do?" My simple answer is "They make the project *happen*." Without a producer, there isn't a project. When I teach university producing classes which focus on no/low-budget filmmaking, there is always a directing student who says, "I can't afford a producer," and I always reply, "You can't afford *not* to have one."

Producer to Producer teaches you how to produce independent low-budget productions—narrative features, digital series, documentaries, short films, music videos, etc. The principles and steps involved are the same whether it is for a 6-day shoot or a 28-day schedule. If you are gathering all the materials, cast, and crew for a short film, you still need to follow all the same rules and regulations as you would for a web series or a feature-length project.

This book is put together in general chronological order for the steps taken to make a film. All aspects of film producing are here and directly reflect my specific background as a producer. I came up through the production ranks as a line producer, so this book will be grounded in that

It's the wanting to know that makes us human.

—*Tom Stoppard,* Arcadia

particular perspective. I'm the type of person who likes to *make* a project and not just *talk* about making one. I find that often, if you can produce it for less money, you can make it happen faster and easier. I'd rather do it and get it done for less than waste time gathering up more resources or collecting more money with strings attached. This book will take you through all the steps to produce your project well—with creativity and finesse.

I think it's helpful to define what a producer does and there are many different kinds of producers with several different titles. Let's go through them here. The Producers Guild of America is a good resource for information. Their website is *www.producersguild.org*. I've included a summary based on their definitions for each title:

Executive Producer—the person who brings in financing for the project or makes a significant contribution to the development of the literary property.

Producer—the person who puts together various elements for the project, such as purchasing the rights to underlying material, coming up with the idea for the project, hiring a screenwriter, optioning and/or purchasing a script, attaching actors (talent) to a film, hiring key department heads, overseeing production and post production, and bringing in financing.

Co-producer—the person who is responsible for the logistics of the production of the film or a particular aspect of the film.

Line Producer—the person who is responsible for the logistics of the production, from pre-production through completion of production.

Associate Producer—the person responsible for one or more producing functions delegated by the producer or coproducer.

Depending on your budget, your project may only have a few of these positions, but the producing *principles* are the same.

Please note that in this book I will refer to any production (no matter what format or genre) as a "project." Most projects are shot on digital video, but to simplify the grammar I'll use the word "film" or "filmmaking" in a generic sense, regardless of what format it was captured on. I will refer to the reader of this book as a *producer*. You may be a director, production manager, screenwriter, filmmaker, or producer (or a combination of several of these), but this book is for the producer or the *producer in you*.

In addition, this book is directed toward low-budget, independent productions. There are other books out there that concentrate on Hollywood and big-budget features. There also are lots of books dedicated to the topics of development, finance, and distribution. I will discuss those topics only insofar as they impact the low-budget side of the spectrum of filmmaking. This book is for the **low-budget, independent filmmaker** and I will assume, throughout the book, that you have limited funds for your project and that the project's ambitions go beyond what those dollars can normally afford. I say "normally" because this book will help you to stretch your dollars as far as humanly possible to give you the highest production values at the lowest cost.

On the philosophical side, as a producer I truly believe that everyone wants to be a part of something that is bigger than themselves. People like being a part of something special that inspires them—and that's what a good project does. And good film producing can provide that experience for all those associated with it. Often that experience is worth more to someone than a paycheck. A good producer can create that and that is what I intend to do with this book.

Throughout each chapter there will be words in **bold** that I'll define along the way. At the end of each chapter there will be points that I wish to highlight and you will find them under the **Recap** heading. Finally, there is the website *www.ProducerToProducer.com* that contains lots of information that you can use, like downloadable documents and templates, essential production information, and important links for you to refer to when making your film.

So let's get started.

For downloadable production templates or to get in touch with Maureen Ryan, please go to *www.ProducerToProducer.com*

For more resources, go to *www.mwp.com* and click *Resources*

CHAPTER 1
DEVELOPMENT

DEVELOPMENT REFERS TO THE time period and resources it takes to bring an idea to full maturation as a final script with full financing. Ideas can be completely original or be derived from underlying material—such as a novel, magazine article, comic book, theater play, television show, web series, or graphic novel. This process involves the creative aspects of writing and revising a script, as well as the legal steps of optioning or purchasing underlying material and procuring the proper releases and contracts. Simultaneously, you are looking for and finalizing the financing, as well. Once you have completed these steps, you will enter the next one—pre-production. The process from first idea/concept to final distribution is usually anywhere from two to five years for a long-form project. Some projects have an even longer gestation period. Keep that in mind as you begin the journey.

Politics is the art of the possible, while art is the art of the possibility of the impossible.

—*Tony Kushner*

Finding the Idea or Material

With the knowledge of how long it will take you to create a project from start to finish, the first thing you want to keep in mind is that you need to love the project. As the producer, it's going to be a part of you for the rest of your life, so choose wisely. Make sure it's a project you are passionate about because there will be many twists and turns on the road to completion. It's just too damn hard otherwise.

Take some time to think about what excites you, energizes you, holds your attention. Figure out what makes you laugh, what's your particular "take" on things. For nonfiction projects, think about what topic inspires you; what do you want to explore? It needs to sustain you intellectually and emotionally for a long, hard time.

When deciding what project you want to produce, also consider where this project fits in with your vision for your career. Is it in keeping with where you want to be in five years? Is it a step forward in the right direction or is it a path down another road that doesn't lead to where you ultimately want to go? Is it the perfect vehicle for you to get from where you are now to where you want to be? When I decided to produce my first feature documentary, *Wisconsin Death Trip,* I was line producing country music videos and commercials in Nashville, Tennessee. I loved the treatment for the film and believed in the project with all my heart. It was also a way for me to move toward my dream of producing documentaries full time. So I worked part time on *Wisconsin Death Trip* for two and a half years while I made a living producing videos for country artists like Dolly Parton and Junior Brown. It was really hard to do, but when the film premiered it was well received, won many awards, and played in theaters and on television … and I had taken a big step toward my goal.

Learning to Say No

Producers are in an enviable place in the film industry. We are the creative engine for any given project, so if you are good at what you do, people will offer you projects and ask for your assistance—often. So talented producers need to learn to say no. Saying yes is kind of easy but saying no for most people is much harder.

Producers need to figure out their own criteria for collaboration and get good at seeing—and then listening to—"red flags," or else your time will be wasted and your plans derailed. By defining your own taste, values, and goals, you can determine if a specific project is right for you and if this is the right time. Be vigilant so you can stay on track and create the kind of work you want to put your talents toward and then stick to those goals.

Study Scripts

Spend time learning what makes a great script. Read lots of already produced scripts and educate yourself by determining what elements compose an excellent one. Find the scripts you love at the library or online and study them. Watching them on screen is *not* the same thing. You need to read them line by line—analyze the structure, figure out the beats, and decide what makes a captivating protagonist and compelling narrative—to really understand what makes a stellar screenplay. Producer Shelby Stone (*Lackawanna Blues, Bessie*) calls it "mapping." She takes a great, already produced script and breaks it down, beat by beat, and maps the beginning and end of each act on paper so she can analyze what makes that particular project work so well. Then she uses that information and compares it to the scripts she is developing to make sure she is on track. You don't need to reinvent the wheel, just use great past work as a template for your great future work.

Better yet, buy books that contain great screenplays in which the author analyzes them and demonstrates how they are crafted. Or take a screenwriting class to learn the principles of the screenplay form. Even if you don't want to be a writer, you will learn the basics of screenwriting and they will be invaluable as you develop a script with a writer. Producers need to know what/how to achieve compelling storytelling at the craft level so they can give excellent script notes and guidance during development.

Lastly, read lots of current scripts—good and bad—in the genre you wish to produce. *Merriam-Webster's Collegiate Dictionary* defines genre as "a category of artistic, musical, or literary composition characterized by a particular style, form, or content." It is the type of project you plan to make, such as horror, comedy, drama, sci-fi, fantasy, documentary, or animation. There are subgenres too, like coming-of-age films, road movies, and buddy films. These genres have a specific set of rules that drive the narrative and character development. The audience gets its enjoyment from the creativity of the project itself, but also how it follows the "rules" of that genre. Learn them so you can combine them in a different way or subvert them. Decide what you want to produce and really go to "school" on it.

Development Process

The development process can be broken down into five steps—1) Rights acquisition of script and/or underlying materials; 2) Screenwriting and revision; 3) Proposal/pitch document creation; 4) Financing procurement; 5) Tentative distribution plan creation. We'll go through them here:

Rights Acquisition of Script and/or Underlying Material

A project may originate as a screenplay or it could come from some other material to be used for adaptation. Such possible materials can include magazine or newspaper articles, short stories, novels, comic books, graphic novels, blogs, theater plays, games, apps, TV shows, web series, screenplays, or another film. If the idea comes from another format, you'll need to obtain the rights to that material to be on solid legal ground. Do this before wasting your time and energy in trying to adapt the material. Inquire first to make sure someone else doesn't already own the film rights. Hollywood studios and film production companies have departments dedicated to discovering new material for potential film projects. They often get a book in pre-publication galley format so they can see it before everyone else and have a chance to purchase the rights first.

Documentaries are often based on already published material about the subject matter. *Man on Wire*, a film I coproduced, is about Philippe Petit, the high-wire artist who walked between the World Trade Center towers in 1974. In 2002, Philippe wrote a book titled *To Reach the Clouds* about the miraculous event. The film's producer, Simon Chinn, purchased the rights to that book and negotiated a deal for Philippe's involvement in the film before he went to financiers to obtain funding for the film. This important step assured the investors that the producer held the proper rights to the underlying material to make the film, without fear of any rights problems further down the line.

Around the same time as Chinn's successful negotiations, Philippe Petit sold the narrative film rights to film director Robert Zemeckis and in 2015 the theatrical 3-D film version titled *The Walk* premiered. This is a great example of how a rights holder can "split the rights" for different kinds of projects. Who knows, there may be an opera or Broadway musical some day from the same underlying materials!

But before we get into the particulars, let's discuss the meaning of the word "rights." **Rights** is short for copyright—or the right to copy. According to Michael Donaldson in his comprehensive book *Clearance and Copyright*, "copyright law does not protect ideas. Copyright law only protects 'the expression of an idea that is fixed in a tangible form.'"

For our discussion in this chapter, we will concentrate on literary-type rights needed for script development. Music rights will be covered in the *Music* chapter, later in this book.

Here's what you need to consider when obtaining the rights for a project:

1. Do you need **exclusive** or **non-exclusive** rights? Is it OK for someone else to also own the rights to material that you use for the basis of your script? Or do you need to own it exclusively? The price will be higher if you require exclusivity.

2. For how long do you need the rights? In perpetuity or a fixed period of time? Generally, you want to own rights **in perpetuity** (forever), but sometimes you may want to purchase rights for a shorter period of time, especially to start with. You could negotiate an **option** for the rights for a year or two with the ability to acquire the rights for a longer period of time, automatically. With an option, you can develop the project more cost effectively and then pay a higher fee for the full rights once you know the project is funded and is going to be produced.

3. Who is the proper and legal rights holder? Do the research to ensure you know who definitively owns the rights. They must own the copyright and be able to prove it so you have a legally binding agreement. Life rights are the rights to the details of a private person's life that are not in the public domain. If you have these rights, the individual can't sue you for using his or her life story.

4. What rights do you need? There are different kinds of rights, based on distribution/viewing format and the country or region: theatrical (domestic and foreign); domestic TV; domestic cable TV; international TV; Video on Demand (VOD); DVD; internet/online; streaming; film festivals; cell phone; and probably a few more since this book was published. Regarding regions, it is usually best to purchase all of them, commonly referred to as **worldwide** rights. But sometimes you don't need all those rights, or you can't afford them, or they are not available. You have to weigh all of these possibilities with what you know and what you anticipate your needs will be, now and in the future. Technology is changing quickly, so make sure to look ahead and stay on top of the current and future state of the industry.

5. Film festival rights are usually affordable. Some of my students option the rights to a short story when producing their short films. Often the

author will give them non-exclusive film festival rights to the story for free or at a small cost. This is helpful and allows you to screen at film festivals for almost no money. But if your film does well and someone wants to buy the rights to your film for a television broadcast or some other distribution, you are going to have to go back to the rights holder and re-negotiate for additional rights. The rights holder could ask for more money than you can afford and then you won't be able to make the deal. *You always want to plan for your film's success!* A good way to future-proof your film is to make an initial deal for the festival rights and simultaneously negotiate fees for the additional rights you would need if your film was successful—internet, DVD, television, streaming, etc. And *get it in writing*—so you'll know the costs before you begin to produce your film and be able to refer to it if you go back to the rights holder later on.

6. Add **future technology rights** to any agreement that you sign. You want to future-proof your ability to exploit your film to your own best advantage. Having rights for "media known and unknown" is necessary to make sure the rights will follow any new technology that has yet to be invented.

All of this should be done with the assistance of an entertainment attorney. Make sure your lawyer approves the final contract *before* you sign it.

Screenplay Creation and Revision

As discussed above, it is important to know what makes a great screenplay. Work hard to get it right and learn to give good, clear, and helpful notes to the screenwriter. "Writing" is actually a misnomer. It's actually *rewriting*. It's the revision process that will make all the difference. Make sure the script is rewritten and rewritten until it is the best you and the writer can possibly create. Benjamin Odell (*Girl in Progress, How To Be a Latin Lover*), the talented producer and cofounder of 3Pas Studios, has a lot of experience regarding script revision and the development process. Following is the transcript of an interview I held with Ben regarding his thoughts and experience with these topics.

> **Maureen: What are the most important steps a producer needs to take to develop a project successfully?**
>
> **Ben:** First and foremost is ownership of material, what will eventually be called "chain of title." One of the first things [a distributor or a studio]

asks for is chain of title, which follows who owns the rights to the underlying material and how those rights were transferred from the original source material, whether it be a novel or a documentary or an idea, to the screenwriter, to the producer, and then to the distributor who's going to control those rights for some period of time.

So when you're developing material, the question you have to ask yourself is: Where are the ideas coming from? Where is the material coming from? And are those rights controlled? If they're not controlled by you, the first thing you have to figure out is how to control them long enough to develop the material into something that you can use to raise the money and make the film.

So many first-time producers get really far into projects—they find a script they like, they develop it with the writer, and they put a lot of energy into sort of shaping the material so it'll work. Then, at some point, when they're ready to do the deal, they haven't discussed and signed and sort of buttoned down the terms of the deal, and the writer walks away or extorts them or feels like he or she deserves more. So buttoning down rights is, by far, the first thing to think about before you think from a creative point of view.

Secondly, as a producer, I think you always have to think about and ask yourself: Who's my audience? Who am I developing this material for? Who is the end user? I think that's the huge difference between a producer and a screenwriter/director. Producers have to really think about the end game where the filmmakers are thinking about their vision and, to some degree, I think producers have the obligation when they're looking for material to say, "*Is this a project I can sell?*" And if it's going to be a hard sell or if you want to take an artistic approach to material, as a producer, you have to go in knowing that.

When you're searching for material ask yourself: "*Who's going to want to see this?*" I think it's important, too, before you get into development, to sort of see where the business is.

If you already have a project you like, I think you have to ask those tough questions before you buy any material or spend any time really developing. People don't really consider this part of development but the truth is, as a producer, I think your obligation first is to understand the reality of the business.

Then sometimes it's like—throw all caution to the wind and do it because there is no logic to it and you don't know if there is an audience there, but you love it and that's fine, too. But I think you have to go into it clear about the reality. I see so many young producers who are perhaps too optimistic about the value of their projects in the marketplace. They're developing material that leaves them so shocked when they can't find anywhere to take their projects and they don't know what to do with them.

Maureen: You are a writer yourself and you've written screenplays. I'd love to hear your philosophy about giving great notes to screenwriters and the revision process.

Ben: First off, when you're in this position of making low-budget films, the one thing you obviously don't have is money to buy scripts. So, more often than not, what you're going to do is option a script for a period of time, while you develop it and then you're going to try to get it made or raise the money.

Draw up an option, negotiate it, and sign it with the writer. Obviously there is going to be very little money involved and I think that inherently changes the nature of the relationship between the producer and the writer, because you have to be much more diplomatic in your approach to development.

Development money is the riskiest money—I don't like to spend money early on. I like to develop at least to a certain point before I spend any money.

One of the first things I'll do if I read a screenplay that I think is 50% there is I'll sit down with the writer and try to understand his or her vision of the screenplay. In other words, not what's on the page but what they tried to get on the page. Because oftentimes I think where the problems come between a producer and a screenwriter is that the producer doesn't try to understand where the screenwriter is going. So when the producer is giving notes to the writer, the writer is fighting those notes because, in her head, the movie is something completely different.

So I think there is a process early on and I think it's pre-option, where you're really trying to figure out what the writer's vision is and then you try to also sort of say, *OK. Is that my vision? Is that what I liked about the screenplay?* And if it isn't, then you need to have that conversation and you have to be very transparent about how you envision the movie, because it has to be all clear beforehand, it's like entering into a marriage. If you don't understand where the writer envisions the movie going and where you envision it and those things aren't cleared up, most likely you'll find yourself, a year later, incredibly frustrated and won't have gotten anywhere. So that's the first process. Try to bring the writer's complete vision to the foreground, even if it's not in the screenplay, and then compare it to your own.

Then, even pre-option, I would recommend that you sort of say, *OK, this is what I feel like the movie needs.* Oftentimes what I'll do is say, *Watch this movie because I feel like that's the tone. The tone that you have isn't right.* Try to find movies or novels or whatever it is that you can give to the other people to express where you think the screenplay needs to go. Then sit down again—and this could take a month or two—and see if you can get on the same page.

At the end of the day, what I do is I keep a log, like a development log. Every time I give notes to a writer I keep those notes in a log so that I know where the script went at the end of the process and I know how I impacted that script—and that's for a lot of reasons. It's also for legal reasons, and I guess, on some level, for my own gratification to understand my impact on the script, and it's also because sometimes you find yourself with a screenplay that's developed and it's gone in a direction that you hadn't imagined.

It's always good to be able to go back and see where it all went wrong and say, *Remember, the original idea that we talked about is that this movie is about a man who will go to all ends to stay … It's the strength of paternal love. And, look, we've gone off. Let's go back and look at these original notes and look at what you said.* You can always go back to that original idea that got things going.

Maureen: Do you ever put your notes in writing and send to the writer? Or is that done in your conversations and they take notes from that meeting?

Ben: I usually go in, take notes, write them down, email them to the writer, get on the phone with the writer, and go through the notes. What I try to do—and I'm not sure that I always succeed—is let them air their complaints because it's such a personal thing. It's people's egos and their lives and their emotions are wrapped up in their characters. So often the main character is some reflection of the writer.

So when you're giving notes it can get very touchy and emotional; so you sort of let them react to your notes. First, let them read them, digest them, you give them a couple days to react to the notes, and then you sit down, chew on them, and then take it from there.

I think every development process with every writer is completely different and part of your job as a producer is to be a psychologist and figure out how to best get where you need to go and the way they need to deliver notes. So, often, if you have an idea that you think would work, the best way to get it to work for the writer is to somehow make her think it's her own idea.

It's just not to make them think it is. It's to somehow get them engaged with the idea in such a way—I can't tell you how many times I'll give a writer an idea and a week later he or she will call me up and say, *I got this idea.* They'll tell you the idea exactly as you proposed it to them and it's hard on the ego but you've got to say, *That's a brilliant idea* and then everything is good.

It's hard as a producer but you have to be prepared on some level that you are going to support this project, creatively, on so many levels that you will never get credit. The only way a producer ever is seen as a creative force is over time with a body of work … but never on a single film will somebody say, *It's obvious that you, the producer, had a great creative impact on the script.*

Maureen: As the producer, you need to know what you really want for the project.

Ben: Definitely. I also think you don't have to be a writer but you should, as a producer, have tried to write and you should read the books. You should read *Save the Cat!* by Blake Snyder, *The Art of Dramatic Writing* by Lajos Egri, and you should read Syd Field and you should read Robert McKee (screenplay teaching gurus). These books can be helpful as a guide as long as you don't become dogmatic. Some great films live beyond the logic of these books. But better to understand the rules and discard them. Also, so many writers live by them today it's useful to understand what they know. You don't have to know how to write but you should be able to at least speak the language. I frankly think any producer should go through the painful act of trying to write a screenplay to understand how bloody hard it is and therefore why you shouldn't beat your writers up when they don't do exactly what you think they should. Because the movie you have in your head is never the movie that ends up on the page. It never translates that fluidly unless you're a genius screenwriter, but there are very few. I think the more you can empathize with the writing process, the easier it is to deal with the writers.

The other thing that I think is really important to mention is the pacing of [the rewriting process]. No good screenplay comes in less than 15 or 20 drafts, but you can't get all your notes in one draft. When you read a screenplay and you love it but it needs a lot of work and it needs structural work and it needs work on character and it needs work on dialogue . . . you have to start with the macro first and fix the structure and make sure there is a through line and a premise and that there are themes and all those sort of larger concepts first and then you go in.

If you send them a 30-page document—and I know this because I've done it and it's a disaster—with every note from like "*the second act, it doesn't work*" to "*on page 33 the line of dialogue—blah-blah-blah—doesn't feel funny enough*," writers will feel so overwhelmed that they'll burn out. You shouldn't try to get everything in one draft and I think that anyone who tries to do that finds it takes much longer to get to a good screenplay. Pace yourself in terms of how you're trying to deconstruct and reconstruct the screenplay.

Also, after a draft let the writer rest and don't come at him three days later with aggressive notes because you can really burn out a writer fast if you don't watch how you're pacing. That's why I [think it's good to] write a screenplay and then you'll understand just how hard it is.

Richard Price, a novelist and screenwriter, said that "writing a screenplay is like carrying a piano up five flights of stairs." He had written a screenplay called *Clockers* for Scorsese and so he got it up the five flights of stairs and then Spike Lee decided to direct the movie. He said it was like all of a sudden you had to take the piano down the five flights and carry it back up again. That's sort of the way it feels, as a writer, to go through a draft. So the more you can put yourself in their heads and realize how difficult it is—I think producers always underestimate how hard it is to be creative and execute those creative ideas. Because of that they sometimes beat the writers up, unnecessarily.

Maureen: Any other advice regarding the rest of the screenwriting process—getting to the point where you finally have a script that's ready to go into production?

Ben: One is if you're dealing with a screenwriter who's not the director, [you need] to know when to bring a director in and you shouldn't bring a director in at the end. If you bring in a director at the end you're losing the advantage. It is a director's medium and the director needs to come in early enough to shape the material.

At the same time, you have to be very clear about who controls the ultimate vision of the screenplay because you may bring in a director who takes control and takes it in a direction you don't want. So you almost have to do the same thing with a director. You have to interview your directors, make sure they have the vision that you want and that they're only going to bring out more of what you had in mind. If it's a writer/director you don't have that problem, necessarily, but you can have other problems because they're so tied to it in so many different ways.

I think the other big piece of advice is patience. Too often producers take their material out too early. They have one connection to one executive at one studio or they have one potential financier and they take the screenplay to them when it's not ready. It's always harder to get that person to read a screenplay a second time. They don't read as carefully. They remember the things they didn't like. Even if they aren't in the screenplay any longer, they still sort of linger in the mind of the reader and so it's very hard to get somebody to become excited about a screenplay the second time. You only have one chance at a first impression.

I think producers so often make the mistake, especially when they're doing it cheaply and they raise the [money] independently where nobody has invested that deeply in it. It's $10,000 here or there and you make it for $200,000. No one contemplates that by not spending those six extra months to get the screenplay right you will have to live with that flawed movie for the rest of your life. Forget about the fact that you have two to three years between pre-production, production, editing, and distribution of just dealing with the project. Why would you not spend those additional six months to get the script further along—first, to raise money and then to go into production? People are really impatient and often young producers will go into production before they should.

Maureen: How do you know when it's time to go into production?

Ben: I think one thing is that you should surround yourself with people you trust. I'll send my screenplays undeveloped out to three or four readers and I ask the screenwriter to do the same. Look for people who are neutral, don't know the story and some who do. Some who've read a previous draft and some who haven't. Every time we feel like the script is taking a giant leap forward, we try to find that little group of people—some of them are the same, some are new, [to read it and give notes]. I never take their advice 100%. I listen and what you'll find, if you take it to enough readers, is the film's patterns. Things that you were feeling and then you hear three people say the same thing and you'll go, *OK, I have to change that.*

Then you'll get a note from somebody whom you really respect but it's the only time you've ever heard that note and, frankly, often—it's not that the person is wrong but it's not the right note for the project you're making and so you have to ignore it. It's a process. [But] don't depend on just your [opinion] and constantly refresh yourself by finding new people to read it. But always keep an arm's length from those notes because they don't always work. They may not like the genre. They may not have been paying attention when they were reading. That's why you need enough readers to really rely on.

Don't rely only on yourself and certainly you have to be very in touch with your ego and the need to make a project. Never discount how much your ego plays into making films because we all want to be recognized as filmmakers and there is always that glamorous side of it. Sometimes we're so hungry for that part that we rush through the rest because we're imagining receiving the Oscar. Frankly, because you rushed through things you won't get close to getting even a theatrical release. It's about getting your ego in check and not being too eager to be a producer and tell everybody that you're making a movie because they'll see it a year later and say, *That sucked,* and then you'll really regret that you didn't take more time.

Maureen: As you're getting ready to go into production, anything else to keep in mind?

Ben: Screenplays are fluid and what's amazing about the process of making films is that when your art director gets involved, when your actors get involved, when your director of photography (DP) gets involved, they all see your movie from their own particular angles and they all bring really interesting energy and ideas. At that point the director really needs to be in control and all of those ideas need to be filtered through the director. But as long as the parameters of the idea of the movie you want are firmly in place, all of that new energy and those new ideas are good. As a producer and then with the director, of course, you create an atmosphere of collaboration where those ideas can be absorbed, because in the process of making the movie you're still writing. I think as a producer you have to stay very alert, especially in the low-budget world, to how the budget is impacting the storytellers.

So it's a process of seeing what's in front of you and being able to weave it into your screenplay, taking advantage of the resources you do have rather than trying to force a screenplay using the resources you don't have. In other words, trying to make a big-budget movie with a low budget. Keep the writing process open as you go into production because you'll find that so many opportunities continue to expand and make the script better.

So often you'll find that the things that are right in front of you, that you have access to, that can work as well or better than what you had imagined in the screenplay and will cost you less money. That process is using your resources and continuing to develop your screenplay as you go and keeping your eyes open to opportunities within the reach of your budget that are functional to low-budget screenwriting. I think all the good, interesting low-budget projects have that story in which there is a lot of exploration that came out of the limitations.

Maureen: If you are open and if you're looking, if you're seeing and hearing and then you just throw out an idea, it could really take the scene to a whole other level and it didn't cost anything. That's probably a major part of my philosophy about producing.

Ben: I think we, the producers, have to establish that atmosphere of collaboration and willingness to change early on. When you talk about development, I think it does leak into pre-production and production and you need a director who's going to have that kind of spirit. Too often you'll find directors who are so set in their ways that, because they're not willing to make changes based on the reality of the budget, they undermine the film and end up with something that doesn't work. It's hard, in low-budget filmmaking especially, to separate the development of the screenplay from the development of the film itself. Honestly, no matter how big the budget, resources are always limited and filmmakers need to tailor their stories to their resources. Imagination has no limits, movies do.

Maureen: How important is a good log line to the development process?

Ben: Screenplays need a focus and usually that focus can be summed up some way in a log line. It may not be in the traditional Hollywood sense of the log line but there is this kind of concept that will carry you through, all the way to the marketing of the movie. It's like that very same thing that hooked you into wanting to make the project is the same thing that, captured properly in a trailer, will hook an audience into going into a movie. That can be very effective.

Producers, from the day they decide to make a project until it's marketed at the end, need to be able to sum up a movie quickly for a hundred different people. First for investors and for actors, then for your director, then for a great DP, and then when you've got to get into a festival and they ask you to send in a log line. If you get in, that log line ends up in the catalog and that catalog ends up being sent to every major distributor. Or it ends up showing up at the festival with people reading the log lines to decide whether or not they're going to see the movie.

So, in a way, if you don't have a quick way of summing [up] your film, it will make it harder every step of the process. I believe that with most great films, you tend, somehow, to catch their essence in a very simple way, even if it's not some sort of Hollywood hook.

I think that as a producer you're constantly forced to reduce your movie to a concept that's salable and so it is effective to figure out how to sell it from the beginning.

The other point is that it also depends who you're talking to as to how you want to sell your movie. So you may want to have sort of different pitches depending on who you're talking to. Certainly if you're trying to pitch name actors, that log line should be about the characters they would be playing.

Maureen: I think that if I can't come up with a log line that makes sense, I find it to be a red flag. You've got to go back and make sure you get it right. Do you agree with that?

Ben: I completely agree. I fully believe that and frankly I won't make a movie unless I feel like there is a really interesting concept in it. Partly it's because I've come to a point where I tend to like movies that are a little more concept driven, even if it ends up *Being John Malkovich*. *Being John Malkovich* is a pretty weird concept, but there was a log line. A guy finds a portal into the brain of John Malkovich.

Now, that's not going to get the masses running to go see it but, certainly for its audience, that log line was brilliant. I definitely feel that's the way to develop screenplays and that, truthfully, once you have that concept you sort of have to ask yourself as you're developing it: *Are you being true to it?* If you find that in the middle of Act II you're off on some tangent that has nothing to do with that original concept, you're probably lost.

But the only reason I don't say that out loud is because you get that, *How would you discover the next Fellini then? How would you pitch Amarcord?* It's true. It's like the exception, in a sense, proves the rule that once in a while there is a movie that's so brilliant and so impossible to sum up in a phrase.

I think as a responsible producer you want to have more than a log line. It's a concept that conveys your movie in some way that's interesting and unique and more often than not—emotional. If there is some sense of emotion in the concept and you're true to that emotion in your movie, it tends to make more sense.

Maureen: I know you've worked with a lot of writer/directors. Is there anything in the development process that would be different if it were a writer/director as opposed to only a writer?

Ben: One thing that I do see happen often is that writer/directors tend to think—young ones, new ones, and some who maybe aren't fully developed—they don't need everything on the page. They say, *No, but I had this in my head and I've envisioned …*

The problem is that a screenplay is a tool that many people who collaborate on a movie have to use and so it does two things. One is that you need to communicate to other people and also it's always better to force your writer/director to articulate his vision on the page first. Because often when they don't, you realize they really didn't have it that clear and when they try to execute, it didn't work.

So it's always better to try to get them to get as much of their vision in screenplay form as possible and that's one of the areas that you can run into problems.

I think there is one other area of development that's hugely important, which is finding your director. How do you find your director based on your material? Obviously you have them read the script. You have them sit down and articulate their vision and then one of the things that I often do is have them list several movies that they feel in some way capture what it is they want to do. Like how many different ways can we have them visualize their vision before you take them on as a director? I think you have to get a sense of what they're going to bring to the table before you get them involved. It's not just about seeing their previous films and thinking that they have the right sensibility. It's also about articulating their vision on that project before you sign them on. Because once you sign a director you now have three people opining about every little nook and cranny and it gets more complicated.

Maureen: Thanks so much for your insights, Ben.

Screenwriting Software

There are many screenwriting software programs out there. Final Draft is one of the most common and is compatible with Movie Magic Scheduling and Budgeting, Showbiz Scheduling, and Gorilla software. There are many others and you can check the *www.ProducertoProducer.com* website for more information.

Getting Feedback on the Script

Once you have a great draft of the screenplay it's a good idea to send it to people who have different tastes from yours to give notes. It can be very enlightening to have a different perspective on the screenplay from someone who may not be a ready cheerleader and yet can give constructive criticism. Don't ask for script notes from family and friends unless they are talented and experienced filmmakers themselves. Otherwise, the chances are slim that anything they say to you will be very useful. No offense, but I wouldn't ask my mom to read my X-rays and give a diagnosis on my broken foot unless she was a trained radiologist. It's fine for family and friends to read your screenplay but I would take whatever they say with many "grains of salt."

Doing a **table read** or a **staged reading** is often invaluable in the final stages of the script-revision process. Ideally, you can persuade great actors to participate in the reading. Send the script a week ahead of time so they can work on their roles. Plan for a few hours of rehearsal time with the director (if attached at that time) or whoever will do the best job. Then invite trusted filmmakers and insightful colleagues and have the actors read the script, start to finish, without stopping. A quiet space that allows the actors to sit proscenium-style in front of the audience works best. Afterward, poll the audience on key questions about the script so you can get insights for the next revision.

It's one thing to read the script and hear the voices in your head. It's a revelation to watch great actors read the dialogue and act it out. Jokes that just laid there on the page can come alive and things that you thought would be incredibly moving or funny might not deliver the dramatic punch or laughs when exposed to the light of a staged reading. Caution—don't get too caught up in the individual performances and gloss over any needed changes in structure and tone. There have been times producers become so enamored with a brilliant actor's performance that it blinds them to the weak third act or the lack of a clear "want or need" in one of the other characters. We've all heard the adage—If it's not on the page, it's never going to get onto the screen. You still need to attend to those issues before you begin official pre-production. Now is the time to do it.

Script Doctors

Sometimes it makes sense to bring in a script doctor to work on the screenplay. A **script doctor** is an experienced screenwriter who is brought in to rewrite parts of a screenplay such as dialogue, pacing, or character development. Often script doctors do not receive screen credit for their work. If you decide to hire one you should consult a lawyer and research any guild rules, if applicable.

Writers Guild of America

The Writers Guild of America (WGA) is the union for screenwriters in the United States. The West Coast chapter is located online at *www.wga.org* and the East Coast chapter can be found online at *www.wgaeast.org*. If you hire a union screenwriter you'll need to follow the guild rules for fees and work regulations.

Log Line—Don't Leave Home Without It

It's never too early to start working on the log line for your project. The **log line** is a sentence (or two) that describes the protagonists and the plot line of the project simply and clearly. Some people insist it must be one sentence only. I believe it can be two if the alternative is a jammed sentence that is grammatically mangled and hard to understand. The log line describes what the film is about, using verbs as much as possible. Verbs are action words and that's what makes a good project.

The log line should capture the essence of your project and elicit the reaction, "I want to see that!" If it's a comedy, the log line should come across as funny. If it's a documentary, then you want it to communicate the topic and narrative approach effectively.

If people aren't interested after hearing the log line, you need to revise it until it works. If you change it and you still get lukewarm responses, then you might not have a great project yet and you'll need to change the script or the treatment until you do. Log lines can be a great reality check to find out if you are onto a good thing. Don't underestimate the power of a good log line.

Log Line Creation

Writing a log line requires skill and there are certain principles for creating a great one. I think Dave Anaxagoras (*www.davidanaxagoras.com*) has come up with the best rules for log line creation. He's been kind enough to let me reproduce his invaluable information in this book.

Here is Dave's advice for the essential elements of effective log lines:

TONE AND GENRE

What is the tone and genre of your screenplay? If your log line describes the humorous adventures of a robot butler, it is a safe assumption you have a sci-fi comedy. But if there is any chance of confusion, explicitly state the genre and tone.

A MOTIVATED PROTAGONIST

Whose story is this? What flaw must your hero overcome? What motivates your protagonist to undertake his or her goal? The subject of your log line (and your screenplay) is the **protagonist**. We must also understand what motivates this protagonist. Why *this* protagonist for *this* story? Protagonists' motivations could be an emotional problem, a character flaw, or an incident in their past that still haunts them.

Sometimes, a single adjective is enough to give us a sense of the protagonist's motivations—not just a pet store clerk, but a lonely pet store clerk. Not just a fourth-grader, but a timid fourth-grader. Remember, these aren't extraneous adjectives; they are relevant to the story and describe motivation. A bald man doesn't suggest motivation ... unless he's stalking the president of the hair club for men.

INCITING INCIDENT

What sets the story in motion? This is the spark that ignites the fire, the event that sets the whole story in motion. It gives your protagonist (and your script) focus and direction. The inciting incident is the meat of our log line.

MAIN OBSTACLE

Without some serious conflict, without an obstacle, you could just write *and they lived happily ever after* and the story would be over. The inciting incident sets the story in motion. The conflict *is* the story. In order to sustain a script for 110 script pages, we need big conflict. This would be a good place to mention the antagonist.

ULTIMATE GOAL

This is the end game, the desired outcome of the protagonist's efforts. This is what the protagonist is after, what he or she truly desires more than anything else in the movie. You have to have it in your script, or the story could meander and end up anywhere.

STAKES

A legitimate question that many people ask is, "Who cares?" or, put another way, "So what?" What they are really asking, for our purposes, is "What's at stake?" The outcome has to matter in a way that we care about. So what hangs in the balance? What happens if the protagonist doesn't reach his or her goal? In other words, we are talking worst case scenario. What catastrophe are we trying to avoid?

The six essential elements of the log line are:

1. Tone and genre
2. The protagonist's identity and motivation
3. The inciting incident
4. The main obstacle or central conflict
5. The protagonist's ultimate goal or desired outcome
6. The stakes, or what happens if the goal is not accomplished

A prototype log line might look like this: TITLE OF MY SCREENPLAY is a GENRE with overtones of TONE about a PROTAGONIST who HAS A FLAW/MOTIVATION when THE INCITING INCIDENT HAPPENS and s/he must then overcome THE MAIN OBSTACLE in order to accomplish THE ULTIMATE GOAL or else there will be CATASTROPHIC CONSEQUENCES.

Don't be a slave to the formula. Not all elements must be explicitly stated, and not always in this order. But the idea is to cover this essential information, one way or another, as economically as possible. I find it easiest to write everything into one long, unwieldy and awkward sentence first and then edit down to something elegant and economical.

Keep in mind that the essential elements in any effective log line are also the essential elements of any viable project. Working out a thorough log line can be an important first step in developing a solid and worthwhile project.

Creating a Proposal

For any project that requires funding you will usually need to put together a proposal. There is a general format for such proposals, although a fiction project has a different format than a nonfiction project. I have included an example of each at the end of this section. Proposals are usually five to ten pages, so keep it clear and concise—you only have one opportunity to make a first impression. Below is the proposal information breakdown. When applicable, the different narrative and documentary elements are outlined:

OVERVIEW OR PROJECT INFORMATION

Narrative format: Describe the project concisely. Include the title, running time, type of project (feature, short, web series, interactive, virtual reality/VR, etc.), and the log line. Any important attachments, such as cast or executive producer, should be stated as well. You can include a pitch line, too. The **pitch line** is constructed with two fairly recent successful projects that have elements of your project: you put the word "meets" between them to create a filmic child that represents your particular project. When you put them together you should get an instant image in your mind of what the project will be, e.g., "*Romeo & Juliet* meets *Mad Max*." Make sure to include the format, production schedule length, and estimated budget.

Documentary format: Similar to the narrative format. Include more information about the project's topic, giving the reader historical and topical background and context. Write in detail about how your project will focus on the topic, the point of view, and the narrative arc.

COMPARISON PROJECTS

Narrative format: The proposal should include budget and box office information about similar past projects to demonstrate similar possible positive financial results for the investor of your project. When picking comparison projects, consider the project's theme, demographic (gender and age of your intended audience), storyline, subject matter, similar characters, casting, scenarios, and genre. In the proposal provide information about the production budget, financing, box office statistics (domestic and international), other sales and awards. If it's a television or VOD project, cite the ratings and subscription information as well. Create a grid and analyze four to six projects for comparison. The programs should be fairly recent, within the last five years is best—so the economics are relevant. There are many websites that provide box office/ratings information about past projects to fill in the grid.

While you are doing the research on possible comparison films, you'll discover other projects that were not financially successful. Use your findings to figure out why. Was the budget too high? Did they spend too much on prints and advertising (P&A)? Was it the wrong distribution plan for the demographic? Were the theatrical numbers low but it was very successful on video on demand (VOD)?

All those factors will be predictors of your possible success and give you ideas as to where to go for funding and how to distribute and market the project when completed. If a strategy worked successfully before on a comparison project, it has a good chance of working for your project, too—as long as the same conditions apply. Remember everything is constantly evolving in the world of film and media so stay informed about the latest information and trends. Consider what factors may impact your project in the marketplace two years down the line and plan for them now. For the proposal, only include the comparison projects that were financially successful.

Documentary format: Comparison projects are important for documentaries, as well. There are many feature documentaries that had strong theatrical or VOD releases that you can use as examples. Your project's topic and scope will be different, so concentrate on the same target audience and not necessarily the content.

INVESTMENT PARTICULARS—

Narrative/Documentary format: Discuss the budget and how the money will be raised—presales, equity investment, other monies—and explain the distribution plan. Lastly, include how the investor will be paid back for each level of investment. When sending out to potential investors, remember to consult your attorney before finishing the investment sections. For legal reasons, there are Securities and Exchange Commission (SEC) rules that need to be followed and specific legal language that needs to be included.

SYNOPSIS—

The synopsis is probably the most critical part of your proposal. Write it and rewrite it until it represents the essence of your narrative arc, concisely and clearly. Keep it visual so that readers are able to "see" your project by the time they finish reading the last paragraph.

Narrative format: Describe the main characters and the key plot points of the film. Keep it to three or four key character descriptions. If there are too many characters, it becomes hard for a first-time reader to keep them all straight in their head when reading. You should list the character's name, then age, and then a quick description, like "petulant teenager" or "biker chick"—instant identification through an adjective and a noun. Highlight the key narrative beats so the readers really understand what happens and what is special about your project.

Documentary format: Use the same principles for a narrative when writing the documentary synopsis. Bring the project to life for the reader. Introduce characters and plot points (if applicable) so the synopsis has the dynamism of a clear narrative arc.

BIOGRAPHIES—
Narrative/Documentary format: Include one paragraph bios of any key personnel—executive producer, director, and producer. If cast is attached include their bios as well. If a key department head (e.g., cinematographer, production designer, editor, composer) has an impressive résumé, make sure to include it.

BACKGROUND/HISTORY OF THE PROJECT—
Narrative format: If there is additional useful information, include it in this section. Add details about any awards or any participation in impressive labs like a Sundance Lab or the Berlin Talent Campus. If there is an interesting back story about the history of the project, add it here.

Documentary format: In addition to the above, you can list any grants your project has been awarded.

BUDGET AND/OR SCHEDULE—
Narrative format: Add the budget's summary page or the top sheet only and a tentative schedule. If there is any important tax information that is relevant, put it here. Many states have tax incentives and the rules should be outlined if you plan to take advantage of them. The proposal is usually accompanied by the script. Don't send out the proposal until you have a final draft of the script. You only have one chance to make a first impression.

Documentary format: Include the budget information as described above. Instead of a script, include a trailer if you have one.

LEGAL DISCLAIMER
As I have stated at the beginning of this book, I am not an attorney and am not dispensing legal advice in this book. You should always consult with your entertainment lawyer before proceeding. In the case of putting together a proposal, you need to be aware that the Securities and Exchange Commission (SEC) has very strict rules about raising money for a business or a project. You need to discuss these issues with your attorney before you send out a proposal to make sure that you do not run afoul of any legal statutes.

Narrative Proposal Example

Private Placement Memorandum

SQUARE UP AND SEND IT

Prepared by Tina Braz

SYNOPSIS

"SQUARE UP AND SEND IT":
1. (White water rafting term) to line the raft up for a rapid and paddle full force into it
2. used colloquially in the rafting community to mean hooking up

Square Up & Send It is the story of a recent college dropout who has found a new home in the Crabapple Rafting community. David, "Woody" Woodsome has escaped the real world to join this mix of quirky social misfits that live and work on the river and college kids on summer break. After a promotion from the amateur level "Fife," to the more advanced "Dry way," Woody is more eager than ever to make a permanent home at Crabapple. He also develops an interest in the spunky new guide, Rosie.

But, when one of Woody's customers falls out of his raft and drowns because he did not follow the "Nose & Toes" rule, Woody's life falls apart. He can't bear to leave the community that has become his home, but there's no job for a guide who's lost a "custy" – even if it wasn't his fault. He becomes a recluse, still living on the Crabapple property, but avoiding all the friends that he counted as family.

One day, Woody hangs around the river, comes across a group of townies that want to go tubing down the river. Drawn to their enthusiasm, he joins their tubing expedition. When they ignore his instructions to end the joyride before hitting a dangerous part of the river and one of the townies ends up trapped under water. Woody rescues her, but the stunt is more than Crabapple's owner, Frank, can take. He tells Woody to pack up his tent and leave.

Living with his mother again and working at a tollbooth, Woody's soul is crushed. His gloom is interrupted when he hears about an encroaching storm that he knows will wipe Crabapple off the riverbanks. He wants to go back to save Rosie and his mentor Money, and redeem himself in the process. But will he be able to get over his pride in their hour of need? These are the stakes – psychological and physical – that drive the suspense in *Square Up & Send It*.

CHAIN OF TITLE

The writer/director, Benjamin Leonberg, has assigned the right to produce a feature film from his screenplay, *Square Up & Send It,* to **SUASI LLC** of which he is a Managing Member.

THE CREATIVE TEAM

WRITER & DIRECTOR: BENJAMIN LEONBERG

Benjamin Leonberg is a filmmaker of many talents! Since 2007, Leonberg has made over 30 short films and has functioned as writer, director, producer, DP, actor and stunt coordinator on nearly all. In his words, "I make movies hard." His body of work reflects this intensity and commitment to filmmaking, and a never-say-die attitude.

Leonberg's ability to tell stories was honed in an unusual setting – on the white water rapids of New England as a rafting guide. With a boat of customers to entertain, Leonberg became adept at the subtleties of story telling – pacing, knowing how to draw in an audience and being able to deliver a dramatic and surprising turn of events.

His experience as a guide prompted his feature-length script, *Square Up & Send It*, the tale of a white-water rafter whose dreams are shattered after one of his customers drowns. Meanwhile, Leonberg is also developing a second feature, *Rhino,* an action-packed drama about poaching in rural South Africa. His latest short, *Bears Discover Fire*, adapted from the short story of the same title by famed science-fiction writer, Terry Bisson, is in production.

Leonberg holds a Bachelor's degree in Communication and Film and Television Production from the University of Massachusetts and a Certificate in Applied Film Making and Television

Production from the New Zealand Film Academy. Before pursuing his Masters of Fine Arts degree in Screenwriting and Directing at Columbia University, he worked in women's apparel advertising for Reebok International.

Leonberg will serve as a Managing Member of **SUASI LLC**, being set up to finance and produce *Square Up & Send It*.

PRODUCER: TINA BRAZ

Originally from Cape Town, South Africa, Tina Braz is an up-and-coming film producer living in New York City.

Braz is developing two movies, *Square Up and Send It*, drama set in the world of white-water rafting, and *Rhino*, an action-adventure about rhino poaching in her native South Africa.

She has produced a variety of short films, including *The Great Kevini* (2012, 5min), about a young magician seeking revenge on his unrequited crush, and *The Last Day of Summer* (2012, 10min), about a mixed-race couple torn apart in Apartheid-era South Africa.

Braz is also interested in art direction and production design, and served as an art department assistant on the movie, *Take Care,* directed by Liz Tucillo, which will have its premiere at the 2014 SXSW Film Festival.

Braz was awarded a BA (with Honors) in Screenwriting from the University of Cape Town in 2011, and is currently pursuing her MFA in Producing from Columbia University's Graduate School of the Arts.

Braz will serve as a Managing Member of **SUASI LLC** being set up to finance and produce *Square Up & Send It*.

TALENT WISH LIST

The film currently has no cast attachments. This list reflects the look and feel of the actors we hope to attract to the project.

WOODY – RYAN EGGOLD

Eggold is best known for his TV roles on *The Blacklist* (2013-2014), *Daybreak* (2012) and *90210* (2008-2011) but he's also been involved in a number of Indie films such as *Driving by Braille* (2011), *Trophy Kids* (2011) and *Lucky Them* (2013).

ROSIE – SAOIRSE RONAN

Ronan has garnered critical acclaim for popular films such as *Atonement* (2007), and *The Host* (2013) but is no stranger to the Indie space. Her Indie projects include *Violet & Daisy* (2011) and *City of Ember* (2008).

FRANK – TERRY O'QUINN

O'Quinn's most famous role with current audiences is on the epic TV show, *Lost* (2004-2010) but he's been involved in a myriad other TV series including *The West Wing* (2003-2004), *Alias* (2002 – 2004), *666 Park Avenue* (2012-2013), and *Hawaii Five-O* (2011-2013). He's had roles in TV movies and small films such as *Taken From Me: The Tiffany Rubin Story* (2011) and *Hometown Legend* (2002).

MONEY – VIGGO MORTENSEN

Mortensen's filmography includes huge films such as *The Lord of The Rings* (trilogy: 2001, 2002, 2003) and *Hidalgo* (2004) as well as smaller projects like *A History of Violence* (2005) and *Good* (2008).

PRODUCTION PLAN

Square Up & Send It is set in the summertime on the Deerfield River, in Massachussetts, but we've decided to shoot in September in West Virginia. The West Virginia location makes sense for the following reasons:

→ West Virgina has a 31% state tax credit
→ West Virginia has 2 suitable rivers: the Gauley River and the New River
→ The Gauley River's flow can be modulated to suit production requirements
→ As September is the beginning of the off-season for white water rafting tour companies, it will be easier and cheaper to get locations, trained safety personnel, and props such as rafts, paddles and life jackets.
→ September is mild enough for white water rafting in West Virginia but not in Massachussetts.

In the event that we have the Minimum Required Financing in place by June 1st 2014, we will begin principal photography on, or as close as possible to, September 1st 2014.

Development: April – May 2014
Pre-Production: June – August 2014
Principal Photography: September 2014
Post Production: October 2014 – January 2015

PRODUCTION COMPANY MANAGEMENT

A single purpose, Limited Liability Company (**SUASI Film LLC.**) will be formed for the sole purpose of developing, producing, and exploiting the film and shall have a One Hundred Percent Ownership Interest in the film. The LLC is managed by the Production Team for *Square Up & Send It*, namely, Tina Braz and Benjamin Leonberg. Investors will not participate in the management of the LLC. The sole business of the LLC will be the production and distribution of *Square Up & Send It*.

The film's producer and writer/director are the Managing Members of the LLC. The Managing Members of the LLC have complete discretion over the production, editing, distribution and exhibition of the film and will control all business decisions with respect the the film. The Managing Members will exploit the film to its full potential in all markets.

BUDGET

It is anticipated that the Production Budget of *Square Up & Send It* will be $1,000,000 US including cast and crew deferments. This budget provides for pre-production, principal photography, post production, delivery costs and a small reserve for initial marketing.

THE ESCROW ACCOUNT

Capital raised from investors will be held in an escrow account, to be released to **SUASI LLC** for production of the film when the Minimum Required Financing (MRF) of $300,000.00 has been raised. The MRF figure of $300,000 US is sufficient to fund pre-production, principal photography and several weeks of editing.

DEVELOPMENT

FINANCING PLAN

The financing for *Square Up & Send It* will come from a variety of sources, as indicated in the following table:

U.S. Private Equity	$500,000.00
Crowd-Funding Campaign	$50,000.00
West Virginia State Tax Credit	$200,000.00
In-Kind Contributions	$50,000.00
Cast & Crew Deferments	$200,000.00
TOTAL	**$1,000,000.00**

The State of West Virginia offers up to 31% transferable tax credits for in-state spend. **SUASI LLC** will satisfy all of the terms and conditions for obtaining this tax credit while making the film. All principal photography will happen within the state and at least a third of the post-production budget will be spent in West Virginia. Although key cast and crew (writer/direcor and producer) will come from outside the state, the majority of the below-the-line cast and crew will be from West Virginia.

The transferable tax credit means that whatever tax credits cannot be spent by **SUASI Film LLC.** within West Virginia, can be sold to other companies who can make use of these credits. Usually, this transfer is done at a rate slightly lower than the dollar value of each credit.

Another benefit of filming in West Virginia is that most state-owned property is fee-free. As much of the film will be shot along the banks of the Gauley River, which is state-owned property, this will dramatically reduce our location costs. The West Virginia State Film Office may also assist with negotiation of discounted fees for other locations and may help us source in-kind contributions in lieu of payment for office and warehouse space, lodging, transportation rentals, etc.

TERMS OF INVESTMENT

One of the virtues of the proposed financing plan is that this $1,000,000 film will utilise only $500,000 of private equity. The other funds are not recoupable. Thus the investor's capital is well-leveraged and this should enhance the investors' chances to recoup and to earn a return on investment should the film be a financial success.

Budget	$1,000,000.00
U.S. Private Equity Portion	$500,000.00
Cost Per Share	$10,000.00
Number of Shares Available	50

DEFERMENTS:

Out of funds received by the LLC from distribution of the film, 10% will be retained by the LLC to pay its management expenses, including the annual accounting and tax filing fees, and 90% will be used to pay any cast or crew deferments.

RECOUPMENT:

After payment of all cast and crew deferments, funds received by the LLC from distribution of the film will be allocated as follows: 10% will be retained by the LLC to pay its management expenses, including the annual accounting and tax filing fees, and 90% will be distributed to the investors on a pro rata/pari passu basis until the investors have recouped 100% of their initial capital contribution.

Thereafter, the LLC will distribute another 30% to the investors in the form of an "equity kicker," until they have recouped 130% of their initial capital contribution.

THE PROFIT SPLIT:

After the investors have recouped 130% of their initial capital contribution, 10% of all revenues received by the LLC will be distributed to the investors on a pro rata/pari passu basis, and 90% will be retained for the benefit of the Managing Members of the LLC and to pay for the ongoing LLC management expenses. Any profit participations that may be due to the key cast and/or crew will be paid out of the Managing Members' 90% share.

THE TERMINATION OF THE LLC:

It is assumed that the majority of the film's revenues will be generated within a three-year period following its first release. Therefore, 36 months after the first release of the film, the film's copyright and distribution rights will be assigned to the Managing Members as individuals. The LLC will make a final revenue report to the investors and the LLC will be shut down. Thereafter, no further accounting will be due to the investors, whether or not they have recouped their investment in the film.

ADDITIONAL INVESTORS:

The LLC reserves the right to raise an additional $500,000 to complete the film. Investors acknowledge that this would dilute their percentage holding in the LLC.

DISTRIBUTION PLAN

SUASI LLC. intends to market the film during its festival run, and follow this festival run closely with a day and date release in theaters and on iTunes and/or Amazon Instant in the USA and appropriate foreign territories. This strategy will make the most of the publicity garnered from the festival run as well as taking advantage of a nationwide audience.

Other markets in which the film will be exploited include:
→ International Streaming platforms
→ International Pay TV platforms
→ DVD and Blue Ray
→ In-flight and On-Ship Entertainment Services

COMPARABLE FILMS

Hide Your Smiling Faces (2014)	Mean Creek (2004)	Brick (2005)
After a neighborhood tragedy, two adolescent brothers confront changing relationships, the mystery of nature, and their own mortality.	When a teen is bullied, his brother and friends lure the bully into the woods to seek vengeance.	A teenage loner pushes his way into the underworld of a high school crime ring to investigate the disappearance of his ex-girlfriend.
81% (Critics) – Rotten Tomatoes	90 % (Critics) – Rotten Tomatoes	80% (Critics) – Rotten Tomatoes
Budget: $100,000	Budget: $500,000	Budget: $475,000
Box Office: $3,576.00	Box Office: $603,000	Box Office: $2,075,743
Won New Director's Award at Denver Intl. Film Festival, Nominated at Tribecca & won 3 awards at Bend Film Festival	Won 2 Independent Spirit Awards, Humanitas Prize & Best Directorial Debut at Stockholm Film Festival.	Won Special Jury Prize at Sundance, won Most Promising Director at Chicago Film Critics Association Awards & Best First Film at Austin Film Critics Association
First Time Writer/Director, Ultra-low Budget, Drama Genre	First Time Writer/Director, Low budget, Drama Genre	First Time Writer/Director, Low budget, Drama Genre

RISKS:

As with any investment, there are risks. Investment in film is particularly high risk because of the unpredictability of the market. The LLC will endeavor to make the film a success but there is no guarantee that the film will generate any income, let alone enough to recoup investors' capital. Investors enter into this subscription with the knowledge that there is no market for shares in the LLC, nor is there ever likely to be one. These shares are not transferable, refundable or liquid in any way. Once paid for, they can only be redeemed by the financial success of the film. As such, no investor should enter into this subscription without the financial ability to lose the entire investment, should the film fail.

In addition to the standard risks associated with investment in film, this film carries additional unique risks that include:
→ First-time writer, director and producer have no experience in these roles on a feature film.
→ 80% of the film requires exterior scenes and locations and, as such, filming can be delayed or halted by unexpected and uncontrollable weather issues.
→ White water rafting is an inherently risky sport and although the production team, cast and crew will take all possible safety precautions, accidents do happen.
→ The film includes a scene where a customer drowns after falling out of a raft. Although the production team, cast and crew, will take all possible safety precautions, this is a dangerous stunt sequence to perform and capture.

PERKS OF INVESTMENT:

Making this film, *Square Up & Send It*, will be an exciting and unforgettable experience for all involved! In addition to being part of making this thrilling film become a reality you'll have access to exclusive, investors-only perks which include:

→ Access to the production blog that will be updated regularly with behind-the-scenes pictures and interviews with the cast and crew

→ The opportunity for you and 3 friends to visit the set and have lunch with the cast!

→ 6 VIP tickets to the film's New York or LA premiere and access to the official after party!

→ If you're unable to make it to the New York or LA premiere, the opportunity to have your own friends and family screening with an introduction by one of the cast or crew members via Skype!

→ A digital download and copy of the DVD before its official release in stores!

→ A Production hamper packed with limited edition merchandise, an autographed copy of the poster, and a digital download and copy of the CD Soundtrack from the film!

IF YOU WOULD LIKE TO TAKE THIS WHITEWATER RAFTING ADVENTURE WITH US, PLEASE CONTACT:

TINA BRAZ

Documentary Proposal Example

RED LIGHT FILMS

E-TEAM

A Feature Length Documentary Film

Katy Chevigny
Director / Producer

Ross Kauffman
Director / Producer

Marilyn Ness
Producer

San Francisco Film Society Documentary Film Fund Proposal

BRIEF SUMMARY

The E-Team follows the intense and courageous work of three intrepid human rights workers on the frontlines of identifying international human rights abuses. Dramatic and crucial, Human Rights Watch's Emergency Team work is custom-made for a compelling documentary film with a global perspective.

DESCRIPTION OF THE FILM

The action of *The E-Team* will be driven by the high stakes investigative work of Anna Neistat, Fred Abrahams and Peter Bouckaert, three key members of the Human Rights Watch Emergency Team. Though very different personalities, Anna, Fred and Peter share a fearless spirit and a deep commitment to exposing and halting human rights abuses around the world. Peter Bouckaert, a savvy strategist and investigator, is a Belgian national living in Geneva with his wife and two children. *Rolling Stone* magazine called him "the James Bond of human rights investigators." Fred Abrahams is a New York City native with a wickedly dry sense of humor and a tireless energy. In the earliest days of his career as a human rights investigator, it was his research that brought down Slobodan Milosevic in the International Criminal Court. Anna Neistat, a Russian national, is as fashionable as she is formidable. She now resides in Paris with her son and a husband, Ole, who is himself learning the ropes of being a human rights investigator. Anna's childhood experiences in the former U.S.S.R. have brought her a righteous indignation about the practices of unaccountable dictatorships. Dedicated and energetic, all three members of the E-Team bring an infectious enthusiasm to their work. Their contrasting characters lend nuance to the film and draw viewers into their collective stories.

The headquarters for this trio is the well-known international organization, Human Rights Watch (HRW). Founded in 1978, HRW is now one of the largest and most respected organizations monitoring human rights abuses worldwide. Currently based in New York, but with offices all over the world, HRW has been on the front lines in the fight for human rights in Rwanda, Kosovo, Chechnya, Chile, Afghanistan, Burma, Sri Lanka and Sudan, among others, monitoring conditions in over seventy countries around the globe. International prosecutors have used HRW's evidence in the trials of Yugoslav President Slobodan Milosevic and Chilean dictator Augusto Pinochet.

The E-Team is a key component of HRW's success and conducts the organization's most dramatic work on the ground. Arriving as soon as possible after allegations of human rights abuses surface, the E-Team uncovers crucial evidence to determine if further investigation is warranted and to capture the world's attention. Even more importantly, they also immediately challenge the responsible decision makers, holding them accountable. Human rights abuses thrive on secrecy and silence, and the work HRW has done in the last thirty years has shone light in dark places and given voice to thousands whose stories would never have been told.

The film's narrative will be fueled by the strong plot structure that springs naturally from the E-Team's investigative process. We are filming Anna, Fred and Peter in the field as they piece together the actual events that take place in various troubled spots around the globe. We are also spending time with each E-Team member at home, exploring the intricacies of managing family and personal relationships within the challenges of their exceptional work life.

We have unprecedented access to the work of the E-Team; this is the first time HRW has ever granted independent access to a film crew. To be perfectly clear, however, we are interested in portraying the complexity, difficulty and importance of human rights work, not in lionizing a well-known organization. Our production model is to travel on missions with each E-Team member, and follow their work as it unfolds, either through further research on a separate mission or through additional research back at home. We also make a point of filming them as they interact with one another and with colleagues, to shed light and bring justice to a particular group or situation. The film draws upon the *cinema vérité* style of filming, interviewing E-Team members in the field and using voiceover to explain the action taking place. We are also using footage of E-Team members being interviewed by the international press as another expository device to clarify story and drama when necessary. This format is the most effective way to vividly convey the immediacy of their work, while providing a window into a type of investigation that most people are entirely unfamiliar with. Throughout the film, we allow the inherent dramatic qualities of their work to drive the story.

Filmmakers Kauffman and Chevigny have extensive experience making documentaries about stories that are unfolding in the field, specializing in narratives that have a complex legal, political or social problem at the core of the plot. Their respective films have demonstrated an ability to tell human rights stories that bring life to the individuals and institutions that are central to the emotional truth of the drama at hand. It is because of their collective experience and credibility with human rights issues that Human Rights Watch has entrusted them to bring their integrity as filmmakers to document this important investigative work.

RECENT PRODUCTION
We are in the midst of principal production of the film. World events, namely, the Arab Spring and the human rights crises it spurred escalated our production timetable.

In January 2011, the filmmakers filmed the E-Team's annual summit in New York City, where the members gathered to discuss upcoming missions. These events shed light on protocols that the E-Team uses to establish a need for investigative research. What constitutes a human rights abuse? How does documentation play a role in throwing open abuses to the attention of the world? These questions are critical to the film's success as a vehicle for broad audiences.

Later in the year, in September 2011, we were able to film Fred and Peter on a mission to Libya. Two days after the fall of Qaddafi, our team landed in Tunisia and drove by land into the newly liberated capital of Tripoli. We spent a week filming Fred and Peter as they investigated alleged abuses in the midst of rapidly changing dynamics while the victorious rebels filled the power vacuum left by the departure of Qaddafi from the capital. Working quickly and efficiently in the war zone, with skilled interpreters and other human rights workers on the ground, they interviewed dozens of individuals throughout Tripoli and its environs. They braved armed checkpoints and stray gunfire throughout the city to investigate the looting of Qaddafi's weapons stores. They traveled to several makeshift prisons -- where rebels took over as the new guards – to question the prisoners and determine what conditions they were enduring as well as the nature of the alleged causes for their detention. They took time to meet with the guards throughout Tripoli to emphasize the importance of establishing protocols that protect human rights in these new prisons and this new country. Later that week, they investigated the abuse of black Africans at the hands of Libyans. Some of these alleged mercenaries of Qaddafi's regime were now imprisoned while entire communities of black Africans had sought refuge in a camp by the port, living in squalor amidst abandoned ships perched precariously on the shore. And finally, they looked into fresh reports of recent killings by Qaddafi supporters in the last days of the regime and interviewed survivors of a mass execution where over forty bodies were found burnt to death at a warehouse detention center. These chilling interviews provide first-hand reports of human rights violations that had only been rumored in the previous days. In each of these cases, the E-Team investigators were among the first to thoroughly investigate and report the findings.

The results of this work were multifold. Several times over the course of the week, Fred and Peter were interviewed by members of the international press about the developing situation in Libya. Due to their strong reputations as rigorous and impartial investigators, their findings were reported in a wide variety of press outlets, including The New York Times, CNN, BBC and Al-Jazeera. In cases where the investigation revealed likely evidence of war crimes, they meticulously collected data that could be reviewed at a later date by members of the International Criminal Court. In cases where the situation was still unfolding – for example, when they saw that the rebels had decided to detain certain Libyan citizens and other African nationals – Fred and Peter informed the newly minted prison guards regarding the needs and rights of prisoners in their care. Through this footage, the viewers immediately come to understand that human rights work involves a variety of important practices including: investigative techniques and an understanding of international law, sharing findings with the world to shed light on abuses and other human rights problems, bringing perpetrators to justice through international justice bodies, and working hand in hand with authorities on the ground to prevent future abuses before they unfold.

At the same time, the personal stories and motivations of our E-Team members provide another layer of interest and give viewers a rare window into the intimate flipside of this intense and fascinating work. Peter is most drawn to the immediate aftermath of war, examining weapons stores and seeking new evidence that explains and proves recent war crimes. Fred, on the other hand, is most effective when he is interacting with people affected on the ground. His interviewing skills, affable manner, the ability to build trust, and meticulous systems of crosschecking victims' accounts enables him to illuminate stories that were previously unknown outside of a small circle. And Anna is most skilled at gaining entry to situations that shut most people out. She frequently works undercover to investigate the living conditions of women in countries where their rights are being withheld. The specific passion that each E-Team member brings to their work allows viewers to engage with and care about the investigators, as well as to empathize with the human rights workers and the victims they seek to support. Their on-the-ground work transforms human rights violations from a problem of statistics and numbing atrocities to a group of people trying their best to solve a problem and bring an injustice to light.

Later in 2011, we began to follow a compelling story conducted by Anna. She spent several months last year working undercover in and around Syria, gathering data on government abuses against the demonstrators that rose up as part of Syria's own chapter in the Arab Spring of 2011. She also met with dozens of defectors from the military, who named their superiors that had ordered them to shoot unarmed demonstrators and inflict other abuses. As a result of this work, she and her partner Ole Solvang published a scathing report that charged Russia with supporting the Assad government as they were committing crimes against humanity. We filmed her working on the report at home in Paris as well in subsequent weeks when she traveled to Moscow to release the report. By directly confronting Russian authorities on their own turf regarding their support of an abusive government, Anna was working to strategically influence Russia's United Nations position on Syria. In addition, this work drew international attention – and reached as high as the International Criminal Court itself – with its credible claims of crimes against humanity being perpetrated in Syria.

Our next chapter in Syria began at the end of April 2012 when Anna, Ole, and our crew were able to smuggle across the Syrian border from Turkey and begin investigations in Keeli, Hazzano, Taftanaz and Maarat Misrin. They gained access to the Free Syrian Army headquarters, recorded stories of civilian casualties, captured footage of destroyed homes from burnings to bombings, and were the first to film testimony of a mass execution from eye-witnesses and survivors. Human Rights Watch is now releasing their findings to the press and we are capturing the media and worldwide response to their investigation.

In February 2012 we filmed the E-TEAM's planning meeting in New York City during which they determine where to allocate their resources for future missions based on current reports of emerging conflicts around the world. In an effort to demonstrate the global nature of human rights investigations, we plan to follow our characters on at least one mission beyond the stories unfolding in the Middle East – to new areas of conflict. We are working to strike a delicate balance, deploying our limited financial resources in regions where we have the highest likelihood of capturing a complete story – from suspicion of human rights abuses to international response. With these parameters in mind, and as we secure additional funding for production, we will select another conflict area into which we will follow the E-TEAM.

Our footage from Libya and Syria has an immediacy and urgency, providing a strong example of the kind of material we will obtain by continuing to film fieldwork with the E-Team. We will also document the personal sacrifices that they make as they leave their families yet again for additional field missions in other parts of the world. The film will ask: what makes this demanding and dangerous work worthwhile for each of these investigators? What drives them to seek justice in these situations and what discourages them?

Another of our central conflicts that the film will draw upon is the difficulty that E-Team members have in finding an effective means of halting a human rights abuse once clearly identified. Frequently, E-Team members are thwarted by government alliances that make it difficult to expose an abuse, or bureaucratic red tape (caused at times by the leadership of HRW itself) that hamstring their attempts to bring the weight of the United Nations or other international bodies to bear on the issue. The struggle for an individual's hard-won discovery of information to be converted into a concrete action is one that is well served by cinema, in fiction as well as documentary. Viewers will empathize and engage with the E-Team's passion to generate tangible change, and their frustration when institutions and rules hinder change; this is the stuff of drama as well as of life itself: easy to empathize with and engaging to watch.

The film in its final form will cover the work of the E-Team in several different locations. Our choices will be dictated by both practical necessity – the E-Team members are often on the move in unexpected ways – and by the desire to tell a story with a broad sweep. We will balance coverage of the heroic members of the E-Team with those of the even more courageous individuals affected by and working to alleviate human rights abuses in their own countries. The basic premise of the E-Team's work dictates that human rights apply equally to everyone, everywhere. Fitting together multiple stories featuring the different members of the E-Team in different locations will help illustrate that premise. No single investigation covers the range of the E-Team's concerns. Through an inclusion of several compelling stories, we will give an overall portrait of the team as the breadth of their fight emerges. The final film will show how the work affects each of the E-Team's lives, and we will have followed at least one international human rights investigation to its conclusion.

CURRENT STATUS OF THE PROJECT

Chevigny and Kauffman began their development work in 2009, meeting extensively with a variety of staff at HRW and thus gaining access to the E-Team members in order to follow them on their missions abroad. HRW Deputy Director for External Affairs Carroll Bogert has signed a letter of commitment (see attached) stating that HRW leadership is prepared to authorize access for a "warts and all" profile of their work, ensuring that the final film will reflect the independent perspective that the project demands.

We continue to pursue funding that would allow the filmmakers to continue production and begin post-production in the fall of 2012. Specifically, we intend to continue following at least three stories: Peter and Fred's work in Libya, assessing the new regime as it develops; Anna's work in Syria, as she continues to research and monitor the ongoing conflict there; and Fred's work covering both areas from New York which serves as "home base" for the global movements of Anna and Peter in 2012, fielding media requests, compiling research and coordinating the "big picture" of the various E-Team projects as they move forward. We continue to monitor the E-Team's movements for a story occurring outside of the bounds of the Middle East that will engage our characters.

We have already raised initial production funds from the following sources: Sundance Documentary Fund, BritDocs Foundation's Creative Catalyst grant, the Still Point Fund, the National Endowment for the Arts, and most recently, Gucci Tribeca Documentary Fund, and the MacArthur Foundation. We will continue to seek funds from foundations and individuals. Numerous donors who care about Human Rights Watch's work have already expressed interest in funding the film. Lastly, Arts Engine, Chevigny and Kauffman have a proven track record of raising funding from co-production partners for their films. We are planning to apply to the IDFA Central Pitch for pre-sales with co-production partners.

PRODUCTION PERSONNEL

Directors Kauffman and Chevigny bring shared and complementary film experience to this project. Both of them are known for making films that bring viewers close to the individuals and organizations that fight human rights abuses, whether fighting for the rights of children in Calcutta's red light district in *Born Into Brothels* or showcasing a historic blow against capital punishment in *Deadline*. Both directors are committed to making films that draw viewers in with compelling characters and an engaging story as a tool to help audiences care about people, places and events about which they may never have heard.

KATY CHEVIGNY, DIRECTOR/PRODUCER

Katy Chevigny is an award-winning filmmaker and co-founder of Arts Engine, a leading independent media nonprofit and its production arm, Big Mouth Films. She directed the film *Election Day* (2007) which premiered at the South By Southwest (SXSW) Film Festival in 2007 and was broadcast on POV in 2008. With Kirsten Johnson, she co-directed *Deadline*, an investigation into Illinois governor George Ryan's commutation of death sentences. After premiering at the 2004 Sundance Film Festival, *Deadline* was broadcast on NBC to an audience of over six million, in an unusual acquisition of an independent film by a major network. It was nominated for an Emmy Award and won the Thurgood Marshall Journalism Award, among others. Chevigny also directed *Journey to the West: Chinese Medicine Today*, a feature-length documentary about traditional Chinese medicine and its influence in the West. She has produced several acclaimed documentaries: *Arctic Son, Innocent Until Proven Guilty, Nuyorican Dream, Brother Born Again, Outside Looking In: Transracial Adoption in America* and *(A)sexual*. Chevigny's films have been shown theatrically, on HBO, Cinemax, POV, Independent Lens, NBC, and Arte/ZDF, among others and have played at film festivals around the world, including Sundance, Full Frame, SXSW, Sheffield and Berlin. Most recently, she produced *Pushing the Elephant,* which premiered on Independent Lens in 2011.

ROSS KAUFFMAN, DIRECTOR/PRODUCER

Ross Kauffman is the director, producer, cinematographer and co-editor of *Born Into Brothels*, winner of the 2005 Academy Award for Best Documentary. Kauffman began as a documentary film editor, and then spent several years at Valkhn Film and Video Inc., a post-production company where he worked on a wide variety of films for HBO, WNET/Thirteen, National Geographic and The Discovery Channel. In 2001, Kauffman formed Red Light Films to direct and produce *Born Into Brothels*, a documentary about the children of Calcutta's prostitutes. It was accepted to over 50 film festivals worldwide and has since received over 40 awards, including National Board of Review Best Documentary 2004, LA Film Critics Best Documentary 2004 and the 2004 Sundance Film Festival Audience Award. Kauffman is currently working on a variety of projects, including: *Exposure*, a scripted television series following the lives of five present day photojournalists around the globe and the documentary *Wait For Me,* chronicling the story of a mother's spiritual and emotional search for her son who went missing twenty-three years ago. Other projects include: *In a Dream*, the story of the Philadelphia mosaic artist Isaiah Zagar which was shortlisted for the 2009 Academy Award for Best Documentary Feature; and *Project Kashmir*, a documentary that takes viewers into the warzone of Kashmir and examines the conflict from emotional and social viewpoints.

MARILYN NESS, PRODUCER

Marilyn Ness is a two-time Emmy Award-winning documentary producer. She is currently producing Ross Kauffman (2005 Academy Award winner) and Katy Chevigny's film E-TEAM as well as Johanna Hamilton's film UNTITLED 1971. Before joining Arts Engine as Director of Production and MediaMaker Services, Marilyn founded Necessary Films in 2005, directing short films for non-profits including the ACLU and the World Federation of Hemophilia and developing documentaries for broadcast. Her most recent film *BAD BLOOD: A Cautionary Tale* broadcast nationally on PBS in 2011 and was the centerpiece of campaign to change US blood donation policies. Prior to that, Ness spent four years as a producer for director Ric Burns, collaborating on four award-winning PBS films: *Ansel Adams*, *The Center of the World*, *Andy Warhol*, and *Eugene O'Neill*. Ness's other credits include films for TLC, Court TV, and National Geographic, as well as films for the PBS series *American Experience*.

DISTRIBUTION AND MARKETING

We anticipate significant attention for *The E-Team*. Given the combination of the high-profile nature of Human Rights Watch's work, the dramatic content of the film and its global significance, we will aim for broad distribution in the United States and internationally. We plan to launch the film with a prominent festival premiere, a subsequent theatrical release, US television broadcast, home video sales, and educational distribution. Throughout the filmmaking process, we will work closely with a wide range of organizations and individuals interested in gaining exposure for international human rights. Our press strategy for the film will be in tandem with key human rights organizations, in order for the film to bring attention to timely international events that speak to the themes of the film.

We see the E-Team's work as a uniquely cinematic vehicle to paint a portrait of the global scope and importance of top-level human rights work. Over the last several years, issues of international human rights have begun to penetrate the American mainstream. *The E-Team* will be an important tool in advancing public understanding and appreciation of international human rights work. The film's global perspective will help initiate conversations about the interconnected nature of human rights work in a significant way.

OUTREACH AND ENGAGEMENT
Chevigny and Kauffman have a strong track record of innovative and effective community engagement and social justice outreach around their past films. Kauffman's *Born Into Brothels* spawned Kids With Cameras, a nonprofit formed in 2002 to raise money and awareness for children of the red light district through print sales, exhibitions, film festivals and a book of their work. The children's images have been exhibited in Calcutta, Europe and all over the U.S. A book of their photos was published in 2004. In order to help more children from Calcutta's red-light district, Kauffman, along with executive producer of *Born Into Brothels*, Geralyn White Dreyfous, has also been raising money to build Hope House, a nurturing home where up to 150 children from Calcutta's red light district will come to live, learn, and grow. The children who live in Hope House will receive a free, first-rate education through high school, courtesy of the Buntain Foundation, which owns and operates eighty schools in India. An educational curriculum based on the film was also created to engage students and teachers across the US and around the world.

The outreach efforts around Chevigny's *Deadline* gave hundreds of organizations, universities, and high schools the chance to grapple with one of the most significant issues of our day. They helped take capital punishment away from the artificiality of a debate team topic and planted it squarely in a moral framework of justice, equality and due process. Through a combination of *Deadline*'s 25 festival screenings, an NBC broadcast that reached six million viewers, a *New York Times* article, 110 house parties during the broadcast, a theatrical release, 100 community screenings nationwide, a DVD release, and an interactive website on death penalty issues, we were able to engage millions of viewers around the world in a moral, political, and philosophical conversation on capital punishment. By leveraging two high-profile events – the premiere at the Sundance Film Festival and the national network broadcast in 2004 – we reached far more viewers than we would have in a more conventional distribution strategy. The film's ultimate Emmy nomination drew further attention to the film and the debate around the death penalty in the United States.

The filmmakers plan to use the lessons learned from the engagement campaigns of their past films to create a timely and effective campaign for *The E-Team*. Due to the international nature of the work, the outreach plan will coordinate with grassroots organizations working on the ground abroad to help bring greater awareness to the issues raised by the E-Team's work.

INTERACTIVE ELEMENTS
Arts Engine will take the lead in creating a tailored interactive campaign for the film that will draw international attention to the need for human rights globally as well as to raise awareness about the specific human rights abuses that *The E-Team* focuses on. Specifically, the website will include a map of the world which highlights the sites visited by E-Team members and specific actions that viewers can take to advance the human rights cause in these areas.

Chevigny is also the co-founder of Arts Engine, which conducts a number of online activities to enhance the social impact and exposure of documentary films. MediaRights.org has more than 27,000 members and connects social justice organizations to thousands of filmmakers and films that can help them promote their cause. Media That Matters, now in its eleventh year, showcases curated short films on social justice issues through a festival, online, screenings at schools and community groups and DVDs. This unique multiplatform model allows Media That Matters to reach millions of people globally, and her experience with it positions Chevigny to use similar strategies for *The E-Team*.

HUMAN RIGHTS WATCH LETTER OF COMMITMENT

HUMAN RIGHTS WATCH

350 Fifth Avenue, 34th Floor
New York, NY 10118-3299
Tel: 212-290-4700
Fax: 212-736-1300
Email: hrwnyc@hrw.org

June 16, 2009

Dear Ross and Katy,

I am writing on behalf of Human Rights Watch to express our commitment to participating in a documentary film directed by you two which focuses primarily on the work of HRW's Emergency Team. To enable you to produce the film, we are willing to grant you access to the Emergency Team's work both in the field and at HRW's offices.

Through meetings and conversations with the two of you and with the members of the Emergency Team, we feel confident in your collective experience as documentary filmmakers and your sensitivity to issues of human rights. I know that your several meetings and conversations with various members of the Emergency Team has built mutual trust in the project.

We have spoken about the issue of editorial control, but I'd like to clarify my position on this in writing. It is perfectly well understood by myself and the members of the Emergency Team that your interest in a film about our work is in no way intended to be a promotional piece for HRW. Rather, we understand your interests are to make a truly independent documentary that may show the Emergency Team's work in a "warts-and-all" approach. We trust in your capacity as fair and thoughtful filmmakers to tell the story in such a way that it will reach a broader audience than any promotional piece could, and we see this as a benefit to HRW. To underscore the point, while we will be happy to facilitate your access to the work of HRW for the purposes of this film, we understand the authorship, copyright and editorial control of the film rests entirely with you two as Directors.

Our only concern is that the filmmaking process in no way hinder the efficacy of the Emergency Team's crucial investigative work, which I know you have discussed with the Team itself. We anticipate that the work of the Team and your coverage may take place under conditions that pose security risks. Human Rights Watch will also need to conduct a legal review of a close-to-final cut of the film to ensure no statements or depictions could raise issues of liability for Human Rights Watch, but such a review is not intended as any form of editorial control.

We're looking forward to having you join us on an Emergency Team mission later this year.

All the best,

Carroll Bogert

IMDb.com

The free online database at *www.IMDb.com* lists all screen credits for most films and television programs produced over the last several decades. It's a great resource and enables anyone to research any individual or project. Make sure to add your project to the database and add confirmed credits to keep it up to date. IMDb has a verification process to make sure credits are accurate. IMDbPro.com contains more industry information including agent information, casting notices, box office numbers, and estimated budgets. Access to the Pro website requires an annual subscription fee.

Creating a Pitch

In addition to the proposal, you'll need to work up a pitch for your film. The purpose of your **pitch** is to verbally inform, engage, and excite the person listening to your project. A pitch is a distillation of the key elements of your project and it is expressed orally. The form and length of the pitch will depend on whom you will be pitching but certain principles apply.

Below I've included an insightful piece written by John McKeel about creating The Winning Pitch.

> "Just the thought of standing in front of an audience scared Jim. He wasn't alone. A recent survey showed more people are afraid of public speaking than dying, so Jim worked very hard to memorize what he thought was a great speech. He wrote and re-wrote it until every word was perfect. Unfortunately, when it came time to deliver his talk, Jim was so nervous he forgot what he was going to say. He stumbled over his words. Jim stopped frequently and his eyes naturally rolled to the top of his head as he tried to remember those perfect phrases he had so meticulously constructed. He lost contact with his audience and the speech was a total bomb.
>
> You've written a great proposal but now you have to pitch it. Never confuse the written word with the spoken word. They are two completely different forms of communication. Beautiful writing can sound stilted and pretentious when read aloud. Great literature doesn't guarantee great performance, so prepare an oral presentation orally. This is so important I'm going to repeat it. Prepare an oral presentation *orally*.
>
> How is that possible? You know your material. You've lived and breathed your project for a long time. You've talked about it with friends, family, and probably perfect strangers, so your first exercise in the preparation of a great oral pitch is to sit down in a room by yourself and just start talking. Let the words come as you describe your passion. As you talk about it, certain sentences will stand out. Quickly jot them down and then keep talking. Again, remember this is an oral presentation, not a written proposal. Don't write down any more words than it will take to

remind you of the thought. The key is to get back to talking as soon as possible. It's an oral presentation, so we are preparing orally for it.

If you are having trouble getting started with your talk, answer these questions *out loud*. Imagine that I am right there with you. Now let's talk:

- Your film is a jewel with many facets. Can you describe some of these facets and some of the characters or themes I will see in your final project?
- Now, if you had to choose only one theme, what is the most important facet? Why?
- Who are you making this film for?
- You seem very passionate about your project. Why?
- Tell me about some of the characters I will meet in your film.
- What do you hope people will take away from watching your project or documentary?

The three most important topics to address in your pitch are:

1. For narrative—Who is the film about and what is the conflict?
2. For documentaries—What is this film about?
3. Why make it now?

You have to convince us that our money (as an investment or grant) won't be wasted. Tell us why you will see this project through to completion.

After an hour you should have pages of great sentences that will trigger great thoughts. Now it's time to find the theme of your project.

Look over those pages of sentences you just wrote down. For the narrative—what is the most compelling way to describe your film or project? For the documentary—do you see any themes? It's time to take out more paper and write a different theme on the top of each page. Now copy all of the sentences that relate to that theme onto that page.

Take a break. Have a cup of coffee. Go for a walk. Play with the kids and then come back to your notebook. Look through all the pages. One will stand out. You've done it! That's your pitch. But how will you organize those random sentences into an organized pitch?

Try giving a four-minute talk from just the notes on that particular page. A couple of things will happen. First, a natural rhythm will develop. You'll discover you need to say this before that. A rough outline will develop. You will also find that some of the sentences aren't as powerful as the others. Discard them and you will be left with pure gold."

Producing a Trailer

Producing a trailer is a great way to raise project financing. It works well for narrative projects when you are going after investor money, but for nonfiction projects it is often an essential part of grant applications and when pitching to a funder.

For narrative projects, filming a scene or two from the project to edit a trailer can be a good investment of time and resources. Sometimes the cast and crew are willing to work for a day or two on a brief section of the film if they think it will benefit them in the long run—like getting the financing to make the feature-length project. If you produce a trailer, make sure it reflects the production values and tone of the longer project. Potential investors will be watching to see how it looks and sounds as much as for the performances and the script. The trailer must be a strong pitch element, otherwise it could be a detriment to your proposal package. Better to leave the script up to the investor's imagination then create a poor trailer.

Some creators produce a stand-alone short film to show the merits of the feature. If the short wins awards at film festivals it may help to garner support for the feature version.

For nonfiction projects, trailers are usually required for any application to a grant-making organization or foundation. Aside from your written proposal/treatment, it is the best way to convey your project to any decision maker, whether a grantor, investor, or network.

The trailer should run between 5 and 10 minutes; shorter is better. Make sure it is well shot and edited and demonstrates your understanding of the topic, your access to the story elements, and the way you plan to tell the story. Production grants are very competitive, so make sure the trailer grabs the viewer's attention and keeps it from the very beginning. Remember that it is part of a whole proposal: The written material is there to help tell the full story and the trailer is there to support and "prove" that you are competent and capable of delivering a strong project.

Trailers can be used in lots of different places besides grant applications and investor meetings. You can post it on your project's website, use it at film festival pitch contests and at fundraising parties. Keep these audiences in mind as you create the trailer.

Distribution Plan

You'll need a general distribution plan for your film at the outset. Of course, things will change as you progress through the steps in producing your project but it's important to make a thorough plan at the beginning. Don't assume that distributors and networks will be knocking down your door after its first screening at a major film festival. Research and determine the best way to release, distribute, and disseminate your particular project. There is no one way to sell or distribute projects, but with the constant evolution and change in our industry, whatever you did on your last project doesn't necessarily pertain to this one. Below is a list of various distribution outlets to consider:

- Domestic theatrical
- International theatrical
- Domestic network or cable television
- International television
- Video on Demand (VOD)
- Subscription Video on Demand (SVOD)
- Online streaming
- Digital downloads
- DVD sales
- Cell phone or mobile Apps
- New future technology models

Stay up-to-date by reading the film industry trades and blogs like *Variety, Hollywood Reporter, Filmmaker, IndieWire* and *Documentary* magazines/websites. Many film festivals offer seminars and panel discussions with the latest distribution models for independent projects. Local film organizations also offer master classes and invite guest speakers to keep their members educated on the constantly changing distribution landscape.

Marketing/Publicity Campaign

During the development process, think about your intended audience and how/where you can reach them with a marketing and publicity campaign. Also consider how much it will cost, in terms of time and money, to communicate with those potential viewers. Can it be done through social media and online media or will it require more expensive advertising and publicity? A tentative plan should be worked out before you move forward with the project.

For nonfiction and some narrative projects, it may be appropriate to create a social outreach media campaign based on the topic or message of the project. If so, think about how best to contact the relevant communities that would most want to support the project and then create a plan.

Presales

A **Presale** is any sale that occurs before you complete the project. Depending on the amount of money you receive from any presales, it could be enough money to produce the entire project. That all depends on your budget and which territories you can sell. For instance, if you had presales for domestic and international television, it would still leave you with the other rights listed above that could be sold after the project's completion

Keep in mind that presales are not that easy to obtain. If you have a firm reputation as a filmmaker or producer, it can help you obtain meetings with networks and other distributors. For instance, the director may have a proven track record of making profitable films, or an A-list actress is attached to your film—these are the kind of things that help to get presales.

Genre films with very low budgets can sometimes get funding before production begins. There are strong, insatiable audiences for horror and sci-fi, so some funders may take a chance on an emerging filmmaker if there is a strong script and plan.

For documentaries, elements like the director's track record, an A-list actor who agrees to do the narration, or the strength of the underlying material may be the key elements that make the project bankable for a presale. For several of the feature documentaries I have produced or coproduced, a few key foreign television rights and the U.S. cable television rights were sold and these presales funded the film entirely. It means you have to keep the budget tight, but at least you know you have all the money necessary to make the film start to finish.

Sometimes you won't be able to get a sale until after you have shot the project and have created a great rough cut. Then you might be able to get some sales. But this is a calculated risk and you should proceed with caution. I don't advise going into any kind of debt for a film. If it is a good enough project you will find the money—or wait until you have saved up the money to cover the entire budget.

For documentaries, there is the added funding option of nonprofit agencies and foundations. Development and production grants are an ideal way to get the project made if it meets the foundation's criteria and you can make a strong application. This takes a lot of time and effort so make sure you and your project fit all the criteria before applying. You'll need to plan for a long fundraising period before production can start. Often the decision from foundations takes several months after the submission deadline.

Sales Agents

Sales agents are people who specialize in selling rights to films. They have connections with the various distribution outlets (domestic and international) and are known for the certain kinds of films/projects that they sell. Some concentrate on narrative features, some on feature documentaries, others focus on digital platforms and a few sell short films.

Deliverables

Deliverables is the list of documents, masters, and other media that need to be delivered to a distributor or broadcaster when a project is finished. It is important to understand the amount of material that will need to be created for a deliverables list. It is time consuming and costly and should be factored into the post production timeline and budget before accepting a distribution deal. (This will be discussed, in depth, in Chapter 15, *Post Production*.)

Development Wrap Up

The process of getting your film from first idea to pre-production is a different adventure with every project. There is no way to know all the twists and turns in the road but by knowing the steps and executing them in the most efficient and logical way possible, it will be easier. By following these guidelines you should be well on your way to moving to the next level with your project.

Final Checklist Before Deciding to Produce the Film

I've put this list together as a final checklist before you take the leap and produce a project. Depending on your answers, you may decide to move forward or not:

1. Are there other films out there—in development, in production, or already released—similar to my project?
2. If so, is my project different enough so it won't be impacted negatively? For a documentary, if it is the same subject matter, is it a different enough "take" from the others so it won't matter? Even the perception that it is too similar could diminish your project's viability. Make sure you research and know what has been produced and what is in the pipeline.
3. Is there an audience for this project? If so, how can it be marketed and publicized to that audience? Is that doable with limited resources?
4. Am *I* the right person to make this film?
5. Can I devote two to five years of my life to this project?
6. What's the preliminary budget?

DEVELOPMENT

7. Can I raise all the money? Do I know exactly where I can get the financing? Or is it just wishful thinking?

8. If not, can I fund it entirely by myself (or with family and friends)? Is that something I am willing to do? Does everyone understand and accept the risks of such an investment?

9. Do I have all the rights I need with the proper documentation?

10. If making a documentary, can I afford all the archive (video and stills) that I need?

11. What format do I plan to use for shooting? What is the *exact* workflow for the finishing of the film? What will be my deliverables? (See Chapter 15, *Post Production*.)

12. Do I trust my key collaborators? Are they people who share my values and work ethics? Will it be fun and rewarding to work with them over the long life of the project?

Depending on how you answered, you are ready to move onto the next step for your project.

RECAP:

1. **Allow 2–5 years for development.**
2. **Read great scripts to learn from the best.**
3. **Nail down the rights.**
4. **Create and memorize your log line.**
5. **Proposals differ for narratives and documentaries. They also differ depending on whom you are sending them to. Make sure it is the best it can be before sending it out. You only have one shot at a first impression.**
6. **Trailers are essential for documentary proposals. They can also be helpful for narrative projects.**
7. **Presales can give you all or some of the money you need to make your film.**
8. **Acquire a sales agent or a very concrete distribution strategy.**
9. **Be sure you *really* want to make this particular film and you know the reasons why. They will sustain you during the long, dark hours.**

CHAPTER 2
SCRIPT BREAKDOWN

A SCRIPT BREAKDOWN IS LIKE a road map for your project. We all know the importance of preparation, so what would you think if you heard this story? A friend decides that she wants to go see her favorite band play in a city that is somewhere half way across the country. She knows the name of the town and the date the band is playing. She decides to just hop in her car without directions, no knowledge of what's the best route to take, and no sense of how much it will all cost. She doesn't know if she'll need to stay at a hotel along the way and hasn't brought any additional supplies, change of clothes, or even tickets to the sold-out concert. What would you say to this friend?

Well, that's what it's like to try to budget and schedule a film without doing a script breakdown first. You've got a great 100-page script—how do you turn that into a 25-day shooting schedule and a detailed, estimated budget? The first step is the **script breakdown**, the tool the producer and assistant director use to analyze a script into its specific elements and then turn them into a plan and budget for the production. Once

First, have a definite, clear practical idea—a goal, an objective. Second, have the necessary means to achieve your ends— wisdom, money, materials, and methods. Third, adjust all your means to the end.

— Aristotle

completed, you'll have a way to wrap your arms around the production details and work out the first draft of the schedule and budget with ease and certainty.

Nuts and Bolts

Creating a script breakdown is a process that allows you to list all the characters, locations, props, special effects (SFX), costumes, etc., required by the project's script. During early prep, in order to create a budget, the producer often makes the script breakdown because the assistant director (AD) hasn't been hired yet.

The script breakdown is always the first step after the script is written, so you can figure out how ambitious and challenging your project will be and how best to produce it. Later in this book we will go more in-depth for the full, detailed breakdown of the final version of the shooting script in Chapter 11, *Scheduling*. Here we will be using a single sheet to list the major production elements of the script. You can access the script breakdown template on the website *www.ProducerToProducer.com* or use any other form that works for you.

Script breakdowns are used for fiction projects or nonfiction projects with narrative elements like re-creations. For documentaries where I produced re-creations like *Man on Wire* (2008) or *1971* (2014), I created a script breakdown before budgeting or scheduling the historical re-creation shoots.

Once you have created a script breakdown, you will use it to create a tentative production schedule laying out how many days or weeks you'll need for the pre-production, production, and post-production phases of your film. The tentative schedule will then allow you to create an estimated budget. (As you get closer to the shoot dates, you'll need to lock a *detailed* schedule and budget—see the *Scheduling* and *Budgeting* chapters for further details.)

Finally, the script breakdown is an effective way of focusing the attention of the director and/or writer to the more ambitious, expensive, and otherwise potentially problematic elements of the script at a relatively early stage in the process. The breakdown allows them to understand the schedule and budget ramifications of the script in a way they can't without one.

For instance, on *Torte Bluma*, a short film I coproduced, the other producers thought the 18-page script could be shot in six days. It's a period piece that takes place in Treblinka, the extermination camp built by Nazi Germany in WW II, and we planned to shoot it all in Brooklyn, NY. Because of all the production design, props, animals, location moves, and costumed extras, the director believed that the film would require seven days to shoot it all. Only after I did the script breakdown did it become clear that the director was right—we had to plan for a seven-day shooting schedule.

Breakdown Details

Creating a breakdown is data-entry intensive and requires a lot of concentration. You may need to do it over the course of several days, depending on the length of the screenplay, so pace yourself. Some scheduling software programs allow you to import the script into the template which can save you time. I personally like to manually input it because I get to know the project in a more detailed way.

Before we go over the breakdown sheet, let's define all the elements that are included in it.

Script Title—Working title for your screenplay.

Scene #—List the scene number from the scene heading. Tracking by scene number allows you to keep track of which elements play in which scenes.

Page Count—List each scene in chronological order. Numbering the page count allows you to build a tentative schedule later on.

Int/Ext and Day/Night—Information taken from the scene heading. It will facilitate scheduling later on.

Location—Information taken from the scene heading. It will facilitate scheduling later on.

Action—A concise description of the character action. It will facilitate scheduling later on.

Cast—List each actor with a speaking role in the scene.

Extras/Background Actors—**Extras** or **background actors** are the people who are in the background of a scene and do not have any script lines or specific action that requires direction from the project's director. List all non-speaking roles with approximate number of each type.

Props, Costumes, Animals, Picture Vehicles, Stunts, Weapons, EFX, Hair/Makeup—Include any of the production elements discussed below:

Props—List all of the production design/art direction elements for the set. Include set dressing, props, signs, wall decorations, etc.

Animals—List any animals required in a scene.

Picture Vehicles—List **picture vehicles** which are the vehicles that will be seen and used by actors on camera.

Stunts—List stunts including fight choreography, car chases and crashes, and actor falls. You need to hire a stunt coordinator, as well.

Weapons—List any prop weapons.

Costumes—List any special costumes.

Hair/Makeup—List any special hair/makeup considerations.

To best illustrate how to create a script breakdown and other pre-production steps later in the book, I am using a short film titled *Sundae* as a case study. Written and directed by Sonya Goddy, produced by Kristin Frost and coproduced by Birgit Gernboeck, the film's log line reads: "An irritated mother bribes her young son with ice cream in exchange for vital information."

The *Sundae* script is only five pages long and it demonstrates beautifully how you can pack a lot into a few minutes if you know what you are doing. As a case study, we'll analyze it to understand the many important pre-production steps outlined in the next few chapters and will use it to create the breakdown, tentative schedule, estimated budget and other pre-production documents.

Please read the screenplay below and then look at the script breakdown sheets that follow. As you will see, the production elements are highlighted in capital letters (CAPS) in the script so they can be added easily to the script breakdown sheet in the next section.

Here is the *Sundae* script:

SUNDAE

Written by

Sonya Goddy

Story by Sonya Goddy & Keola Racela

1   INT. CAR - DAY   1

    MARY (40s), is driving through a residential neighborhood
    with her son TIM (6), in the backseat.

    Tim's little legs fidget, dangling miles from the car floor.
    He looks out the window for a bit.

    The SUBURBAN CAR stops. Mary looks at her son.

                            MARY
                Which way now?

    Tim hesitates. He points to the right.

    Mary nods and turns the car, focused.

    They cruise past lawns, some YOUNG KIDS (Tim's age) playing
    outside, a MIDDLE-AGED MAN in a DOWN JACKET taking out the
    GARBAGE. MUSIC blares from one of the houses as they pass.

    After a beat:

                            TIM
                Mommy.

                            MARY
                Mm.

                            TIM
                Can we get ice cream after this?

                            MARY
                    (distracted)
                Maybe.

                            TIM
                Can I get an ice cream sundae?

                            MARY
                I said maybe.

    They've reached another intersection.

                            MARY (CONT'D)
                Which way now?

    He looks out at the street, uncertain. Shakes his head.

                            TIM
                I don't know.

                            MARY
                Try to remember.

Tim peers out the window. He looks back at his Mom, blank. She swivels around in her seat.

> MARY (CONT'D)
> How about this. If you can remember, then we'll get ice cream after this.

She has her son's attention.

> TIM
> Sundae?

> MARY
> Anything you want.

Tim's eyes widen. He thinks.

The car idles for a moment. He points in a direction. The car ACCELERATES.

> MARY (CONT'D)
> (quietly)
> Good boy.

They drive -- going a little too fast for this residential street.

> TIM
> Here!

> MARY
> (alert)
> Here? This block? Are you sure?

> TIM
> Yeah.

He gazes out the window, scrutinizing the houses, trying hard now.

> MARY
> What color is the house?

> TIM
> Yellow.

Mary nods and slows down. Both mother and son peer out the windows as they cruise past house after house.

Then, like magic, it appears: A LARGE, YELLOW HOUSE. Mary smiles.

2   INT/EXT. CAR CURBSIDE AT YELLOW HOUSE - DAY   2

The car peels over to the SIDE OF THE ROAD. She unbuckles her seatbelt.

                    MARY
            I'll be right back.

She smooths her shirt, checks herself in the rearview mirror. Takes off her EYEGLASSES and puts them on the dashboard.

3   INT/EXT. YELLOW HOUSE/LAWN - DAY   3

Shuts the car door and walks up to the house. She rings the BELL. Tim fidgets in the car, absent-mindedly. From the car window, we see the scene play out:

A WOMAN in a BATHROBE AND SLIPPERS opens the front door. Mary and the Woman exchange a few words before Mary GRABS the Woman and KNOCKS HER TO HER FEET. She starts wailing on her.

The Woman SCREAMS and FIGHTS BACK.

                    WOMAN
            Help! SOMEONE! STOP!

4   INT/EXT. CAR CURBSIDE AT YELLOW HOUSE - DAY   4

Next door, a dog starts BARKING. Tim looks away from the scene. He plays with the lock button next to him. Lock, unlock. Lock, unlock.

5   INT/EXT. YELLOW HOUSE/LAWN - DAY   5

                    WOMAN (O.S.
            Get off of me! Help!

The Woman lies crumpled against the side of the house and slowly stumbles inside.

Mary WALKS briskly back to the car. Her hair and clothing is disheveled.

Instead of getting back into the car, however, she goes to the trunk, OPENS IT, SHUTS IT.

She starts to march BACK to the house, now carrying a CEMENT BLOCK. The Woman is nowhere in sight and the door is closed. Mary throws the block at the living room window.

4.

6   INT/EXT. CAR CURBSIDE AT YELLOW HOUSE - DAY   6

   We stay in the car with Tim as we hear the SOUND of a GLASS
   WINDOW BREAKING -- with a SCREAM. Followed by the SOUND of an
   ALARM. Tim ignores the chaotic noises.

   Tim looks up as the car door OPENS. He looks at the back of
   his mom's head as she gets inside.

   Mary sits for a moment, breathing heavy. She looks upset,
   but then she exhales -- almost giddy. She LAUGHS out loud.
   Takes the eyeglasses off the dashboard and puts them back on.
   Put the KEY in the ignition.

7   EXT. NEIGHBORHOOD STREET - DAY   7

   The car ZOOMS OFF.

8   INT. ICE CREAM PARLOR COUNTER - 15 MINUTES LATER - DAY   8

   The SOUND of a can of WHIPPED CREAM over Top 40 MUSIC on the
   radio.

   Tim watches a TEENAGE EMPLOYEE build a HUGE SUNDAE with ICE
   CREAM, whipped cream, HOT FUDGE, SPRINKLES AND A CHERRY.

9   INT/EXT. ICE CREAM PARLOR TABLE - DAY   9

   Mary sits next to him at the table and starts to fix her hair
   in a SMALL COMPACT. She uses a WET NAPKIN to blot at her
   eyes.

   She has a relaxed air about her now. She puts away the
   compact and smiles at Tim.

10 INT. ICE CREAM PARLOR TABLE - DAY   10

   Tim's hands fidget with anticipation as he clutches his BIG
   SPOON then digs in and starts to eat rapidly, without a word.
   Mary looks on.

   Mary sighs, almost looking happy herself. She gazes out the
   window at the streets.

   Suddenly she stops. Her eyes fixed on a point outside.

11   INT/EXT. STREET CORNER - DAY   11

In her vision, a MAN (40s), walks across the street hand-in-hand with a BLONDE WOMAN (40s). She stares at the Man's face. Then at Blonde Woman, perfectly coiffed, put-together. PEOPLE pass by on the street.

Blonde Woman is laughing at something -- the two of them intimate, romantic.

He guides Blonde Woman to a LINCOLN TOWN CAR, opens the passenger seat for her and then climbs in the back after her. After a moment the TOWN CAR DRIVER pulls the sedan away.

12   INT/EXT. ICE CREAM PARLOR TABLE - DAY   12

Mary's face has gone from tranquil to frozen. Tim is still going at his sundae, humming to himself.

13   INT. ICE CREAM PARLOR TABLE - DAY   13

                    MARY
               (hoarse)
          Honey?

He doesn't answer.

                    MARY (CONT'D)
          Timmy.

                    TIM
          Mm hmm?

She slowly turns to her son.

                    MARY
          Are you sure it was a yellow house?

His face is completely covered in HOT FUDGE, NUTS and WHIPPED CREAM. MELTED ICE CREAM drips from his chin.

He looks at her with big eyes. Swallows his bite with a gulp.

                                                    CUT TO TITLE:

          SUNDAE

MUSIC PLAYS OVER CREDITS.

Filling In the Script Breakdown Sheet

As mentioned earlier, before making the script breakdown, you'll need to add consecutive numbers to the scene headings to create the shooting script. Then you'll do a page count for each scene. **Page counts** are recorded in 1/8th-page increments. A quarter of a page is 2/8ths and a half page is 4/8ths, and so on. Remember to keep the numbering in eighths: Don't turn 4/8ths into ½ or 2/8ths into ¼. When the count gets to 8/8ths of a page, you'll count it as one page. For instance, if you counted 11/8ths of a page, it will be noted as 1-3/8ths.

Below is the *Sundae* breakdown. It has 13 scenes and they are each listed in the breakdown sheet. By looking at each one of these factors you can determine your production requirements and discover the more challenging and expensive elements of your film. With this information you can discuss the elements with the director and/or writer during the development and pre-production stages. Before looking at this breakdown we'll discuss the specifics for each element of *Sundae*.

Scene #s—*Sundae* has 13 scenes.

Page Count—The rule of thumb for an independent low-budget production is to shoot three to five pages a day. *Sundae* is planned as a two-day shoot.

Int/Ext and Day/Night—*Sundae* has 4-2/8 pages of interior/exterior day scenes, and 7/8 pages of interior day scenes.

Location—*Sundae* has four locations—Neighborhood Streets, Yellow House, Ice Cream Parlor, and Street Corner.

Cast—*Sundae* has two principal actors. Mary and Tim are in every scene. There are four non-speaking featured roles—Woman, Teenage Employee, Blond Woman, and Man. Note that Tim is a minor actor (under 18 years old).

Extras/Background Actors—*Sundae* needed one extra to play a town car driver and eight others to fill out the scenes in the Neighborhood Streets and Street Corner.

Props—*Sundae* was written with very few props required. The Prop Cement Block and the Ice Cream Sundae are the biggest requirements.

Vehicles—*Sundae* needed two picture vehicles: a Suburban Car and a Town Car. Both could be rented from a local car rental company for one day each.

Stunts—The cement block crashing through the window and the women fighting will require a stunt coordinator.

Animals—There were no animals in *Sundae*.

EFX—There are no post effects in *Sundae*.

Costumes—There are no special/particular costumes except for the bathrobe and slippers and the possible need to "double" Tim's shirt when he is eating the sundae—one clean and one covered in ice cream and hot fudge.

Here is the *Sundae* script breakdown:

SCRIPT BREAKDOWN

Scene #	Page Count	INT/EXT Day/Night	Location	Description	Cast	Background Actors	Props/Animals/Vehicles/Costumes/Stunts/SFX/Weapons
1	2	INT. Day	Car	Mary drives her son around a neighbor asking for directions	Mary, Tim	2 Young Kids, Middle-aged man	Suburban Car, Down Jacket, Garbage Can
2	2/8	INT/EXT. Day	Car curbside at Yellow House	Car pulls to the side, Mary takes of glasses	Mary, Tim	0	Suburban Car, Eyeglasses
3	2/8	INT/EXT. Day	Yellow House/Lawn	Mary rings bell and fights with woman at door	Mary, Tim, Woman	0	Suburban Car, Doorbell, Woman's bathrobe & Slippers, Fight Stunt
4	1/8	INT/EXT. Day	Car curbside at Yellow House	Tim plays for car's lock button distracted	Tim	0	Suburban Car
5	3/8	INT/EXT. Day	Yellow House/Lawn	Woman stumbles inside. Mary get cement block from car, marches back to house & throws at front window	Mary, Woman	0	Suburban Car, Prop Cement Block
6	2/8	INT/EXT. Day	Car curbside at Yellow House	Tim sits in car and watches Mary sits in seat. Mary laughs and puts glasses back on	Mary, Tim	0	Suburban Car, Eyeglasses, Ignition Key
7	1/8	EXT. Day	Neighborhood Street	Car zooms off	Mary, Tim	0	Suburban Car
8	1/8	INT. Day	Ice Cream Parlor Counter	Teenage Employee builds huge sundae	Teenage Employee	0	Sundae with Ice cream, Whipped cream, Hot Fudge, Sprinkles & Cherry
9	2/8	INT/EXT. Day	Ice Cream Parlor Table	Mary fixes hair, relaxes & smiles at Tim	Mary, Tim	0	Sundae, Small compact, Wet Napkin
10	2/8	INT. Day	Ice Cream Parlor Table	Tim eats sundae rapidly while Mary sees something out the parlor window on the street	Mary, Tim	0	Sundae, Big Spoon
11	3/8	INT/EXT. Day	Street Corner	Man & Blonde Woman walk hand-in-hand, get into Town Car and drive away	Man, Blonde Woman	5 People on street, Town Car Driver	Lincoln Town Car
12	1/8	INT/EXT. Day	Ice Cream Parlor Table	Mary is frozen while Tim eats sundae	Mary, Tim	0	Sundae, Big Spoon
13	4/8	INT. Day	Ice Cream Parlor Table	Mary asks Tim about Yellow House and he swallows a big gulp	Mary, Tim	0	Sundae, Big Spoon, Hot Fudge, Nuts, Whipped cream, Soiled shirt for Tim(?)

Schedule Analysis of *Sundae*

Before putting the script scenes into a shooting order, analyze all the factors that will affect scheduling decisions. We'll discuss the principles first and then use them to analyze *Sundae* specifically.

PAGES PER DAY

Most low-budget independent projects can shoot no more than three to five pages per day (for a 12-hour shoot day.) The *Sundae* script is five pages long, so the filmmakers planned for a two-day shooting schedule (one of the great things about really short scripts). Day 1 would be the Neighborhood Streets and Yellow House locations and Day 2 would be the Ice Cream Parlor and Street Corner locations.

LOCATIONS

For the shooting schedule, you'll want to group all the scenes together that are shot in one location. Ideally you don't want to do a company move during each shoot day. A **company move** requires everyone to pack up the equipment into vans and trucks, drive to the next location, unload, and set up the equipment again. It usually kills at least two hours in a shooting schedule so it's always optimal to avoid them if possible when scheduling. Lastly, to keep the costs down, it's usually cheaper to film in locations versus building a set in a studio.

As mentioned before, in *Sundae* there are four locations: interior/exterior Neighborhood Streets driving shots, Yellow House exteriors, Ice Cream Parlor interior/exteriors, and Street Corner exterior. This script is unusual because two of the sets are interior/exterior. For the driving scenes, the camera is positioned inside the car most of the time but the outside is seen in each shot; and for some of the Ice Cream Parlor scenes, the camera is inside the location but the actors and picture vehicle are directed outside on the corner. Note that neither shoot day had a company move.

The filmmakers scouted for the yellow house and the ice cream parlor six weeks in advance. The director approached a local ice cream shop in Brooklyn and a friend who had a house nearby. Both owners said yes! For the exterior street corner across from the ice cream parlor, the filmmakers were able to utilize the real street across from the ice cream parlor so that kept continuity fairly simple.

In New York City, the Mayor's Office for Film, Theatre & Broadcasting is the local film commission and they require a $300 permit fee if it is necessary to take over a public space or sidewalk with personnel and equipment or if you need parking permits for production vehicles. For the exterior shots, the filmmakers used available light and didn't need extra lighting or grip equipment. When they were shooting the wide shots, PAs asked the public to wait on the sidewalk until the director yelled "Cut." They used parking permits for their vehicles in this neighborhood and for the Yellow House neighborhood. It allowed them to secure public parking spaces overnight.

DAY VS. NIGHT SHOOTING

Generally it is much easier to shoot during the day than at night. For night shoots, cast/crew are a little more tired and often more lighting is required. Additionally, I'm always concerned about safety and when cast/crew get tired, it can sometimes lead to accidents.

For *Sundae,* all scenes take place during the day so it was relatively easy to schedule. It was shot during the winter so the days were short which impacted how much daylight the crew had to work with on each shoot day.

WEATHER

Weather contingency refers to the production plan if the production gets bad weather that would negatively impact the schedule. Usually the production team would procure a **cover set** (a different location that can be shot at on short notice) if there is bad weather, like rain or snow. Exterior shoot days are always scheduled at the beginning of the shooting schedule in case you have to switch to a cover set. The cover set allows you to shoot interiors on the bad weather day and then go back to the original location on a different day later when the weather is good.

For *Sundae,* filming in the winter with exteriors on both days, weather was a big concern. Many discussions between the assistant director (AD), producer, and director revolved around what to do if it rained or snowed on one or both of the days. If there was snow between the two weekend shoot days, there could be continuity problems—what to do? What if it started raining in the middle of Day 1 filming in the car? What was the weather contingency plan?

The producers of *Sundae* decided to film rain or shine. They calculated that each major location—Yellow House/Neighborhood on Day 1 and Ice Cream Parlor/Street Corner on Day 2—was a discrete, self-contained "place" in the viewer's eye, and if the weather was different, the narrative could handle the slight inconsistencies that would occur on screen. Having said that, they much preferred to have no precipitation for either day and watched the weather forecasts closely in the days leading up to the shoot. The filmmakers did have a catastrophic weather contingency; if they had a snow blizzard the cast/crew would plan to shoot the following weekend.

CAST AVAILABILITY

Sometimes certain cast members have availability issues that need to be factored into scheduling. Maybe one actor stars in a play on Broadway and has to be wrapped every day by 5 p.m. or another actor has to go to her brother's wedding one Saturday during the principal photography period. If so, these caveats have to be worked around during the scheduling process.

For *Sundae,* all cast members were available for all shooting days so they didn't have to adjust the schedule at all. But for the minor actor they needed to follow the New York state child performer rules. The actor playing Tim was 7 years old and the law restricts his work time to eight hours on set and only four hours of that time can he work. This would affect certain scheduling decisions because the character Tim is in 60% of the scenes.

Summary

Based on an analysis of all of these factors, there is a good understanding of what it will take to make this project—two shooting days, four sets, three locations, two picture vehicles, two principal actors (one is a minor), four non-speaking featured actors, nine extras, a fight, a stunt, and no weather contingency. This is a doable film for a low-budget but there are a few issues that could be problematic so a smart and detailed production plan and schedule will be important.

Using the Breakdown to Adjust Your Script

Now that you or the Assistant Director have completed the script breakdown, it is time to have a conversation with the director to obtain more specific details so you can plan and budget. The breakdown has enabled you to target the more challenging (logistically and financially) elements of the script. By discussing these issues early with the director and writer, some of those elements can be re-written to make the film more doable with the resources/finances available. This is a critical step. If you don't engage with possible script changes now, you may put the project's overall success at risk.

Depending on the specifics for each prop, set dressing, or picture vehicle written in the script, the budget can vary widely. Ask the questions now so you can budget accordingly. For instance, if the script says "car," does it mean a cheap, beat-up car that would be inexpensive and easy to acquire from a junk yard? If so, does it have to run or can it just be towed to the location and sit there?

If the script calls for a "period" vehicle—what period in history? Does it have to be an authentic period car in perfect condition or is there flexibility on how historically accurate it needs to be? Does it have to be a particular color?

Location costs can vary widely too. Perhaps the script requires three days of shooting in an airport lounge—a location that is potentially very expensive and difficult to acquire for multiple days. Depending on the story, there may be a different location that would work for those scenes—perhaps an abandoned warehouse, a much cheaper and easier location to procure.

I was an advisor on a low-budget production where the script called for an actor to fall off a motorcycle in the middle of a busy New York City street. The character, who is drunk, grabs the bike, drives down the block, hears a police car siren and crashes the motorcycle, after which his mother runs up and yells at him.

This would require a lot of resources: a stunt double for the actor, a motorcycle to be ridden by the actor, another motorcycle that has been "propped" to show the damage after the accident, a costume for the actor and another for the stunt person, another set of costumes that show damage to the clothes post-accident, permits to close down the street, police officers for security, and extra crew on walkie-talkies to "lock up" and control the location during filming.

Once we mapped out all the requirements for the scene, it became clear that the production could not afford it. As a result, the director and the writer rewrote the scene. In the final version, the character grabs the motorcycle and tries to start it up but it won't start. So he jumps off the bike, runs down the street, and nearly gets hit by a cab before his mother (who was chasing him) pushes him out of the way and he falls to the ground. As you can see, this is a much cheaper way to stage the scene that nevertheless preserves the dramatic action. Once you have a good script breakdown you can use the information to really tighten your script, production plan, and budget.

RECAP

1. A script breakdown is a list of all the production elements in a film's script on a scene-by-scene basis.

2. Download a script breakdown template from www.ProducerToProducer.com or create your own template.

3. Outline all the elements for each scene on the breakdown sheet.

4. Analyze the script breakdown and discuss the important elements with the director for specifics necessary to begin budgeting the film's costs. Refer to the list in this chapter.

5. If an element in a scene is proving to be too expensive or difficult, discuss alternatives with the director and/or writer to find out if more affordable options can be included in the next revision of the script.

6. For scheduling purposes, generally a low-budget project can shoot three to five pages on a 12-hour day schedule.

CHAPTER 3
BUDGETING

Budgeting Overview

Now it's time to prepare a budget. Don't panic—it will be fine and it can actually be fun. In fact, budgeting is one of my favorite things to do. Seriously. It's fun, creative—even relaxing. Here are my reasons why:

1. Numbers don't lie.
2. Numbers don't have an attitude.
3. Numbers don't have an agenda.
4. Numbers can be changed easily.
5. Numbers reflect the producer's vision for the project.
6. Numbers lead you to concrete decisions, which are the building blocks of creativity.
7. Numbers—meaning money—can sometimes be stretched by a good producer in a way that is deeply satisfying and, at times, thrilling.

Every excellent producer needs great budgeting skills. Limitations (e.g., lack of money and resources) are just an opportunity for creative problem solving. By knowing how

> *I have become my own version of an optimist; if I can't make it through one door, I'll go to another door—or I'll make a door.*
>
> —Joan Rivers

to create and understand budgets, you can figure out how to solve the issues that any production will face.

First and foremost, budgeting is a great organizing tool. An estimated budget will give you a good idea of the scope—not just financial, but also logistical—of the film, which allows you to begin conceptualizing the project on many different levels. By creating an estimated budget, you can begin to visualize the size of the production, the number of locations and studio days, the number of cast and crew, all the production design elements, and everything else outlined in the script breakdown. Without a budget, you have no idea how much to estimate for production costs and no concrete plans to make the project happen.

For those of you who become nervous, uncomfortable, or downright terrified when interacting with numbers, have no fear—we'll go through the budget, line by line. Keep in mind that the more often you create budgets, the more facile you will become with them.

If you don't anticipate a full-time career as a producer—maybe you are a director or a screenwriter—learning how to make or, at least, understand a budget is invaluable and raises your confidence level. Occasionally I've encountered directors who are intimidated by budgets and are afraid to engage with the producer about their specific creative and production requirements. Knowledge is power and the more you understand the numbers, the better informed you will be about where all the money is going—and this will help you make better decisions on the creative side.

Once you have prepared an estimated budget, you can begin to figure out how and where to save money. The first draft of your budget is going to be "fat" and probably unaffordable. Don't panic, as the first draft is just a benchmark to use as a worst-case scenario. You'll then start to whittle that down as you move through the pre-production process.

When Should You Create a First Budget?

As soon as you have a script that you want to produce, you need to create a budget. Why so early in the process? You need to decide what resources you'll require and figure out what is possible. You can shoot your project on so many different kinds of digital and film formats—all of which have very different costs. Once there is a ballpark budget number, you can compare it to the amount of funding you have raised. If there is a big difference, it will enable you to ascertain if the project is doable or not. It may also impact the creative assumptions. More on that later in this chapter.

Everything but the Kitchen Sink

There are many ways to approach budgeting. I think the best way is to first create the "kitchen sink" version of the budget, which comes from the American colloquial phrase "throw in everything but the kitchen sink." Create a budget for the most expensive format you *might* be able to shoot in. If you really want to shoot with an expensive, hi-resolution digital camera, create a budget for that format first. You can always create another one for a less expensive format later.

Think out everything you could possibly need and put a number to it. Don't factor in possible donations or favors in this first pass. If you know you are *definitely* getting a free camera rental, then you can factor that into the budget as an assumption. Put everything in there so you don't forget any possible elements. When you do the next iteration you can reduce things and tighten it up.

Budgeting Software

The best way to prepare a production budget is to use computer budgeting software specifically created for film/video productions. It will have a pre-formatted template that will contain all the necessary line items already listed in numerical order.

I've created a budgeting template based on the line numbers we'll discuss in this chapter. It is free with the purchase of this book and can be downloaded at *www.ProducerToProducer.com*. As a Microsoft Excel spreadsheet, it is a comprehensive template for budgeting, ideal for anyone who doesn't want or need a complicated program. I recommend it for short films, music videos, documentaries, series projects and some feature films because it is simple, user-friendly, and based on the industry standard for line-item names and numbers. Other companies sell proprietary software such as *Showbiz Budgeting* and *Movie Magic Budgeting*.

Movie Magic Budgeting is software specifically created for budgeting feature films. It is the industry standard and provides templates that correspond to various film studios and television networks. It is proprietary software (*www.entertainmentpartners.com*) that does not allow multiple people to share one application. *Movie Magic Budgeting* is companion software to *Final Draft* (screenplay software) and *Movie Magic Scheduling* (discussed in Chapter 11, *Scheduling*), so you can break down a feature script written in *Final Draft*, put it into a schedule with *Movie Magic Scheduling* and then import directly into *Movie Magic Budgeting*. Naturally, this can save you time transferring info from one format and stage to the next. This is a robust piece of software which also allows you to create budgets with various currencies, globals and in-depth fringe rates (see later in this chapter).

For lots of projects like short films, music videos or documentaries, I don't use *Movie Magic Budgeting*—it's a little cumbersome and has a longer learning curve. But it is indispensable for feature films, television series, or anything that requires more line items and additional customization. In addition to the *Producer to Producer* template, I often use *Showbiz Budgeting* because it has actualization capabilities, something we will discuss later in the book. Go to *www.ProducerToProducer.com* for more information.

Budget Breakdown

A budget breakdown utilizes all the information in the script and the script breakdown so you can do the first pass of the budget.

Go back to the two documents and figure out the following:

1. How many days to shoot? The rule of thumb is three to five pages per day for a low-budget indie production.

2. How many days to scout? This will depend on how many locations you have to visit.

3. What crew positions do you need? What will you be paying each of them? This can range from free (for those who volunteer) to deferred compensation to a daily or weekly rate. We'll discuss these options later in this chapter.

4. How many cast members? SAG-AFTRA or non-union? What SAG-AFTRA agreement will you be working under? Does it require pay or deferred pay? If pay, does it require the payment of a flat fee (with deferred for OT) or does it require OT to be factored in? (We'll discuss the different SAG-AFTRA agreements in Chapter 5, *Casting*.)

5. Set build or locations? If you need to build a set, how elaborate must it be? You'll need to budget for a studio, as well. If locations, list them in detail. If both, you'll need to know what you will build and what you will shoot on location and how many days for each.

6. Cast and crew numbers—How many cast and crew do you plan to hire for the project? How many days do you require for each actor and crew person for pre-production, rehearsal, shoot, and wrap?

7. Travel and transportation costs—Will you need to hire vans to transport cast and crew? Do you have to book airfare for anyone? Do you need to rent hotel rooms for any cast or crew? What about production vans and trucks for equipment, props, and costume departments?

8. Catering/food costs—How many people and days do you need to budget for lunch and craft service? Will you need to budget for 2nd meals or per diems?

9. Props/art/picture vehicles—What will you need to purchase/rent for these elements in the film?

10. Equipment—What format? Digital or film? Which camera and accessories for which technology? Do you need a dolly, crane, underwater housing, or Steadicam? What is required for grip and lighting equipment? Are walkie-talkies needed?

11. Sound recording—Will it be sync sound recording or MOS (without sync sound recording)? Will there be a need for audio and video playback?

12. Shooting Ratio—How many digital media storage drives do you need to budget for? Calculate how much digital material you'll be acquiring during the entire shooting period and make sure you have enough hard drives and backup drives to suffice. If shooting film, remember to budget for film stock purchase, film stock processing, and the film-to-digital transfer. Also keep in mind that digital material may need to be down converted, backed up, and archived and that will have a cost, as well.

13. Post production—How do you plan to finish? What kind of digital master? Any film prints? Color correct session? Digital intermediate? Archival research and footage acquisition? How do you plan to do the audio editing and mix?

14. Music—Will you hire a composer, plan to license music, or both?

15. Film festivals/Marketing and Publicity—What do you need to spend for film festival application fees, posters, postcards, website creation, travel expenses, and other marketing materials?

16. Miscellaneous—What do you need to budget for legal costs, overhead costs like office rental, office equipment, insurance, and accounting?

Before creating a budget, answer these questions on a piece of paper and refer to it as you work your way through all the budget sections.

Estimated Budget

Now you are ready to create a first draft of your estimated budget. Just like a writer, you need to get it all down on paper and then start to revise. At this stage you may decide to create two budgets to test out different production and post production scenarios. Perhaps you have access to a "free" camera for a lower resolution digital format but you would also like to consider shooting on a higher res format if you can get the money. Be prepared to do a full budget one way, then duplicate it and make some format changes to see the cost differences.

As I said above, always start with your most realistic "kitchen sink" budget. Decide what is the highest-quality format you can realistically afford to shoot in, and budget for that format first.

So let's build a spreadsheet for a budget. The easiest way to do that is to go through each line item on the *ProducerToProducer.com* budget spreadsheet template and plug in realistic numbers for each.

Spreadsheet Mechanics

The *ProducerToProducer.com* budget spreadsheet template utilizes Microsoft Excel, so you will need to make sure you have the software on your computer and that you have a basic proficiency in that program. There are formulas (mathematical equations) across each line item to create subtotals and totals throughout the document. Each line has a number on the far left side that is called a **line number**. To the right of that number is a line name, and there are some columns to the right of that. You should not change the names of the line items because they are standardized for the film industry and are rather comprehensive. If you want to add something, look for an empty line item in the correct section and type in a new name.

Each subtotal column has a formula. It is important to keep the integrity of each formula, so don't change them or it will corrupt the mathematics of the spreadsheet. Each row uses certain columns to allow you to add up multiple elements for computation. For instance—Amount column × Rate column = Salary Total. Or Days column × Rate column = Rental Total.

Geography of the Budget

This budget is eight pages long. It is organized as follows:

Page 1—Referred to as the **Top Sheet**—is divided into three sections. The top section contains the contact details, lists the shooting format, number and types of locations, and the number of shooting days. The middle section contains the subtotals for each of the sections later in the budget. It also has line items for the insurance fee, production fee, and other contractual fees. The bottom section is for the Comments/Assumptions—a place to state what assumptions the budget is based on, e.g., a union or non-union crew, what is included or not included in the budget.

Page 2—Pre-production and Wrap Crew Labor costs

Page 3—Production/Shooting Crew Labor costs

Page 4—Pre-production costs, Location and Travel costs, and Props/Wardrobe/Hair/Makeup costs

Page 5—Studio costs, Set Construction costs

Page 6—Equipment costs, Media/Storage costs, Miscellaneous costs, Creative fee costs

Page 7—Talent Labor costs and Talent expenses

Page 8—Post Production costs

Let's go through it page by page:

Top Sheet

On the Top Sheet, fill in the following pertinent info:

Title/Length: Title and total running time of project.

Client, Production company, address, phone, cell, and email address: Put all your contact information here.

Job #: If this project has an internal job number put it here.

Executive Producer: Name, if known.

Director: Name, if known.

Producer: Your name.

Director of Photography: Name, if known.

Editor: Name, if known.

Pre-Production days: The total number of pre-pro days.

Pre-Light days: If applicable, the total number of days for lighting/grip work only.

Studio days: The total number of days that you plan to shoot on a stage.

Location days: The total number of days that you plan to shoot on location.

Locations: State where in the world you plan to shoot: cities/states/countries.

Format: Digital or film. Camera type, if known.

Shoot dates: The inclusive dates of the shooting period.

It's important to put all this info here so that anyone who reads the budget will understand the parameters you have set for this estimated budget and the production. If you have planned for a 24-day shoot, then when someone looks at the labor sections, most of the labor costs will reflect 24 days for shooting and some time for prep and wrap.

Don't touch the middle part of the Top Sheet! As you enter in numbers on the subsequent budget pages, the subtotals will be automatically totaled and transferred to the front, section by section. The only formulas you will use/change in this section will be for the insurance fees, the production fees, and any other contractual fees that you need to compute. The final total is posted at the bottom of this middle section.

The bottom part of the Top Sheet is the place for your comments/assumptions. Here you should write sentences that explain your reasoning for creating the budget (e.g., "the budget assumes that the DP fee includes the use of his/her own camera as part of the total fee"). This explains to the reader why there is no money budgeted for camera rental on line 193. It should also include details about what guild contracts you are using ("Production will be working under the Modified Low-Budget SAG-AFTRA agreement" or "All labor will be non-union"). Any other details regarding post production should be outlined here (e.g., "Budget does not contain money for color correction. Will be done by editor on editing system").

Creating the Estimated Budget

When you create a budget, go through each line item and decide if you need to put a cost there. For this first pass, if you are not sure exactly how much something costs, put a good guesstimate there (you can always change it later). Keep a running list of all the line items that you will need to research later. That way you can go back to the budget and insert the correct numbers when you obtain them.

Let's say your project takes place in an art gallery and a house. For the house, you can shoot for free at a friend's place. (The director and DP have seen it and think it will work fine.) For the art gallery, though, you'll need to location scout. If you are shooting in New York City, you might go to Chelsea or SoHo one afternoon with a digital still/video camera and shoot a few galleries that look right for the scene. After the director picks two options, you'll call the galleries and discuss what kind of fee they would charge to shoot on a Sunday (when the gallery is usually closed.) One gallery says $3,000 (including a security person to watch you and the art during the shoot) and the other says $1,000 plus $500 for a security guard for 10 hours. For the budget line item, write in $3,000 for now. That way you know that you have enough in the budget to rent either place. Later, when you need to tighten the budget you can reduce down to $1,500 if you need to. Continue line by line in this way.

When creating an estimated budget, everything goes in the Estimated columns only. The Actual column is used once you start spending money and need to start entering your real costs from your production's receipts. (See the *Actualization* section later in this chapter.)

Detailed Line Items

In this portion of the chapter we will go through the budget, line by line (with line numbers corresponding to the *Producer To Producer* template) and give you all the information you need to know to budget for your project.

LABOR CONSIDERATIONS

This section is for labor costs for your shoot days only. Please note that at the bottom of each of these two Labor pages there is a P&W line below the Labor subtotal line. P&W stands for Pension and Welfare and it is where you calculate the Fringe rate if you are going through a payroll service for your crew payments. **Fringes** is the word used for the total amount of federal tax, state tax, city tax, unemployment tax, social security tax, Medicaid tax, union pension charges, and payroll fees that need to be computed and paid for each employee on your production. Check with your accountant to determine if you will be required to pay out fringes/P&W. If so, contact a payroll service to find out what the rate should be—usually between 19%–22% of non-union labor costs on top of the day-rate salaries. If working with union crew, there will be higher fringe rates to accommodate the additional P&W costs. Overtime is computed in the 1.5× column or 2× column for the two different overtime computation rates.

Regarding labor costs, these are the deals you can make with your crew (from the least expensive to the most):

1. Everyone works for free or deferred.

2. Pay only certain key crew/skilled crew positions, and everyone else works for free or deferred.

3. Pay all crew a small stipend per day.

4. Pay all crew a flat day rate.

5. Pay all crew (union or non-union) a day rate plus overtime (OT) (and if union, then add the union P&W charge, as well).

Your labor costs (along with travel costs, food, office rental, and phone charges) will account for a big chunk of your budget. So try to keep your labor costs down as much as possible. This is not done to exploit the people who are working on the project, but it's one of the few areas where you can save money. Hire the best people you can afford, but there are additional ways to compensate someone besides money.

I've done many productions where very skilled crews have worked for free or for a small stipend (a fraction of what they would normally receive) because they believed in the project and wanted to be a part of it. If you have a great script, or if a crew person will get to do a job he or she normally doesn't do, that might be the "payment." To the right person, it might be enough compensation.

On the other hand, don't be "penny wise and pound foolish." I coproduced a short film several years ago—a very ambitious project with a very tight budget. We paid the skilled labor but we didn't have the money to pay the production assistants (PAs), so I decided to recruit PAs who could work for free. We advertised online and received many résumés from people with little or no production experience, conducted interviews, and picked the best of the bunch. They were enthusiastic and helpful, but you get what you pay for. The volunteer PAs lacked the experience of veteran PAs and on our fifth day of shooting, one of the PAs drove a production truck into a low-hanging heater in a parking garage and it cost $2,500 to fix it! I often think of how many experienced PAs I could have hired for that amount of money.

Keep in mind that on shorter-term projects (less than six shooting days) you can often find a DP to shoot your project for free because short films and music videos are a great way to build up their demo reels. They may work for free but they will ask for the production to pay their assistant cameraperson, DIT, gaffer, and/or key grip to work on the production with them. Sound recordists rarely work for free, but you can often get a production designer, props, and hair/makeup for free or at a reduced rate. A production manager could be someone who usually works as a production coordinator and will work for free/reduced so they can get the screen credit. You should be able to find PAs by referrals, contacting local film schools and other producers. One of the best PAs I ever worked with was a 15-year-old high school sophomore—he was smart, highly motivated, and had energy to burn. He was the son of one of the executive producers and was a delight to work with.

LABOR RATES AND MOST FAVORED NATION

These A & B sections are for labor costs only. Depending on the budget version you use there may or may not be overtime or fringes computed. Labor rates are open to negotiation with each individual crew person, but most of the time it is done on a most favored nation basis.

Most favored nation is a legal term used to describe the universal pay rate that each corresponding labor rank is paid. So each department head (i.e., Director of Photography [DP], Production Designer, Costume Designer, Head Hair/Makeup) are paid the same rate. Then the next level in each department gets the same rate (i.e., Ass't Director [AD], Ass't Camera, Gaffer, Key Grip, Sound Recordist, Script Supervisor). Then the next level gets paid the same rate (Best Boy Electric, Best Boy Grip, Costume Ass't, Hair/Makeup Ass't, 2nd AC, etc.).

This creates universality across each corresponding position in each department. That way everyone at the same level in the crew hierarchy gets the same rate. This industry standard is based on fairness and fosters harmony among the ranks and I work this way for all of my productions. If you don't pay crew on a most favored nation basis, it can lead to anger and resentment. If you make a side deal with some and expect them to keep the secret, forget about it! Crews talk to each other and compare rates all the time. I highly recommend most favored nation for all productions.

Below is a breakdown by budget section of what to include in each section:

SECTIONS A & B (LINES #1-50, #51-100)

This section consists of the line items for your labor costs for all of your crew. Each line item breaks down by the number of days and rate per day. Section A is used to estimate labor costs for Prep and Wrap, including time and money for crew during location scouting, tech scouting, set build, shopping, pre-light and wrap. Section B is for labor costs for Production, including time and money for all shoot days. The computation equals the # of days × day rate. Overtime is computed in the 1.5× (1.5 times the hourly rate) column or 2× (2 times the hourly rate) column for the two different overtime rates.

Below are the key crew positions to consider for your production:

Producer
Director
Director of Photography
Camera Operators
1st Assistant Director (AD)
2nd AD
Assistant Camera
Loader
Gaffer
Electrics
Key Grip
Grips
Sound Recordist/Production Mixer
Boom Operator
Production Designer
Art Director
Props
Props Ass't/Set Dresser
Costume Designer
Costume Ass't
Key Hair and Key Makeup
Hair/Makeup Ass't

Casting Director
Digital Imaging Technician (DIT) or Video Engineer
Audio Playback (for music videos or musicals only)
Video Playback
Location Scout
Script Supervisor (Scriptie)
Production Manager
Production Coordinator
Production Assistants (preferably with their own cars)
Police
Fire
Tutor
Still Photographer
Weaponer/Pyrotechnics

Depending on the size of your production and your project's specific needs, this list may expand or contract.

Once you decide on the configuration of your crew, you'll pick what kind of pay scale you can afford and start entering the number of days and hours in each line. Remember to factor in the costs for a tech scout for your crew in *Section A* (we'll discuss tech scout in Chapter 6, *Pre-production*). Usually you'll need the Producer, Director, DP, AD, Production Designer, Sound, Gaffer, Key Grip, Location Manager, and Production Manager on the tech scout. You'll also need to hire various departments to prep and wrap for the film, i.e., Production Designer, Art Dept., Set Dressers, Costume Designer, Hair and Makeup, Location Scout, UPM, Production Coordinator and PAs. In *Section A* you'll need to estimate how many people and how much time for prep and wrap in these departments. In *Section B* you'll estimate the number of shoot days and if you'll need to put in for overtime. Most non-union crews will work on a 10-hour day so overtime (OT) will start after 10 hours. Usually the 11th and 12th hours are computed at 1.5× the per-hour rate of the day rate. After 12 hours, it is 2× the per-hour rate of the day rate. For instance, if the pay rate is $500/10 hr. then the per hour rate is $50; 1.5× = $75/hr; 2× = $100/hr. A 10-hour day = $500, 12-hour day = $650 and a 13-hour day = $750.

If you are paying fringes (federal, state, city taxes, social security tax, etc.), it's best to contact a payroll company and they can calculate the total taxes for each person. They will also charge a small fee for the work they do. The rates are generally 19%–22% on top of each person's gross salary.

SECTION C #101–113 PRE-PRODUCTION/SCOUTING EXPENSES

Hotels—Costs for hotel nights when scouting and prepping. Call or go online to get prices. Computed by # of nights × cost/night × # of rooms.

Airfares—Airfare costs for scouting and prepping. Computed by # of round trips (RT) × cost/trip × # of people.

Per Diem—(Latin for "by the day")—A daily fee to reimburse crew for out-of-town costs during scouting and prepping, (e.g., meals, wi-fi charges, parking, and laundry costs) . Computed by # of days × cost/day × # of people. Cost/day depends on what city you are visiting. Certain cities (domestic or international) are more expensive than others and per diem will reflect the relative costs.

Auto Rentals—Car rental costs for scouting and prepping. Can be computed as daily, weekly, or monthly rentals. Depending on your production insurance coverage, you may need to budget for the daily Collision Damage Waiver (CDW) fee to cover the vehicle in case of any accident. Check your policy and make sure you are covered or supplemented through the rental company. There are other kinds of insurance you can purchase from the car rental agencies. Read the fine print ahead of time on their websites so you can make the decision quickly when the car is picked up. Computed by # of days × cost/day × # of cars. Car rental on an hourly basis is another cost effective option.

Messengers—Costs for messengers for scouting and prepping. Computed by estimated total.

Office Rental—Costs to rent office space to prep, shoot, and wrap the production. Computed by weekly or monthly rate.

Taxis—Costs for taxis for scouting and prepping. Computed by estimated total.

Office Supplies—Costs for binders, paper, pens, pencils, markers, staples, rubber bands, envelopes, stationery, printers, etc. Computed by estimated total.

Copies—Costs for copying documents and/or copier rental. Computed by estimated total.

Phones/Cells—Telephone and cell charges. May include phone installation costs, Skype, and international calls. Computed by estimated total.

Casting Director—Casting director's fee. Computed by # days × cost/day.

Casting Expenses—Costs for audition facilities rental, videotaping expenses, website fee to upload casting sessions, etc. Computed by # days × cost/day.

Working Meals—Costs for lunches or coffee with people when prepping the project. Computed by estimated total.

SECTION D #114-137 LOCATION EXPENSES

Location fees—Put in your high estimate for all locations. Don't forget to base all figures on how many hours you plan to shoot at a location. Some locations have a flat rate for 10 hours, then overtime (OT) after that, at time and a half. Don't forget to budget for a "minder" for each location—someone provided by the owner who will be your liaison. They will be familiar with the location, can answer questions, have keys to all the doors and closets and know how to turn off the noisy air conditioner when recording sound. You'll need to pay for this person, in addition to a location rental fee but they are usually worth the expense. Computed by # of locations × cost/location.

Permits—Some municipalities or locations will require a permit fee or fees. (We'll discuss this further in Chapter 7, *Locations*.). Computed by estimated total.

Auto rentals—Car rental costs to transport cast/crew during the production period. Can be computed as daily, weekly, or monthly rentals. Depending on your production insurance coverage, you may need to budget for the daily Collision Damage Waiver (CDW) fee to cover the vehicle in case of any accident. Check your policy and make sure you are covered or supplemented through the rental company. There are other kinds of insurance you can purchase from the rental agencies. Read the fine print ahead of time on their websites so you can make the decision quickly when the car is picked up. Computed by # of days × cost/day × # of cars. Car rental on an hourly basis can be a cost effective option.

Van rentals—Van rental costs for minivans, 15-passenger vans, or cargo vans. Some larger cities have van rental companies that cater to film companies. They allow PAs to pick up the vans easily and will take the back seats out without a hassle. See *Auto rentals* above for additional information about insurance.

RV/Winnebago—RV/Winnebago rental costs. Computed by # of days × cost/day × # of vehicles.

Parking/Tolls/Gas—Costs for parking, tolls, and gas for all vehicles including possible crew-owned vehicles. Computed by estimated total.

Truck rentals—Truck rental costs for grip, lighting and production design/props department needs. See *Auto rentals* above for additional insurance info. Depending on the size of the truck you may need to hire a driver with a CDL (commercial driver's license).

Hotels—Hotel room costs for cast and crew during the shooting period. Call or go online to get prices. Computed by # of nights × cost/night × # of rooms.

Airfares—Call or go online to get prices. Computed by # of roundtrips (RT) × cost/trip × # of people.

Per Diem—(Latin for "by the day")—A daily fee to reimburse crew for out-of-town costs during shooting, (e.g., meals, wi-fi charges, parking, and laundry costs). Computed by # of days × cost/day × # of people. Cost/day depends on what city you are visiting. Certain cities (domestic or international) are more expensive than others and per diem will reflect the relative costs.

Train fares—Train fare costs. Call or go online to get prices. Computed by # of roundtrips (RT) × cost/trip × # of people.

Airport Transfers—Costs for people to get to and from the airport. Computed by # of roundtrips (RT) × cost/trip × # of people.

Breakfast, Lunch, Dinner Catering—Number of days × rate per person × number of people for breakfast, lunch, and/or dinner. *You have to feed your crew every six hours.* For a 12-hour day, ideally you'd serve a hot breakfast prior to the call time, then work 6 hours; have a hot lunch, then work 6 hours and complete the wrap. That way the crew would be finished working for the day and there would be no need to serve dinner. (Discussed further in Chapter 12, *Production.*)

If you work past 6 hours after finishing the lunch meal, then you'll have to serve dinner, as well. I usually budget for breakfast and lunch for each shoot day and maybe a few dinners, in case we go over 12 hours on a few days (depending on how many total days/weeks for the entire shooting period). Remember to plan for meals on set build and pre-light days too. On those days, if the crew is small you can give each person money to go off set and have lunch and then come back. (Have lots of paper money if you decide to do this option.)

Craft Service—Costs for the cast/crew snacks to munch on throughout the day. Generally it consists of coffee, tea, juice, soda, and water for beverages. In the morning, fruit, muffins, bagels, croissants with butter and cream cheese are served. Later you can offer bite-size sandwiches, or, if you have access to a stove or microwave, little quiches, spring rolls, etc. For afternoon snacks you might have crudités, cheese and crackers, gum, mints, cookies, and candy. Additionally, the craft service table should always provide a first aid kit with bandages, aspirin/ibuprofen, and disinfectant. If applicable, you should provide sunscreen and bug spray, too. There is a full craft service list in Chapter 6, *Pre-production*.

You can make your craft service table as minimal or as lavish as your budget allows. Shopping at a discount warehouse can help stretch your dollars much further.

Taxis and Other Transport—For taxis or other transport charges not included above. Calculate the number of rides × rate per ride × number of people—and remember to count each trip separately, so a roundtrip equals two rides.

Kit Rentals—Costs for kit rentals for hair/makeup kits and tech kits (e.g. grip/electric, assistant camera, DIT). Computed by # of days × cost/day × # of kits.

Cell phones—Costs if the production purchases cell phones for any cast/crew members or if you plan to reimburse any crew person for their cell phone usage.

Gratuities—Tips at hotels, for skycaps at airports, janitors, etc.

Table & Chair rental—Charges to rent tables and chairs for cast/crew meals on location.

SECTION E #138–150 PROPS/WARDROBE/SFX

Prop Rental/Prop Purchase—Costs to rent and purchase props and other scenic elements for all the sets and locations.

Wardrobe Rental/Wardrobe Purchase—Costs to rent or buy the costumes/wardrobe.

Wardrobe Cleaning—Costs to dry clean any costumes.

Picture Vehicle Rentals—Costs to rent any vehicles that appear or are driven on camera in the film.

Animals and Handlers—Costs to rent a trained animal, the time for the animal prep and training, and the trainer/handler's costs.

Hair/Makeup Expenses—Costs to rent or purchase wigs, makeup, haircuts, etc.

Weapons Rentals—Costs to rent prop weapons, squibs, etc.

Special Effects (SFX) Expenses—The costs of any effects like fires, explosions, or fireworks. Depending on the effect, you may need to obtain a permit from the local fire department. (See Chapter 6, *Pre-Production,* for more information.) (The SFX operator, Pyrotechnician, and Weaponer will be in the Labor costs in Sections A & B.)

SECTION F #151-167 STUDIO RENTAL AND EXPENSES

Studio Rental—Compute how many days you'll need to shoot in a studio, if any. There are often different rates for Build, Pre-Light, Shoot, and Strike days. There is usually overtime after 10 or 12 hours, but make sure you check to find out the rules for the studio you are using.

Electricity/Power Charges—Studios usually have an additional charge for the Pre-Light and Shoot days to cover the cost of using lights.

Hair/Makeup/Wardrobe/Green Room—Often these rooms are included in the Studio rental fee. If not, this line will cover those costs.

Studio Parking—particularly in Los Angeles, there may be an additional charge for parking cast/crew/production vehicles.

Studio Manager—Some studios charge for managers to be on duty during your work time or sometimes there is only a labor charge for overtime.

Phone/Internet/Copies—There is usually a charge for these services. Often they are flat fees with the copier on a pay-as-used basis.

Cartage/Dumpster Rentals—Costs to rent dumpsters for discarding set construction materials and other debris.

Miscellaneous Equipment—If you need to rent additional equipment like a scissor lift or ladders you should put them here.

Studio Painting—Your production may need to paint the studio walls and/or floor a different color. Usually the studio will charge a fee to have it painted to your color and then to paint it back to the regular color.

Trash Removal—costs for daily trash removal and clean up after usage.

SECTION G #168-182 SET CONSTRUCTION LABOR

Set Designer—Fees for a designer to create the set and construction plans: # of days × day rate × # of people.

Art Dept. Coordinator—Labor costs to hire a coordinator for the art department: # of days × day rate × # of people.

Set Decorator—Labor costs to hire the person to place furnishings, lighting fixtures, drapery, and artwork on set: # of days × day rate × # of people.

Leadperson—This person works under the set decorator to dress the set: # of days × day rate × # of people.

Set Dressers—These people work under the Leadperson to dress the set: # of days × day rate × # of people.

Greensperson—Labor costs to hire the person in charge of anything "green" on set like flowers, grass, plants, rocks, gravel and landscaping: # of days × day rate × # of people.

Draftsperson—Labor costs to hire the person to draw the set designs and construction plans: # of days × day rate × # of people.

Lead Scenic—Lead person in charge of the Scenics who paint and create scenic effects: # of days × day rate × # of people.

Scenics—The crew who work under the Lead Scenic = # of days × day rate × # of people.

Painters—Costs for skilled crew to paint the set = # of days × day rate × # of people.

Construction Coordinator—The person who plans and hires the crew to construct the set = # of days × day rate × # of people.

Carpenters—Costs for skilled crew to build the set = # of days × day rate × # of people.

Grips—The grips who work on the construction crew = # of days × day rate × # of people.

Strike Crew—Crew members that come in for the strike of the set only by dismantling and disposing of it safely. Because of turnaround time and safety issues, you may need to hire a different crew than the one that put it up. A strike crew can be a lower day rate because it does not require the same skill level of those who built the set = # of days × day rate × # of people.

Art Production Assistants—Specific PAs to work in the Art department = # of days × day rate × # of people.

SECTION H #183-192 SET CONSTRUCTION MATERIALS

Set Dressing/Props Rentals—To rent set dressing like furniture, artwork, lamps, wallpaper, etc. and to rent Props like dinnerware, drinking glasses, reading materials, etc.

Set Dressing/Props Purchases—To purchase the materials described above.

Lumber—Material to build the set.

Paint—Necessary to cover the set surfaces.

Special Effects—Costs for any special effects.

Hardware—Whatever needs to be purchased to build the set.

Construction Materials/Rentals—Any additional materials or equipment rentals needed to build the set.

Art Trucking—Costs associated with trucking something for the set.

Meals/Parking—Meal or parking costs for set construction.

SECTION I #193–210 EQUIPMENT RENTAL

NOTE: If you are shooting more than two consecutive days, it is common to get a "2- or 3-day week" for equipment rentals. If you are renting for a total of three consecutive days, you can ask for a 2-day rental. If you are picking up on a Friday and returning on a Monday, you should only be charged for a 1-day rental.

Camera Rental—Costs to rent the camera equipment. This includes the camera bodies, lenses, and tripods. Additional accessories are listed in separate line items: = # of days/weeks × daily/weekly rate.

Sound Rental—Costs to rent the sound equipment. This includes microphones, digital audio recorder, boom pole, audio mixer, backup audio recorder, etc.: = # of days/weeks × daily/weekly rate.

Lighting Rental—Costs to rent the lighting and electrical equipment. This includes light fixtures, light stands, electrical cable, electric distribution boxes and ballasts: = # of days/weeks × daily/weekly rate.

Grip Rental—Costs to rent the grip equipment. This includes grip stands, heads and arms, flags and nets, reflector boards, grip clips and apple boxes, etc.: = # of days/weeks × daily/weekly rate.

Generator Rental—Costs to rent an electric generator. Generators can be as small as a 45-amp "putt-putt" genny that you can rent from a hardware store or it can be a large truck with enough gasoline to power 750 amps. They come in different sizes and are priced accordingly. If you rent a truck you'll need to hire a generator operator who will drive the truck to location, hook up the electrical cables, and monitor the electrical power situation throughout the shoot day. Their fee would be computed in *Section B: Crew Shoot Labor.*

Camera Lens Rental—Costs to rent lenses for all the cameras on the production = # of days/weeks × daily/weekly rate.

Camera Accessories Rental—Costs to rent accessories like monitors, playback, etc. = # of days/weeks × daily/weekly rate.

DIT Equipment Rental—Costs to rent DIT equipment like computers, monitors, digital recording devices, hard drives, etc. = # of days/weeks × daily/weekly rate.

Walkie-Talkie Rental—Costs to rent walkie-talkies, batteries, and chargers = # of days/weeks × daily/weekly rate.

Dolly Rental + Accessories—Costs to rent a dolly, track, and other accessories. There are several different kinds with different price points: = # of days/weeks × daily/weekly rate.

Crane/Jib Rental—Costs to rent a crane or jib and track = # of days/weeks × daily/weekly rate.

Drone Rental—Costs to rent a drone and accessories. The drone operator labor costs will be computed in *Section B*: = # of days/weeks × daily/weekly rate.

Production Supplies—Costs for miscellaneous supplies like batteries, garbage bags, traffic cones, cleaning supplies, tissues, padlocks to secure equipment trucks, etc.

Expendables—Costs for supplies for the grip, electrical, and camera departments. Gaffer's tape, gels/diffusion, clothespins, sash cord, etc. Can be charged on a pay-as-used basis whereby you only pay for the amount that you consume.

Aerial Photography—Costs for helicopter, pilot, mounting equipment, fuel, landing fees, etc. = # of days/weeks × daily/weekly rate.

Green Screen Rental—Costs to rent a green screen = # of days/weeks × daily/weekly rate.

Underwater Housing Rental—Costs to rent underwater housing for the camera = # of days/weeks × daily/weekly rate.

Missing & Damaged—An estimated cost for possible charges for missing and/or damaged equipment and repair charges. Set aside money for these costs, then hire a professional crew so these costs will be as minimal as possible.

SECTION J #211–216 MEDIA/STORAGE

Digital Storage Purchase—Costs to purchase digital storage, like hard drives or memory disks. Have the assistant cameraperson and DIT compute how much storage you'll need and remember to have at least one or two backup drives.

Film Stock Purchase—Costs to purchase film stock = amount of footage × cost/ft.

Film Stock Process and Prep—Costs to process and prep exposed film stock = amount of footage × cost/ft.

Telecine/Film to Digital Transfer—Costs to transfer processed film to digital files = amount of footage × cost/ft or a per-hour rate.

Videotape/Audiotape Stock—Costs to purchase video or audio tape stock = # of tapes × cost/tape.

HOW TO COMPUTE SHOOTING RATIO

Shooting ratio is an important concept because it impacts the budget exponentially. Once you know the shooting ratio that you plan to use for the project, you can create a solid estimate of how much digital media memory, storage drives or film will be required.

The shooting ratio is the total number of minutes of footage acquired vs. the final total running time (TRT) of the project. That formula is expressed as two numbers—like 10:1 or 15:1. That means, on average, you plan to shoot 10 or 15 times the material for that one moment in the project. If the final TRT of your project is 100 minutes, then for a 10:1 shooting ratio, you would plan to shoot 1,000 minutes of material. At 15:1 you will budget for 1,500 minutes of material.

For digital, you'd need to know the camera model you are using and other important tech spec decisions (discussed in Chapter 15, *Post Production*) and compute how much digital storage space (plus backup drives) are needed for 1,000–1,500 minutes of material. For film, you would need to know how much stock to purchase (1,000–1,500 minutes). For a low-budget project, a shooting ratio of 10:1 or 15:1 is usually the norm. Higher-budget projects can often afford higher shooting ratios.

Remember, your shooting ratio represents not only materials you'll need to purchase, but also hours/days you'll need to account for in your shooting schedule. The higher the shooting ratio, the longer the schedule.

SECTION K #217–226 MISCELLANEOUS COSTS

Rights purchase—Costs to purchase the rights to the script or other underlying rights for the project.

Air Shipping—Costs for using air courier services.

Accounting Fees—Costs for accounting services.

Bank Charges—Costs for bank transfers and other fees.

Production Insurance—Costs for general liability and all other production insurance, including workers' compensation insurance.

E&O Insurance—Costs for Errors & Omissions insurance.

Legal Fees—Costs for legal services and fees.

Business License/Taxes—Costs for incorporation and/or business taxes.

Film Festival Fees/Expenses—Costs for film festival applications and travel expenses.

Publicity/Marketing—Costs to hire or create publicity and marketing for the project.

SECTION L #227–233 CREATIVE FEES

Writer Fee—Fee for writer.

Director Fee: Prep—Fee for director's prep days.

Director Fee: Travel—Fee for director's travel days.

Director Fee: Shoot—Fee for director's shoot days.

Director Fee: Post—Fee for director's post production days.

Fringes for Labor Costs—Payroll taxes/fees for the above labor costs.

SECTION M #234–262 TALENT FEES

O/C Principal—Salary for on-camera principal actors = # of days × day rate. Could be a weekly rate on certain projects.

Day Player—Salary for day player actors = # of days × day rate.

Background Actors—Salary for background actors (extras) = # of days × day rate.

Voice-Over Talent—Salary for voice-over talent. Computed by the hour or half hour = # of hours × hourly rate.

Dialect Coach—Salary for coach to work with actors on dialects or accents = # of days × day rate.

Choreographer—Salary for fight or dance choreographers = # of days × day rate.

Stunt Coordinator—Salary for stunt coordinator = # of days × day rate.

Stunt Players—Salary for stunt players who do the stunts = # of days × day rate.

Fitting Fee—Additional actor fee for a costume fitting = # of hours/days × rate.

Rehearsal Fee—Additional actor fee for rehearsal time = # of hours/days × rate.

Pension & Welfare—Computation for P&W and fringes for total actor salaries. The *Section M* subtotal multiplied by the P&W/Fringe rate (see earlier in chapter). Put the P&W/Fringe rate in the Rate column.

SECTION N #263–276 TALENT EXPENSES

Airfares—Costs for actor airfares = # of roundtrips (RT) × cost/trip.

Hotels—Costs for actor hotel charges = # of nights × cost/night.

Per Diem—Costs for actor per diem = # of days × day rate.

Cabs and Transportation—# of trips × cost/trip.

Extras Casting Director—Salary for casting director to find Background Actors/Extras = # of days × day rate.

Work Visa Fees—Fees for legal and application fees if any actors require work visas.

Talent Agency Fee—Usually a 10% markup paid to the agent for each actor. Computed by total actor salary × 10%.

SECTION P #277-322 POST PRODUCTION

EDITORIAL

Editor—# of days/weeks × day/weekly rate.

Assistant Editor—# of days/weeks × day/weekly rate.

Post Production Supervisor—# of days/weeks × day/weekly rate.

Editing Room Rental—# of weeks × weekly rate.

Editing System Rental—# of weeks × weekly rate.

Transcription—Computed per minute of running time of audio material.

Online Edit/Conform—# of hours × hourly rate.

Screening Room Rental— # of hours × hourly rate.

MUSIC

Music Composition—For musical composer fee.

Music Licensing/Clearance—Costs to clear and purchase the rights to music for the audio track. Rights need to match the usage you require for the project. (See Chapter 17, *Music*).

Music Recording—Costs to record the musical composition. Includes studio rental, audio recording personnel, and musician fees.

Recording Expenses/Rentals—Costs for recording studio, musicians, instrument rentals, etc.

Music Supervisor—Computed by # of weeks × weekly rate or a flat fee.

Audiotape Stock/Files—Costs for audiotape stock or computer drives for files and copies.

POST PRODUCTION SOUND

Sound Editor—Costs to add and edit the audio tracks = # of hours/days × hourly/daily rate.

Assistant Sound Editor—Assistant to the Sound Editor = # of hours/days × hourly/daily rate.

Music Editor—Editor of the music audio tracks = # of hours/days × hourly/daily rate.

Automated Dialogue Replacement (ADR)—Costs for rental recording studio and technician for ADR = # of hours/days × hourly/daily rate.

Foley Stage/Editor—Costs to rent foley stage and editor for foley work = # of hours/days × hourly/daily rate.

Foley Artists—Salary for the foley artists to create sound effects = # of hours/days × hourly/daily rate.

Narration Recording—Rental costs for audio recording booth and recordist for narration = # of hours/days × hourly/daily rate.

Audio Mix—Costs for audio mix room and audio equipment = # of hours/days × hourly/daily rate.

Audio Layback—Costs to layback audio tracks to master = # of hours/days × hourly/daily rate.

Dolby/DTS License—Fee for Dolby or DTS audio technology license.

DIGITAL INTERMEDIATE

Color Grading/Digital Intermediate—Costs for the color grading session and DI work at a post facility = # of hours/days × hourly/daily rate.

Hard Drive Purchases/Storage—Costs for purchases of data storage and back up, including cloud storage.

POST PRODUCTION—DIGITAL/FILM

Archival Footage/Photos—Costs to license the stock footage used in your project. Often charged per second of footage with a 30-second minimum.

Archival Researcher—Salary for researcher to locate archival materials = # of days/weeks × daily/weekly rate or a flat rate.

Clearance Supervisor—Salary for person to license archival and other rights = # of days/weeks × daily/weekly rate or a flat rate.

Screeners = Costs to purchase screener copies to look at archival material.

Film Prints—Costs to print a film master from digital master. Charges based on the project's total running time.

Masters/Clones—Costs to make master copies in various formats. Charges based on the project's total running time and media cost.

TITLING/GRAPHICS/ANIMATION—Costs to create and place screen credits and "lower thirds" on final master.

Graphic Designer—Fee to design and create graphics, including titles.

Visual Effects (VFX)—Fee to design, shoot and create visual effects.

Animation—Fee to design, shoot, and create animation.

Motion Control—Fee for MC operator and equipment.

Closed Captioning—Fee to create and place closed captioning on final master. Charges based on the project's total running time.

Subtitling—Fee to translate, create, and place subtitles on final master.

MISCELLANEOUS

Shipping—Costs for air shipping and/or postal costs.

Messengers—Costs for messenger services.

Post Working Meals—Costs for post production working meals.

Sundae Budgeting Case Study

We'll use the *Sundae* short film script breakdown that we described in the last chapter to help with the budgeting now. If you recall, we planned for a two-day shoot. This project represents many of the things that a typical feature length or series indie project would have to grapple with, but it is a shorter production timeline. Of course, a long format project is much more complicated, but the short film will allow us to go through the budget, line by line, with concision. *Sundae* was produced as a student no/low-budget project—so very few crew were paid and the actors' salaries were deferred under the SAG-AFTRA Student Film agreement.

Following is the *Sundae* estimated budget.

Producer To Producer Budget Template

Title	SUNDAE		
Length	5:00		
Client			
Production Co.			
Address			
Address			
Telephone			
Cel			
Email			
Job #			
Exec. Producer			
Director	Sonya Goddy		
Producer	Kristin Frost/Co-producer-Birgit Gernboeck		
DP	Andrew Ellmaker		
Editor			
Pre-Prod. Days			
Pre-Lite Days			
Studio Days			
Location Days	2		
Location(s)	Brooklyn, NY		
Format	RED Dragon		
Shoot Date(s)	January 22-23		
	SUMMARY	ESTIMATED	ACTUAL
1	Pre-Production and wrap costs (Totals A & C)	700	0
2	Shooting Crew Labor (Total B)	1,000	0
3	Location and travel expenses (Total D)	2,618	0
4	Props. Wardrobe and animals (Total E)	1,150	0
5	Studio & set construction costs (Total F/G/H)	0	0
6	Equipment costs (Total I)	2,650	0
7	Media/Storage costs (Total J)	300	0
8	Miscellaneous Costs (Total K)	230	0
9	Talent costs and expenses (Total M & N)	360	0
10	Post Production costs (Total O-T)	3,000	0
	SUBTOTAL	12,008	0
11	Insurance (2%)	0	0
	SUBTOTAL Direct Costs	12,008	0
12	Director/Creative Fees (Total L-Not including Direct Costs)	0	0
13	Production Fee		
14	Contingency		
15	Weather Day		
	GRAND TOTAL	12,008	0

COMMENTS

Budget for 2 day shoot in Brooklyn, NY.
DP will work for free - will rent his camera.
SAG-AFTRA actors will work under the Student Film contract.
Music licensing will be free.

Producer to Producer Budget Template

A	PRE-PROD & WRAP LABOR	Days	Rate	OT (1.5)	OT sub	OT (2.0)	OT sub	ESTIMATED	ACTUAL
1	Producer				0		0	0	0
2	1st Assistant Director				0		0	0	0
3	Director of Photography				0		0	0	0
4	Camera Operator(s)				0		0	0	0
5	2nd Assistant Director				0		0	0	0
6	Assistant Camera				0		0	0	0
7	Loader				0		0	0	0
8	Production Designer				0		0	0	0
9	Art Director				0		0	0	0
10	Set Decorator				0		0	0	0
11	Props				0		0	0	0
12	Props Assistant				0		0	0	0
13	Gaffer				0		0	0	0
14	Best Boy Electrician				0		0	0	0
15	Electrician				0		0	0	0
16	Key Grip				0		0	0	0
17	Best Boy Grip				0		0	0	0
18	Grip				0		0	0	0
19	DIT				0		0	0	0
20	Swing				0		0	0	0
21	Sound Recordist				0		0	0	0
22	Boom Operator				0		0	0	0
23	Key Hair/Makeup				0		0	0	0
24	Hair/Makeup Assistant				0		0	0	0
25	Hair/Makeup Assistant				0		0	0	0
26	Stylist				0		0	0	0
27	Costume Designer				0		0	0	0
28	Wardrobe Supervisor				0		0	0	0
29	Wardrobe Assistant				0		0	0	0
30	Script Supervisor				0		0	0	0
31	Food Stylist				0		0	0	0
32	Assistant Food Stylist				0		0	0	0
33	Video Engineer				0		0	0	0
34	Line Producer				0		0	0	0
35	Production Manager				0		0	0	0
36	Production Coordinator				0		0	0	0
37	Location Manager				0		0	0	0
38	Location Scout				0		0	0	0
39	Police				0		0	0	0
40	Fire				0		0	0	0
41	On Set Tutor				0		0	0	0
42	Motorhome Driver				0		0	0	0
43	Craft Service				0		0	0	0
44	Still Photographer				0		0	0	0
45	Weaponer/Pyrotechnics				0		0	0	0
46	Key PA				0		0	0	0
47	Production Assistant				0		0	0	0
48	Production Assistant				0		0	0	0
49	Production Assistant				0		0	0	0
50	Production Assistant				0		0	0	0
	TOTAL A				0		0	0	0

BUDGETING

Producer To Producer Budget Template

B	SHOOTING LABOR	Days	Rate	OT (1.5)	OT sub	OT (2.0)	OT sub	ESTIMATED	ACTUAL
51	Producer				0		0	0	0
52	1st Assistant Director				0		0	0	0
53	Director of Photography				0		0	0	0
54	Camera Operator(s)				0		0	0	0
55	2nd Assistant Director				0		0	0	0
56	Assistant Camera				0		0	0	0
57	Loader				0		0	0	0
58	Production Designer				0		0	0	0
59	Art Director				0		0	0	0
60	Set Decorator				0		0	0	0
61	Props				0		0	0	0
62	Props Assistant				0		0	0	0
63	Gaffer				0		0	0	0
64	Best Boy Electrician				0		0	0	0
65	Electrician				0		0	0	0
66	Key Grip	2	100		0		0	200	0
67	Best Boy Grip	1	100		0		0	100	0
68	Grip				0		0	0	0
69	DIT				0		0	0	0
70	Swing				0		0	0	0
71	Sound Recordist	2	150		0		0	300	0
72	Boom Operator				0		0	0	0
73	Key Hair/Makeup	2	100		0		0	200	0
74	Hair/Makeup Assistant				0		0	0	0
75	Hair/Makeup Assistant				0		0	0	0
76	Stylist				0		0	0	0
77	Costume Designer				0		0	0	0
78	Wardrobe Supervisor				0		0	0	0
79	Wardrobe Assistant				0		0	0	0
80	Script Supervisor				0		0	0	0
81	Food Stylist				0		0	0	0
82	Assistant Food Stylist				0		0	0	0
83	Video Engineer				0		0	0	0
84	Line Producer				0		0	0	0
85	Production Manager				0		0	0	0
86	Production Coordinator				0		0	0	0
87	Location Manager				0		0	0	0
88	Location Scout				0		0	0	0
89	Police				0		0	0	0
90	Fire				0		0	0	0
91	On Set Tutor				0		0	0	0
92	Motorhome Driver				0		0	0	0
93	Craft Service				0		0	0	0
94	Still Photographer				0		0	0	0
95	Weaponer/Pyrotechnics	2	100		0		0	200	0
96	Key PA				0		0	0	0
97	Production Assistant				0		0	0	0
98	Production Assistant				0		0	0	0
99	Production Assistant				0		0	0	0
100	Production Assistant				0		0	0	0
	TOTAL B				0		0	1000	0

Producer To Producer Budget Template

C	PRE-PROD./WRAP EXPENSES		Amount	Rate	x	ESTIMATED	ACTUAL
101	Hotel(s)					0	0
102	Airfare(s)					0	0
103	Per Diem					0	0
104	Auto Rental(s)					0	0
105	Messengers					0	0
106	Office Rental					0	0
107	Taxis					0	0
108	Office Supplies					0	0
109	Copies						
110	Phones/Cel					0	0
111	Casting Director	flat fee	1	500	1	500	0
112	Casting Expenses					0	0
113	Working Meals		1	200	1	200	0
	TOTAL C					700	0

D	LOCATION/TRAVEL EXPENSES		Amount	Rate	x	ESTIMATED	ACTUAL
114	Location Fees	Ice cream parlor	1	400	1	400	0
115	Permits		1	300	1	300	0
116	Auto Rental(s)					0	0
117	Van Rental(s)		1	190	1	190	0
118	RV/Winnebago Rental					0	
119	Parking, Tolls & Gas	prod. & picture vehicles	1	200	1	200	0
120	Truck Rental(s)					0	0
121	Other Vehicles					0	0
122	Other Trucking					0	0
123	Hotel(s)					0	0
124	Airfare(s)					0	0
125	Per Diem					0	0
126	Train fare(s)					0	0
127	Airport Transfers					0	0
128	Breakfast	20 people	2	7	20	280	0
129	Lunch	22 people	2	8	22	352	0
130	Dinner	22 people	2	9	22	396	0
131	Craft Service		2	100	1	200	0
132	Taxis & Other Transport	cast transport	1	175	1	175	0
133	Kit Rental(s)	crew transport	1	125	1	125	0
134	Cel phone(s)					0	0
135	Gratuities					0	0
136	Table & Chair rental					0	0
137						0	0
	TOTAL D					2618	0

E	PROPS/RELATED EXPENSES		Amount	Rate	x	ESTIMATED	ACTUAL
138	Prop Rental					0	0
139	Prop Purchase		1	150	1	150	0
140	Wardrobe Rental					0	0
141	Wardrobe Purchase		1	150	1	150	0
142	Wardrobe Cleaning						
143	Picture Vehicles	2 picture vehicles/1 day each	1	375	2	750	0
144	Animals & Handlers					0	0
145	Hair/Makeup Expenses		1	100	1	100	0
146	Weapons Rentals					0	0
147	SFX Expenses					0	0
148						0	0
149						0	0
150						0	0

BUDGETING

Producer To Producer Budget Template

F	STUDIO RENTAL & EXPENSES	Amount	Rate	x	ESTIMATED	ACTUAL
151	Build Day Rental				0	0
152	Build Day OT				0	0
153	Pre-Lite Day Rental				0	0
154	Pre-Lite Day OT				0	0
155	Shoot Day Rental				0	0
156	Shoot Day OT				0	0
157	Strike Day Rental				0	0
158	Strike Day OT				0	0
159	Electricity/Power Charges				0	0
160	Hair/MU/Wardrobe/Green Room				0	0
161	Studio Parking				0	0
162	Studio Manager				0	0
163	Phone/Internet/Copies				0	0
164	Cartage/Dumpster Rental				0	0
165	Miscellaneous Equipment				0	0
166	Studio Painting				0	0
167	Trash Removal				0	0
	TOTAL F				0	0

G	SET CONSTRUCTION LABOR	Amount	Rate	x	ESTIMATED	ACTUAL
168	Set Designer				0	0
169	Art Department Coordinator				0	0
170	Set Decorator				0	0
171	Lead Person				0	0
172	Set Dresser(s)				0	0
173	Greensperson				0	0
174	Draftsperson				0	0
175	Lead Scenic				0	0
176	Scenics				0	0
177	Painters				0	0
178	Construction Coordinator				0	0
179	Carpenter(s)				0	0
180	Grip(s)				0	0
181	Strike Crew				0	0
182	Art Production Assistant(s)				0	0
	TOTAL G				0	0

H	SET CONSTRUCTION MATERIALS	Amount	Rate	x	ESTIMATED	ACTUAL
183	Set Dressing/Props Rentals				0	0
184	Set Dressing/Props Purchases				0	0
185	Lumber				0	0
186	Paint				0	0
187	Hardware				0	0
188	Special Effects				0	0
189	Construction Materials/Rentals				0	0
190	Art Trucking				0	0
191	Meals, Parking				0	0
192					0	0
	TOTAL H				0	0

Producer To Producer Budget Template

I	EQUIPMENT/EXPENSES		Amount	Rate	x	ESTIMATED	ACTUAL
193	Camera Rental	flat	1	500	1	500	0
194	Sound Rental					0	0
195	Lighting Rental					0	0
196	Grip Rental	flat	1	1000	1	1000	0
197	Generator Rental					0	0
198	Camera Lens Rental	flat	1	200	1	200	0
199	Camera Accessories Rental					0	0
200	DIT Equipment Rental					0	0
201	Walkie Talkie Rental	flat	1	100	1	100	0
202	Dolly Rental + Accessories					0	0
203	Crane/Jib Rental					0	0
204	Drone Rental					0	0
205	Production Supplies		1	150	1	150	0
206	Expendables		1	200	1	200	0
207	Aerial Photography					0	0
208	Green Screen Rental					0	0
209	Underwater Housing Rental					0	0
210	Missing & Damaged		1	500	1	500	0
	TOTAL I					2650	0

J	MEDIA/STORAGE		Amount	Rate	x	ESTIMATED	ACTUAL
211	Digital storage purchase	2 hard drives	1	150	2	300	0
212	Film Stock Purchase					0	0
213	Film stock Prep & Process					0	0
214	Telecine/Film to Digital Transfer					0	0
215	Videotape/Audiotape Stock					0	0
216						0	0
	TOTAL J					300	0

K	MISCELLANEOUS COSTS		Amount	Rate	x	ESTIMATED	ACTUAL
217	Rights purchase	Rate for non-students				0	0
218	Air Shipping					0	0
219	Accounting Fees					0	0
220	Bank Charges					0	0
221	Production Insurance	school rate/workers comp	1	230	1	230	
222	E & O Insurance					0	0
223	Legal Fees					0	0
224	Business License/Taxes					0	0
225	Film Festival Fees/Expenses					0	0
226	Publicity/Marketing					0	0
	TOTAL K					230	0

L	CREATIVE FEES		Amount	Rate	x	ESTIMATED	ACTUAL
227	Writer Fee					0	0
228	Director Fee – Prep					0	0
229	Director Fee – Travel					0	0
230	Director Fee – Shoot					0	0
231	Director Fee – Post					0	0
232	Fringes for Labor Costs					0	0
233						0	0
	TOTAL L					0	0

BUDGETING

Producer To Producer Budget Template

M	TALENT LABOR	Days	Rate	OT (1.5)	OT sub	OT (2.0)	OT sub	ESTIMATED	ACTUAL
234	O/C Principal				0		0	0	0
235	O/C Principal				0		0	0	0
236	O/C Principal				0		0	0	0
237	O/C Principal				0		0	0	0
238	O/C Principal				0		0	0	0
239	O/C Principal				0		0	0	0
240	O/C Principal				0		0	0	0
241	O/C Principal				0		0	0	0
242	O/C Principal				0		0	0	0
243	O/C Principal				0		0	0	0
244					0		0	0	0
245	Day Player				0		0	0	0
246	Day Player				0		0	0	0
247	Day Player				0		0	0	0
248	Day Player				0		0	0	0
249					0		0	0	0
250	Background Actor				0		0	0	0
251	Background Actor				0		0	0	0
252	Background Actor				0		0	0	0
253	Voice Over Talent				0		0	0	0
254	Voice Over Talent				0		0	0	0
255	Dialect Coach				0		0	0	0
256	Choreographer				0		0	0	0
257	Stunt Coordinator	1	150		0		0	150	0
258	Stunt Player(s)				0		0	0	0
259	Fitting Fee				0		0	0	0
260	Rehearsal Fee				0		0	0	0
261					0		0	0	0
262	Pension & Welfare				0		0	0	0
	TOTAL M							150	0

N	TALENT EXPENSES	Days	Rate	OT (1.5)	OT sub	OT (2.0)	OT sub	ESTIMATED	ACTUAL
263	Airfare(s)				0		0	0	0
264	Hotel(s)				0		0	0	0
265	Per Diem	2	30		0		0	60	0
266	Cabs and Transportation	1	150		0		0	150	0
267	Extras Casting Director				0		0	0	0
268	Work Visa Fees				0		0	0	0
269					0		0	0	0
270	Talent Agency Fee (10%)				0		0	0	0
271					0		0	0	0
272					0		0	0	0
273					0		0	0	0
274					0		0	0	0
275					0		0	0	0
276					0		0	0	0
	TOTAL N							210	0

Producer To Producer Budget Template

O EDITORIAL	Amount	Rate	X	ESTIMATED	ACTUAL
277 Editor				0	0
278 Assistant Editor				0	0
279 Post Production Supervisor				0	0
280 Editing Room Rental				0	0
281 Editing System Rental				0	0
282 Transcription				0	0
283 Online Edit/Conform				0	0
284 Screening Room Rental				0	0
TOTAL O				0	0

P MUSIC	Amount	Rate	X	ESTIMATED	ACTUAL
285 Music Composition				0	0
286 Music Licensing/Clearance				0	0
287 Music Recording				0	0
288 Recording Expenses/Rentals				0	0
289 Music Supervisor				0	0
290 Audiotape Stock/Files				0	0
TOTAL P				0	0

Q POST PRODUCTION SOUND	Amount	Rate	X	ESTIMATED	ACTUAL
292 Sound Editor				0	0
293 Assistant Sound Editor				0	0
294 Music Editor				0	0
295 ADR				0	0
296 Foley Stage/Editor				0	0
297 Foley Artists				0	0
298 Narration Recording				0	0
299 Audio Mix	1	1500	1	1500	0
300 Audio Layback				0	0
301 Dolby/DTS License				0	0
TOTAL Q				1500	0

R DIGITAL INTERMEDIATE	Amount	Rate	X	ESTIMATED	ACTUAL
302 Color Grading/Digital Intermediate	1	1500	1	1500	0
303 Hard Drive Purchase(s)/Storage				0	0
TOTAL R				1500	0

S POST PRODUCTION-DIGITAL/FILM	Amount	Rate	X	ESTIMATED	ACTUAL
304 Archival Footage/Photos				0	0
305 Archival Researcher				0	0
306 Clearance Supervisor				0	0
307 Screeners				0	0
308 Film Prints				0	0
309 Masters/Clones				0	0
310				0	0
TOTAL S				0	0

T TITLING/GRAPHICS/ANIMATION	Amount	Rate	X	ESTIMATED	ACTUAL
311 Titling				0	0
312 Graphic Designer				0	0
313 Visual Effects (VHX)				0	0
314 Animation				0	0
315 Motion Control				0	0
316 Closed Captioning				0	0
317 Subtitling				0	0
TOTAL T				0	0

U MISCELLANEOUS	Amount	Rate	X	ESTIMATED	ACTUAL
318 Shipping				0	0
319 Messengers				0	0
320 Post Working Meals				0	0
TOTAL T				0	0
TOTAL POST PRODUCTION				3000	0

Sundae Budget Analysis

The budget above assumes several things and they are written on the Top Sheet in the Comments section as follows:

Budget for 2-day shoot in Brooklyn, NY.

DP will work for free but will rent his camera to production.

SAG-AFTRA actors will work under the Student Film contract.

Music licensing will be free (friends of director).

Budget includes money for audio mix and color correct.

The filmmakers were enrolled in Columbia University's graduate film program so they were able get their classmates to work for free. They planned to pay for key grip, best boy grip, sound recordist, hair/makeup and a casting director. There was money in for a small location fee, the NYC film permit, transportation, catering, craft service, and some props, wardrobe, and picture vehicles.

For equipment they paid the DP for the camera rental, budgeted to rent some additional equipment including walkie-talkies, production supplies and expendables. They budgeted for missing & damaged (M&D) expenses and workers' comp (for non-school cast and crew) and a nominal insurance fee.

In the Talent section, they budgeted for one day with a stunt coordinator who would play the Woman role (for the fight scene) and coordinate the cement block throw and planned for some additional transportation costs.

Lastly, in the Post Production section, they assumed the director could ask her friends to license some music for free, but they would need to pay for a professional audio mix and color correct.

Cash-Flow Schedule

Once you have created the estimated budget, you need to create a cash-flow schedule to match that budget. A **cash-flow schedule** states when you are going to need certain amounts of money to cover the specific costs tied to the prep, production, and post production stages of the project. You'll need option money and writer's fees early in the process, then scouting/casting costs; next will be salary costs, as you hire cast and crew.

After that, you'll have equipment rental costs, location fees, production and costume design expenses, catering, etc. These stages usually happen in a particular and predictable order. Once you know your shoot dates, you can create a cash-flow schedule that dictates how much money needs to be available in any given week to cover the costs for those line items. Then in post production you'll need to adjust your cash flow based on where you are in that phase.

Locked Budget and Working Budget

Once you finalize the financing for the project, you will complete your estimated budget to meet the total amount of funds you have available for your project. Up until that point the estimated budget has fluctuated as prep and funding are finalized. Then you **lock the budget** and that version is the one that is considered the Final Estimated one. This is always a big moment—it's both exhilarating and terrifying. I'm always relieved that after months/years of development and prep we finally have committed to a locked budget and plan. But at the same time it means you and the rest of the team have to make it happen at this budget level. There's no going back. Once the budget is locked you will never change the numbers in the estimated column again. As pre-production and production continues you start to build a working budget. The **working budget** is in the column next to the estimated column and reflects any budget changes that may be occurring as you start to finalize choices such as specific locations and final equipment lists and you receive final numbers on the true costs for your project. It's imperative that you input these new, and more accurate, numbers into a working budget. Some budget templates have a button you can push that allows the software to switch to a working budget format or a column you can click that reveals a Working column. If the one you are using doesn't have this feature, then make a copy of your locked Estimated Budget and rename it as the Working Budget and start moving the numbers around to reflect the new numbers you are getting for your actual needs.

This step is essential to be able to keep a running tally of how your estimated budget is being adjusted in a concrete way. You'll start to see very quickly if you are over or under in individual line items and budget sections. You may have estimated that you'd need $3,000 for location costs to rent a house for a few days. But then your parents give you permission to use their home and you now have a $3,000 savings on that line number. But then the DP completes the tech scout and realizes that your parents' home is very dark with little ambient light and will need additional lighting equipment, so your lighting order increases by $1,000. You can see how costs start to shift around once you lock in and make final decisions.

Padding and Contingency

Although your budget is based on what you think it will take to make your project, you can never know for sure until you have completed it. That's why it is always good to pad or put in a contingency amount to cover any overages that may occur during the production. A **pad** refers to areas or line items in the budget that you know you have overestimated and you can draw upon those extra dollars if you need to pay for additional costs in other areas. I always do this so I know I have a little extra in case things change. A **contingency** is a line item on the top sheet that is usually set at 10% of the total budget, which is added just in case things go over budget. The funder understands to expect that the budget could go up to the amount of the locked estimated budget and the contingency combined.

Budget Actualization

I wanted to mention **budget actualization** here but will go into more depth in Chapter 14 (*Wrap*) later in the book.

Budget actualization occurs when you enter each paid or payable invoice into the budget in the Actual column (next to the Estimated column) in your budget. Each invoice is entered into the line item that it matches, e.g., airfares are on the airfare line item, lighting rental is on the lighting line item, etc. This process should be done as soon as you begin to receive invoices to be paid. As you enter each invoice into the budget, the formula will total it up and you can track it in real time.

Once this process is completed and all of your invoices have been entered into the budget, you can compare the difference between the estimated and actual columns. Sometimes you are over in certain sections and under in others and they offset each other. This is to be expected. The goal is to come in *under* in the overall budget total.

Tax Resale Certificates

Each state allows for production companies to use resale certificates when purchasing goods or services that contribute to the production of a film production. This allows the production company to avoid paying state sales tax on these items at the time of purchase if they are used to make the project. This is because when the project is completed and sold, sales tax will be paid at that time and if sales tax was paid at the time for project creation as well, it would be a double tax situation. You can obtain the resale certificate form from each state's tax authority. Fill it out and give it to the vendor you are purchasing goods or services from and they will omit the sales tax from your invoice.

Tax Incentives/Credits

Many states in the United States have tax incentives or tax credits for film productions that are produced in their states. Some incentives equal 5%–25% of the total monies spent in the specific state. Some give you tax credits that are used against the production company's tax returns for several years and some states actually give you cash back. Some states allow productions to be exempt from hotel sales taxes for nights at hotels for cast/crew and some tax credits you can sell through a tax credit broker and turn them into cash instead of waiting to use them in your upcoming tax returns over the next few years.

There are very specific rules that you need to follow in order to be assured that you are eligible for the tax credit. The best place to start to research is the film commission for the state you want to shoot in. They often have the information on the state film commission website and the contact info for follow-up queries.

If you think you qualify and want to take advantage of the incentive programs, meet with the state authority months ahead of the production to learn the eligibility requirements and accounting procedures. They will also advise you on what the timeline will be once you apply for the credit. Many states have a "minimum spend" which means that you can't be eligible unless you spend a certain minimum amount in state. Do the research so you understand the rules, timeline, budget requirements and procedures before committing to the state's program.

RECAP

1. **Don't be intimidated about budgeting. Follow the steps in this chapter and go line by line through the budget.**

2. **Use a budgeting software template to help you estimate each element of the production and put it in an organized form.**

3. Overestimate on the first pass by creating the "kitchen sink" version, so you don't forget any projected need.

4. After you have completed the first draft of the budget, discuss your assumptions with the director and key department heads for any questions about the production requirements. Refine and tighten the budget according to what is needed and what you anticipate your total funding will be.

5. Once you know the final funding amount and all the producers and the director have agreed, lock the estimated budget.

6. Once you have a realistic locked budget, create a cash-flow schedule so you know when you need money in the bank in order to fund the key phases of filmmaking—development, pre-production, production, and post production.

7. Continue to revise the budget as assumptions and reality change to create updated "working" budgets.

8. If filming in the United States or internationally, explore tax incentive programs to maximize your funding.

9. For more in-depth information and additional sample production budgets, read my book *Film + Video Budgets, 6th edition* (*http://www.producertoproducer.com* or *http://www.mwp.com*).

CHAPTER 4
FUNDING

Now that you know how much money it will take to produce your project, you need to find the capital to fund it. Financing your project is one of the hardest (maybe *the* hardest) aspects of making it. This chapter provides a guide to the most common ways producers use to fund their independent productions.

Presales

Although we discussed presales in Chapter 1 (*Development*), it's helpful to review them here.

Presales happen when you sell certain rights to the project in order to finance the production. You could sell to a U.S. cable network and maybe an international television network and it might provide enough money to make the film. Then you'd still have the ability to sell theatrical, DVD, and digital rights after the project is completed. It all depends on your budget.

It's difficult to obtain presales for indie filmmakers. Maybe the director has a proven track record of making profitable films and television, or you have an A-list actress attached to your project or an Academy-nominated

> *I think there's only one or two films where I've had all the financial support I needed. All the rest, I wish I'd had the money to shoot another 10 days.*
>
> —Martin Scorsese

writer has written the script. These are the kind of things that help you to get presales.

For documentaries, elements like the director's track record, an A-list actor who agrees to do the narration or the strength of the underlying material may be the key element that makes the project bankable for a presale. For several of the feature documentaries I have produced, a few key foreign television rights and U.S. cable television rights were sold that covered the entire production budget. Then additional rights were sold after the film premiered at film festivals.

Often you won't be able to get a sale until after you have shot the project and created a great rough cut. Then you might be able to get some sales. But this is a calculated risk and you should proceed with caution. I don't advise going into any kind of debt for any project. If it is good enough, you will find the money—or wait until you have saved up the money to cover the entire budget.

For documentaries, there is the added funding option of nonprofit agencies and foundations. Development and production grants are ideal ways to get the project made if it meets the foundation's criteria and you can make a strong application. This takes a lot of time and effort, so make sure you and your project fit all the criteria before applying.

Sales Agents

Sales agents are people who specialize in selling rights to projects. They have connections with various distribution outlets and are known for the kinds of projects they sell. They may focus on narrative projects or non-fiction projects, and a few concentrate on short films.

To understand the types of rights available, here is a list:

U.S. (domestic) television rights—These can be television networks like ABC, CBS, NBC, and Fox, or to cable networks like HBO, TLC, IFC, and Sundance Channel.

International (foreign) television rights—These would be networks like the BBC (British Broadcasting Corporation), CBC (Canadian Broadcasting Corporation), ZDF (Germany), and ARTE (France).

Domestic DVD rights—Rights to license the DVD for the U.S. market.

International DVD rights—Rights to license the DVD for the international markets—usually a separate deal for each country.

U.S. theatrical rights—Rights for a run in theaters in the United States.

International theatrical rights—Rights for a run in theaters internationally.

Digital rights—Rights to broadcast the project digitally, which may include mobile and other future technologies.

Mobile rights (iPods, cell phones, etc.)—Rights to broadcast via cell phones, apps, etc.

Equity Investors

Equity financing is funding by investors who put up the cash for the project. When the project becomes profitable, the investors' deals stipulate the recoupment plan and timeline. The repayment formula is usually based on a certain number of "points."

Points are usually divided into Producer points and Investor points—two different "pots" of investment within the ownership structure. An example of a type of deal is when an investor is paid back up to 125% of the original investment initially. After that repayment, then the Producer Points holders are paid back, and then if there is more profit after that, everyone receives profits on a **pari passu** basis. The Latin phrase means "of equal step" and signifies that each entity is paid back with the same rights as every other entity.

Producer points are usually divided according to the producer's deals with various cast, crew, and other important people who helped get the film made. Sometimes points are given out to the cast and crew who work for free or deferred as a way of sharing profit participation on the "back end."

NOTE: Whenever creating an investment deal, make sure you contact an attorney who can advise you on the legalities and any Securities and Exchange Commission (S.E.C.) rules or regulations that you need to follow.

Deferred Payment Deals

Another type of deal is called **deferred payment**. This means that cast/crew are paid less than their normal salary and the rest is deferred until the time the film becomes profitable. Deals can be completely deferred (cast/crew working for free) or partially deferred (cast/crew are paid something now and paid the rest later if the project becomes profitable).

Like equity investments, it should be made very clear to the cast and crew on a deferred deal that chances are slim that the film will be profitable and that they will be paid back. Advise everyone that they should never expect to see a dime and if they do, it's a bonus. Remember that cast/crew won't be paid until all the costs to make and market the project are recouped. The lower those total costs, the better chance that cast/crew will be paid their deferments.

When a deferred salary is finally paid, it is usually done on a pari passu basis, so if you have $10,000 worth of deferred salaries but only $5,000 worth of profit, then each person is paid 50% of the money they are owed. Then if you make another $5,000 of profit a year later, the rest of the deferred salary owed is paid back to the cast/crew.

Union Signatory Film Agreements

SAG Indie is a section of the Screen Actors Guild-American Federation of Television and Radio Artists (SAG-AFTRA) that facilitates several low-budget agreements for films that are made with budgets from $50,000–$2.5 million. There are four of them—short film (up to $50,000), ultra low-budget (up to $250,000), modified low-budget (up to $625,000) and low-budget (up to $2,500,000). Each agreement outlines a reduced salary for each union actor. Uniquely, the SAG-AFTRA Student, Short and New Media agreements allow for salary deferments for the guild actors, which means the producer only pays the actors' salaries if the film is sold. The union actors are in **first position** to be paid, so whatever money comes in, they need to be paid before all others. You can find all the relevant information at *www.SAGindie.org*.

Donations and Fiscal Sponsorship

Often, independent productions are fully or partially funded by "friends and family" money. Perhaps the film director's grandmother wants to donate money to support the project and writes you a check for that amount. You can take that money and say "thank you," but if the project has a fiscal sponsor, the grandmother can write a check to a non-profit organization and get a tax deduction for her generous contribution. This can be really helpful when asking for cash donations to a project.

Certain non-profits called 501(c)3 organizations (because of the numbers and letters that it refers to in the U.S. tax code) allow projects to apply for fiscal sponsorship. They usually request information via an application—the storyline, the production plan, the schedule, and the budget. Each non-profit has its specific application criteria and administrative guidelines. Be sure to read and follow them carefully.

Donors to your project will send their donation to the non-profit organization and will then receive a tax-deduction letter that they can use when doing their tax return. Then you will contact the fiscal sponsor and follow their process to request the money. Each fiscal sponsor charges an administrative fee of 5%–8% that is deducted from any monies that come into your account. If they have a 5% charge and receive a $1,000 donation (on your project's behalf), you'll be able to use $950 and the institution will keep $50 for administrative and accounting costs.

For donors who give money to your project, ask if they work for companies that have matching contribution policies for employees who make charitable donations. Some corporations match donations, dollar for dollar, so a $1,000 donation can equal $2,000.

Not all fiscal sponsorships are the same. You'll need to research which organization best fits your project. Some groups have specific criteria geared toward their missions or areas of interest, such as films made by women or topic-based projects, etc. Check *www.ProducerToProducer.com* for more information.

Another kind of donation is called an in-kind donation. An **in-kind donation** is for goods or services, not money. Some fiscal sponsors accept in-kind donations and give a donor a tax deduction letter for the value of what they gave to the production. So if a costume rental company donates $500 worth of rental costumes, they can get a tax deduction letter for $500. Check with the individual fiscal sponsor to find out their specific rules and regulations.

Some vendors will donate in exchange for a screen credit. On my last short film we needed two dozen cupcakes for a scene we were shooting. I live around the corner from one of New York City's famous cupcake emporiums. I met with the manager in the store and then sent a follow up request via emails and explained the company would get a screen credit at the end of the film. He approved my request and we got $60 worth of cupcakes for free—and then we all ate them for dessert after lunch!

Many years ago, I produced a two-day music video shoot on Super 16mm for $256 total. Everyone donated everything (we only needed to pay for lunch for two days) and we all had a blast. We really believed in the musical artist and his indie music label and we all wanted to help them by making a great music video that was worth at least $60,000. We asked lots of favors of people and they all said "yes." It can be done, but it takes a lot of time and effort to get donations, so be sure to give yourself enough time in pre-production.

Lastly, when you receive fiscal sponsorship from organizations, check to see if they have any negotiated discount arrangements with certain vendors in your area. This can be helpful in stretching your donated dollars.

Reaching Out to Interested Communities

Fostering community involvement is another way to get much needed assistance (financial and logistical) for your project. If your script revolves around a certain ethnic group or a specific theme or political cause, you should contact the communities that would support it. There are often mutual benefits for creating outreach to specific groups.

Several years ago one of my students produced a film that had an Armenian protagonist and a major scene that took place during an Armenian-American wedding ceremony. Knowing that this ethnic group is underrepresented in American films, the student reached out to the local Armenian community in Brooklyn to see if they would be interested in helping out. They were excited to have their culture represented in his film and allowed the filmmaker to shoot his scenes before and after an actual wedding reception! He got tremendous production values and verisimilitude and the community enjoyed being extras in the film. It's a great example of how helpful groups can be if they want to see your project get made.

Alternatively, you may have a documentary about a specific subject that complements a non-profit organization's mission. The organization might sponsor a fundraiser for your project and help get the word out to the community who would be most interested.

Requesting donations and discounts requires skill and thoughtfulness. Below are ideas to keep in mind to increase your chances of success.

How to Ask for Donations and Discounts

WHAT: KNOW WHAT YOU ARE ASKING FOR

Do the math. Figure out what you really need to make your project happen. You only get one opportunity to ask for a deal so make sure it is the right amount. Be specific with your request and see what response you receive.

For people who are giving you a donation (cash or in-kind) make sure they know what/how their money is being used. Be specific about what their donation is buying—the costumes or food for the crew for one day or the camera rental, etc. It makes them feel more connected to the project and they understand how their donation will benefit your project.

WHY: KNOW WHY YOU ARE ASKING

Be specific. "I'm asking to borrow a dolly for the weekend because we are shooting the climax of the movie and it will make a huge impact on that scene in the project." "I'm asking for a cash donation because we have already raised X dollars and just need another X dollars to be able to fully finance the project." "I'm asking for a donation because I am a student and this is part of my education." You need to be clear about why you need it and make sure you let the potential donor know why it is so important.

HOW: KNOW WHAT THEY WILL GET IN RETURN

Once again, be specific. Here are some possible rewards or exchanges:

1. A screen credit at the end of the film
2. A sponsorship credit in all advertising and press releases
3. A DVD or digital download
4. A promise to shoot their child's bat mitzvah party the following March
5. An offer for their sister to be an extra in the film
6. A promise of your undying devotion forever
7. A commitment to tell everyone to rent from them in the future or eat at their restaurant
8. An understanding that you will rent from them when you produce a commercial shoot with a bigger budget next month
9. A commitment to keep the person or company informed about the progress of the project through periodic emails
10. An invitation to the local premiere

You may not have a lot of money but there are many ways of "paying" someone back. Let them know what you plan to do, put it in writing and then make sure you do it. I often use a donation sheet so I can keep track of who gave what, when it needs to be returned, and the contact details for that person. That way I have all the info on one sheet and I can refer back to it later. It also helps to track the "Thanks/Special Thanks" screen credits for the end of the film.

WHO: FIND OUT WHOM YOU NEED TO ASK

The receptionist at the rental house probably does not have the authority to give out a free camera package for four days. The person in the rental department probably doesn't either. But you should pitch to them to gauge their reaction. They might respond, "We are booked for the next three weeks but after the first of the month we don't have anything reserved." Or, "The owner got burned last time because the filmmaker didn't return it on time and we lost out on a rental for the next day." So now you know several details that will help you modify your pitch when you do approach the owner—change your shoot dates to after the first of the month and make sure you put down a deposit for the cost of the rental so if it comes back late they won't lose money. This way you can address some of the obstacles so the owner can get to "yes."

HOW: CREATE YOUR BEST PITCH

Rehearse your pitch ahead of time so you are ready and then just ask. Once you have finished, be silent and wait for the response. If they are not sure and hesitate, offer to follow up with a letter, proposal, or email. Then follow up again. As long as you don't get a "no," you still have a chance for a "yes."

Carole Dean (*www.fromtheheartproductions.com*) has written a great book that includes important information about film fundraising titled *The Art of Funding Your Film: Alternate Financing Concepts*. She created the Roy W. Dean grant in 1992 and has given away over $2 million in goods and services to deserving filmmakers over the last two decades. When discussing this subject of fundraising she advises: "Filmmakers [that I work with] usually get up to 70% of their donations from individuals and company owners and about 30% from grant organizations and other places. That's about a 3:1 ratio. I think it's important to figure out what percentage of your budget can come from which kind of donor and then put the appropriate amount of time and energy in each area. Divide the budget pie up and then go after the different pieces of the pie."

Grants

National and local independent film organizations offer grants to fiction and nonfiction projects on an annual basis. Read film industry magazines, blogs, and websites to keep up-to-date on grant cycles and deadlines.

In addition to the above there are many non-profit organizations that give grants to film projects that are tied to the organization's mission. This is particularly useful for documentary filmmakers. Depending on your project's theme or subject matter, there may be grant opportunities. Research for foundations supportive of the subject matter. Also check out the Foundation Center (*www.foundationcenter.org*), a comprehensive clearinghouse for information about non-profit organizations across the country. You can take workshops on how to use their databases and how to apply for grants.

Creative Labs

Labs are another way to get access to materials for your project. Many film organizations like the Sundance Institute and film festivals like Hamptons and Nantucket offer extremely selective programs that provide highly regarded mentors to work with the lab participants to hone and improve their projects/scripts. The labs offer crucial creative and institutional support to the lab alumni and work hard to oversee their work so the project can get made or finished or distributed. These programs are difficult to get into but are open to anyone who fits the application criteria. Do your research to decide if any of them are right for you.

Fundraising Trailers

As discussed in Chapter 1 (*Development*), trailers are often required for grant applications and are a very helpful fundraising tool whether your film is a narrative or a documentary. Trailers are usually two to seven minutes long and are edited from your acquired footage and cut to accurately reflect what kind of project you plan to make. Like writing a strong proposal for your film, it is a real challenge to create a good trailer that will get investors and grant organizations to give you money. But a good trailer can allow you to raise all the money you need.

Find a Mentor or Executive Producer

If you can attach a mentor or supporter to your project they can help with getting it made. A well-known producer or director can send out your proposal/trailer to funders and networks that you can't access. Their name recognition and reputation can assure a potential funder that someone with more industry experience will help oversee the project and get it made properly—on time and on budget. Research who may be a good fit for your project, either someone who has done similar work to what you are creating or someone who is attracted to the subject or some other aspect of the project.

Crowdfunding

Crowdfunding websites allow you to raise money through cash donations, which unlike money from investors, will not be paid back. Filmmakers can create a project page on a crowdfunding website, solicit donations, and offer certain rewards based on the amount of the donation. This direct donation relationship is expanding and now, under some very specific legal parameters, filmmakers can use crowdfunding sites to find investors as well. The SEC has created legal guidelines, so make sure you research the laws before you use crowdfunding for an investor model (see earlier in this chapter.)

Lastly, crowdfunding websites can be a great way to create attention for your project that can be helpful with financing. I know one young film producer who used a crowdfunding website to try to raise $50K to produce her first feature film. A veteran producer saw the project on a crowdfunding website and was very intrigued by the project. They had a meeting to discuss the script, budget, and production plans and it went well. So well that he funded their film for $500K!

IndieGoGo and Kickstarter are two websites used often by filmmakers to raise funds for their projects. New websites, apps, and digital platforms are created frequently so stay on top of the latest technology that will help you access possible funders for your project. If you decide to do a crowdfunding campaign, understand that it's really a *full-time job* for the fundraising time period!

Here are some helpful tips for crowdfunding:

- Pick a time period that is long enough to access your potential funders but not too long. It's important for potential donors to feel the immediacy of the deadline so they don't forget.
- Understand the crowdfunding website's rules regarding your goal amount. Pick a goal that is doable and be aware of what will happen if you *don't* reach your goal. Some websites will charge you a higher fee to receive whatever money you raised. Some websites won't allow you to access any of the money and thus don't charge the donor at the end of the campaign. Based on the rules/options, pick the right amount for your project.
- Contact everyone you know from grade school to the present. Often people are interested to hear what you are up to, even if you haven't been in touch in awhile.

- Create a short crowdfunding trailer that represents whatever you want to emphasize about your project. That may include creative collaborators, your personal story, production design, or anything else that can be a captivating story.
- Before you launch the campaign, work out an "updates" schedule that you can use throughout the time period to keep people interested in progression of the crowdfunding.
- Decide what rewards you plan to offer and how difficult it will be to send/mail/provide them after the campaign is over. Giving a "Thanks" screen credit is a fairly easy thing to do, but designing, knitting, and mailing out a hat with the film's logo is a very labor-intensive gift that may get in the way of you actually making the project.
- Understand the fee structure of the crowdfunding site you are using. What percentage of each donation does the site take? What credit card interface do they use and what is the transaction charge? Do they offer the option for donors to receive a tax deduction? As we discussed earlier in this chapter, a tax deduction can be very motivating for certain donors and some crowdfunding websites can facilitate a fiscal sponsorship.
- Remember that these sites take several percentage points as a fee for every donation. Decide if you want all of your donors to use the crowdfunding site or if some should give you a check or bank transfer directly, allowing you to save that money.

After the campaign is over, remember to make/send/do whatever you promised as rewards/gifts. It's important for the donor to receive it when/how it is promised.

Beware of Credit Cards as a Way of Funding Your Project's Budget

We've all heard the stories about maverick filmmakers who make their first feature for $50,000, put it all on their credit cards and then sell it at a film festival for ten times that amount. Great for them, but the odds of being able to pull that off are extremely low (the cinematic version of winning the lottery).

It's such a competitive industry that making a project is a risky proposition, so it's important to have realistic expectations so you don't accumulate debt that could haunt you long after your project is completed.

If you put your production costs on credit cards, you'll be paying them off for years. *Don't do it!* Find another way. Postpone your production until you have raised *all* the money and then shoot.

I wrote "all" the money. Lots of people decide to go forward with a film based on having enough money "to get it in and out of the lab"—basically enough money to shoot it and get to an edited rough cut. They expect to edit the film on their own and then figure out how to finish it after that. Finishing costs for additional editing, audio work, sound mix, music, color correct, and mastering can be quite a hefty number. It can be very hard to raise this money after the production has been completed and you can get yourself into a horrible Catch 22—you don't have enough to properly finish the project and you can't make any money from the project until you do. Make sure you have a solid plan on how to finish it completely and properly before you start the production.

RECAP

1. **If you can get presales for various rights to your film, it's a great way to fund your film.**

2. **There are many deals you can create to attract equity investment in your film. Define investor points, producer points, and deferment deals clearly in legal contracts.**

3. **Explore what SAG-AFTRA low-budget contract your budget qualifies for and apply to SAG-AFTRA for approval.**

4. **Fiscal sponsorship is a good way to attract tax deductible donations to your project. Some organizations facilitate in-kind donations as well, so research what is possible.**

5. **Know "who, what, when, how, and why" before you approach vendors for free or discounted goods and services.**

6. **Consider applying for grants and creative labs if your film meets the criteria.**

7. **Crowdfunding may be a good way to access funding for your project. Research how each website or app works before deciding to use it.**

8. **Do not use credit cards to finance your project. There are other ways to make a film. Don't take on personal debt—it's only a movie.**

CHAPTER 5
CASTING

CASTING IS AN EXTREMELY important part of your project. You can have a fabulous script but if it isn't well cast with the right actor for each role, you won't have a good film. Getting the best possible actor for each role is essential, so if that means postponing production until you have the right cast, then you might need to consider it. Casting is *that* important.

As discussed in Chapter 1 (*Development*), casting is often a key factor in raising funds for your project. Well-known actors or stars can cinch the deal with investors. Distribution is impacted by what recognizable talent is attached to the project. A star's name and face on the movie poster and advertising can make all the difference when someone is making the decision to buy, rent, or download your film.

Hiring a Casting Director

As mentioned above, a well-known actor can make all the difference when seeking funding for your project. Ideally you would bring a casting director on board to help you attach talent to your film. Sometimes a casting director will work on a deferred basis and agree to work during the

"Ninety percent of directing is casting."

—*Milos Forman*

"Casting is everything."

—*Albert Maysles*

development phase and then get paid when the financing is secured. Other casting directors will require payment when they begin work during development.

Once you decide which casting directors you'd like to work with, contact them and discuss the project. *IMDb.com* is a great place to research who cast your favorite films. Make a short list of your top casting directors and contact them. If a director is attached to the project, he or she will need to be a part of the decision-making process, as well. If a casting director is interested, send them the script. Once they have had time to read the script, follow up and find out if they want to work on the project.

The next step is to make sure you are both on the same creative wavelength. Ask them who they imagine for the lead roles and listen to which actors they suggest. Do those match the ones on your short list? Do they understand the specific tone of the project? It is critical that you both have the same vision regarding the actor choices. Good casting directors have the ability to read the dialogue and extrapolate who that character is and who the best actors are to realize that role. Make sure you feel comfortable and don't just go with a casting director who is willing to work on your project. Find the one who is the best fit creatively.

Next discuss the schedule and expectations. Sometimes a well-known/established casting director may want to cast your project but is too busy; they might offer to have one of their assistants to do it through their office. That can be a good deal because the assistant will be calling agents and actors with the clout and name recognition of the lead casting director and you will get direct contact and attention from the assistant throughout the process. It's up to you to weigh all the factors and decide if it is the right answer. Once you have made the decision, create a written contract stating the casting fees, timeline, and payment schedule so everyone understands the expectations.

If you don't know whom you'd like to cast the film, you can contact the local film commission and obtain a list of casting directors. Depending on the size of your city, there will be various people available in your area. Research what kind of casting they do. Some may specialize in certain areas like children or extras or maybe a certain type of project, like commercials. If you don't personally know their work, ask for their reel and watch it. If you like what you see, start the process outlined above.

Attaching an Actor or "Star" to Your Project

Attaching an actor to your project is different from holding casting sessions during pre-production. **Attaching an actor** means you have a verbal and/or written agreement with a recognizable actor who agrees to play one of the roles if you get the specified financing for the project. This allows you to shop your film around to potential investors with the knowledge that you have that specific actor attached to your project. For independent filmmakers, a talented and well-known actor can make a big difference regarding financing.

To attach an actor to your film you'll need to draw up a short list of the actors you'd like for the various roles in your project. Discuss them with your casting director to get a reality check on which actors might be available and interested. For a cameo role that only requires a day or two of work, you might be able to go for a bigger name because it won't require a long time commitment. Short films often can cast well-known actors because they only shoot for a few days.

Once you come up with the game plan for whom you want to approach, you need to work out the offer to the actor. If you are working under one of the union talent contracts (see later in this chapter), the minimum salary for an actor will be dictated by the agreement. You and the casting director may decide to offer the guild rate or you may decide to offer a higher fee to the actor. Whatever the deal, put it in a brief deal memo so it can be sent out to the actor's agent. Depending on each individual actor's recognition factor, you may increase or decrease the offer.

Once you have decided which actor you want to make an offer to, the casting director will contact the actor's agent or, if he doesn't have an agent, will contact the actor directly and send the script, the offer, and a deadline for a response. For this kind of offer, there is no audition; you know the actor is excellent and it is a straight offer.

For each role, you'll need to wait until the actor's agent responds before moving on to the next actor on the list. It can be a slow process so the response deadline is important. The casting director will stay in touch with the agent to find out if the actor has read the script and their reaction. If the actor is interested, the agent will also be able to let you know what dates the actor would be available, based on their current schedule. This is important information to have. If you plan to shoot in the spring but the actor will be in production on another film all spring, it could be a deal breaker. You need to weigh how important that actor is to the project vs.

how locked in you are to the shoot dates. Sometimes you can change your production timeline to accommodate an actor's schedule. Continue to go through the list until you have attached all the actors you need.

Pay-or-Play Deal

Depending on the level of the actor you have attached to the project, they may want a pay-or-play deal. In a **pay-or-play deal** you agree to pay them a certain fee, regardless of whether or not the project gets produced. With certain name actors, this is a worthwhile deal because their name brings enough to the table to be worth the investment and the risk. Pay-or-play deals happen most frequently on big budget projects and very infrequently on an independent production.

Attaching Talent and Casting Without a Casting Director

If you can't hire a casting director, you can cast a project yourself. It means that you will do the process outlined above by yourself, and you won't have the benefit of a casting director's reputation when contacting actors' agents. On the other hand, going through agents can sometimes be a hindrance if you have a very low budget. Agents are paid based on a percentage of their clients' salaries. If an actor takes a no- or low-budget project, the agent might not receive any money because the actor isn't earning anything from the project. Depending on the agent and his or her vision for the client's career, this may be a disincentive for the agent to champion your project to the actor.

In this case, it might be better to get the script and offer it directly to the actor if you can. For instance, maybe the screenwriter wrote the script and while writing it she had Edie Falco in mind for the female lead. Without a casting director, the best way to give an offer to an actor is to get the script directly into her hands. Maybe you have a friend who has a friend who is Edie's hair stylist on her films and maybe this person would be willing to get the script to the hair stylist. The hair stylist reads it and thinks Edie would like it and then passes it to her. She may or may not read it, but if she reads it and likes it, you may get a phone call from her or her agent. The chances are very, very slim, but it's worth a try.

When you put out an offer you need to wait to hear back from that actor before you can offer it to another actor. This can take up valuable time, but that is the protocol. You'll need to decide if you have the time to wait for a response before your project goes into production. It may be better to put in an offer and simultaneously do a casting session for all the roles so you have a great cast regardless of the star's answer. If you decide to do that, make the actor's agent aware of the deadline so you can get a final answer before you move on.

The Casting Process

For those roles that need to be cast through casting sessions, the process is fairly straightforward. You will first want to create a **casting breakdown sheet** for your project. It is a list of each role and a brief description of the age, gender, ethnicity, and physical attributes of each one. For instance, "24-year-old Asian male, fit condition, and must be able to ride a mountain bike," or "65-year-old African American female who can do a southern accent." Once you have the breakdown, the casting director will send it to appropriate agents and also post it to actors via online casting sites. If you are casting outside of your home city, contact the local film commission for recommendations about the best places to publish your casting notice to get the greatest response to your posting.

If you plan to work under one of the guild contracts (more later in this chapter), then you will need to register your production with the guild and get approval of your application. Once approved, the guild will give you a registration number—many of the online casting websites will need this number before they will post your casting breakdown for guild actors to read/view. Make sure you give yourself enough lead time to apply and register your project with the guild before you plan to post your casting breakdown.

Once the posting is online, actors and agents will submit headshots, résumés and demo reels to be considered for a particular role. A **headshot** is a photograph of the actor, with a résumé usually attached. This information allows the casting director to make decisions about who would be right to audition for each role. Photos can be deceiving, so it's always best to meet the actor in an audition before making a final decision. Depending on the number of good actors to be auditioned, the casting schedule may be multiple days or weeks.

Auditions/Casting Sessions

Casting sessions or auditions are usually held in a space that is either in the casting director's office or in a space that is rented or borrowed for that purpose. The space needs to be big enough to accommodate an actor or two, the casting director, director, producer, and a casting assistant. The room should have a video camera on a tripod with a monitor and it should have soundproofing so conversations can't be heard out in the hallway. Ideally there are several chairs outside the room for actors who are waiting, reading the sides, and prepping before their audition time.

Sides is the term used for a portion or scene from the film's screenplay that is copied and given to actors before they audition for the role. Often there is a side for each role—something that, when performed, will give the casting director, director, and producer an idea of the talent and appropriateness of the actor for the role. The side is emailed ahead of time to the actor when the audition is booked so they can prepare their audition. Usually hard copies are also put on a table outside the audition room, where the actors sign in. Most online casting websites have an email component or the ability to post the sides so the actors can access them through the website.

The director, casting director, and/or producer, and casting assistant are usually present for each casting session. Sometimes the first session is conducted with only the casting director present and is recorded so the director and producer can look at the video afterward and make decisions. For an audition video recording, each actor is given a consecutive number written on a card and there is a log taken by the assistant. Once the camera is rolling, the actor says their name, phone number or agency, and holds up the number on the card so the camera can film it. This numbering system allows a person to save time by scrolling quickly through the auditions and track them by the number. After the session, the video files, log, and all the headshots/résumés are uploaded (with password protection) to the director and producer, along with the casting director's notes. The director will look at the audition and make notes using the log to keep track of which actors he or she likes enough to pick for callbacks.

If an actor can't make it for an in-person audition, they could send in a digital recording of themselves as a second-best option. They can record themselves on their cell phone or have a friend record it for them and then upload the digital file to the casting director so it can be included with the other auditions. Although it's not ideal, I've cast actors off these kinds of recordings and they can be useful.

Callbacks

Creating a callback list is a process that is usually done by the director in consultation with the producer and the casting director. **Callbacks** are second auditions where you can see the actor work more in-depth with the material, allowing for more interaction between director and actor. Asking actors to come in for callbacks means that they are among the finalists in the search for that particular role. Sometimes the director will pair up one actor with another to see how they look or work together. Directors may pair certain actors with several different partners to see how different pairs play out. Callbacks are used to give directors enough information so they can make their final selections for each role.

Labor Rules for Minors

Minors are not actors with "minor" roles but a legal term for any actor under the age of 18. Every state has minor labor laws or child performer laws that must be followed when filming. Depending on where you shoot your project, there will be different labor laws and permit requirements to follow. Every state will require that the parent or legal guardian of the minor be with them on set at all times. Some states like California will require an on-set tutor on school days so the minor actors can study on set. The parent or guardian will need to provide a copy of the child labor permit to the producer before the child can work on the project. Contact your state's film commission to find out the legal rules and permit application process.

Extras/Background Actor Casting

Extras or **Background actors** are any roles that do not require speaking lines or very detailed action that would require specific direction from the director. They are the people in a restaurant sitting at tables behind the principal actors—thus background actors. They are the people walking down the street, standing in line at the hot dog stand, and cheering in the bleachers when you are shooting a scene that takes place at a ball game. There are casting agencies and casting directors that specialize in extras casting—creating the background action so that it looks and works well is a special skill.

Casting for extras is usually done closer to the shooting dates, not when casting the principal roles. As you get close to the production dates, the director will be able to quantify and describe what kind of actors she wants. Extras casting is usually done completely from headshots unless you are in a remote filming area that does not have a ready-made pool of extras to work on your project. In that case, you can do an open call and announce a casting session to the local community. An **open call** means that anyone can show up and audition. Pick a time and place and then get the information out with an article in the local newspaper, online blogs, newsletters, and community websites.

On the film *Bomber*, we shot on location in Bad Zwischenahn, Germany. It's a small town near Oldenburg and they had never had a film shot there before. We were able to get an article in the local newspaper and then set up casting sessions at a room in a nearby hotel. People arrived and filled out information cards and had their pictures taken. Then they met with the director and he got a sense of how they might work in the various scenes that required extras. Those notes were put on the cards and he used them later to determine whom he wanted in the background for specific scenes in the movie.

Casting, scheduling, feeding, and coordinating background actors requires time and energy. But for independent filmmaking, nothing says low-budget more then shooting a restaurant scene with only your two principal actors in the location. You need to fill the frame with enough people to make it believable, so it's important to invest the time and money to get the right people for your scenes.

Casting Schedule and Backups

You want to cast as far in advance as possible before your first day of shooting. Ideally, for a feature you'd want to have a minimum of one month to spend time rehearsing and doing a wardrobe fitting and hair/makeup tests. Starting the auditions weeks or months before rehearsals will allow you to find the best actors for the roles.

Always have backups in mind for your key roles. Actors' schedules can change quickly and you always want to have a good alternative if you have to make a last-minute change.

To Be Union or Not to Be Union…

Screen Actors Guild-American Federation of Television and Radio Artists (SAG-AFTRA) is a guild[*] whose members are film and television actors. This guild includes voice-over talent and on-screen stunt performers as

---

[*] A *guild* is a collective bargaining organization for independent contractors, while a *union* is a collective bargaining organization for employees. However, the film industry uses the terms interchangeably and often the guilds are referred to as unions, like "union" and "non-union" talent. I interchange the terms so you are aware of how the film industry uses them.

well. SAG-AFTRA negotiates a new contract with motion picture and television producers every three years. That contract outlines the minimum payment for each kind of acting job, residual payments, and the conditions and rules that must be followed by all signatories to the contract. A **signatory** is a company or individual who signs the contract and agrees to all the conditions of the contract for all of their productions during the contract period.

Most (not all) of the SAG-AFTRA contracts require all actors to be guild members. There is one exception called a **Taft Hartley waiver** (named after the Taft-Hartley Labor Act of 1947) that allows a producer to petition to the union to use a specific person who is not yet in the union for very specific reasons. Those reasons allow for people who have not yet joined the guild to work on a union project—such as children who are just starting out in the acting business, specific ethnic requirements that can't be met by local guild members, or shooting in a remote area of the country where there are no union actors in the local community. If you want the waiver, you'll need to fill out a form and submit it to SAG-AFTRA for their approval prior to hiring.

To cast guild members for your project, you'll need to sign and follow the union contract. SAG-AFTRA has created several low-budget contracts specifically geared to independent film productions. The agreements are tied to the size of your project's budget.

As mentioned in Chapter 4 (*Funding*), SAGindie is a section of SAG-AFTRA that facilitates several low-budget agreements for projects that are made with budgets from $50,000–$2.5 million. There are four of them: short film (up to $50,000), ultra low-budget (up to $250,000), modified low-budget (up to $625,000) and low-budget (up to $2,500,000). Each agreement outlines reduced union actor salary rates and the short-film and new media agreements allow for salary deferments for the actors. When working under a salary deferment deal, the producer pays the actor's salary only if the film is sold. The SAG-AFTRA agreements put the union actors in **first position** to be paid. That means that whatever money comes in, they need to be paid before all others.

Go to www.SAGindie.org to check out the various contracts and determine which one is right for your production. Keep in mind that it takes some time to file the proper paperwork/application for the SAG-AFTRA contracts. Send in the online application at least six weeks before you plan to start principal photography on a feature-length project or series. If it is a short film, SAG-AFTRA suggests you send in the application one month in advance. As mentioned above, some casting breakdown services require proof of your SAG-AFTRA registration before they will allow you to send out your listing to SAG-AFTRA actors. If that is the case, make sure you give yourself enough time to get registered before posting your actor breakdown.

Remember that if you decide to work under a guild contract you will need to abide by the contract rules and salary rates. It's your choice and generally union actors have more experience than non-union talent. For actors to join the union they have to work on at least two union projects before they can apply for membership. That means they generally have a certain level of proficiency and talent. This is not to denigrate non-union actors—there are lots of fantastic non-union actors. If you do get Edie Falco to be in your film, she will definitely be a guild member and you will need to be a signatory in order to work with her and the rest of the cast.

In smaller cities and markets, most of the available talent may be non-union so that is something to consider. A few of the SAGindie contracts allow you to mix guild and non-guild actors, so it might be beneficial for you to sign up, so you have both options when casting.

SAG-AFTRA Bond/Escrow

Once you are approved as a SAG-AFTRA signatory, you'll need to send the guild budgetary estimates for how many days of shooting, how many actors will work and what your total estimated actor payroll will be. SAG-AFTRA will then inform you of the bond amount that you must put in their escrow account for your production. One of the things that a union does for its members is to make sure they get paid all of their wages and their Pension & Health (P&H) fees. By requiring every signatory to put aside a significant amount of money in the escrow account, the guild can access those funds if the production company doesn't pay all the monies due to the actors.

For low-budget productions, the bond is a relatively large amount of capital that is locked away for a significant period of time. As soon as all the actors have been paid their final payroll (including P&H fees), you need to send all the paperwork to SAG-AFTRA so you can get your security bond back as soon as possible. You'll need that money for post production!

Union Paperwork/Station 12

Once you are approved and registered as a guild signatory, you will be given paperwork to use during pre-production, production, and the wrap of your film. There are individual short-form actor contracts that need to be signed by each actor and copies given to the actors, their agents, and the union. Another form requires the actors to approve and sign for each day's work schedule when they are wrapped at the end of every work day. After you wrap, you upload all the signed paperwork to close out your SAG-AFTRA account. Any payments you make to your actors should be paid within 14 days of their work on your project.

For all SAG-AFTRA productions (except short films) you'll need to "Station 12" your film before the first day of shooting. **Station 12** is "SAG-speak" for checking to make sure each SAG-AFTRA actor is fully paid up on their guild dues. Send SAG-AFTRA a list of every guild actor you have cast for your project and they will look them up on the dues database. If they are in arrears, SAG-AFTRA will contact the actor and give them a chance to pay in full. If the actor decides not to pay up, they won't be able to be in your film and you'll have to re-cast. Don't leave this step to the last minute.

RECAP

1. **Hire a casting director based on their reputation and a shared vision for the roles in your project.**

2. **Attaching a name actor to your film can be a critical factor in attracting investors to your project.**

3. **Pay-or-Play deals allow you to lock in an actor to your project based on specific contractual elements like salary and schedule.**

4. **Post a casting breakdown online for the roles you are looking for. Auditions and callbacks allow the director to decide which actor is best for each role.**

5. **Extras casting is an important step in making your film the best it can be. Make sure to give this process the time and attention it requires.**

6. **If you wish to work with union actors, you'll need to become a signatory to a SAG-AFTRA contract. There are several deferred salary agreements available at *www.SAGindie.org*.**

7. **Remember to submit all of your SAG-AFTRA paperwork properly and wrap out the documents they require so your production company can receive the required security bond as quickly as possible.**

CHAPTER 6
PRE-PRODUCTION

NOW THAT YOU HAVE a great script that is ready to shoot and all the necessary funding for the entire project, you are ready to start pre-production. Practically speaking, pre-production begins the moment you decide to do a project. From that point on, everything you do is, in some way, prepping for it.

But for the purposes of this chapter, the pre-production phase begins when enough funding is in place to begin scouting, setting up a production office, hiring cast and crew—the final countdown weeks or months when you are taking concrete and specific steps to make your project happen. Your timeline will depend on what needs to be done and how much time and help you have to do it. The pre-production phase ends on the last day before the start of principal photography.

Production Triangle

Pre-production is the most important period in the life of a film and can make or break the entire project. So many films have gone off the rails because they didn't have enough pre-production time or didn't

Eye, mind and heart—
you need the balance of
all three.

—Henri Cartier-Bresson

get everything accomplished that they needed to do during that period. Now is the time to discuss one of those immutable laws of nature. Like Murphy's Law or the 80/20 Rule, this is another Undeniable Truth and it's called the **Production Triangle**.

THE PRODUCTION TRIANGLE—You only get 2 out of 3

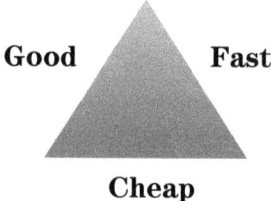

Good   Fast

Cheap

Going through all the sides of the Production Triangle: If you want it **Good and Fast,** it **won't be Cheap** and if you want it **Fast and Cheap,** it **won't be any Good**. But if you want it to be **Good and Cheap**, it **won't be Fast**—and this is where all low-budget productions live! And the only way to achieve **Good and Cheap** is to use time during pre-production to get everything right.

So make sure you get as much time as you can for pre-production. If the schedule is unrealistic, then push back your shooting dates and take more time to prepare. One of the regrets I hear most often is lack of pre-production time—"I shouldn't have rushed into production." "I wish I had waited longer to find a better actor for the lead." "If I had only taken more time to wait until the DP I really wanted became available…."

You only get one shot, so make it count and take the time and get the help you need to prep your film properly—because you can't make excuses for the film after it is completed. It costs more to repair or cover up a mistake then to get it right the first time.

Don't get me wrong. I'm not advocating to prep forever and never make the film. At some point you must "pull the trigger" and decide on your shoot dates. Just make sure you've done everything in your power to maximize your project's resources. Because every day spent on good pre-production adds up to a better film in the end.

Need to Get the Money in the Bank

As mentioned earlier, you need to have a final version of the script (no changes to production but there may be additional dialogue changes) and a *locked* budget before you begin final pre-production. As mentioned in Chapter 2

(*Script Breakdown*), you'll have to create a cash-flow schedule—the document that states when you will need certain amounts of money to cover the specific costs tied to the prep, production, and post production stages of the project. A production is funded as each phase of the project progresses. This schedule is given to the funders and is used to transfer money to the production company's bank account on certain dates based on the next stage of the project that needs to be funded. For instance, the finishing/master stage of a project doesn't happen until many months after it is shot.

As the producer you'll need to be clear that if you don't have that sum available (i.e., in a bank account) on that day, you'll have to delay the project until the money has arrived. This is a tough position to take but as the producer it is your responsibility. Remember that *your* reputation is at stake and if you can't follow through on your commitments, then you can't move forward. Maintaining your integrity and the trust of your cast, crew, and vendors is crucial.

Pre-production Countdown

Here is a general guide on a timeline for doing various pre-production tasks. Your project may require less time or more depending on its unique parameters. Following is a quick reference list. Later in the chapter, each one is explained in detail.

12–9 WEEKS BEFORE PRINCIPAL PHOTOGRAPHY
- Obtain demo reels for all key department heads—director of photography, assistant director, production designer, costume designer, and sound
- Create initial shot lists and storyboards
- Scout for locations and studio space
- Finalize script revisions (for production elements)
- Purchase domain name and create website
- Pick social media handles and set up accounts
- Begin to create the production book
- Obtain production insurance package quotes

8 WEEKS BEFORE PRINCIPAL PHOTOGRAPHY
- Fill out the SAG-AFTRA application/paperwork for the production and submit to the guild
- Post breakdowns for cast and/or hire casting director and begin auditions
- Hire key department heads (listed above)

- Finalize and lock all locations
- Lock script (for production elements)
- Decide on cell phone purchase/reimbursement for key creatives and production team
- Finalize and purchase production insurance coverage
- Test the workflow for the media formats you are considering for the production

7 WEEKS BEFORE PRINCIPAL PHOTOGRAPHY

- Hold auditions for all roles
- Have DP generate tentative camera, lighting, and grip lists for the production
- Negotiate location fees/deals
- Research which permits you will need
- Production designer creates props lists and set designs
- Begin shopping for props

6 WEEKS BEFORE PRINCIPAL PHOTOGRAPHY

- Hold Callbacks
- Post ads for crew positions and begin crew interviews
- Begin signing location deal memos and release forms
- Finalize security bond with SAG-AFTRA and any other completion bonds, if necessary
- Create first draft of the production book
- Set up a private photo/video sharing service and file hosting service for the production

5 WEEKS BEFORE PRINCIPAL PHOTOGRAPHY

- Hire cast and negotiate with agents
- Put out equipment lists to vendors for bids
- Get bids for studio rentals
- Discuss/finalize wardrobe budget estimate with costume designer
- Discuss/finalize production design/props budget estimate with production designer
- Hire a still photographer and/or videographer to create set publicity photos, electronic press kit (EPK) and/or "making of" video

4 WEEKS BEFORE PRINCIPAL PHOTOGRAPHY

- Sign/finalize SAG-AFTRA contract paperwork
- Start actor rehearsals

- Sign cast deal memos
- Hire assistant camera, DIT and/or video engineer
- Obtain caterer bids
- Begin wardrobe purchases/rentals
- Finalize credit card authorizations/security deposit paperwork for all vendors
- Pick studio/stage facility
- Pick equipment vendors
- Assistant director creates first draft of production schedule

3 WEEKS BEFORE PRINCIPAL PHOTOGRAPHY
- Sign crew deal memos
- Finalize vendor deals and payment details
- Obtain location permits
- Obtain insurance certificates for locations and equipment and send to certificate holders
- Hire transportation vehicles
- Pick caterer/figure out how you will feed your crew good meals
- Coordinate extras casting

2 WEEKS BEFORE PRINCIPAL PHOTOGRAPHY
- Do tech scout
- Obtain final equipment lists and send to your vendor
- Confirm credit card authorization/payment paperwork with all vendors
- Confirm insurance certificates with all vendors
- Fill out tax resale certificates and send to vendors
- Create transportation personnel lists

1 WEEK BEFORE PRINCIPAL PHOTOGRAPHY
- Buy craft service food and supplies
- Finalize the production book
- Buy production supplies/expendables
- Copy final scripts
- Have final pre-production meeting with key department heads
- Create accurate driving directions for all locations and stages
- Pre-visualize/create "who's-doing-what" lists

FINAL DAYS COUNTDOWN
- Create pick-up/runs lists
- Crew perform check outs on rental equipment

- Finalize call sheet and directions for first day of shooting and send/confirm with all cast and crew

Pre-production Countdown Explanations
12–9 weeks before principal photography
- **Obtain demo reels for all key department heads—director of photography, assistant director, production designer, costume designer and sound**

These creative collaborators are essential to making a great project. For the producer, this is how you "cast" your crew. It's important to spend the time and energy to get the right people for each key position. There are various ways to find great talent. In larger cities, there are agents who specialize in representing "below the line" creatives—DPs, costume designers, production designers, hair/makeup people, and editors. Get in touch with them and discuss your project, outlining which positions you are looking to fill. Give them your shoot dates (some of their clients may be on long-term projects and not available for your dates) and the salary rate. Depending on the pay scale, the agent will be able to recommend clients. If it is very low pay/no pay, the agent may not have any clients who would accept non-paying gigs, but they can sometimes recommend an assistant costume designer who would be willing to work for free to "move up" and get more experience.

Research the screen credits for films/television you like on *IMDb.com* to create a short list of crew you want to reach out to. Go to film festivals and meet key creatives who have films playing and network with them. Consult colleagues and your mentor to get introductions to talented key department heads whom you are interested in for your project. Posting a job on local production-related websites is also a useful way to see résumés and reels for available local talent.

- **Create initial shot lists and storyboards**

The director and the director of photography will create the shot list for the film. Many directors like to create storyboards to work out how the film will look on paper when cut together. **Storyboards** are drawings that illustrate the director's shot list in the narrative order of the film. Each drawing represents the film language the director and DP envision for each shot, e.g., medium shot, wide shot, close-up, over the shoulder (OTS), etc. Each drawing is created within a box that is the approximate aspect ratio of your project. You can read them like a comic strip to see how each shot would cut together to make up the scene.

You can hire a storyboard artist or purchase a storyboard computer software program to create them. Some programs can provide 3-D dimensionality and camera movements to more closely approximate how the camera would move on the frame. Go to *www.ProducerToProducer.com* for more information.

Some directors like to use a storyboard artist who draws each frame according to their description. This works well but, depending on the artist's rate, it may be expensive for your budget. Check out art schools and art programs where you may be able to find an art student who would be willing to do it for an affordable rate. And there is also the old "stick figure" option. As long as the director and DP can communicate the exact shot to the rest of the crew, it doesn't need to be fancy.

- **Scout for locations and studio space**

This will be discussed at length in Chapter 7 (*Locations*).

- **Finalize script revisions (for production elements)**

It's extremely important to finalize the script for production issues as soon as possible during pre-production. If you don't, you'll have unanswered questions that will plague all departments such as locations, production design, props, costumes, and hair/makeup. It's essential to get these elements finalized now or your budget and departments will have a moving target throughout their prep which will cost time and money. If necessary, most dialogue changes can happen up until the final minutes before shooting and won't affect the production issues.

Getting to a final script from a production perspective means the following:

— Locations should be locked. If your script calls for a suburban house, a high school, a restaurant, and an office building … at this stage, you want to lock those in and only be concentrating on *which* one of each type you will choose to meet the aesthetic and production demands.

— You know what happens in each scene and the general action will not change

— Principal roles are locked in the screenplay—no additional key characters will be added to the cast

— Key production design concepts and key/hard-to-find props are finalized

— Costume needs for all characters are finalized

— Time of day or night is locked

— The key equipment needs (format, lighting, grip, and camera) are finalized

It's important for you, the director and the writer to have these elements locked in the screenplay before you start approaching key department heads. When they start reading the script they will be assessing the potential of the script creatively and from a production point of view. They need to decide if they are interested in the project on both counts and will have lots of questions for you and the director.

From the director they will want to know what the look and feel of the film is. What is the time period, the characters' motivations, and the creative vision for the film? From there, the key department heads will have questions for the producer regarding schedule and budget. On *Man on Wire*, many of the historical recreation scenes take place on the roof of the World Trade Center where the tightrope walk occurred. A long-running discussion in pre-production between the director, the director of photography (DP), and the production designer was whether or not we would shoot those scenes on top of an actual roof—80 or more stories in the sky—or build it in a studio. This decision would have a big impact on the production designer's schedule and budget and those of the lighting and grip departments. Ultimately, we chose to build a large set in a studio and put the time and resources into set construction, set dressing, and props.

- **Purchase domain name and create website**

Decide what web domain name you wish to purchase for the film. Most projects use *www."title"themovie.com* or *www."title"thefilm.com*. Then create an inexpensive website that you can build on as the film progresses. You can use it for publicity, for donations, for blogging, and for dissemination of information to the cast and crew.

- **Pick social media handles and set up accounts**

Decide what you want as your handle and set up the various social media accounts you plan to use. Ideally they will all be the same name to keep things simple. Add the logos/feeds to your website so you are coordinating across all platforms at the beginning of your project. Consistency is key.

- **Begin to create production book**

The production book is the "bible" for the project. It contains all the important info that the production team needs—the cast/crew contact info (names, phone numbers, email addresses), the schedule, vendor information, and driving directions. Create it now and add more information as it is received. Here is the *Sundae* production book.

SUNDAE
Crew List

Producers

Producer	Kristin Marie Frost	Cel Email
Co-Producer	Birgit 'Bitz' Gernbock	Cel Email
UPM	Giovanni Ferrari	Cel Email

Key Creatives

Director	Sonya Goddy	Cel Email
Director of Photography	Andrew Ellmaker	Cel Email

1st Assistant Director	Connor Gaffey	Cel Email
Script Supervisor	Bettina Kadoorie	Cel Email

Casting

Casting Director	Judy Bowman, CSA	Cel Email

Camera Department

1st AC	Chris Cruz	Cel Email
2nd AC	Blaine Dunkley	Cel Email
DIT	Ben Kegan	Cel Email

G&E

Gaffer	Gordon Christmas	Cel Email
Key Grip	Miguel Martinez	Cel Email
Grip/Rigging	Zack Frank	Cel Email

Sound Department

Sound Recordist	Michael McMenomy	Cel Email

Art Department

Prop Master	Michael Piech	Cel Email
Weapons / Specialty Props	Address	Cel Email

Production / Transportation

Production Assistant Temisanren Okotieuro Cel
Email

Production Assistant Amelia Eimert Cel
Email

Catering – Craft Service Brendan Bouzard Cel
Email

Editorial

Editor Souliman Schelfout Cel
Email

Key Vendors/Vehicles

CC Rentals Address Cel
Email

Edge Auto Rental Address Cel
Email

Adorama Rentals Address Cel
Email

Locations

Permits Address Cel
Email

Yellow House Address Cel
Email

Ice Cream Parlor Address Cel
Email

SUNDAE
Cast List

Mary (Mother)	Finnerty Steeves	Cel Email
	Agent Info:	Cel Email
Tim (Son)	Julian Antonio de Leon Mother/Guardian: Francine de Leon	Cel Email
Woman (Stunt woman)	Jenna Hellmuth	Cel Email
	Via Drew Leary	Cel Email
Man	Teddy Canez	Cel Email
Blonde Woman	Laura Gragtmans	Cel Email

PREPRODUCTION

8 weeks before principal photography

- Fill out the SAG-AFTRA application/paperwork for the production and submit to the guild

See Chapter 5 (*Casting*) for details on guild application and paperwork.

- **Post breakdowns for cast/hire casting director and begin auditions**

See Chapter 5 (*Casting*) for how to hire a casting director, advertise for the roles, and begin auditions.

- **Hire key department heads**

Pick the department heads as early as possible because they have a big impact on the vision for the project and estimated budgets for their departments. See Chapter 8 (*Hiring Crew*).

- **Finalize and lock all locations**

See Chapter 7 (*Locations*).

- **Lock script (for all production elements)**

As described earlier, you need to lock the script regarding production elements (except for dialogue changes), as soon as you can. If you make major changes after a certain point, it can cause big problems for each department, create delays in the schedule, and add cost overruns for the budget.

- **Decide on cell phone purchase/reimbursement for key creatives and production team**

Cell phones—phone, text, and data—are the lifeblood of any production. It is essential for all key creatives and the production team to have the use of a phone for the duration of the prep/production/wrap of your project. Discuss with each crew member what is best. Most times, production will pay a flat fee for the crew person's cell phone use. Occasionally production will purchase cell phones on a pay-as-you-go basis. Discuss ahead of time and finalize how this will be done with each key creative and production staff member.

Invest in a headset or earbud for your cell and/or land line phones. It saves your neck and shoulders a lot of strain and also allows your hands to be free when you need to write or carry something. Regardless of state laws, get a headset/ear buds if you plan to drive a vehicle during the prep or production periods; it's a safer way to go. **Remember: Never text while driving!** It's extremely dangerous and has caused many fatal vehicular accidents. Either pull over to use the phone or ask someone else to drive if you need to be on the phone.

- **Finalize and purchase production insurance coverage**

Make sure to purchase the production insurance so you have coverage for all the things that are going on in pre-production—renting vehicles, renting office space, hiring personnel, renting equipment for camera tests, etc. See Chapter 10 (*Insurance*) for more information.

- **Test the workflow for the media formats you are considering for the production**

Test the workflow for production and post production for whatever formats you are considering for your project. Discuss with the director, DP, editor and DIT and then test *all* the steps in the process—media acquisition, down conversions, editing, outputting, and mastering. This test is vital and should not be ignored. You need to know the whole process, any problems and any cost implications *now* or it could have big negative implications for your project. See Chapter 15 (*Post Production*) for more information.

7 weeks before principal photography

- **Hold auditions for all roles**

See Chapter 5 (*Casting*) for more information.

- **Have your Director of Photography (DP) generate tentative camera, lighting, and grip lists for the production**

At this point you should have picked your best two choices for each location and the director has been able to visit them all with the DP. The DP knows what format you are shooting in and the general size of the production so you can get general equipment orders from the DP now and send to vendors for bids. Later, when you have your tech scout with the director, DP, gaffer, and key grip, you can get the final, exact lists.

- **Negotiate location fees/deals**

Now that you have your first and second choices for each location in your script, it's important to negotiate your best rate. Chapter 7 (*Locations*) goes into detail but don't forget to negotiate access for your key department heads to visit the locations soon after you have finalized the deals. They will need to visit the locations to take measurements and photos for the necessary prep work. You'll also want to be able to go back for a tech scout at a later date.

- **Find out about what permits you will need**

Each town, city, county, and state has its own rules about shooting on public property. Make sure you do the proper research and paperwork for any locations that require permits, fees, or other paperwork. See Chapter 7 (*Locations*) for more information.

- **Update script breakdown**

See Chapter 2 (*Script Breakdown*) for more information.

- **Production designer creates props lists and set designs**

At this point, with close-to-finalized locations and an updated script breakdown, the production designer (PD) can finalize the production design budget with an estimate for costs to rent and buy what is needed for the production design, props, landscaping, and set construction. As the producer you take that list and compare it to the estimates in your overall production budget to see where you stand. If any set building is required, the production designer should have drawings for the design and several bids from builders.

You then take all these estimates and figure out if you have enough money to pay for it all. Often you won't, so you'll need to discuss with the director and PD ways that you can tighten the budget. How many period picture vehicles do you really need for that exterior street scene? Can you shoot a scene in one corner of a big room so there is less set dressing needed? Instead of building a complicated set, can you use one of the locations that was ruled out before? These critical discussions at this stage of pre-production allow everyone to come up with solutions creatively to meet the financial reality.

- **Begin shopping for props**

The props master, in consultation with the production designer, will need to begin shopping for props. They will go to prop rental shops, online websites, flea markets, furniture stores, discount stores, retail stores, and everything in between to source what is required for the film. By now, they will have discussed the look in minute detail with the director and DP. Is it a period piece or does it take place in the present day? Does it have a look that is very upscale or does it take place in a dingy, low-rent world? They will take lots of digital photos to show the director, DP, and production designer to determine the right props for the project. Once the director indicates her preference, the props master will price out those items to come up with an estimated budget.

6 weeks before principal photography
- **Hold callbacks**

See Chapter 5 (*Casting*).

- **Post ads for crew positions and begin crew interviews**

You can never start too soon looking for crew for your film. It's the "other" casting you do on a project—you cast your crew much as you would cast the actors. And it's just as important.

You need to consider experience, talent, personality, and availability (see the Department Heads list), but because you have limited resources, there are other factors, as well. For instance, one gaffer may have his own lighting/grip truck but the other one is easier to work with. Or one assistant director (AD) is available for the shoot dates but not the tech scout and the other one is usually a 2nd AD and wants to move up and get experience as a 1st AD. Or the best key grip who is willing to work for the rate you can afford is a real pain and will bring down the rest of the crew's morale. Your alternate choice is a grip with less experience but who doesn't have an attitude problem. These are the kind of decisions that you have to grapple with.

With an independent film you'll be asking crew members to work for very much below their normal rates so you often have to work hard to *sell* the film to each and every potential crew member. And this is where it is important to be clear about the strengths and merits of the film.

If Edie Falco is going to be the lead actor, then tell the potential crew member as soon as you get on the phone. If the screenplay was picked as a finalist for a screenplay competition recently, then mention it. If you've got a well-known DP on the project, that should be of interest to the AC, DIT, grips, and electrics. As producer, you have to be a good sales person but you also need to know if the crew person is good for your project. As mentioned earlier, read their résumés and call their references. A bad or uncooperative crew member is a liability to your production and you need to work hard to insure against it.

Ultimately it is a numbers game. Sometimes you have to call five people to fill one position and sometimes you have to call fifty (no joke). Once I'm on the phone with someone, even if they aren't interested or available for the shoot dates, I always ask for at least two names/contact info for other people who might be interested. That way, you never run out of people to call. Eventually you'll get to the "yes."

When hiring crew, *always go with your gut*. Even on the phone, you'll pick up on a vibe or get an inkling about a person. I always ask enough questions to make sure I know if they know what they are doing. You can often tell by *how* they answer the questions if they have enough experience. Even if you are desperate, don't hire someone you don't feel confident about.

Lastly, there are several crew positions that are notoriously difficult to fill with great people. They are 1st Assistant Director (1st AD), Assistant Cameraperson (AC), Digital Imaging Technician (DIT), and Sound Recordist. You may have to pay them more than you originally budgeted but they are crucial and if you don't pay now, you'll end up paying more later in post production to fix mistakes.

- **Begin signing location deal memos and release forms**
See Chapter 7 (*Locations*).

- **Finalize security bond with SAG-AFTRA and any other completion bonds, if necessary**
As discussed in Chapter 5 (*Casting*), you'll need to put up a security bond with SAG-AFTRA if you become a signatory to one of their guild agreements. The guild will tell you how much you'll need to transfer into the escrow account.

If you are using a **completion bond** with your project, the bond company will require you to put a certain amount of money in an escrow account as well. This ensures that if the producer can't deliver the film, the bond company can step in to finish the film properly so the financiers/distribution company get a completed film per their legal agreements. See Chapter 10 (*Insurance*) for more information about a completion bond.

- **Create first draft of the production book**
The production book is a critical document that the production team uses to keep track of all the key information for cast, crew, vendors, and schedules. It works well to keep the document on a password-protected "cloud" computing site so only the production team can access it and amend the document in real time. As you cast actors, hire new crew, and add new vendor information, the book is revised so it has the most up-to-date info.

- **Set up a private photo/video sharing service and file hosting service for the production**
Use a password-protected photo/video/file sharing service to set up a project folder for the production. Key department heads can upload visual material to facilitate creative dialogue and decision making about locations, production design, props, hair/makeup, wardrobe, etc. Production staff should use one to share project documents and for dissemination to

cast and crew. Make sure you research the security features of whatever service you decide to use.

5 weeks before principal photography
- **Hire cast/negotiate with agents**

Once the director makes his final casting choices, you'll need to book the actors. It's fun to make the phone calls to the final cast picks, but don't forget to call the ones who were in callbacks but who didn't get the roles. If you have a casting director, she usually takes care of this job. If you don't have one, as the producer, you will need to do it. Remember that the actors took the time to prepare for the auditions and callbacks and deserve an answer, one way or the other. Thank them for their time and talent and let them know that you have gone with someone else for the role. No need to get into specifics and no need to give false hope, just inform them and thank them for their time and talent. There are times when the first choice has to drop out and you may have to recast with someone from your callback list.

If you are working under a deferred payment SAG-AFTRA contract or a non-union production with actors deferring their salaries, you will not be paying any of the actors during the production period. But you may still need to negotiate other deal points with your cast or their agents. If you have cast a "name" actor to your project or if the talent's agent has some deal points to discuss, you'll need to get the negotiations going as soon as possible. You never want to be a week out from shooting and still not have a signed deal memo with one of your lead actors!

Remember that *everything* is negotiable, so don't despair if the star's agent wants lots of potentially expensive conditions on behalf of their client. That's an agent's job—to get the most for his or her client. Your job is to figure out what your production can and cannot afford to do for the actor and let the agent know. For instance, you may not be able to give them their own trailer for the length of the shoot, but you can offer them a room at the back of the townhouse you'll be shooting in to be used as a special, dedicated room for their own peace and quiet. You can make sure it has a couch, fresh fruit, bottled water, and the actor's favorite magazines. It doesn't cost the production anything extra but it gives actors the privacy they were asking for.

Remember to keep your eye on the final outcome you want—to work with that actor for your film. The negotiating process may be a bit trying, but if you keep focused on the end result, it will be easier for you and best for the production.

- **Put out equipment lists to vendors for bids**

As mentioned earlier, you will have researched equipment rental houses and the DP may have some recommendations or places she rents from on a regular basis. Email the list to the person in charge of the rental department at each place. They will take your list and "bid it out." The bid will list every piece of equipment, the list price and then usually a discount percentage which can be anywhere from 5%–40%. No one ever pays the list price, but it's the size of the discount that is most important. If you, the director or DP have a personal connection to the vendor, let the rental agent know before they do the estimate; that way they can give you the best discount possible.

Depending on the format you are shooting in, you may consider buying a camera, tripod, or other piece of equipment. Prices to purchase certain equipment might make the most financial sense—it might be more cost-effective to buy and resell afterwards or rent it out to others after you are finished shooting your project. Do the research and get bids for purchases so you can make the best decision.

THE IMPORTANCE OF VENDOR RELATIONSHIPS

Having good long-term relationships with the people and companies that rent equipment, locations, vehicles, props, etc., is extremely important for a producer. Vendors are your partners in the making of the project, in the same way as the cast and crew. If you have a respectful working relationship, vendors can really help you regarding service and budget.

It's important to be loyal to vendors who help you out. I've been working with the same vendors for decades and we have an ebb and flow to what kind of deals I make for each project. There are some projects where I can pay full rate and I do. There are other projects that I do for "love," not money, and then I'll ask the vendor for a favor/discount in order to make the project happen budget-wise.

Another way to pay back such a favor is to recommend the vendor to other producers for their productions. If you like the vendors, it's great to recommend them. I ask the other producers to let the vendors know I suggested them so the vendors know that I am serious about supporting and building up their businesses.

Keep in mind that you can't ask for a favor *every* time or vendors will get resentful and balk. But if you rent from them over the long term, you build up trust and understanding and help each other out.

- **Get bids for studio rentals**

At this point in pre-production you'll know if you will need to shoot in a studio or on location, or a combination of the two. If you need to do a set build, you'll need to rent a studio. Figure which stages will work for your production and get a few bids so you can compare estimates.

- **Discuss/finalize wardrobe budget estimate with costume designer**

By now the costume designer will have priced out all the wardrobe for the film. If the film is not a period piece then, hopefully, the costume designer can augment the costume list with clothing that the actors bring to set from their closets. This will save you wardrobe rentals/purchases and it means that the clothes will already fit the actor well. Note: the SAG-AFTRA contract requires nominal fees to be paid to an actor for each outfit you rent from them. With non-union actors you may pay them fees or they may allow you to borrow their clothing for the shoot at no charge.

Double check to see if you need "multiples" for any pieces of clothing. Anything that is going to get damaged or altered during a scene will require you to have more than one for multiple takes.

Anything that can't be acquired from the actors' closets will need to be purchased or rented. The costume designer will do the research and send you a line-by-line estimated budget for clothes, shoes, accessories, and cleaning to cover all of the outfits needed for the entire production.

Bigger cities will have costume rental houses and they ship throughout the United States too. There are many online websites where you can purchase/bid on used or new clothing. After the production ends, the purchased wardrobe will be saved for a period of time in case there will be a re-shoot. After the re-shoot period is over, production will either sell or donate the clothing.

At this point, if the wardrobe budget is too large, you and the costume designer will discuss ways to reduce it. If any of those ideas have creative implications you'll need to consult with the director and DP to get their approval of proposed costume changes.

- **Discuss/finalize production design/props budget estimate with production designer, props master, and set designer (if applicable)**

Like the costume designer, you'll need a line-by-line estimate from the production designer. This master budget will include any prop rental/purchases, set dressing, and set construction costs. Once you have the estimate you can start brainstorming on how to lower the dollar amount—either through discounts and donations or any cheaper alternatives that the PD and director can approve.

The production design section of the budget is often a large percentage of your total costs. Anything you can do to reduce costs in this area will have a big impact on the rest of the budget. The production design/props/set departments also have some flexibility on what they choose to purchase/rent to achieve the creative vision for the film. Discuss the budget targets and figure out where there are areas that can be reduced in the budget. If any of those ideas have creative implications, you'll need to consult with the director and DP to get their approval of proposed production design changes.

On the feature documentary *Wisconsin Death Trip*, the film recreates stories from a newspaper that was published in the 1890s. It was a period film and we had a very low budget, so one of our smart solutions was to shoot almost entirely at historical sites throughout the state of Wisconsin. Every state has many historic homes and locations that have been preserved by local, state, and federal organizations. Visited by thousands of people each year, they are filled with historically correct, and sometimes priceless, antiques. We were granted permission to shoot at almost every site that we requested and were happy to pay a small donation fee to obtain incredible production values!

- **Hire a still photographer and/or videographer to create set publicity photos, electronic press kits (EPK) and/or "making of" video**

Most distributors will expect 50-plus high-resolution (300 dpi or higher) still photos from the set of your film. It's important for publicity purposes to have photos that show the director, DP, crew, and actors working on the set. Some deliverables lists may ask for an EPK or a "making of" video. These videos are not always required for low-budget productions, but if you have the resources, now would be the time to hire a photographer and videographer so they can visit your set for a few days during the production period.

4 weeks before principal photography
- **Sign/finalize SAG-AFTRA contract paperwork**

You'll want to get all of the signed paperwork into the guild by now. Once approved, SAG-AFTRA will then send you all of the forms and contracts you need to use for your production. You'll want to know the security bond amount too, because it will be a relatively large sum and you'll need to finalize your cash-flow schedule.

- **Sign cast deal memos**

Now that you have negotiated the deals, make sure you obtain all the signed documents and send copies to the actors and agents. You'll need to keep copies for your paper deliverables (see the section on deliverables in Chapter 15, *Post Production*).

If you are working under a union agreement you will use a union work contract for each actor. This contract is tied to the guild agreement you would have signed previously (see Chapter 5, *Casting*) and will cover the rights to the use of their appearance in your project. If you are using non-union actors they will sign a talent appearance release form in addition to the deal memo, so you have the proper rights to use their images in your film.

In addition to the union contract or appearance release form, you may negotiate a cast deal memo that outlines other deal points that aren't covered. Perhaps you have agreed to put them in their own hotel room while on location (whereas all the crew are sharing a room). Or you might have agreed to rent a small recreation vehicle (RV) for the location shooting for the actors. These are the kind of deal points you would put into a simple deal memo agreement. You can download a template at *www.ProducerToProducer.com* that can be customized for your production. Usually talent agreements are negotiated on a most favored nation basis (see Chapter 3, *Budgeting*). That means whatever you negotiate for one actor, the other actors will receive the same deal. Make sure you are clear about each deal with your actors ahead of time.

- **Start actor rehearsals**

Once the proper paperwork is signed, you'll be free to schedule rehearsals. Talk to the director to find out how often she would like to rehearse with the actors and how. What kind of space would she like—an apartment or "black box" rehearsal space? You can rent a space, but to save money you can often borrow a space or classroom. Or perhaps you can borrow a friend's apartment during the day (if they work outside their home) or use an office conference room if you decide to do rehearsals on a weekend.

As you get closer to shooting, it may be helpful to rehearse in the actual locations. If that's not possible, you can put tape on the floor of a studio to mark off the exact spacing. The director may decide to work separately with each actor and then bring them together later in the process. Check with the director and find out how she likes to do it. Be careful about *over* rehearsing—that can be as bad as not having enough rehearsal time.

- **Hire assistant cameraperson, DIT, and/or video engineer**

You'll want to have the assistant cameraperson (AC), digital imaging technician (DIT), or video engineer locked in by now. These positions are critical to the film and directly interact with the DP. Often the DP will recommend good and trusted crew people for you to call. Make sure you check references and that the DP approves each person before you finally decide to hire.

Every crew person is critical but department heads are particularly important as key collaborators and managers of the crew who work in their departments.

- **Obtain caterer bids**

You'll want to get recommendations for good and affordable caterers for your crew/cast meals on set. Providing good, hot, and nutritious meals each day is an incredibly important task for the production department. You want everyone to have good food so they can do their best on the project and it's another way you can let them know how much you appreciate their time and talent.

Give the catering companies the number of cast/crew, the number of days and general budget for what you want. As you hire cast/crew you'll need to collect information about allergies and food diets, e.g., vegetarian, kosher, etc., and you'll want to give that info to the caterer so they can price out what it will cost to provide the food your production requires. Inquire about any costs for transportation, setup, catering personnel, plates, cutlery, etc., so their estimate is as complete as possible.

- **Begin wardrobe purchases/rentals**

Once you have approved the wardrobe budget you need to communicate the bottom line number to the costume designer and make sure he agrees to keep to that budget. It's very important to be clear about what you expect. Let him know that you are signing off on a specific amount of money for costume rentals/purchases to clothe everyone in the film and it can't cost more than the stipulated amount. The costume designer should sign off on this amount and agree that if he thinks he may be going above this amount for any reason, he has to let you know *immediately*, because *only you* can authorize him to spend any more money.

In each crew person's deal memo there should be a section that outlines this procedure. You never want to be in the position of a department head handing you a bunch of receipts at the end of the shoot with the expectation of reimbursement, even it they exceeded the allotted budget.

Keep in mind that sometimes things change. Maybe new costumes must be added to your list or an affordable costume becomes unavailable and you must substitute a more expensive garment. The costume designer needs to inform you immediately so you can be aware of potential overages. Then you, the director, and the costume designer can discuss it and decide what to do.

- **Finalize credit card authorizations/security deposit paperwork for all vendors**

When renting from vendors (equipment, costumes, props, etc.) you'll need to fill out paperwork to set up an account and scan/email a copy of the production's credit card for the security deposits. The deposit protects the vendor in case there is damage/loss to their rentals. To avoid fraud, the vendor usually requires a copy of the front and back of the credit card and a copy of the credit card holder's driver's license.

A few days before the rentals are picked up, remember to confirm that all the paperwork is in order to avoid any delays on the pick up day.

- **Sign out petty cash/debit cards to key department heads**

At this point in pre-production, several departments will need petty cash for their purchases as well. They will "sign out" on a Petty Cash Sign Out Sheet for the amount of money they are given. The department heads will make the purchases and keep all the receipts. Anything they do not use for the production will be returned to the production. It is the department's job to reconcile all the petty cash on a Petty Cash Sheet, including all of the receipts.

Keep a revolving line of petty cash for each department. Once a certain amount of money has been reconciled, a new infusion of cash can be given out so you never have a large amount of unreconciled cash at any given time. It allows you to track spending and keep on top of your actualized budget so you know where you stand.

Some productions prefer to issue debit cards to departments for petty cash usage. That way every transaction is immediately tracked online and the department can't spend more than the limit on the debit card before they reconcile and request more petty cash. There are still some instances when actual cash is required, e.g., gratuities, some parking meters, and certain vendors, so you'll probably have to sign out some cash in addition to the debit card.

HOW TO RECONCILE PETTY CASH

Reconciling petty cash is an important skill. It may seem like an easy thing to do but I can't tell you how many people have trouble with it. Here are the steps to follow for petty cash reconciliation:

1. Count out the money that you are given and then sign out for that amount with the producer/UPM/production coordinator/accountant.

2. Keep petty cash separate from your own personal money.

3. Pay for production-related expenses with cash and obtain a receipt for everything you pay for. If you can't get a receipt (e.g., parking meters, gratuities), write down the amount on a piece of paper with the date, the amount, and what it was used for.

4. When you are ready to give the money back to the production department, tape up each receipt on scrap paper and number them.

5. Get a petty cash reconciliation envelope from the production department and fill in the info for each receipt.

6. Add up each receipt and total it for the receipt total column.

7. Add up the total cash you have on hand for the cash-on-hand total.

8. The receipt total and the cash-on-hand total should equal the total amount you were initially given.

9. If the amounts do not total correctly, go back and check your math or find missing receipts until the totals are correct.

10. Hand in all the paperwork, receipts, and cash to the production department and make sure they take your name off the petty cash sign-out sheet and close out the amount. It's a good idea to scan/take photos of all of your paperwork so you have a copy of everything you handed over.

- **Pick studio/stage facility**

Once you have bid out your job to several studios you'll have an idea of the various costs. Make sure to go over the bids thoroughly. One studio may charge a flat fee for 10 hours and another stage may charge a higher fee for 12 hours. But when you add in the 2 hours of overtime (OT) for the first facility, you realize it is more expensive if you plan to use the studio for 12 hours or more.

Remember to factor in the other costs like **green rooms** (holding areas for actors), tables and chairs, hair, makeup and wardrobe rooms, electricity, dumpster fee, cartage, and studio manager rates, so you know you can make accurate comparisons between the three bids.

There are other factors to consider. How far a distance do cast/crew have to travel? If they are driving their own vehicles and you need to reimburse them for gas and tolls for each day of filming, it could really add up and make the studio rental less cost effective. Or the travel time to get there and back adds two hours to each shoot day and blows your tight shooting schedule. Once you have analyzed the bids, discuss them with the director and key department heads to find out if there are any other mitigating factors that concern them.

Then make your decision and negotiate the best rate you can. Use the other bids you received as leverage in your negotiation. If it's a multiple-day shoot, maybe you can get the build or strike day for free. When booking always put the studio "on hold" but don't "confirm" until you must and you know you are definitely going to use it. See the distinctions below.

HOLD/CONFIRMATION PROTOCOL

Reserving equipment, studios, and locations all work on a **hold, confirm,** and **challenge** system. You need to know these terms and understand them so you don't put yourself on the hook for commitments you can't keep.

Confirm means you have "bought" the reservation and the vendor will not rent the stage/location/equipment to anyone else. If the shoot gets canceled or postponed, you will still owe the studio/equipment house for the rental costs for those days you confirmed.

So the best thing to do is put a **hold** on the facility for all the dates you need. Ask if you have a **1st** or **2nd hold.** If you are reserving far enough in advance, you'll probably have a 1st hold. The next person/company that wants the same dates will have a 2nd hold. As the dates get closer, the other production may decide they want to book/confirm and will put in a **challenge** for those dates. The studio/rental house will then call you and give you 24 hours to confirm or you lose the dates to the other production company. If you confirm, then you "own" the dates and will need to pay for them whether you shoot or not (see above).

This is the way it works for equipment rentals, wardrobe/props rentals, studios, locations, and freelance personnel. It's a pretty fair system and it's important to understand and follow the rules of the game. Your word is your bond in this business. Make sure you understand the language and honor your commitments.

- **Pick equipment vendors**

Picking equipment vendors is very similar to picking a studio/stage. You'll be making the decision based on price, availability of what you require, and other factors like reputation for service, quality, and reliability.

Consider this—you are shooting far out of town on location and an important light stops working on the set. If the vendor can't replace it until the next day, they may not be the best company for your production. Maybe it makes sense to pay more for the equipment rentals if it means you'll be given better service or they'll give you some backup lights as part of the deal. These are the kind of factors to consider before you pick your equipment vendors. For studio shooting, check the rules because often the facility requires you to rent their own lighting and grip equipment—you'll need to know their rates.

- **Assistant director creates first draft of production schedule**
The 1st assistant director (AD) creates the project's production schedule. If you can't hire the AD until later in pre-production then you, as the producer, might need to create the first draft yourself.

The schedule will be based on the latest draft of the script. Each scene will be given a consecutive scene number that will be locked in from this point forward. If scenes are added or subtracted they will receive scene numbers like 1A or 2A, then 1B or 2B. Shooting chronologically by what happens in the script is rarely the most economical way to shoot a film, so the AD will break the scenes down into the smartest and most efficient way of shooting. Considering factors like location availability, weather conditions, geographic considerations, actor availability, and technical requirements, the shooting schedule will most likely be "out of sequence."

Once the first shooting schedule is created, it is disseminated to the key department heads who go through it and give back notes. Maybe a set needs to be built and it won't be completed until the second week of principal photography or a certain location can only be shot on weekdays. Based on the feedback, the AD makes adjustments to the schedule. For the film *Man on Wire,* we had a seven-day shoot for our NYC historical recreations. Because another film was shooting in our interior apartment location at the beginning of our production schedule, we had to shoot there on our last days. Our two days of shooting at the 7 World Trade Center office building could only happen on a weekend. So it meant that we *had* to shoot the big set construction in a studio as our first shoot day. We would have much preferred to shoot that later in the schedule, but we were forced to make it our first day of principal photography by default.

3 Weeks before principal photography
- **Sign crew deal memos**

At *www.ProducerToProducer.com* you'll find a sample crew deal memo. You can amend that one or create your own. At the very least, it should state the crewperson's name, address, phone, social security number, paid rate for the job, dates of employment, title, screen credit, and rules of employment.

- **Finalize vendor deals and payment details**

Make sure to finalize your vendor deals for now. Give the vendors the most accurate info about your equipment rental lists and let them know when you'll have the final, final list (usually as soon as the tech scout is completed.) Work out your money deals at this point so you know what to expect.

Find out the exact language each vendor requires for the insurance certificate for their company so you can make sure it is correct. Finalize *how* you will pay for it, too. If this is your first rental with this company, they may require you to pay on a C.O.D. (cash on delivery) basis. Do they accept credit cards or must it be a certified check or some other form of payment? Work out these details now and make sure you have done all the proper paperwork for each vendor so there are no problems when your crew picks up the equipment, props, etc. on the pick-up day.

- **Obtain location permits**

If you are shooting on location, the production may need to acquire filming permits. Contact the film commission that has jurisdiction for the towns, cities and/or states where you will be shooting. The Association of Film Commissioners International (*www.afci.org*) has the listings for U.S. and international film commissions. See Chapter 7 (*Locations*) for more information.

- **Obtain insurance certificates for locations and equipment**

Insurance is a critical part of producing any film production. Chapter 10 (*Insurance*) has a wealth of important information—be sure to read it carefully. Any individual or company can obtain insurance for a production and there are many insurance brokers that cater to the film business. Some of them allow you to fill out a form online and then get a quote via email. Go to *www.ProducerToProducer.com* to get a list of insurance companies/brokers.

At this point in pre-production, you'll start to issue the insurance certificates for all your vendors and locations. Usually the insurance broker will provide the production with an online portal so you can type in the vendor's information and obtain an insurance certificate that you can forward to the rental house or location owner, etc. This certificate assures them that your general liability and production insurance are in effect and will cover any loss or damage caused by the production, less the deductible that your policy dictates.

- **Hire transportation vehicles**

At this point you'll need to figure out how many vehicles to rent for the production. Certain departments may need their own vehicles, such as art, camera, grip & lighting, and wardrobe. These may need passenger vans, cargo vans, and/or trucks. Depending on your studio or locations, you may need to transport cast and crew to/from the set each day. Add up how many people you need to transport and then put the appropriate number of vehicles on hold.

Remember that not all cast and crew will have the same call times, so you have to figure out how many people will travel at the same time. Perhaps you can do two "runs" to the set in the morning in the same vehicles if there is enough turnaround time, but that is not always feasible. Keep in mind that you'll need to rent vehicles for errands and pick ups/returns. Sometimes the cheapest way to cover this situation is to hire production assistants who have their own cars and pay them for the mileage traveled or the gas and tolls during the production.

When renting vehicles (vans and trucks), be sure to hire only *qualified* people to drive them. Make sure the PA (or other crew person) has experience and is comfortable driving a van or truck—14-foot trucks can be a daunting challenge for uninitiated drivers—so you can prevent accidents. You may need to hire professional drivers with commercial driver's licenses (CDL) for some of the vehicles.

Early in my career, on the first shoot day of a short film I produced, we had to drive 45 minutes across the Lake Pontchartrain Causeway Bridge out of New Orleans. The night before I had worked out with all the PAs who was picking up which cast and crew member and driving which vehicle. We all set out at 5 a.m. the next morning, crossed the bridge and arrived at the location right on time at 6 a.m. As we were setting up, we realized that our lead actor was not on set. I queried the assigned PA/driver and she let out a gasp when she realized she had picked up the other two actors but had forgotten the lead who was still waiting for her back in his apartment in downtown New Orleans! As we waited an hour-and-a-half for the PA to go back and pick him up and bring him to set, we had already blown our first day's shooting schedule before the day had even begun.

- **Pick caterer, figure out how you will feed your crew good meals**

I almost titled this book *Feed Your Crew Every 6 Hours* because I believe that is one of the most important things to do as a producer on any project. I'm not kidding and I'll tell you why.

Every production runs on the stomachs of the crew. Sometimes your crew is not being paid at all or very little, so the only thing they are getting each day for their hard work is food. So make it good as it demonstrates that you value and respect their contributions by serving good food at meal time and on the craft service table. It won't be cheap but it will be the best money you spend on your film. A well-fed crew is a happy crew. And a happy crew gives its all to you and your project.

If you choose not to hire a caterer you can hire a friend or family member who is a great cook to buy all the ingredients and make home-cooked meals for your crew. They will need a place to prepare the food for a cast and crew of 20 to 40-plus people and be expected to serve the food at the specified time and keep it hot.

For some of my productions, I'll canvas the neighborhood we are shooting ahead of time and decide which restaurants can make platters of good food that we can serve for lunch and dinner on set. Different kinds of foods work well this way, but make sure it is high quality and does not have any MSG, in case crew members have reactions to that ingredient. Serving "fast food" is not acceptable.

Lastly, remember to poll your crew prior to finalizing the menu to find out any about food allergies and special dietary requirements. You want to know this information ahead of time so you can plan properly for everyone's dietary needs.

- **Coordinate extras casting**

If your film requires **background actors** or **extras** (non-speaking actors who appear in the background), you will need to cast and coordinate them. Depending on how many you need for each shoot day and how specific they need to look, this often is a separate casting job.

Ideally, you'd have an extras casting director. If that is not possible, you'll need to get a coordinator to take on this challenge. The key is to find a very organized person for this job. (See Chapter 5, *Casting*.)

2 Weeks before principal photography

- **Do tech scout**

The **tech scout** is when the director, producer, and department heads go to each location and work out all the logistics for each shoot day. The crew should include the director, producer, DP, 1st AD, gaffer, key grip, sound recordist/production mixer, production designer, location manager, production manager, and PA/driver.

The director and DP should have a close-to-final shot list and will "walk through" what will happen in each space. The DP will discuss lighting and grip requirements with the gaffer and key grip. The production designer will go over the plans for what will be in each space and how it will look.

If you have a location manager, he will be there and will discuss the rules for shooting in the space—e.g., no smoking, garbage disposal, what entrance can be used, shooting times, parking, etc. If you don't have a location manager, the producer should have all the pertinent details.

The sound recordist will be listening to the space and deciding if there are any problems that need to be addressed, such as turning off central air conditioning, refrigeration, or a background music system. If there is a construction project nearby, it may impact your shoot during the day. Try to go to the location on the same day/time of the week that you plan to shoot so you can learn if there are certain things that might affect your production. Discuss with the location owner anything that might have consequences for your filming—garbage pick-up schedule, landscaping/lawn mowing, building construction, apartment renovations, school children playing in a nearby playground, freight elevator operation schedule, parking regulations, etc.

The producer and the production manager will be listening to all of these issues and concerns and taking complete notes. Each key department head will have his or her own specific questions, concerns, and requests that you will need to follow up on. Don't let them talk to the location owner or else the owner may get overwhelmed with requests; have it all funnel through the production team.

Don't worry, at some point on the tech scout your head will want to explode with all the specific requests and details that each department head is bringing up. But it's OK, because you want to know about all these things *now*. This will allow you to address them and work them out so they do not plague you on the shoot day when you have scores of people, lots of pressure, a tight shooting schedule, and a lot of money at stake. I promise, it will all work out.

HOW TO DO A TECH SCOUT

1. Schedule the tech scout far enough in advance so that you can have all the key department heads there—director, producer, production manager, 1st AD, DP, camera assistant/video engineer, gaffer, key grip, sound recordist/production mixer, production designer, and PA/driver. Usually you'll rent a 15-passenger van and have the PA drive from location to location. This will keep everyone together so you all arrive at each location at the same time and allow people to discuss questions with each other while in transit.

2. Check with each location owner and make sure they can accommodate the date and time you wish to scout. Tell them that you will have a small posse in tow so they don't freak out when you arrive with so many people. Non-film people are always surprised that it takes a small army to make a film and it's best to prep them so they are not overwhelmed by the crew's arrival.

3. Arrange the scout in the most time-saving way. Start south and move north or start east and move west—whatever makes sense for the city or town you are scouting. Keep in mind traffic patterns—don't schedule the scout to start in the middle of rush hour—and avoid as much of it as you can with canny scheduling.

4. Create a schedule on paper that reflects travel time and how much time you'll need at each location. If you are shooting at a suburban house in four different rooms and a backyard, it will take more time to scout than a small Manhattan apartment. Allow enough time for a full discussion in each location with the director. The crew will need to take measurements and notes so they can plan appropriately for their departments.

5. If there is a house electrician or maintenance person who will be a key interface for the location, ask the owner if that person can be available during your visit. The gaffer will need to talk to the house electrician and other crew may have questions of a technical nature for the maintenance person. Some office buildings have HVAC (Heating, Ventilation, and Air Conditioning) personnel and it would be good for the sound recordist to talk to them about any sound issues.

6. Once you arrive at the locations, meet with the owners and introduce them to the crew. Then move to the first area/room you plan to shoot in and start the tech-scout discussions.

7. The director and DP will go through the shot list for the area so everyone knows what will happen in the scene, where actors will move to, where the camera will be, and what shots are planned for the scene. The 1st AD may add info that is relevant for the crew, like the sequence of scenes that are scheduled for that day. After the director has taken everyone through the sequence, the crew will quickly and succinctly ask pertinent questions. Certain issues/problems will come up and often they can be solved on the spot. If the discussion gets too long, you may suggest that it be tabled until another time so you can keep on schedule. Continue in this way until you complete all the locations scheduled for the day.

8. If you fall behind, call the next location to inform them of your delay.

9. Schedule enough travel time between each location or you will fall behind. After 6 hours, schedule a lunch break. With a crew of about 10 people you'll need to make a reservation somewhere so you can get in and out easily. Keep in mind the crew's food preferences/allergies, choose a restaurant/diner that can accommodate them, and don't consider drive-thru or a fast-food restaurant. Everyone needs to sit down and have a proper meal to fuel themselves for the rest of the day.

10. Make sure to bring bottled water for everyone so no one gets dehydrated. You may decide to do a coffee/tea run sometime during the day, too—it keeps everyone's energy up.

- **Obtain final equipment lists and send to your vendor**

After the tech scout, the gaffer, key grip, and assistant camera/video tech will send you their final detailed equipment lists within 24 hours. Hopefully, they are not too different from the original guesstimates. Take the lists and forward them to your equipment vendors. The vendors will tweak their bids and you will negotiate the final deals for all of your equipment.

- **Confirm credit card authorization/payment paperwork with all vendors**

Check with each vendor one last time to make sure they have all the proper paperwork for your order. Nothing can destroy a tightly packed pick-up schedule the day before principal photography faster than PAs waiting at the rental house because the correct paperwork is missing.

When you do get confirmation of your order and the paperwork, make sure to get the name of the person you spoke to so you can give it to the PA when they pick it up 2 weeks later.

- **Confirm insurance certificates with all vendors**

For all the above reasons, make sure each vendor confirms that they have the proper certificate from your insurance company. Often vendors have very specific wording for how the certificate needs to read so make sure you put it down correctly or the vendor won't accept it. If you have any questions, contact your insurance broker so you can deal with the issue now so it doesn't derail your production.

- **Fill out tax resale certificates and send to vendors**

As mentioned in Chapter 3 (*Budgeting*), each state allows production companies to use resale certificates when purchasing goods or services that contribute to the production of a film/media project. Obtain your state's resale certificate form, fill it out, and send it to all the vendors so they will not charge state sales tax for your transactions.

- **Create transportation personnel lists**

Transportation of cast, crew, equipment, props, and costumes can be a surprisingly complex task. If the location and/or studio are not easily accessible by reliable and cheap public transportation, or if your crew don't have access to their own vehicles, you will be responsible for getting them to and from set every day. If you have a transportation captain, she will coordinate the schedules and vehicles for the daily production. If you don't have a dedicated crew person, then the job falls under the production staff duties. This is a critical job and needs to be taken care of properly. Transportation problems are the number one reason why schedules get delayed on shoot days. Make sure a very organized someone is on top of this job on a daily basis.

Keep in mind the individual cast and crew call times for each shoot day. One actor may need to be on set at 7:00 a.m. and another one has a call time of 12:00 p.m. You'll have to make separate arrangements for each actor. For people (cast and crew) who have the same call times, it works best to have a central place where everyone meets and then have a 7- or 15-passenger van take them to the location. Depending on the size of your cast/crew, you may need more than one van. Also remember that you will need to have a competent and experienced driver armed with accurate driving instructions to set for every shoot day. You don't want the production's driver to get lost on the way to set.

The other vehicles you need to coordinate are the vans and trucks that will be used for picking up and delivering equipment, props, set pieces, and wardrobe. Certain departments (art, camera, wardrobe, construction) may rent vehicles for exclusive use by their departments. But the production department will need at least one van for pre-shoot day pick ups and errands throughout the production. Figure out who will be driving it each day and make a schedule with all the necessary driving directions, addresses, phone numbers, and contact personnel.

Remember that there are two designations of license plates—commercial and personal. Certain trucks and large vans have commercial license plates and there are different regulations that pertain to that vehicle when on the road. In most states, 15-passenger vans, cargo vans, and trucks have commercial license plates. For parking areas that are designated "commercial" only, vehicles with commercial license plates can load and unload. Often commercial vehicles pay different tolls on roads and bridges.

When transporting people and equipment in and around the greater New York City area, there are special rules for vehicles that have commercial plates: they are *not* allowed on any road designated as a parkway and on certain other roads. In other cities and states, vehicles can be banned from using certain roads or bridges due to license designations, or height and weight limits. Make sure all production drivers know and follow these rules. Otherwise, you'll get a very expensive citation and in some cases a truck could get stuck under a low underpass—an absolute nightmare.

1 Week before principal photography
- **Buy craft service food and supplies**

Craft service refers to the food and beverages provided to the hardworking crew and extras throughout each shoot day. The origin comes from the phrase to provide "service for the crafts." Usually, it is laid out on a table and it can be anything from a minimal setup (coffee, tea, water, fruit, and bagels) to an elaborate and expensive smorgasbord (handmade gourmet treats and made-to-order cappuccinos). Your budget will probably be more along the lines of the former but it's still important to have craft service and keep it stocked during every day of shooting. Cast/crew work very hard and need to have snacks and beverages available throughout the day for energy and hydration.

When affordable, hire a professional craft service person to buy, prepare, and serve craft service. On tighter-budget films, you may assign a PA to purchase the food and supplies and to set them up as a self-service table.

GREEN PRACTICES IN FILM PRODUCTION
Following green and eco-friendly practices when producing a film is good for the environment and can save money. The Producers Guild of America (PGA) provides helpful and important information at *www.pgagreen.org*.

Green practices impact craft service in several ways. Providing water to everyone throughout the day is an important job for the production team as dehydration is a serious issue. To save money and keep plastic bottles out of the landfill, ask cast/crew to bring refillable water bottles and hot beverage containers and/or provide them with these at the beginning of the shoot. Then provide large containers of chilled water on the craft service table and people can fill up their bottles throughout the day. If cast/crew use refillable hot beverage containers for coffee and tea, you can reduce the number of paper coffee cups you need to purchase as well.

ESSENTIAL CRAFT SERVICE SUPPLIES LIST

Coffee
Tea
Water
Juice
Soda
Breakfast snacks, e.g., bagels, muffins, croissants
Butter
Cream cheese
Jam
Milk/Half and Half
Sugar
Fruit
Trail mix/energy bars
Cheese and crackers
Hummus and pita bread slices
Chips and salsa
Small vegetables and dip
Small chocolate candies (never put out on the craft service table until *after* lunch)
Cookies
Nuts and raisin mix
Gum
Paper plates
Paper cups
Paper towels
Napkins
Utensils
Electric coffee maker
Electric hot water kettle
Portable beverage cooler
Small fire extinguisher
First Aid kit
Aspirin, Ibuprofen
Sunscreen
Hand sanitizer

Shopping for craft service is best done at a discount warehouse store; you can buy in bulk to save money and reduce packaging. In many cities you can order online and have the supplies delivered for a nominal charge.

- **Finalize production book**

Now it's time to finalize the production book with the overall schedule, the names and contact info for all cast and crew, the vendor information list, and location contact information. You can email this to all the cast and crew or post it online securely so it can only be accessed by cast and crew.

- **Buy production supplies/expendables**

Unlike office supplies, production supplies and expendables are the materials you'll need for the production phase of the project. It will include office supplies but also much more. You should check with department heads to find out if they need anything that should be ordered/acquired by the production department.

Grip and Lighting department expendables	*Production design/art/props*
Various rolls of adhesive tape (gaffer's, camera, double stick, paper tape, etc.) in different colors and sizes	Tarps to protect floors
	Paper tape
	Bubble wrap to protect props
Gels and Diffusions (for use on lights and windows)	*Sound*
	Batteries
Show cards/Foam core	*AD*
Dust-Off/canned air	Pads of paper
Clothespins	Portable printer
Rope	Printer paper
Twine	Toner/ink
Monofilament (fishing line)	*Production*
Fabrics	Portable file boxes
Rubber matting	File folders
Camera department expendables	Pens
Various adhesive tapes	Pencils
Dust off/canned air	Office supplies
Empty film cans and bags (if shooting film)	Stapler + staples
	Sharpies
Eyepiece covers	Petty cash receipt book
Camera reports (digital or paper)	Rubber bands
Script Supervisor	Paper clips
Digital camera for continuity photos	Stationery
Any Report paperwork	Envelopes
Wardrobe/Costume	Reams of printing paper
Digital still camera	Reams of colored printing paper
Hangers	Portable printer
Steam iron	Toner/ink
Wardrobe racks	Locks for securing the back door of any rental trucks

- **Copy final scripts**

It's time to make multiple copies of the script for all department heads, actors, etc. If changes are made after this time they should be printed on colored paper and given out to all department heads and actors each day they occur. One color will be used for each revision so that everyone can keep track of the changes and add them to their scripts. This is done digitally as well for those who use an electronic device to read scripts and other materials.

- **Send out final vendor lists/create pick-up day instructions**

This is the time to amend any last-minute changes to your vendor equipment lists. The department head should confirm the final list. Then you can lock it and make/send copies to the PAs for their pick-up day runs. This will reduce confusion at the rental house as well.

Create one document that contains all necessary information—vendor addresses, phone numbers, contact names, driving directions, and a list of what needs to be done or picked up at each location. Include any paperwork (e.g., credit card authorizations, etc.) that need to be given to the vendors. Then hand/send a copy to each of the PAs doing the pick-ups in the rental van/truck. If there is an exterior locking mechanism on the back of the trucks, make sure to give the PAs locks with keys so they can lock them up between pick-ups.

- **Have final pre-production meeting with key department heads**

This is a very important meeting to schedule the week before principal photography begins. With the director, production team, and all key department heads present, the assistant director will run through the overall shooting plan for the film. For a feature film the focus will be on the first few days of the shooting schedule, but if there are any potential conflicts with the extended shooting schedule they can be addressed as well.

Go through the first day's schedule in detail. Transportation, how to get to the location, set-up times, etc. Department heads will bring up any specific questions, concerns, or problems. Crew across all departments can discuss, problem solve, and come up with final solutions. This is the last time to sit down and discuss together in detail before the hectic pace of the shoot starts.

- **Create accurate driving directions for all locations and stages**

Accurate driving directions for all locations and stages are essential. *I can't stress this enough!* Many a shooting schedule has been destroyed because production vehicles got lost on the way to location and the whole shoot was negatively impacted. The location manager should create the driving directions. If you do not have a location manager, then have a trusted member of the AD department or production team drive to each location and write down detailed directions with the correct mileage, etc. Online directions can be a good starting place but you *must* have someone drive and amend them to make sure they are correct.

Remember that some roadways and bridges may have restrictions on what kind of vehicles can legally be driven there. In that case, you'll have two sets of driving directions—one for cars and small vans and one for commercial vehicles. In certain locations, there may be limits to how big or heavy a truck can be. There have been times where I've had to cross a bridge and our grip truck is too big or heavy. In that case, you'll need to find a different route to get the truck to that location or you'll rent multiple smaller/lighter vehicles to get the equipment to the location. The alternate directions may take longer for the journey, so do the research and give those vehicles an earlier departure time for the location.

In some cities, public transportation may be the best way for the cast and crew to travel to the shooting location. This can save you a lot of time and money but if there is a problem with the subway or metro on the morning of your shoot, your production could be delayed by late arrivals. In those situations, I often have the key cast and crew driven to set and the other production personnel take public transportation.

- **Pre-visualize/create "who's-doing-what" lists**

There are so many details that need to be attended to for a successful production. It's important to make sure you don't forget any of them or it can have a perilous impact on the film. To avoid this predicament, I sit down with the production manager periodically throughout pre-production (at least one week before our first day of principal photography) and pre-visualize the entire first few days of production to make sure we have not forgotten anything.

I "see" every step in the process for the final pre-production day and the first day of shooting—the PAs arriving at the van rental place and picking up the vehicles and driving to the location, the production and craft service people arriving and setting up, the DP and other departments arriving and beginning to work, the hair/makeup crew moving into their trailers or rooms and setting up their departments. Next, the cast with the first call times arriving, then checking in with the AD and the director and then heading to the hair/makeup and wardrobe rooms to get ready, etc.

By meticulously visualizing each step, the production manager and I can pick up on things we may have forgotten and have the time to take care of them. For instance, we may discover we don't have enough PAs for the first shoot day. Or the hair/makeup crew doesn't have a designated room at the first location. Or we forgot to schedule a car to pick up the actors for the early call time. Pre-visualization is incredibly helpful and a great way to catch potentially catastrophic mistakes. We have a week to rectify and make adjustments.

Pre-visualization also allows you to "see" the whole day in your mind and you will feel as if you have already "lived" it. On the actual shoot day, you are able to stay present because you have already "seen" how the day is supposed to happen and now you can concentrate on what is happening in the moment. This may sound "new-agey" but I've been doing it for years and find it to be a very helpful tool.

This is also the time to work out "who is doing what" lists. Assign tasks to the production team personnel and check in with the AD to make sure every little detail and task has been taken care of.

Final Days Countdown
- **Lock pickup lists**

The day before the start of principal photography is the pickup day of all equipment, props, etc. You'll need two production assistants for each vehicle you rent—one person to sit in the van while the other PA does the pickups at the rental house. Someone is *always* in the vehicle, so the equipment, props, etc. can't be stolen, and in case the vehicle needs to be moved while the other PA is picking up.

At this point I want to mention a disturbing scam that has happened in New York City in the past. This happened to a student of mine who, with some quick thinking and fast running, was able to foil the robbers. Here's how it worked: The robbers loitered outside of known equipment rental houses and waited while the PA returning equipment brought in the first load. While the other PA was up front in the driver's seat, they opened the back door of the van and took the camera cases before the other PA had returned. You can never be too careful, so always have one PA guard the equipment and make sure the van doors are locked between trips. Review this protocol with all of your production assistants before they go out on their runs and give them a lock if the van/truck has a slot in the back.

For the pickup list, create a realistic schedule based on the start time and end time for the work day. That way you can time out how long it will take to get from one place to another and to load in the equipment/

props. This list should have the name of the businesses, the addresses (with cross streets), phone numbers, and the contact names. Include a comprehensive list of everything that needs to be picked up at each location. This allows the PAs to check off each item on the list before leaving the rental house. If they have any questions (is it OK to replace one kind of tripod with another because it is not available on pickup day?) they should call you to double check. Make sure you have taken care of payment (cash, credit card, on account) ahead of time so there are no delays.

Organize everything in the most efficient and streamlined way. Start from where the PAs will pick up the van/truck/car. Remember to check ahead of time that they have their driver's licenses and are old enough to drive the rental vehicles (some rental companies require the driver to be at least 25 years old to rent/drive a vehicle). Also find out if you need to register each person who will be driving the vehicle or if the company allows any employee on the shoot to use the vehicle and receive insurance coverage.

Schedule the pickups so the runs closest to the vehicle rental place are done first, then fanning outward from there. Usually the equipment houses don't allow pickups until later in the afternoon (remember to check their rules), so often it's best to purchase/pick up food, craft service, expendables, film stock, props, and other supplies earlier in the day.

When picking up equipment make sure you have determined that the van/truck will have enough time and space to get it all done. If not, you'll need to alter your plan and maybe rent an additional vehicle and hire two more PAs to get it all done in one day. The pickup day is critical—it's the day you put together all the means of production that you need for the next day... the first day of principal photography.

- **Crew perform check outs on rental equipment**

When renting any camera equipment, you'll need to hire the assistant cameraperson to do a check out at the rental facility. During the **check out**, the AC will go through *every* piece of equipment—camera body, lenses, follow focus, matte box, filters, tripod, etc.—and make sure it is all working properly. If not, the AC will alert the rental company so it can replace the equipment with a properly working one. This process usually takes a full day and you'll need to budget for the AC salary and contact the rental house ahead of time so you can reserve space there for the check out.

- **Finalize call sheet and directions for 1st day of shooting and send/confirm with all cast and crew**

The AD will create a call sheet for the production. A **call sheet** is one sheet that lists the name, phone number, and email address for each cast and crew member and it designates each person's individual call time for that shoot day. The AD or a member of the production staff will need to call and/or email each cast/crew member with the call time and directions for the first shoot day. This needs to be done no later than 24 hours before the call time the next day. It should be clear in the email that everyone needs to email back or call/text a specific phone number to confirm. For those cast/crew members who have not confirmed by early afternoon, the AD/production person will call/text them to get a confirmation. Keeping a running tally, the AD must confirm each person by the end of the day. If someone is missing from the list, they need to alert the producer because it means that person may not show up the next day and the producer will need to decide how to handle it.

For future shoot days, the call time/directions information will be given out at the end of the shoot day via the new call sheet, so you only need to do this on the day before principal photography or for any cast/crew members who are coming in to work for the first time after principal photography has begun. For cast members, the call times/directions are usually sent to and confirmed by their agents. If actors don't have agents/managers, then they are contacted directly. I also recommend that you call the cast personally on the day before the first shoot day just to be assured that they received the correct information from their agents.

On the following pages are the *Sundae* call sheets.

RECAP

1. **Remember the Production Triangle—Fast, Good, and Cheap— you only get two out of three.**

2. **Make sure to get the funding into a bank account based on the cash-flow schedule so you can stay on schedule for pre-production.**

3. **Follow the detailed pre-production timeline for the months leading up to the start of principal photography.**

PREPRODUCTION

	Sundae			1/22/20XX	Day 1 of 2

Producer	Kristin	(xxx) xxx-xxxx
Producer	Birgit	(xxx) xxx-xxxx
Director	Sonya	(xxx) xxx-xxxx
1st AD	Connor	(xxx) xxx-xxxx
UPM	Giovanni	

SUNDAE

DAY 1

BREAKFAST	6:30 AM	
LUNCH	1:00 PM	
SUNRISE		SUNSET
6:15 AM		7:50 PM
WEATHER	30° AM 40° NOON	32° PM
Humidity	20%	Partly Cloudy

Production Office	(xxx) xxx-xxxx
Address Line 1	
Address Line 2	

CALL 7:00am

Nearest Hospital	(xxx) xxx-xxxx
SUNY Downstate Medical Center	
811 New York Avenue, Brooklyn, NY 11203	

Filming interior/exterior ALL DAY. Wear warm clothes and boots.
First Aid Kit and Fire Extinguisher at craft service table.

PRODUCTION CEL PHONE- BIRGIT - # XXX-XXX-XXXX
NO SOCIAL MEDIACLOSED SET**

SCENE #s	SET AND DESCRIPTION	CHARACTER #	D/N	PAGES	LOCATION/NOTES
1	Suburban Car	1, 2	D		3 Extras, Picture Vehicle
	Mary drives Tim around a neighborhood asking for directions.				
2	Car Curbside at Yellow House	1, 2	D		Picture Vehicle
	Car pulls to the curb and Mary takes off glasses.				
4	Car Curbside at Yellow House	2	D		Picture Vehicle
	Tim plays distractedly with car lock button.				
6	Car Curbside at Yellow House	1, 2	D		Picture Vehicle
	Tim watches Mary get into car and sit in front seat. Mary laughs and puts glasses back on.				
3	Yellow House/Lawn	1, 2, 3	D		Stunt Coordinator, Picture Vehicle
	Mary rings bell and fights with Woman at door.				
5	Yellow House/Lawn	1, 3	D		Cement Block, Picture Vehicle
	Woman stumbles into house. Mary gets cement block from car, marches back & throws at house.				
7	Neighborhood Street	1, 2	D		Picture Vehicle
	Car zooms off.				
			TOTAL PAGES	0	

#	CAST	CHARACTER	SWHF	MU	SET	MINOR?	SPECIAL INSTRUCTIONS
1	xxx	Mary	SW	7.30am	8.30am	Y	
2	xxx	Tim	SW	7.30am	8.30am	N	
3	xxx	Woman	SWF	8.00am	9.00am	N	

EXTRAS		PRODUCTION NOTES	
EXTRAS	REPORT AT:	PROPS:	Garbage can, Eyeglasses, Doorbell, Ignition Key
2 Young Kids	8.00 AM	SFX:	Cement block
Middle-aged Man	8.00AM	LOCATION:	Exterior
		PICTURE VEHICLE:	Suburban Car
		STUNTS:	Fight and Cement Block throw
		ADDL LABOR:	
		WARD:	
		MAKEUP:	
	UNION	CAMERA:	
	NON-UNION x	NOTES:	

ADVANCE SHOOTING SCHEDULE					
SCENE #s	SET AND DESCRIPTION	CHARACTER #	D/N	PAGES	LOCATION/NOTES
8	Ice Cream Parlor Counter	4	D		Ice Cream Sundae
	Teenage Employee builds huge sundae.				
11	Street Corner	5, 6	D		Picture Vehicle
	Man and Blonde Woman walk hand-in-hand, get into Town Car and drive away.				
9	Ice Cream Parlor Table	1, 2	D		Ice Cream Sundae
	Mary fixes hair, relaxes and smiles at Tim.				
10	Ice Cream Parlor Table	1, 2	D		Ice Cream Sundae
	Tim eats sundae rapidly while Mary sees something out the parlor window on the street.				
12	Ice Cream Parlor Counter	1, 2	D		Ice Cream Sundae
	Mary is frozen whil Tim eats sundae.				
13	Ice Cream Parlor Counter	1, 2	D		Ice Cream Sundae
	Mary asks Tim about Yellow House and he swallows a big gulp.				
			TOTAL PAGES		

Production Company   Production Title   [Shoot Date]

#	POSITION	NAME	PHONE	IN	#	POSITION	NAME	PHONE	IN	#	POSITION	NAME	PHONE	IN
	PRODUCTION					**PROPERTY DEPT.**					**TRANSPORTATION**			
	Director	Sonya		6:30		Propmaster					Transportation Coord.			
	Producer	Kristin		6:30		Asst. Propmaster					Transportation Captain			
	Producer	Birgit		6:30		On Set Props					Driver			
	UPM	Giovanni		6:30		On Set Props					Driver			
						On Set Props					Camera			
	1st AD	Connor		6:45							Grip/Lighting			
	2nd AD					**PRODUCTION DESIGN**					Prod. Design			
						Production Designer	Michael		7:00		Set Decoration			
	DGA Trainee/Key PA					Art Director					Wardrobe			
	Set PA	Temisanren		6:30		Set Designer					Hair/MU			
	Set PA					Ass't Art Director					Trailer			
						Art Dept. Coordinator					Trailer			
	Script Supervisor	Bettina		7:00		Art Dept. PA					Prod. Office Trailer			
						Art Dept. PA					RV			
	CAMERA DEPT.					Set Decorator					Production			
	Dir. Of Photography	Andrew		7:00		Leadman					Catering/Craft Service			
	Camera Operator					Buyer								
	1st AC	Chris		7:00		On Set Dresser					**STUNTS**			
	2nd AC/Loader	Blaine		7:00		On Set Dresser					Stunt Coordinator	Sally		9:00
	B Camera					Swing Gang					Stunt person			
	B Camera 1st AC					Swing Gang					Stunt person			
	B Cam. 2nd AC/Loader					**CONSTRUCTION**					**ADDITIONAL LABOR/CREW**			
	Steadicam					Construction Head					Studio Teacher			
						Construction Coord.					Studio Teacher			
	DIT	Bob				Constr. Foreperson					Medic @ Location			
	DIT Utility					Carpenter					Fire Captain			
	Still Photographer					Carpenter					Police			
						Carpenter								
	GRIP/RIGGING					Prop maker					**CASTING**			
	Key Grip	Miguel		7:00							Casting Director			
	Best Boy Grip	Zach		7:00		Greensperson					Casting Ass't			
	3rd Grip					Scenic					Extras Casting			
	4th Grip					Scenic					Extras Casting Ass't			
	Dolly Grip					Construction PA								
	Addl Grip										**ACCOUNTING**			
	Addl Grip					**MAKE-UP/HAIR**					Prod. Accountant			
	Addl Grip					Makeup Dept. Head					Accounting Ass't			
						Key Makeup Artist					Payroll			
	Key Rigging Grip					Add'l Makeup Artist					Accounting Clerk			
	Rigging Grip					Makeup Ass't								
	Rigging Grip					SFX Makeup					**POST PROD.**			
											Post Prod. Supervisor			
						Hair Dept. Head					Post Prod. Coordinator			
	LIGHTING					Key Hairstylist								
	Gaffer	Gordon		7:00		Add'l Hairstylist					Editor			
	Best Boy Electric					Hair Ass't					Asst. Editor			
	3rd Electric					Wig person					Add'l Editor			
	4th Electric										Add'l Asst. Editor			
	Addl Electric					**COSTUMES**					Post Prod. PA			
	Addl Electric					Costume Designer								
	Addl Electric					Key Costumer					Music Supervisor			
	Swing					Add'l Costumer								
						Costume Ass't					**EXECUTIVES/CREATIVES**			
	SOUND DEPT.					Costume Ass't					Executive Producer			
	Sound Mixer	Michael		7:00		Set Costumer					Executive Producer			
	Boom Operator					Costume Ass't					Co-Executive Producer			
	Sound Utility										Co-Executive Producer			
						PRODUCTION OFFICE					Production Executive			
	PLAYBACK					Production Coordinator					Writer			
	Video Playback					Asst. Prod. Coord.					Story Consultant			
						Office PA								
	LOCATIONS					Office PA								
	Locations Manager					Office PA								
	Key Asst Loc Manager					Script Coordinator								
	Key Asst Loc Manager					Director's Ass't								
	VISUAL FX					Producer's Ass't								
	VFX Supervisor													
	On Set VFX					**CATERING/CRAFT SERVICES**								
	SPECIAL FX					Caterer	Brendon							
	SPFX					Craft Service								
						Addl Craft Service								

STUDIO ANONYMOUS SAFETY HOTLINE
STUDIO PRODUCTION SAFETY INFORMATION CAN BE VIEWED ON-LINE AT WEBSITE:
SAFETY MEETING AT CALL EVERYDAY ON NEW LOCATIONFOOD SAFETY HOTLINE
STUDIO INJURY & ILLNESS PREVENTION PROGRAM BOOKLET CAN BE FOUND IN THE
***PLEASE REPORT ANY NAME CHANGES / ADDITIONS / DELETIONS TO:
GREEN SET INFO AT:
WALKIE CHANNELS: #1 PRODUCTION, WARDROBE, PROPS, #2 OPEN, #3 TRANSPO, #4 OPEN, #5 GRIPS, #6 CAMERA, #7 SET LIGHTING

PREPRODUCTION

Sundae 1/23/20XX Day 2 of 2

Producer	Kristin	(xxx) xxx-xxxx
Producer	Birgit	(xxx) xxx-xxxx
Director	Sonya	(xxx) xxx-xxxx
1st AD	Connor	(xxx) xxx-xxxx
UPM	Giovanni	

SUNDAE
DAY 2

BREAKFAST	6:30 AM
LUNCH	1:00 PM
SUNRISE / SUNSET	6:15 AM / 7:50 PM
WEATHER	30° AM 40° NOON 32° PM
Humidity	20% Partly Cloudy

Production Office (xxx) xxx-xxxx
Address Line 1
Address Line 2

Nearest Hospital (xxx) xxx-xxxx
SUNY Downstate Medical Center
811 New York Avenue, Brooklyn, NY 11203

CALL 7:00am

Filming interior/exterior ALL DAY. Wear warm clothes and boots.
First Aid Kit and Fire Extinguisher at craft service table.

PRODUCTION CEL PHONE- BIRGIT - # XXX-XXX-XXXX
NO SOCIAL MEDIACLOSED SET**

SCENE #s	SET AND DESCRIPTION	CHARACTER #	D/N	PAGES	LOCATION/NOTES
8	Ice Cream Parlor Counter Teenage Employee builds huge sundae.	4	D		Ice Cream Sundae
11	Street Corner Man and Blonde Woman walk hand-in-hand, get into Town Car and drive away.	5, 6	D		Picture Vehicle
9	Ice Cream Parlor Table Mary fixes hair, relaxes and smiles at Tim.	1, 2	D		Ice Cream Sundae
10	Ice Cream Parlor Table Tim eats sundae rapidly while Mary sees something out the parlor window on the street.	1, 2	D		Ice Cream Sundae
12	Ice Cream Parlor Counter Mary is frozen whil Tim eats sundae.	1, 2	D		Ice Cream Sundae
13	Ice Cream Parlor Counter Mary asks Tim about Yellow House and he swallows a big gulp.	1, 2	D		Ice Cream Sundae
			TOTAL PAGES	0	

#	CAST	CHARACTER	SWHF	MU	SET	MINOR?	SPECIAL INSTRUCTIONS
1	xxx	Mary	WF	7.30am	8.30am	Y	
2	xxx	Tim	WF	7.30am	8.30am	N	
4	xxx	Teenage Employee	SWF	7:30am	8:30am	Y	
5	xxx	Blonde Woman	SWF	9:00am	10:00am	N	cold weather exterior
6	xxx	Man	SWF	9:00am	10:00am	N	cold weather exterior

EXTRAS		PRODUCTION NOTES	
EXTRAS	REPORT AT:	PROPS:	Ice cream sundae, Hot fudge, Sprinkles, Cherry, Whipped Cream
Town Car driver	9:30 AM		sundae dish, small compact, wet napkin, big spoon
5 people walking down street	9:30 AM	SFX:	
		LOCATION:	Interior and Exterior. Cold Weather precautions
		PICTURE VEHICLE:	Town Car
		STUNTS:	
		ADDL LABOR:	
		WARD:	
	UNION	MAKEUP:	
	NON-UNION x	NOTES:	Set up exterior heater for crew when outside

ADVANCE SHOOTING SCHEDULE

SCENE #s	SET AND DESCRIPTION	CHARACTER #	D/N	PAGES	LOCATION/NOTES
	SET 1 Description 1				
	SET 2 Description 2				
	SET 3 Description 3				
	SET 4 Description 4				
	SET 5 Description 5				
	SET 6 Description 6				
	SET 8 Description 8				
			TOTAL PAGES		

Production Company | Production Title | [Shoot Date]

#	POSITION	NAME	PHONE	IN	#	POSITION	NAME	PHONE	IN	#	POSITION	NAME	PHONE	IN
	PRODUCTION					**PROPERTY DEPT.**					**TRANSPORTATION**			
	Director	Sonya		6:30		Propmaster					Transportation Coord.			
	Producer	Kristin		6:30		Asst. Propmaster					Transportation Captain			
	Producer	Birgit		6:30		On Set Props					Driver			
	UPM	Giovanni		6:30		On Set Props					Driver			
						On Set Props								
	1st AD	Connor		6:45							Camera			
	2nd AD					**PRODUCTION DESIGN**					Grip/Lighting			
						Production Designer	Michael		7:00		Prod. Design			
	DGA Trainee/Key PA					Art Director					Set Decoration			
	Set PA	Temisanren		6:30		Set Designer					Wardrobe			
	Set PA					Ass't Art Director					Hair/MU			
						Art Dept. Coordinator					Trailer			
	Script Supervisor	Bettina		7:00		Art Dept. PA					Trailer			
						Art Dept. PA					Prod. Office Trailer			
	CAMERA DEPT.										RV			
	Dir. Of Photography	Andrew		7:00		Set Decorator					Production			
	Camera Operator					Leadman					Catering/Craft Service			
	1st AC	Chris		7:00		Buyer								
	2nd AC/Loader	Blaine		7:00		On Set Dresser					**STUNTS**			
						On Set Dresser					Stunt Coordinator			
	B Camera					Swing Gang					Stunt person			
	B Camera 1st AC					Swing Gang					Stunt person			
	B Cam. 2nd AC/Loader													
						CONSTRUCTION					**ADDITIONAL LABOR/CREW**			
	Steadicam					Construction Head					Studio Teacher			
						Construction Coord.					Studio Teacher			
	DIT	Bob				Constr. Foreperson					Medic @ Location			
	DIT Utility					Carpenter					Fire Captain			
	Still Photographer					Carpenter					Police			
						Carpenter								
	GRIP/RIGGING					Prop maker					**CASTING**			
	Key Grip	Miguel		7:00							Casting Director			
	Best Boy Grip	Zach		7:00		Greensperson					Casting Ass't			
	3rd Grip					Scenic					Extras Casting			
	4th Grip					Scenic					Extras Casting Ass't			
	Dolly Grip					Construction PA								
	Addl Grip										**ACCOUNTING**			
	Addl Grip					**MAKE-UP/HAIR**					Prod. Accountant			
	Addl Grip					Makeup Dept. Head					Accounting Ass't			
						Key Makeup Artist					Payroll			
	Key Rigging Grip					Add'l Makeup Artist					Accounting Clerk			
	Rigging Grip					Makeup Ass't								
	Rigging Grip					SFX Makeup					**POST PROD.**			
											Post Prod. Supervisor			
						Hair Dept. Head					Post Prod. Coordinator			
	LIGHTING					Key Hairstylist								
	Gaffer	Gordon		7:00		Add'l Hairstylist					Editor			
	Best Boy Electric					Hair Ass't					Asst. Editor			
	3rd Electric					Wig person					Add'l Editor			
	4th Electric										Add'l Asst. Editor			
	Addl Electric					**COSTUMES**					Post Prod. PA			
	Addl Electric					Costume Designer								
	Addl Electric					Key Costumer					Music Supervisor			
	Swing					Add'l Costumer								
						Costume Ass't					**EXECUTIVES/CREATIVES**			
	SOUND DEPT.					Costume Ass't					Executive Producer			
	Sound Mixer	Michael		7:00		Set Costumer					Executive Producer			
	Boom Operator					Costume Ass't					Co-Executive Producer			
	Sound Utility										Co-Executive Producer			
						PRODUCTION OFFICE					Production Executive			
	PLAYBACK					Production Coordinator					Writer			
	Video Playback					Asst. Prod. Coord.					Story Consultant			
						Office PA								
	LOCATIONS					Office PA								
	Locations Manager					Office PA								
	Key Asst Loc Manager					Script Coordinator								
	Key Asst Loc Manager					Director's Ass't								
	VISUAL FX					Producer's Ass't								
	VFX Supervisor													
	On Set VFX					**CATERING/CRAFT SERVICES**								
	SPECIAL FX					Caterer	Brendon							
	SPFX					Craft Service								
						Addl Craft Service								

STUDIO ANONYMOUS SAFETY HOTLINE
STUDIO PRODUCTION SAFETY INFORMATION CAN BE VIEWED ON-LINE AT WEBSITE:
SAFETY MEETING AT CALL EVERYDAY ON NEW LOCATIONFOOD SAFETY HOTLINE
STUDIO INJURY & ILLNESS PREVENTION PROGRAM BOOKLET CAN BE FOUND IN THE
***PLEASE REPORT ANY NAME CHANGES / ADDITIONS / DELETIONS TO:
GREEN SET INFO AT:
WALKIE CHANNELS: #1 PRODUCTION, WARDROBE, PROPS, #2 OPEN, #3 TRANSPO, #4 OPEN, #5 GRIPS, #6 CAMERA, #7 SET LIGHTING

CHAPTER 7
LOCATIONS

FINDING THE RIGHT LOCATIONS for your film is always a big challenge. By hiring a location scout, you'll be able to access their contacts and experience to help you find the best locations for your project. If you are on a tight budget and can't hire a scout, you'll need to devise other strategies to find your locations.

Create Location Lists

Go to your script breakdown and determine how many sets you require for your film. Then discuss with the director, DP, and production designer whether the set will be built in a studio or shot on location. It is often cheaper to shoot in a location than to rent a stage and build a set. In some cases there may be flexibility—the preference may be to shoot on a stage unless the right location is found.

Discuss if other locations could be used to replicate the real thing. For instance, it is usually very difficult to procure a working hospital room for a shoot day but a hospital-like room in a nursing home or veterinarian's office may be more doable and affordable.

> *The essential thing 'in heaven and earth' is ... that there should be a long obedience in the same direction; there thereby results, and has always resulted in the long run, something which has made life worth living.*
>
> —*Friedrich Nietzsche*

Talk out these options ahead of time so the location scout has as much flexibility as possible when scouting.

Discuss what the visual and logistical priorities are for each location. Explain to the scout that you'll need certain things, e.g., a bathroom for cast and crew, running water, a place to set up tables and chairs for the crew meals, nearby parking, a freight elevator to load in equipment, etc.

The scout will request a tentative budget—the amount you can pay for each shoot day so the scout can plan accordingly. For example, if you are looking for a luxury loft space and can't afford a fully furnished, high-end condo, you might be able to dress a low-rent artist's loft further from the center of town and bring in all your own props and a coat of paint. Your strategy will start to emerge.

The Specifics of Location Scouting

Once you have the list, you and the location scout should come up with a game plan for scouting locations to maximize time and money. Consult with them on where they have filmed in the past that may work for your film. Decide which locations are the priority—some will be more important to find than others. You may decide that the office location may be the most important one because it will be used the majority of the shooting days but you can use a friend's apartment as a backup location if you don't find the "bedroom set." It's amazing how helpful it is to the creative process to get photos of actual locations so the creative teams can start to make specific plans.

The location scout will be hired based on a day rate (the rate may or may not include the use of a personal car) and will charge for travel expenses (gas, tolls, parking) as well. Agree to a timeline based on your budget—how many sites to be scouted and photographed per day and when you'll receive the location photos (usually uploaded each night or the next morning to a password-protected website).

Give all the vital information you can to the scout before she begins her work. Include info like: 1) day or night; 2) tentative shoot dates; 3) how many cast and crew; 4) the need for a place to feed crew; 5) the need for running water or electricity; 6) bathroom [or are you bringing an RV/trailer?]; 7) specific looks or shots that are required (e.g., what you see when looking out a window); 8) sync sound or MOS (no sound recording).

Location Photo Folders

The location scout will post the photos from each location in their own folder on a password-protected website that can be accessed by all members of the creative team and production staff. There should be a 360-degree picture of the room and then individual photos that show every aspect of the room. If the director/DP/production designer needs specific angles or elements, the scout will be sure to photograph those too. The producer should make certain to have access to all pertinent information:

1. The address, phone number, email address, and contact person name.

2. Time of day when photo was taken.

3. Notes describing what direction the location windows are facing—north, south, east, and west. This helps the DP to determine where the light would be at a specific time on a specific day.

4. The usual location rental fee. (You may or may not want the scout to inquire about the rental fee.)

5. Any restrictions or caveats that are important to know when considering that particular location (e.g., it's not available on Sundays, or only available weekdays from 6:00 a.m. to 2:00 p.m.).

Once you receive the first batch of photos, you can determine if the scout is on the right track. Discuss with the creative team and then give specific feedback to the scout for the next day and allow her to be more accurate when she is scouting. You'll repeat this process until all of the locations are found for your project.

Check with Local Film Commissions for Leads

Every state has a film commission and most large cities and regions have one as well. Created to support all productions in the area or state, they can give helpful leads and information about potential locations and often have a photographic locations archive that is viewable on their website. To find the local city/region, state and international film commissions go to the Association of Film Commissioners International at *www.afci.org*.

Check out the website for the city or region that is closest to where you are shooting for all pertinent information about services they provide and film permit rules (if applicable.) Then call and briefly explain your project to the appropriate person at the office. See if they have any other ideas or information that isn't on their website so you get as much free assistance as you can —your tax dollars pay for it—when looking for your locations.

I've had great experiences with many film commissions over the years. They are usually very knowledgeable and are a big help if you are shooting in an area that you are not familiar with. Once you do find your locations, they will give you the rules and regulations for the area and help coordinate the permit application process.

City parks, public housing, and other local governmental land are often free or almost free for filming purposes. The film commission will have the contact info for the various agencies and personnel so you can follow up on those possibilities. On the short film *Torte Bluma*, we had to re-create the WW II Nazi concentration camp Treblinka somewhere in New York City on a very tight budget. For several scenes, we chose to shoot in Brooklyn, NY, at the Floyd Bennett Field in the Gateway National Park. The permit was very affordable and we were able to get the looks/locations we needed.

Federal, state, and local historical societies are another affordable way to find great locations with built-in production design. Often charging a nominal rental fee, all of the furnishings are historically correct and in good condition—a real boon for a low-budget period production. As mentioned before, we shot the majority of *Wisconsin Death Trip* at Wisconsin historical sites. My favorite one was the nineteenth century steam locomotive restored by the community of Eagle, WI, who were kind enough to let us shoot on it for two different scenes.

Alternatives to Hiring a Location Scout

If your budget is too tight to hire a location scout, I suggest two other options: 1) pay a fee to a professional location scout to share his or her location archives with you, or 2) you and the director scout for yourselves. Many scouts maintain comprehensive picture files of the thousands of locations they have scouted over the years and will go through their databases and share the ones that might work for your project. Each location file will contain photos of all angles of the site, address, contact name and number, and the requested location fee. This can jump-start your scouting and save a lot of time for a relatively low fee to the scout.

If you can't afford that option, the task will fall to the producer and director to find the locations on their own. This is where resourcefulness, serendipity, negotiating experience, and good people skills come into play.

Send out an email to family/friends and use social media to let everyone know what you are looking for. Be as specific as you can about what/where/when you plan to shoot. People can forward your email to others and get the word out. I've gotten great leads this way and often people think of places that you might not have considered. Sometimes people find the prospect of having a movie shot at their home an exciting idea and will volunteer it for free.

The other thing to remember is the power of production design. An available and affordable location may not look like the right place, but with some paint, props, and clever art direction, it could work very nicely. Writer/director Paul Cotter (*Bomber, Shameless*) likes to be flexible when scouting for low-budget productions. He'll re-write a scene to fit a location as long as "the essential dramatic thrust of the scene remains the same, just in a different place with its own sense of character."

Finalizing Location Decisions

Once you have several good location possibilities and you have narrowed down your choices, you need to make some decisions. You'll want to go visit your first and second choices with the director (and director of photography if possible) to see if those choices are appropriate for the project. Plan to look at no less than two places for each location in your film; that way you'll have a possible back-up option.

When you visit the property you need to consider many things at once. Here's a checklist:

— Is there any new or ongoing construction in the area that could impact your shoot?
— Any limitations (days or times) on when it is available?
— Is this the right "look" for the film?
— Is it big enough for your shooting purposes?
— Does it have all the props/set dressing you need or will you have to buy/rent more or different ones?
— Are there bathroom facilities for cast/crew use?
— Is there a holding area for talent? A place for hair/makeup and wardrobe to set up and work?

- Where will cast and crew be able to sit and eat for lunch? Do you need to bring in tables and chairs? Or procure a separate nearby location for the catered meal?
- Where can you park the trucks and/or vans for the production? Is it safe or will you need a security person to watch the vehicles all day/night long?
- Is there room to stage equipment when it's not in use?
- Is there an internet connection for the production staff's laptop computers? Do you get good cell phone service?
- Are there any sound issues with the location—noisy radiators or ventilation systems that can't be turned off or quieted or an active construction site across the street?
- Is the location affordable for your budget?
- If it is a "period" production, does the location have any attributes that will be problematic for the historical period you are shooting for?

Once you have all the answers for each location, you can make your decision. A location may look perfect and be affordable, but if there are no bathroom facilities, you may have to rent an RV or trailer and that will add to the overall cost. The location you want may not be available for the shoot dates you had in mind; can you change the schedule so you can shoot there when it is rentable? What if you and the director love a location but the rental rate is beyond your budget? Negotiation is the next step in the process.

Negotiating the Deal

Everything is open to negotiation. If both parties in a negotiation want something to happen and can get enough of what they want, then it can happen. If you are asking for a reduction (sometimes a significant reduction) in a rental price then you need to come up with other ways to compensate for the requested discount. Here are a few possibilities to consider:

1. Name or company name in the screen credits of the film.
2. A DVD/digital link of the finished project.
3. The owner's son wants to be in a film. Do you have a role for an extra?
4. The owner's daughter wants to get into film school. Can she work on your film as a PA to get some experience?

5. Advertising for their company. One of my students bartered with a restaurant that was near campus. In exchange for shooting at the location for free, he put up flyers around campus one afternoon to advertise the restaurant to students.

6. Offer to pay for the location's employee to stay with you overnight during the shoot to make sure everything runs smoothly. This works really well because the employee knows where everything is and can be helpful while shooting at the location

7. If the location serves food, promise to purchase the cast/crew lunches for each shoot day—that will add to their bottom line.

8. Offer to shoot some digital footage of the location for promo purposes to use on their website and social media.

9. Offer to shoot the owner's niece's wedding video the following summer in exchange for a free location now.

10. Get creative—there are many ways to provide compensation other than money.

Back-up Locations

Having back-up locations for all of your top choices is essential. I always negotiate a good deal with the back-up location first. Once that is in place I then negotiate with the first choice to get the best deal possible. Having the alternate location in your "back pocket" gives you confidence and leverage when trying to make a deal with your number one choice. Once you have a deal for your first choice, let the back-up location know that you are going with a different location but really loved their location and will keep it in mind for other projects. Make sure you are professional and considerate, because sometimes your preferred location pulls out while in final pre-production and you'll need to return to the back-up and shoot there. This happens more often than one would like, so always be prepared.

Paperwork

Once you have negotiated the terms you'll need to agree on a payment schedule. Then both parties will sign a location release form and possible contract. The owner will require an insurance certificate for the shoot dates as well.

Location Release Form

A location release form should state the shoot dates (and alternate/back-up dates), address, rental rate per hour, number of hours (e.g., $1,000 for a 12-hour day, then $150/hour after 12 hours). The form will include other information, like whether you have to hire someone to oversee the production, liability issues, a hold-harmless clause (see Chapter 9, *Legal*), who has responsibility for what, a payment schedule, security deposit amount and when/how it will be returned, access to certain areas at the location including a freight elevator and parking, and when the key department heads can have access to the location prior to the shoot dates for a tech scout and other prep. Once negotiated, both parties need to sign and keep a copy for their records. It's important to sign the deal as soon as possible so you know you are locked far enough in advance of shooting.

If the owner hesitates to sign the contract in a timely manner, it may be a warning sign and you may need to go with your back-up location. The more lead time you have, the better you will be able to switch to another location if necessary.

Notice that I keep referring to the *owner* of the location. You must get the owner's signature (not a manager or relative or employee) because that is the only person who has the legally binding authority to sign the location agreement.

General Liability Insurance Certificate

Insurance is a critical part of covering your liability for all of the production's locations. (See Chapter 10, *Insurance*.) **Liability** is another word for things that you and the production are responsible for, legally. Each location's owner will require a general liability insurance certificate before they will let you onto their premises. Often the owners will have specific language as to how they want the certificate to read. This is often the case when you shoot in a city, state, or federal property, requiring a certificate written out to the public authority itself.

Every production insurance policy specifies a certain dollar amount for the limits (usually between $1–2 million). If the owner requires a higher limit, you will need to either buy an additional amount of insurance (a rider) or you will have to find another location that will accept your insurance coverage.

Co-ops and Condos

While we are talking about property ownership we should also cover the issue of co-ops and condos and their boards. In many U.S. cities, apartment owners live in buildings that are run as co-ops or condominiums. For these types of properties, there are **co-op and condo boards or homeowner associations** that run the management of the buildings and uphold the buildings' rules and regulations.

In these cases, the co-op or condo owner is not the only entity you need to get permission from to enter and film on the premises. You'll need to contact the boards/associations to get approval as well. Usually co-op/condo boards meet once a month, so you should contact them *at least six to eight weeks* before you plan to shoot so you get on the agenda for the next board meeting. They may ask you to submit an application with a letter, budget, script, and production plan and require you to appear at the next meeting in person.

If you get approval, you will need to create an insurance certificate for the co-op/condo association as well as the individual homeowner. Usually there will be a list of rules you must follow and/or a fee to be paid to the co-op/condo association. If you agree to the terms, make sure to get a signed permission letter from the co-op/condo board for your files.

"Gated" communities or developments in the United States will have associations that operate in a similar way to coop/condo boards. Sometimes the homeowners don't even understand that there are rules they have to follow for a film-shoot request, so do your research to find out if the location has such a governing body.

One of my students shot a short film at her uncle's home in a development outside of Washington, D.C. She asked if there were any other approvals needed to shoot in his home and he said no. On the morning of the film shoot, as the production van and assorted cars descended upon her uncle's home, she was promptly visited by two condo association board members who tried to shut her down because she didn't get their permission! She explained that she was told that she didn't have to and it was her uncle who got in trouble. They worked it all out, but it was a stressful way to start the production.

Permits

Filming permits are often required when you shoot in U.S. cities and towns. Permits are usually required for public exteriors in many cities/

towns (e.g., sidewalks, roadways, public parks). It's also a way for municipalities to track productions that are shooting in the area and to make sure that the production crew is following the local regulations and supplying a general liability insurance certificate during the production period. As discussed earlier in this chapter, film commissions will provide you with this information. Go to the website or call the office to discuss your specific production needs and how to apply for a permit.

Some cities require a fee for a permit and others do not. Los Angeles has a rather expensive fee structure for filming permits (although qualified students pay a small nominal fee). New York has a free Optional Permit for certain kinds of low-impact filming and a flat nominal fee for a permit for larger productions.

Police/Fire/Sheriff's Departments

Depending on your production's filming requirements, you may need to involve the police, fire, or sheriff's departments of the local municipality. If you need to stop traffic, block off a street, or shoot with equipment on the outside of a vehicle, you'll need to contact the police or the sheriff for permission and coordination. Working with the local authority, they will determine if you need to pay a permit fee, hire local officers, and follow any other safety regulations. The New York Police Department's Film and TV unit is an exception, and provides police officers for free, per the determination of the Mayor's Office of Media and Entertainment.

If you need to open a hydrant to access water for a **wet down** (watering down a street) or if you are planning to use pyrotechnics, you will need permission and in most cases pay a fee to the local fire department. Give yourself several weeks to complete the application to request permission.

Tech Scout

We discussed this in depth in Chapter 6, *Pre-Production*. Please refer to that section.

Shoot-day Protocol

On the shoot day, the location manager (if you don't have one, then the 1st Assistant Director will usually perform this role) will arrive one half hour prior to anyone else's call time. She will have decided where each vehicle will be parked, where to load in, and where each department will set up at the location. Each crew/cast person needs to check in with the location manager/AD and follow their instructions. Otherwise, anarchy will reign.

Run Through with Owner

At the beginning of the shoot day or the day before, the location manager (or producer) will do a "run through" of the location with the owner. After taking digital photos/video of the entire location and close-ups of any details that show prior damage, the location manager/producer will write up a list describing any pre-existing damage to the location and both the owner and location manager/producer must sign it.

Remind each department that it is important to treat the location with utmost care. Protective boards should be put down on the floors if necessary, sound blankets wrapped around fragile furniture, and protective material affixed to walls to protect them. Grips and art department crew should be knowledgeable of what kind of tape they can use on certain surfaces and check in with the AD if there are any questions or concerns.

Remind the crew to report any problems or damage to the location as soon as it occurs so the location manager/producer is aware of it immediately. It's vital to know about damage as soon as it happens, rather than finding out about it afterwards or having the owner point it out later. If the production team learns about the damage as soon as it happens, they can come up with a solution or try to fix it immediately before the shoot is over.

Leave It Better Than You Found It

The best mantra for location shooting is "Leave it better than you found it." The location manager or production manager should inform the crew of the rules for proper garbage disposal at the location. Most locations will require you to take all of your garbage with you when you leave (or they may allow you to use their dumpster for a fee). Film production normally creates a lot of trash and you should expect to make arrangements to take it away. In most cities it is illegal to dump your garbage in public garbage cans on the street.

Green Set Protocols

In running a "green set" you'll plan to recycle as much as you can. Most communities have public rules for recycling glass, metal, plastic, and paper. There are often places in a city were you can recycle or donate set construction materials. Research ahead of time and refer to the PGA's Green Production Guide website at *http://www.greenproductionguide.com*.

Idiot Check

An **idiot check** is when you go around a location (every nook and cranny) looking for any equipment or materials that have been left behind. Forgetting equipment is a nuisance at the least and expensive at the most—requiring someone to retrieve it the next day or causing you to pay to replace it. Best to check the location thoroughly before departing so you don't leave anything behind.

At the end of the shoot day after the crew has wrapped, the owner and location manager will do the same "run through" together again. The owner will point out any new damage caused by the filming. If there is any damage, it will be noted on the sheet. Photos/video should be taken to document it. (Depending on the circumstances, these could also be used for an insurance claim.) If it is slight damage, the owner may request immediate repairs or a small payment from the production company as compensation. If so, this deal can be written onto the location sheet and signed by the owner and producer to finalize the agreement.

If the damage is extensive, then an insurance claim will be necessary. The producer should make a claim the next day and begin the paperwork process with the insurance company (see Chapter 10, *Insurance*). To begin the process, photos and descriptions will be needed and an explanation provided to the insurance agent. Remember that each insurance policy has a deductible, so confirm that the estimate for the claim is larger than the deductible limit before contacting the insurance company.

The Day After the Location Shoot

Always remember to call and thank the owners the next day. Make sure they are satisfied with how everything turned out and follow up on any outstanding issues. You want to leave a good impression and do the right thing. By leaving on good terms you'll be able to go back there and film again. And it's not just your reputation but also the film industry's reputation that is at stake. There have been many times in the past when I approached a potentially great location and they refused to let us shoot there because they had a bad experience with another film production a few months before. It's horrible to have a good location ruined by inept and unprofessional productions. Be courteous and responsible when you shoot.

Tax Incentive Programs

As mentioned in Chapter 4 (*Funding*), many states and cities in the United States have tax incentive programs to entice film productions to film in their area. Film production can bring in a lot of money and jobs, so many states have created rebates ranging from 5%–25%. Some states give cash back at the end of the production and other states give a tax rebate to the production company over a period of years. Some require you to shoot a certain portion of the budget in the state and others have less rigid regulations. Most have a minimum "spend" so very low-budget productions may not be eligible. Go to *www.ProducerToProducer.com* to learn about the various film tax incentive programs in the areas you are interested in for your production.

RECAP

1. **Create your list of required locations and hire a location scout familiar with the area. If you can't hire a scout, the scouting will be done by the production staff.**

2. **The location scout will post digital photos online so the producer, director, and other key department heads can look at them and give back notes to the producer.**

3. **Check with local film commissions for information about possible locations and permits.**

4. **Finalize your location choices. Secure a deal for your back-up location first and then negotiate for your first-choice location.**

5. **Get a signed location release form and obtain an insurance certificate for your general liability coverage for the locations.**

6. **Have the location manager (production manager or assistant director if you don't have a location manager) coordinate the cast/crew/equipment on the shoot day for all logistics.**

7. **Contact the local police and fire departments if you have any production issues that fall under their jurisdictions.**

8. **Utilize tax incentive programs for the areas you are shooting in to stretch your production dollars.**

CHAPTER 8
HIRING CREW

H IRING CREW IS ONE of the producer's most important and creative tasks. Finding the best and brightest for your project requires patience, research, instinct, and vision. It's important to learn what each job entails and discuss what attributes the director is looking for in each key creative position. You will also need to factor in the budget and other resources and requirements when "casting" the crew. How each crew position fits in with the overall production is a bit of a puzzle. Let's start with an overall understanding of crew jobs and organization.

Crew Positions: Who Does What

Here's a quick reference for all the crew positions that contribute to a production. Depending on the size and budget of a production, the crew configuration will change. Each low-budget independent project, based on budget and other factors, will have some of these positions and not others. Here is a master list of the key crew positions to consider for your production:

If you want to go fast, go alone. If you want to go far, go together.

—*African proverb*

Producer(s) – As outlined at the beginning of the book, the producer puts together most elements of a project to make it happen. The list of producer credits can be found on page xxiii.

Director – creates and implements the creative ideas to bring the project to fruition

Writer – writes the script and/or treatment and revises drafts based on notes from producer and director

Director of Photography (DP) – collaborates with director, production designer and costume designer to create the visual ideas and images and oversees the camera, lighting and grip departments

Camera Operator – collaborates with the DP and films the project by operating the camera

1st Assistant Director (AD) – collaborates with the director and producer, breaks down the script, schedules the project, runs the set and keeps track of all cast and crew

2nd AD – assists the 1st AD, often concentrates on coordinating and supporting the cast

Camera Assistant – checks out the camera equipment, pulls focus and manages the camera equipment on set

Gaffer – collaborates with the DP, creates and implements the lighting plan, including rental decisions and electrical requirements, and oversees the electrical department

Electrics – implements the lighting plan per gaffer instructions

Key Grip – collaborates with the DP, creates and implements the grip plan, including support equipment for the lighting and camera departments (e.g. tripods, dollies and cranes), and oversees the grip department

Grips – implements the grip plan per key grip instructions

Sound Recordist/Mixer – records and mixes audio on set in coordination with boom operator (if necessary)

Boom Operator – holds and operates the sound boom pole in coordination with sound recordist

Production Designer – collaborates with director, DP and costume designer to create the visual ideas and images and oversees the production design department, including art direction, props, set dressing and construction

Art Director – collaborates with production design team to implement the creative vision

Props Master – collaborates with production design team to create and procure all props (objects touched by cast)

Set Dresser – collaborates with production design team to create and procure all set dressing (furniture, wall and floor coverings)

Costume Designer – collaborates with director, DP and production designer to create the visual ideas and images and oversees the costume department, including the creation and procurement of all costumes

Hair/Makeup Artist – collaborates with director and DP to create the hair and makeup for all cast

Casting Director – collaborates with director and producer to audition and hire the right actor for each role

Digital Imaging Technician (DIT) – collaborates with DP to build LUTs and advise on data media management on set

Media Manager – downloads, transcodes and backs up all media on set

Playback – records and plays back audio and video on set and manages all video monitors

Location Manager/Scout – based on information from the director and producer, researches and procures the locations for scenes in the script

Script Supervisor (Scriptie) – tracks continuity and takes director notes for each camera take on set. Notes are sent to the editor to guide their work in post production

Line Producer – collaborates with producer to create the budget, hire cast and crew, schedule and organize every aspect of the film's production

Production Manager – works with the line producer to manage all production logistics

Production Coordinator – works with the production manager and tracks all production paperwork and coordinates logistics

Production Assistants – entry level position that assists various film departments to support their work

Police/Fire – police and fire personnel to oversee all safety and security issues

Tutor – teaches academic lessons for any minor-age actors during non-working periods on the set

Still Photographer – takes production still photos of cast and crew working on the film for publicity purposes

Stunt Coordinator – plans and implements any stunts and hires additional stunt people to execute any stunt

Weaponer – plans, advises, coordinates and controls all weapons on set

Pyrotech – plans, advises, coordinates and controls all fire and explosives on set

Special FX (SFX) – plans, advises and coordinates special effects on set or in post production

Editor – collaborates with director to edit acquired footage to final, locked picture master

Assistant Editor – ingests, breaks down and organizes all acquired footage, backs up working cuts and assists editor during post production

Post Production Supervisor – schedules and coordinates all aspects of post production, hires post personnel and creates all tech deliverables

Music Supervisor – collaborates with director to build the film's soundtrack through music acquisition and music composition and licenses all music

Composer – based on notes from the director, composes music for the film's soundtrack

Colorist – collaborates with DP to digitally manipulate the master to create the final cinematic look of the film

Graphics Designer – creates graphics and titles for the film

Sound Editor – edits all audio tracks and adds sound elements to build the film's soundtrack

Audio Mixer – collaborates with director to mix the audio tracks and music to locked audio master

Finding Talented Crew

What kind of production are you creating? Really low-budget, with a very small crew? A production with very high production values so you'll need to hire very experienced key department heads? A production that needs to stretch the budget so you want to discover new talent that will work for less money than more-established key creatives? These are discussions you need to have with the director to manage expectations and set a strategy for who/how you'll hire crew.

Where to Find Crew

There is no "one" way to find talented crew people. If you have worked with good crew members in the past, you'll often hire them for the next gig. It's always great to work alongside people with whom you have a shared production history—you have a shorthand of common experience and know the person's strengths and weaknesses and feel comfortable working together.

Asking trusted colleagues for recommendations is a good way to find possible hires. Look at favorite films and read the screen credits. Visit online resources like *www.ProductionHub.com, www.ShootingPeople.com,* and location film commissions' websites. Film schools can also be a good place to find affordable crew members.

There are "below-the-line" agents who focus on representing the key department heads like line producers, cinematographers, production designers, hair/makeup, costume designers, and editors. If you have a large enough budget, contact them for recommendations and demo reels.

Hiring Criteria

This is where the "casting" of your crew begins and here's a short list of criteria:

1. Talent
2. Previous experience
3. Excellent references
4. Availability for prep and shooting period
5. Interest and vision for the project
6. Work ethic
7. Good connections for potential vendor discounts and favors
8. Good contacts for other crew members in the department
9. Compatibility with director
10. Plays well with others
11. Not a yeller and treats everyone with mutual respect
12. Does not lie
13. Communicates effectively

You can place the emphasis anywhere you'd like in this list. But for me, personality, work ethic, and honesty pretty much trump talent and experience every time.

I'm not saying I'd hire someone who was not right for the job, but those other factors are just as important—and even more so—when you have limited resources and everyone has to pull together to create a miracle. I've changed my feelings about this over the years. I used to tolerate a--holes more, but I've gotten older and now realize that there are tons of talented people who are decent and true as well. So I work just with those people—life really is too short. The nice talented people need to be rewarded for their decency and I support them, one production at a time.

Watch Demo Reels

Each semester I teach a class on how to watch demo reels and how to decide who is best to hire for your production. Most crew have either a website with their video portfolio posted or a link to a password-protected demo reel. If you are hiring for a narrative project, it's best to watch scenes from past narrative work and not only a "montage" reel. Why should you watch clips from scenes? Because it allows you to see if the person did work that was appropriate for what you think is required for that particular scene. A montage reel doesn't give you any context for analysis of their work.

For DP reels, even if I am hiring for a narrative project, I will often watch the person's documentary work as well (if available). Why? Because it gives you insight to how they frame and shoot material when it is not specifically created ahead of time (i.e., storyboards). It can be helpful in making a decision about the person's talent. If the DP owns equipment like a camera and/or lenses and offers it to the production at a discount, don't factor that into your decision to hire the person! I've seen so many filmmakers make their decision based on a "hot" new camera and not base their hiring decision on the cinematographer's talent.

Check References

Always check references. My (very few) bad crew hires over the years only happened when I was too desperate or felt I didn't have enough time to check references. Learn from my pain. Check them out!

Ask each of your top potential crew hires for two references. The crew person should be more than happy to give them to you and if they balk, that's a red flag and you should walk away. It's standard practice for crew to have several references available upon request.

Once given the references' contact info, email them with a short introduction of who you are and ask if there is a good time for a quick call to discuss their reference for that crew person. Producers and directors are busy people so when you call them have your questions ready to go. Then call them at the appointed time and thank them for taking the time to speak. Here's a good list of questions to ask:

1. How long have you known the person?

2. What position did the person fill on your film? What kind of job did they do—great, good, bad?

3. Describe any specific issues you are concerned about on your particular production, e.g., "we don't have much set-up time or we have a very temperamental lead actor, etc." and ask the person if they think the crew person could handle that particular situation.

4. Would you hire them again? If so, why? If not, why not?

5. What are their strengths?

6. What are their weaknesses?

7. Anything else I should know? Any final insights regarding working with this person?

Understand that it is human nature to say nice things about people even if the person was just "OK." So the question "what are their weaknesses?" is the *most* important question in the list. Many people get uncomfortable when answering this question. You have to wait it out until they answer that question, because what they say in that answer will probably determine if you hire that person or not. If their weakness is a minor thing, no worries. But if it's a major thing like, "every day we were behind schedule by an hour because they were really slow at lighting," then you may decide you can't hire the person.

I always respond to producers when they ask for references on crew people. Because if they are good, I want to help get them more work and if they are not up to standard, I want to share helpful information in a professional way so that producer can make their best hiring decision.

On Hold/Confirm or Book/Release

Clear communication when hiring crew is essential. There is a protocol for hiring film crew based on *very specific words* and it's important to know the words and their meaning to avoid any confusion. You are putting together a crew made up of freelancers so it's important to be clear about the status of a potential hire.

On Hold means that the crew person is keeping the date available for your production but is not officially hired. I always send an email to the crew person with the on hold language and the dates so I'm clear that it's a hold and not a booking yet. The written email helps to remind everyone of the hiring status.

Confirm or Book means that you are committing to pay the crew person for those dates whether or not your production moves forward. This occurs when you are 100% certain that the production will happen on that particular date and you want to ensure the crew person is locked in for your production. This is a crucial moment for a producer: It means that there is a firm commitment to pay that crew person no matter what. After someone is confirmed, you can't un-book them. If the shoot cancels, you still owe them their salary. A confirmation/booking may happen because the shoot is finalized and is a "go" or it may occur when there is a "challenge" (see below).

Release means that the producer no longer needs or wishes to hire the crew person for the dates that were on hold. The production may have been canceled or the decision made to hire a different person for the position. If you decide not to shoot or change the dates, you need to release the crew person as soon as possible so they can become available for other work on those dates.

Challenge occurs when a crew person says you are on a "first hold" or a "second hold." If you are a first hold, then if you book them, you'll get them. If it's a second hold and you want to book them, you'll need to challenge for their availability. They will need to go back to their first hold client, explain that you are ready to confirm them, and give the client 24 hours to make a decision to confirm or release them. If you get them, it's an automatic confirmation and you'll have to pay the crew person even if the production cancels (see above.)

Salary Negotiation/Most Favored Nation

When hiring cast and crew, I always recommend using Most Favored Nation as the way of keeping rates the same across each department. As discussed in Chapter 6 (*Pre-production*), each crew person at the same rank has the same salary rate. This protocol keeps salaries equitable.

Hiring Paperwork

When you hire crew and cast there will be paperwork that needs to be filled out and signed before the person can work on your project and get paid. Have this paperwork ready for each hire to sign when they come onto the project so you have the legal right to their work and can pay each person promptly. Below are the key documents:

DEAL MEMO

A **deal memo** is the agreement that states the rules that the production company and crew/cast person agree to for the length of the production. The deal points should include: 1) Crew contact info and emergency contact info, 2) Compensation, payment schedule, and tax paperwork requirements, 3) Insurance coverage, petty cash and kit rental rules, 4) "Work-for hire" language and publicity requirements or limitations. It is signed between the crew/cast member and the production company. The agreement should be created and approved by an entertainment attorney.

NON-DISCLOSURE AGREEMENT (NDA) OR CONFIDENTIALITY AGREEMENT

An **NDA** codifies the confidentiality requirements for a crew/cast person when they are hired onto a project. It is signed between the crew/cast member and the production company. The agreement should be created and approved by an entertainment attorney.

PAYROLL COMPANY PAPERWORK DOCUMENTS

If you are using a payroll company to pay the crew/cast, there will be **start paperwork** to fill out so the payroll company can set up each crew/cast member into the computer system. Additionally, the crew/cast member will need to fill out federal tax documents including a W-2 or W-4 (states social security number or federal tax ID number and the amount of deductions), an I-9 (states that the crew/cast member is legally eligible to work in the U.S.) and proper photo ID.

RECAP

1. **Hiring crew is one of the most important steps in producing a project. Make sure to "cast" the crew with the best personnel you can hire. Use personal contacts, industry job listing sites, and social media to put together a hard-working, talented and dedicated crew.**

2. **Watch demo reels carefully and always check at least two references before hiring someone for the crew. This helps you bring the best people onto the team to make the project.**

3. **Follow the proper protocol for On Hold/Confirm/Release when hiring crew. Clear communication in writing will make sure that the crew knows when they are officially hired or not and reduces confusion or misunderstandings.**

4. **Hiring of all cast and crew requires several signed documents. Have the paperwork ready to expedite each hire and the prompt payment of their salary.**

CHAPTER 9
LEGAL

When most people are confronted with a 20-page legal document, they can be overwhelmed—which leads to feelings of anxiety, frustration, or outright fear. If you are not a trained lawyer, the language and concepts can be confusing, even intimidating. As the producer, it is your job to deal with various legal concepts and documents, but you don't have to be an attorney to understand them. As with all things, the more you learn, the easier it becomes.

For this chapter, I've asked George Rush, an entertainment attorney and sales agent based in San Francisco, to share his expertise and guidance (*www.gmrush.com*). We will break down the most common legal concepts that you will encounter in the documents that come your way. Then we'll outline the specific documents that are most often used in film productions. At the end of the chapter we'll go over additional documents that may be of use to you in specific cases. You'll find templates for some of these documents at *www.ProducerToProducer.com* to help when creating your own forms, deal memos, and contracts for your production.

> *Determine the thing that can and shall be done and then we shall find a way.*
>
> —*Abraham Lincoln*

And now for the legal disclaimer: **This chapter is for informational purposes only and is not intended as legal advice.**

It's All About Rights

As discussed in Chapter 1 (*Development*), one of the tenets of film producing revolves around the understanding, negotiation, and acquisition of rights. **Rights** is a derivative of the word "copyright" and copyright refers to the "right to copy." Copyright is exactly what it sounds like—rights pertaining to the copying of something someone else owns. For example, if one were to copy this book, you would need the rights from me, the owner/author. The producer needs to have the rights to the property (e.g., novel, comic book, play, etc.) he wishes to develop *before* moving forward with the project. Generally, this is done by acquiring an option to purchase the rights. This is usually a nominal sum that gives you the exclusive rights to purchase the motion picture rights to a property for a fixed period of time. Do not spend a lot of resources developing a story unless you are certain you can obtain the rights. Work with an attorney to make sure you have all the signed legal documents for the rights you require *before* spending time on writing or looking for financing or talent attachments.

It's All About Liability

Another major aspect of a producer's responsibilities has to do with liability. **Liability** is your legal risk and exposure. As a producer, you need to eliminate or mitigate the circumstances under which you may be liable or at risk for an occurrence. For instance, a distributor will not be interested in your film (regardless of its merits) unless there is zero or next-to-no liability.

This is done in several ways:

1. Written agreements that seek to eliminate or set limits on liability for the producer/production entity. This ranges from contracts with your cast and crew to music/archival licenses to financial agreements with your investors. You want a written agreement for everything you can think of where there may be liability.

2. Incorporation to shield a producer and the film's personnel from any damages if a liability arises during the producing of a film. You, as an individual, do not want to be party to any of these agreements. If

there is a dispute about an agreement, that means the other party would go after you and—if you lose—your personal assets. You want the party to these agreements to be your company, which will be the legally responsible party and whose only asset will be this one film.

3. Acquisition of proper insurance so the production and its cast, crew, and resources are covered for possible risk factors. We will discuss this in detail in Chapter 10, *Insurance*.

In this chapter we will discuss general legal concepts and then outline specific legal documents. At the end of the chapter, we'll discuss how to incorporate for a film production.

Breakdown of a Legal Document

Most legal documents related to film producing contain specific legal components. Below is a breakdown of those concepts that you will find in the various kinds of documents you will come across.

PARTIES
State who/what are the two or more parties that are signing the agreement.

TERM
State the date when the agreement commences and the period of time that the contract covers.

RIGHTS
If it is an agreement covering rights, state which rights are being covered by the document. Examples include broadcast rights (right to broadcast on TV), music composition rights (rights to a piece of music), theatrical distribution rights (rights to distribute a film in theaters), DVD rights (rights to create and sell a DVD of a work), and streaming rights (rights to the digital streaming of the project).

SERVICES
What exactly you are obligated to do, and what exactly the other party is obligated to do.

FEES
For lawyers, this is often called a **consideration**—the benefit of the bargain or the amount of money paid for the purchase, usage, or rental of

something. This could be a location rental fee—how much will be paid for the use of a location for a certain period of time or acquisition fee—or money paid for a period of time for certain rights to a project. It could also be the day rate of a cast or crew member.

LIABILITY
Who/what is responsible for any problem, damage, or accident that may occur during a production.

LIMITATIONS
What the document does and does not cover regarding the agreement.

RIGHT TO ENTER INTO AGREEMENT
All parties signing agreements must verify that they are legally responsible for the parties they are signing for.

CAN OR CANNOT ASSIGN TO OTHERS
Need to state if the parties can or cannot assign rights in the agreement to others.

RECOURSE OR REMEDY
How and where the parties will be able to go to remedy a situation if they have problems with an outcome, or if something has changed.

CONTACT INFORMATION
How and where each party can be contacted in the future, usually via written and/or delivered mail.

Legal Concepts

There are several concepts or legal terms that play a role in some of the legal documents in the film industry. Here's a short list:

FAIR USE
Fair Use is a legal concept whereby a filmmaker can use copyrighted material in their project (without asking permission or paying a licensing fee to the copyright holder) because it falls under one of the four criteria for fair use under U.S. copyright law. The criteria focus on "transformative use" often used in scholarship, criticism, and education. An excellent document outlining the legal concepts for filmmakers can be found at American University's Center for Social Media website, *www.centerforsocialmedia.org*. Fair use is a defense against someone suing you for copyright

infringement. It is a shield, not a sword. There are a lot of grey areas and misconceptions regarding fair use. In a very basic sense, you need to be "commenting" on a copyrighted work for it to even be considered fair use.

Another good organization for information about fair use is Stanford University's Copyright and Fair Use Center at *www.fairuse.stanford.edu*. This is a definition from the Stanford website: "fair use is a copyright principle based on the belief that the public is entitled to freely use portions of copyrighted materials for purposes of commentary and criticism. For example, if you wish to criticize a novelist, you should have the freedom to quote a portion of the novelist's work without asking permission. Absent this freedom, copyright owners could stifle any negative comments about their work."

Unfortunately for filmmakers, there is not a lot of case law or an easy, bright-line test for what is or is not fair use. There are a number of legal/academic groups (including Stanford University and American University) that advocate best practices for fair use and/or advocate a broadening of fair use. If you are consulting with one of these group's websites, read their information very carefully, since the criteria is specific and narrow. You never want to intentionally overstep the copyright laws because it could result in a lawsuit. If you have any concerns or questions, hire an entertainment attorney who specializes in copyright law to assist you in decision-making about material licensing.

Generally, unlicensed copyrighted material used in a fictional narrative film will not qualify as fair use. However, as more narratives incorporate elements of documentary, the issue does come up. Most distributors will require a copyright report as one of your deliverables: If certain material is not licensed, they will want to know if it is fair use.

PARI PASSU
This means "at the same time, at the same rate." This concept is often used regarding investor payback clauses.

MOST FAVORED NATION
The term most favored nation (MFN) refers to the concept of everyone in a certain category receiving the same deal as everyone else in that category. The concept is commonly used in international trade agreements where each country signed to an agreement has the same terms as every other country. As an example, any crew person hired as a key department head will receive the same salary rate as every other person who is a key department head.

List of Agreements During Each Phase

Below is a list of individual agreements that are most often used in the course of producing a project. Each document is used during a specific phase in the filmmaking process, as outlined below:

DEVELOPMENT

Option Agreement

As discussed in Chapter 1 (*Development*), an option agreement gives a producer an "option" to own the rights to creative material that has been previously produced, e.g., book, short story, play, comic book, or screenplay. It will cover a fixed period of time for a certain fee and usually there is a renewal feature built into the agreement.
Signature by Creator of the Work and the Purchaser of the Work

Writer's Contract

This agreement commissions a writer to write a screenplay, either original or based on other material. If the screenwriter is a member of the Writers Guild of America (WGA), it will be a WGA contract. If the writer is non-union, then the purchaser will draw up a specific agreement. Outlined in the agreement will be the writing schedule, the payment schedule, re-writes, details about the ownership of the work, and how long the rights are owned by the purchaser before they revert back to the screenwriter.
Signature by Screenwriter and Purchaser of the Script

Non-Disclosure Agreement

This agreement is between two parties to treat information confidentially and to not share it with third parties. It is often used by companies when reading unsolicited scripts and treatments and is used to limit liability in regard to producing work that is similar to past submitted materials.
Signature by Crew/Cast Member and Production Company

Investor's Agreement

This proposal is the document sent out to possible investors for your project and must be in compliance with Securities and Exchange Commission (SEC) regulations. The document states all of the potential risks involved for those investing in the film in clear detail. Attorney George Rush advises: "Independent film, unlike investing in other businesses, is the worst business. The likelihood of the investors making their money back are like slim to none, and because of that you need to give them full disclosure about the risks, in particular. It is absolutely necessary to disclose [all the details]. So, if they sign on the dotted line, they know what they're getting into."

If you accept money from an individual outside the state in which you are incorporated, then you have to make sure you are complying with their particular state's security laws. You'll need an attorney to ensure you are compliant with all relevant legal rules. *Do not try this on your own, as one of your biggest liabilities will be the money received from investors.*

Signature by Investor and Production Company

PRE-PRODUCTION
Crew/Cast Deal Memo
As discussed in Chapter 6 (*Pre-production*), this document covers the employment details for each crew/cast person. It should state screen credit, payment, time period, job responsibility, and work rules and regulations. It should also include language about confidentiality or non-disclosure—the production's expectations about what a crew/cast member is or is not allowed to discuss about the project with others, including through social media, etc.

Signature by Producer and Crew/Cast Person

Location Release Form
As discussed in Chapter 7 (*Locations*), this form covers the deal for each location you use during the production of your project. It should state the fee, the rental time period, and the liability for the producer and the location's owner.

Signature by Producer and Property Owner

Producer/Director Agreement
This may be a "work for hire" agreement or some other document between the producer and the director of the project. The document should solidify the expectations and responsibilities that you and the director agree to meet during each phase of the project. Areas to be covered should include: 1) funding; 2) screen credit; 3) responsibilities; 4) cash flow; 5) ownership of the project and ownership of the work done by the producer and the director; and 6) "points" or profit participation on the film.

Signed by Producer and Director

PRODUCTION
Union Contracts—Crew and Cast
If your production company is a signatory to any crew or cast unions, the negotiated union contract will be signed.

Signed by Producer and Union Cast/Crew Member

Non-union Appearance Release Form
This form is signed by non-union talent who appear in your project. If you are filming in public, this may be signed by people walking by on the street who appear (recognizable for who they are) in your project. The form allows you to use their image and voice in your film (usually in perpetuity, worldwide, in any current and future media).
Signature by Producer and Non-union Cast Member or Person on Screen

Music License Agreement
Most films/videos use some kind of music for the soundtracks—either previously recorded compositions or original work composed specifically for the project. There are two kinds of music rights that you need to obtain with regards to music—Synchronization license (publishing) and Master Use license (recording). (See Chapter 17, *Music*.)

Make sure to get both rights for each composition and for the correct usage that you need, e.g., film festival, DVD, theatrical, television, online, digital, etc.
Signed by Producer and Music Rights Holder or Representative

Logo Release Form
To be signed when you use the logo or brand of a product on screen in your film. Because logos are trademarked, obtaining the rights holder's permission is required. The logo owner may ask to read the script to make sure their product/logo/reputation is not being defamed before agreeing to give permission.
Signature by Producer and Trademark Holder or Representative

Legal Corporate Entities
A producer wants to limit any kind of damages that could arise from a liability issue on a project. For instance, if on a shoot a heavy piece of equipment falls on a picture vehicle (like a restored classic automobile in pristine condition) and causes $25,000 worth of damage, the insurance policy should cover the cost of repairs, minus the deductible. But if the car's owner decides to sue for loss of rental income while the car is being repaired, the producer could be responsible for the legal costs and a monetary award for the owner if he or she wins the suit. In such a situation, you want to make sure a legal judgment can't go after your personal money or assets (like your home or car). Consequently, it is wise to set up a corporate entity to protect yourself and the project. The most

common options are either a corporation or a limited liability company (LLC). The key points of each entity are outlined below.

CORPORATION
A **corporation** is a business entity that has many of the rights and responsibilities of a person, but is distinct from the persons who own it. Corporations provide structure so that groups of individuals may conduct business as an individual entity. There are S Corps and C Corps, which have different set-ups and tax consequences. In addition, film projects often use limited partnerships and limited liability companies. These entities, for the most part, shield their members from liability. You should contact an attorney and an accountant before you decide on which entity to create for your project.

LIMITED PARTNERSHIP (LP)
A limited partnership is made up of a general partner (usually the producer) and limited partners (usually the investors.) The investors have limited liability, while the general partner has all the liability. Attorney George Rush instead suggests a limited liability company for films.

LIMITED LIABILITY CORPORATION (LLC)
An LLC is almost like a hybrid of corporation and partnership, and as the name suggests, limits your liability. The terms of the LLC are analogous to that of a corporation—instead of articles of incorporation, you have articles of organization. Instead of stockholders, an LLC has members. LLCs are the most common entity used by filmmakers, as they are set up for just one film (the manager is usually the filmmaker) and they are easy to create.

Never Sign Anything Without Proper Legal Advice
Legal counsel is essential when making a film and reading this chapter of *Producer To Producer* does not eliminate your need to obtain proper legal counsel. If anyone gives you a document to sign, you should hire a knowledgeable entertainment attorney to look it over and/or amend before you sign.

There are many different areas of specialty in law. Entertainment law is very different from corporate law or divorce law, etc. Make sure you hire an entertainment lawyer who will be familiar with issues specific to the film industry.

To find a good attorney, you can ask fellow filmmakers for recommendations and go to legal seminars offered by local film organizations. Take meetings with several candidates before you select your attorney: most attorneys will give you a 20- to 30-minute free consultation. Lawyers charge by the hour or 1/10th of an hour.

If you cannot afford an attorney, there are organizations that provide legal counsel for reduced fees to artists throughout the country. Volunteer Lawyers for the Arts (VLA) is a organization that offers pro bono/greatly discounted legal services to low-income artists and non-profit organizations. Go to *www.vlany.org* for more information.

Your Lawyer Is an Extension of You

Remember that your attorney represents you, particularly when negotiating on your behalf. Your attorney's interaction and behavior in each negotiation reflects directly on you and I think it is important to factor that into your selection criteria. What kind of person do you want working on your behalf?

A businesswoman I know had four different lawyers whom she used to help run her business. She had a tough, bulldog attorney to collect monies from late-to-pay clients and a corporate attorney for leases, business dealings, and contracts. In addition, she had a liability attorney to protect her against risk inherent in her business and to create and keep current her invoice disclaimer. She also had an accident attorney to analyze and collect on other people's insurance policies and handle accident suits. She found that by choosing a professional in each field, she saved money and had excellent results.

I picked my attorney because she's intelligent, experienced, steady-as-a-rock, fearless, and a good negotiator. I know she will negotiate hard on my behalf, but she is reasonable and forthright. She's not a bully and doesn't play games. I also like the way she writes. Her legal writing style is clear—not overblown with too much legalese—and it's efficient.

People who know me might say that I just described myself because I want my attorney to reflect my style and values. Hey, but that's me. Some people feel you should get someone who is the opposite of you. If you are kind and decent, then get a shark to negotiate for you. That's your choice.

Attorney as Financier/Executive Producer/Producer's Rep

This chapter has discussed the legal issues and documents used to produce a project. There is another area in entertainment law that concentrates on film financing and packaging. Some attorneys work as Producer's Reps and you should look into those kinds of services if appropriate for your project. Often an entertainment law firm will have many attorneys that focus on different aspects of the business.

RECAP

1. **Negotiate, sign, and keep copies of all necessary legal documents throughout each phase of producing your project. You'll need to keep them on file and include copies of the agreements as part of your deliverables list.**

2. **Create a corporate entity for the project to protect yourself and others from liability.**

3. **Learn about legal terms and concepts for negotiation purposes.**

4. **Hire a good entertainment lawyer to review and amend any legal documents before they are signed.**

5. **Your lawyer is an extension of you. Pick one who represents you in the way you wish to be seen.**

CHAPTER 10
INSURANCE

Why Do You Need Insurance?

THE SHORT ANSWER IS SO you and your collaborators can financially transfer the liability for any accidents, mishaps, or damage that may occur to a person or thing during your production to an insurance company. That's not to say that you don't have *responsibility* for all aspects of your production. But if a grip breaks her leg while stepping off a ladder and you have workers' compensation insurance coverage in place, the insurance will be able to pay for her medical bills for a cast, rehabilitation, and a percentage of her lost wages if she cannot work for several weeks.

As producer, it's your responsibility to obtain all the necessary insurance policies, such as General Liability, Hired or Non-owned Auto Liability, Auto Physical Damage, and Workers' Compensation. You may also need DBL (Disability Benefits Law), Production Insurance (covering the props, sets, wardrobe, equipment, locations, and final master copy of your project), Umbrella Liability, Travel Accident Insurance and Errors

> *Doubt is not an agreeable condition but certainty is absurd.*
>
> —Voltaire

& Omissions Insurance. From an insurance standpoint, you protect yourself and the production by acquiring the proper insurance coverage for your project.

Do not produce a film or video unless you have the proper insurance! No matter how small or low-budget your project, no film is worth the potential financial ruin a lawsuit could cause you and your fellow collaborators.

For this chapter I enlisted Christine Sadofsky, the president of Ventura Insurance (*www.venturainsurance.com*) to illuminate the world of production insurance coverage.

Common Insurance Policies

COMMERCIAL GENERAL LIABILITY INSURANCE

General Liability insurance will protect you from claims alleging bodily injury, property damage, personal injury, and advertising injury (such as libel, slander, and copyright infringement) that you cause to a third party. A third party is someone other than your employees, unpaid volunteers, independent contractors, or freelancers. This basic general liability coverage will be required before you can obtain permits, rent locations, and rent equipment. The premium for this coverage will be based on Gross Production Costs for the policy period for the project. A **premium** is the fee you pay for your policy to the insurance company. Insurance brokers are paid a commission by the insurance company when they sell you the policies. Since a premium is an estimated number, many insurers will audit the figures and require you to provide the actual Gross Production Costs after the policy term is over and send you an adjustment if the estimate was incorrect.

Limits are typically $1,000,000/Each Occurrence with a $2,000,000 General Aggregate (maximum the policy will pay). Higher limits are available by purchasing an Umbrella Policy. The reasons for higher limits will be discussed in the Umbrella Liability section that follows.

Deductibles are not usually found on General Liability policies issued to producers. A **deductible** is the amount of money you need to pay out-of-pocket before the insurance company will pay an approved claim. Usually the higher the deductible amount, the less expensive the policy costs.

WORKERS' COMPENSATION INSURANCE

Workers' Compensation insurance covers workers/employees (including freelancers and independent contractors who do not have their own policies) in case they have an accident on a job that requires medical attention. The policy provides for full reimbursement of all medical costs and a percentage of lost wages if the employee cannot work. There is a minimum number of days that the employee must be out of work for lost wages to kick in.

This policy also provides Employer's Liability coverage to protect the production company/employer for third party claims against the production company/employer arising out of an injury to an employee (e.g., a spouse who brings a lawsuit against the employer). It's important to note that if you decide to use a payroll service company which becomes the employer of record for the production, you still need to obtain a basic workers' compensation policy for the minimum premium, since the Employer's Liability coverage under the payroll service company *does not* extend to your company, leaving you exposed. Also, if you have a volunteer or someone you pay cash to and this person is injured while working for you, the payroll service company will not cover that loss, since they have no record of paying that person.

The premium for this policy is based on the actual compensation you will pay to all full-time employees, freelancers, and independent contractors. This compensation is multiplied by a rate for a certain class of employee (the rate is higher for a gaffer than it is for a production office coordinator). Then there are taxes and fees that are calculated to develop the final deposit premium.

This policy is auditable at the end of the policy period because the compensation given upfront most likely was an estimate and will need to be adjusted at the end of the 12 months. It's important to keep good bank records and accounts payables so you know how much you spent on Gross Production Costs during that 12-month period.

The law in all fifty states requires workers' comp coverage, so make sure you obtain it. Often it can be purchased directly from a state authority for relatively low cost, so do the research before you go into production. Each state levies fines for entities that are found to not carry this important insurance coverage.

DISABILITY INSURANCE

This policy is also **statutory** (required by law) and employers need to provide coverage for employees for injuries that occur off the job. The cost of this kind of policy is rather inexpensive. There are several states that require disability insurance for employees. Failure to have this policy will also result in a fine.

AUTO INSURANCE

Whether you own, rent, borrow, or hire an automobile, you will need Auto Liability to protect the production from claims alleging bodily injury and/or property damage that may have been caused by the operation of an automobile. In addition, most owners of the vehicles will require the production company to protect their vehicles from physical damage in case of accidents.

The primary limit of liability found under an auto policy is $1,000,000 and the coverage for physical damage will vary by insurance company. The damage to the auto will also be subject to a deductible (see above). For instance if an employee damages an auto and the total cost to repair is $3,500 and your deductible is $1,000, the insurance company will pay $2,500.

The premium for this type of insurance will depend upon whether you own, lease, or rent the vehicle. If you own or lease the vehicle, you will need to provide the year, make, model, VIN (Vehicle Identification Number), what it costs for a new model, garaging location, and the driver information. If you are renting the vehicles, you will need to provide the total cost of rental charges you expect to incur during the 12-month policy period.

NEGATIVE FILM/VIDEOTAPE/DIGITALIZED IMAGE PRODUCTION COVERAGE

The policy starts with coverage to protect your "master," whether this is film, video, or digital. If after completion of shooting for the day, the "master" is destroyed, lost, or stolen, the policy will give you the funds to reshoot the work if the claim is approved. Example: If someone leaves the laptop computer with the only copy of the project's digital footage at the airport by accident, the insurance should pay for the reshoot costs, less the deductible.

FAULTY STOCK, CAMERA, & PROCESSING COVERAGE

If the camera or other media acquisition elements or processes are damaged, you will need to reshoot the segments and the coverage will provide the funds to do so, less your deductible. Example: If the camera lens is defective, the hard drive fails, or the film lab destroys your film negative while processing it.

EXTRA EXPENSE COVERAGE

If any of the property being used for the production is damaged or destroyed and you have to cancel or postpone the production, you may incur extra expenses because of this loss. The policy will reimburse you for any *extra expense* you incur as a result, less your deductible. Example: If there is a fire at your location the night before your shoot and you have to reschedule the shoot day.

PROPS, SETS, & WARDROBE COVERAGE

If the production either owns or rents props, sets, or wardrobe, the policy will provide coverage in case there is a loss and these items have to be replaced, less the deductible. Example: If someone drops and breaks a prop and it needs to be replaced.

THIRD-PARTY PROPERTY DAMAGE COVERAGE

Provides protection to the production company in case a cast/crew member damages the location they are working in, less the deductible. Example: A grip accidentally ruins a location's wooden floor by using the wrong tape and destroying the finish.

CAST INSURANCE COVERAGE

If a declared cast member has an accident or becomes ill and cannot work, this coverage will reimburse the production company for any extra expense that is incurred due to the interruption, postponement, or cancellation of the production, less the deductible. In order to have sickness coverage apply, each declared person must undergo a medical exam by a doctor approved by the insurer. This coverage is not an automatic part of the policy so this must be discussed with your broker. This kind of coverage is usually purchased for a television series and $3 million (or higher) film productions.

FAMILY BEREAVEMENT COVERAGE

This coverage extends the coverage to include reimbursement to the production company in case a declared cast member must leave the production due to the death of an immediate family member, subject to a limit per loss and/or a specified number of days and less the deductible.

UMBRELLA INSURANCE

This policy will provide higher limits of liability over several policies. If you decide to purchase a $5,000,000 Umbrella, this limit will be available for claims over and above the primary General Liability, Employer's

Liability, and Auto Liability (as discussed above). The reasons for this coverage will vary but sometimes a production is contractually required to have more than $1,000,000; or you have a big production with many autos, cast, crew, and hazardous activities and you want the higher limits to provide better protection.

The premium for this is actually based on the premiums for the coverage that "sit underneath" this policy. So the insurance company will look at what the premium is for General Liability, Auto Liability and, sometimes, Employer's Liability and price it accordingly.

ERRORS & OMISSION (E&O) INSURANCE

Errors & Omissions (E&O) insurance provides defense and indemnity from claims alleging copyright infringement, trademark infringement, plagiarism, libel, slander, defamation, and other media perils that arise from the *content of your media*. This coverage can start the moment your project begins filming, but typically, unless there is a definitive distribution agreement in place, a producer would not purchase this coverage until it is required by the distribution company. The premium is based on the entities—both domestic and international—where your film will be screened. Worldwide distribution coverage costs more than if the film is only playing on a domestic cable television network.

The limits will start at $1,000,000/Each Occurrence and will go as high as $5,000,000/Each Occurrence—this will depend upon your contract with the distributor. The policy period is usually for multiple years and/or will include a rights period endorsement so that the distributor is covered throughout the contract period. The premium for this type of policy will depend upon the size of the budget, the length of the production, the territories for distribution, the type of production (for example: a documentary vs. a narrative theatrical feature film), and the answers to the questions in the application. This coverage will require a completed media application and the answers in this application become a **warranty** under the policy, so it's critical that the application be completed accurately. If you fill out the form and say you have certain signed releases and licenses when you don't, then if there is a claim it will not be covered. This policy can also be extended to cover the title of the production, music, film clips, and merchandise.

UNION TRAVEL ACCIDENT INSURANCE

When productions employ various union personnel there will be requirements that the production company provide travel/accident insurance for its members. This coverage and the benefits paid are in addition to the workers' compensation policy. The premium is based on the total number of union vs. non-union personnel, their travel plans (if any), and the type of hazard/work they will be performing. The limit for the insurance will be determined by the various union contracts.

FOREIGN PACKAGE POLICY

If the production requires traveling outside of the United States, Canada, Puerto Rico, or any of the U.S. territories, you will need to obtain a foreign policy in order to have all the same coverage while filming abroad. This policy provides Foreign General Liability, Foreign Excess Auto Liability (excess over the coverage on the auto you are renting), and Foreign Workers' Compensation. The premium for this is based upon the foreign budget figures, the number of cast and crew traveling, the duration of the trip, and the concentration of people traveling together. The more individuals you have traveling together on the same aircraft, the higher the premium for the foreign workers' compensation.

Keep in mind that workers' compensation insurance does not exist in countries other than the United States. Many countries have national health care coverage for their citizens but it will not cover U.S. personnel filming there. Consequently you'll want to make sure that any U.S. citizens traveling to another country have medical insurance that covers them abroad. Ask them to check before they travel. There are many good affordable international travel health insurance companies that sell short-term medical insurance for individuals.

Sometimes it makes sense to hire a local production services company in the local foreign city where you are filming. They are aware of the various regulations for that particular country and can arrange for the proper coverage for all cast and crew.

OTHER SPECIALTY COVERAGE

1. Stunts and hazardous activities need to be discussed, up front, with your insurance company so they can fully understand the nature of the hazard and work with you to control the potential for loss.

2. If animals are a part of your production, you would need to include coverage for any extra expenses the production may incur if the animals cannot perform, causing you to shut down your production. In addition, you may be required to have Animal Mortality insurance

in case the animal dies during the production while in your care, custody, and control.

3. If you need to film on train platforms or in the actual train cars, Railroad Protective liability insurance is required by most municipal public transport operations. This is a separate policy that requires extra time to obtain, and this insurance is usually for the benefit of the municipal authority and to protect your production and its personnel.

4. Watercraft insurance is required if you rent watercraft to be used in the production. You will need non-owned watercraft liability and hull coverage (for damage to the boat). This is a separate policy, so give yourself enough time to purchase it if necessary.

5. Aircraft insurance is more common than you think. If your production requires aerial photography, you will need to obtain quotes for non-owned aircraft liability insurance. Most times, you can request a Waiver of Subrogation on the aircraft hull (the body of the plane), because trying to obtain coverage for this hull is cost prohibitive. Again, this takes some time to arrange, so plan ahead. Don't just work under the pilot's insurance for your production because it won't protect you if someone is hurt by something that your production did to the aircraft.

6. Weather insurance is very important if you are filming live outdoor events. Unexpected bad weather may cause the event to be cancelled and without this coverage, you will incur costs for the shooting days and will not have any means of reimbursement. The premium is determined by the number of hours you need the protection and by the type of weather you are either insuring against or insuring for. (For example, if you need complete sunshine in Seattle, WA, it will cost more than if you plan to shoot a sunny day in Florida.)

Completion Bond/Guaranty

A **completion bond** is a written agreement that guarantees that a film will be completed on time and on budget. It is for the benefit of the investors but is very often *not* required for low-budget, independent films. If your investors require a completion bond you will need to contact a bond company and go through a rigorous process to get approval. The bond company will want to see the script, the schedule, the budget, résumés of key department heads and cast, and information about the investors and their financial commitments. They will also want to meet/interview the director and the key production team to determine their ability to deliver the film as promised. The fee for a bond (usually about 3%–5% of the total budget) may be a flat fee on a low-budget film.

FORCE MAJEURE AND ACT OF GOD
Force majeure and act of God are legal terms used in most contracts regarding liability. **Force majeure** is a French phrase meaning "superior force" and refers to an extraordinary event beyond anyone's control (e.g., riots, strikes, or war) and may include incidents that are considered an **act of God** such as a tornado, hurricane, earthquake, or flood. When used in a legal document, force majeure is used to describe what kind of extraordinary occurrence would allow a suspension of liability for one or both parties. A specific definition of force majeure is important, especially in insurance policy language. Keep in mind that liability is not suspended if the production company was neglectful or didn't plan a contingency for a bad rainstorm, etc. The criteria for force majeure are quite extreme and narrow.

How Do You Obtain Insurance?

A production insurance program, including all of the insurance discussed above, is usually purchased through an insurance company that specializes in this kind of coverage. Go to *www.ProducerToProducer.com* for more information about insurance companies.

When you are ready to purchase a policy, you need to work with an insurance broker who also specializes in production insurance. She will ask you to fill out a production application. You'll need to decide on how many months you will need coverage (up to a year), what kind of coverage you require, and what deductibles and limits of coverage you need. It's best to ask for a bid for small deductibles and high limits and find out what that will cost—you can always adjust those factors to decrease the premium cost later. The longer the duration of the policy, the cheaper it will cost on a per-month basis. Getting a one-month policy is the least cost-effective option, but if you will only need it for one month, it will be cheaper than an annual policy. If you think you will have more than one project over the course of the coming year, an annual policy may be the best option. You can amortize it across the 12 months. It pays to have the broker **market** (bid out) your insurance to all the insurance companies that she works with so you can get the best deal. Many brokers have an online quote system which allows you to answer questions online and then receive an estimate via email. Some insurance companies also allow you to finance the payments over a longer period of time.

Based upon the information in the production application, you may also be asked for résumés of the principals or key employees, a list of projects that you have worked on in the past and whether or not you have had production insurance before. If you are actually **remarketing** (bidding out for a renewal) your insurance, you will also be asked for a **loss run**, which is a report that your insurance company produces that will show whether or not you have had past claims.

Once the broker has all the information and receives quotes from the various insurance companies, you will receive a formal proposal with all the options so you and the broker can decide which is the best insurance program for you.

How Insurance Brokers Work

Each bid may be different regarding the limits and exemptions, so make sure you read them carefully. Don't just go with the cheapest quote—it needs to be the right coverage and your broker will advise you.

Once you have decided to purchase the policy, the broker will take your full payment for the premium or offer you a financing plan with a monthly payment schedule with an initial down payment. Upon receipt of the payment and written approval from you, the agency will **bind** (make it effective) your policy and issue you the certificates as proof of coverage.

Once the insurance is in place, the broker's job isn't finished. Brokers will answer any questions you have during the process of buying the policy or any questions that arise during the period that you carry the coverage. Brokers will also facilitate any claims that may occur during the policy period. The servicing of your insurance is one factor that distinguishes brokers from one another. When picking an insurance broker I always consider the location of their office (what time zone they are in), how readily they respond to my requests/questions, and how much they truly understand my business. Always ask colleagues for recommendations or contact a local film commission for information about good, reputable production insurance brokers. You can see a short list of brokers at *www.ProducerToProducer.com*.

Certificate Issuance

When renting equipment or a location, you'll need to provide proof of your insurance coverage to the vendor or owner. This will be done by obtaining certificates for vendors with the correct language and emailing them prior to the shoot. Once the vendors or owners receive the certificates, they know they are covered and will allow you to pick up the equipment or enter the location premises.

Your insurance broker will explain the procedure for obtaining certificates. Usually the broker has an online system so you can type in the name and address of the company and any specific insurance language they require (see below) and email the certificate to the vendor and yourself directly.

When you add an entity to your insurance policy as an **Additional Insured,** you are actually offering to protect them in case your employees cause an injury to a third party and that third party decides to sue you and them. That company will want your insurance company to defend them since "you" caused the claim.

When you are adding an entity to your insurance policy as a **Loss Payee**, you are recognizing that you have their property in your care, custody, and control and if you damage it, you will be responsible to them for its replacement.

There are several types of certificates that can be requested:

Evidence Only—this certificate simply shows the coverage you have purchased as proof only.

Equipment Rental Certificate—where the certificate will include your general liability and equipment coverage and it will include the rental company as an Additional Insured and Loss Payee.

Location Certificate—where the certificate will include your general liability and workers' compensation coverage and it will include the owner of the location as an Additional Insured on the general liability policy.

Permit Certificate—can be a very specific form issued to the municipality, or a standard certificate, but with specific wording. In most cases, brokers must issue these certificates even if they have online systems. The certificate will list your general liability policy and sometimes, the auto, workers' compensation, and umbrella coverage, depending upon who is asking, and the municipality will be added as an Additional Insured and Loss Payee.

Auto Certificates—are issued for the rental of cars, vans, honey wagons, prop cars, etc. These companies also want to be listed as Additional Insured and Loss Payee, too.

Insurance Audits

Unlike an audit from the IRS, an insurance audit is a way for the insurance company to obtain the actual exposure during the past period of coverage and change the premium accordingly. Since some of the policies are based on production costs and compensation, and each of these figures will change throughout the 12-month policy period, the audit simply adjusts the premium to reflect the actual exposure. For example, if you estimated $1,000,000 of production costs and you actually had $1,500,000, you will owe more money for the premium for the additional $500,000. Conversely, if you only had $800,000 of production costs at the end of the policy term, then you would receive a return premium for the $200,000 underage.

An insurance audit occurs at the end of your policy's coverage period. The insurance company will have you answer a questionnaire about how much money you spent on cast/crew salaries and production costs throughout the policy period. It's important to keep accurate records of all of your financial transactions so you can answer the questions quickly and accurately.

What to Do When You Have a Claim

Insurance brokers play a key role if you ever have an insurance **claim**. As soon as an accident occurs or something is lost, stolen, or damaged, you will need to notify your insurance broker. She will ask you specific questions and let you know how to proceed. You'll need to fill out a claim report, giving very specific details (e.g., how/where the accident occurred, what piece of equipment [with serial numbers] was stolen or how/what damage was done to a location). You may need to file a police report, substantiate the equipment's value, send in copies of medical reports, take photos, etc., and she will advise you on what is required to submit the claim.

Insurance brokers also determine if the claim equals an amount that is higher than your deductible. If the cost of replacement is less than your policy's deductible, then you don't have a claim to report, since this portion is your responsibility. But if the costs exceed the deductible amount, it will probably be worthwhile. One caveat—once you put in a claim on a policy, it will be noted the next time you go to renew your policy.

Insurance carriers may determine that your company is a higher risk and your premium may be more expensive next time because of the former claim. Keep that in mind when you are deciding what to do but always discuss all the options with your broker.

Things You Should Know

1. You can't "sell" or "rent" your insurance policy to anyone else. The coverage afforded under the policy was issued to you and your company only. Coverage will not respond to a claim if you try to allow another production company to "use your insurance."

2. You can't cover your equipment rental business (something you just started to do because producing was slow) using your production policy. A production policy is not going to cover the operations of a rental facility—you must call your broker to obtain additional or different coverage.

3. You can't change a certificate of insurance, once it is issued, to reflect higher limits, or coverage that you forgot to buy. Since this evidence of insurance is on record with the broker, if a claim occurs the parties will realize the certificate was illegally modified.

4. You can't buy coverage today and then put in a claim for something that already happened. A known loss is not going to be covered unless the loss occurs after the insurance period goes into effect.

5. Your homeowner's or renter's coverage won't cover your business.

6. There is no insurance to cover investors if the completed film does not do well in theaters or during distribution.

7. Production Insurance policies don't cover the personal effects (e.g., jewelry, jackets, laptops) of your employees.

Never Go into Production Without Insurance

It is vitally important that you obtain the proper insurance coverage for every production, every time. If you don't have insurance, it will be virtually impossible to rent equipment, props, or a location for your production. But even if you don't have those immediate considerations, there are greater liability issues that you need to cover through insurance. You never want to take the chance that someone gets hurt or a very expensive piece of equipment gets broken and your future personal financial health is affected by a lawsuit or your credit ruined by a collection agency. It's only a film and nothing is ever worth the risk. It's important to sleep well at night and protect yourself and everyone you work with.

RECAP

1. **Do not go into production without the proper insurance coverage.**

2. **Obtain insurance many weeks before you plan to shoot so you can discuss your production needs with your insurance broker.**

3. **The insurance broker will bid out to insurance companies for your needs and make recommendations about what coverage to purchase.**

4. **Commercial General Liability, Workers' Compensation, Disability, Auto, Production, Umbrella, E&O, Union Travel Accident, Foreign Package, and Specialty Insurance are all options for your production needs.**

5. **Certificates are usually issued online when you send the correct information for each certificate holder request.**

6. **When the insurance policy expires you will send in total gross production costs to the insurance company to comply with the audit.**

7. **Your insurance broker will assist you if you ever have a claim.**

CHAPTER 11
SCHEDULING

Overview

SCHEDULING IS ONE OF the most critical steps in the pre-production process. It's the road map for the project. Once you have a solid working draft of the shooting schedule, the various departments can start to plan when they need to do certain work or acquire equipment or props for certain days. The schedule will also dictate which actors work on which days, and that affects the schedule for the costume, hair, and makeup departments.

Scheduling is a paradox—a fixed set of plans and assumptions that the entire production works with, but a schedule has to be flexible to deal with changes and adjustments in real time. For instance, you plan on shooting a day of exterior scenes in the local park, but if 24 hours before the call time the weather forecast calls for torrential rain, you will have to switch to the cover set and the production will have to film inside all day. All departments must be alerted to the change so they can prep the new scenes in the revised schedule.

The production's shooting schedule is usually created by the film's assistant director (AD). On very

> "No matter. Try again. Fail again. Fail better."
>
> —Samuel Becket,
>
> Worstward Ho

low-budget projects you may not be able to afford to hire an AD or they may come onto the project very late with little prep time. In that case, the producer or production manager usually creates the first pass of the shooting schedule. That's what we did on *Man on Wire*—I created the first draft of the schedule so we could get a general idea of how to plan for the film. Then, a week before we started production, 1st AD Curtis Smith and 2nd AD Eric Berkal came on board and finalized the schedule. Thankfully, my original plan was close to what Curtis created, so we were able to move forward quickly. For the purposes of this chapter, we will assume the AD is on board to prep the project.

Script Breakdown

In Chapter 2 we discussed the script breakdown. If you created an initial script breakdown, now several weeks before commencement of principal photography the AD will do the final breakdown. The script should be locked at this point—any additional changes will only be dialogue/word changes and nothing that affects locations, props, wardrobe, lighting, and hair/makeup.

To create a script breakdown, the AD can use computer software programs or do it with custom-made forms. There are many film scheduling computer software programs on the market. One of the most common scheduling programs—Movie Magic Scheduling— will be used now for the case study film, *Sundae*. Easy to learn, it allows the AD to create a script breakdown, shooting schedule, and all of the other forms required.

Element Sheet Creation

With a computer software program, each scene will have a separate breakdown elements sheet. The AD enters all of the elements from each scene in the script into the elements sheet. The elements include: cast; background actors (extras); vehicles; stunts; SFX; props; wardrobe; hair/makeup; animals; locations; and set.

Following is the set of element sheets for the case study film *Sundae*. The short film has 13 scenes and there are 13 sheets, one for each scene. All of the element sheets and stripboards utilize Movie Magic Scheduling software.* Take a look at the documents, then we will discuss them.

---

* Screen shot created using Movie Magic Scheduling software owned by Entertainment Partners. For more information, go to *https://www.ep.com/home/managing-production/movie-magic-scheduling/*

Scene # 1		Date: _____
		Bkdown Page # 1
Script Page _____	Breakdown Sheet	INT
Page Count 2		DAY

Scene Description: Mary drives Tim around a neighborhood asking for directions.
Setting: Car
Location: Suburban Car
Sequence: _____ Script Day: _____

Cast Members	Extras	Props
1. Mary 2. Tim	2 Young Kids Middle-aged man	Garbage Can
		Vehicles Suburban Car
	Costumes Down Jacket	

SCHEDULING

Scene # 2

Script Page
Page Count 2/8

Breakdown Sheet

Date:
Bkdown Page # 2
EXT
DAY

Scene Description: Car pulls to the curb and Mary takes off glasses.
Setting: Car Curbside at Yellow House
Location: Yellow House Curb
Sequence: _____ Script Day: _____

Cast Members 1. Mary 2. Tim		**Props** Eyeglasses
		Vehicles Suburban Car

Scene # 3

Script Page

Page Count 2/8

Breakdown Sheet

Date: _____
Bkdown Page # 3
EXT
DAY

Scene Description: Mary rings bell and fights with Woman at door.
Setting: Yellow House/Lawn
Location: Yellow House
Sequence: _____ Script Day: 1

Cast Members 1. Mary 2. Tim 3. Woman		
		Vehicles Suburban Car
Set Dressing Doorbell		

SCHEDULING

Scene # 4
Script Page
Page Count 1/8

Breakdown Sheet

Date: _____
Bkdown Page # 4
EXT
DAY

Scene Description: Tim plays distractedly with car lock button.
Setting: Car Curbside at Yellow House
Location: Yellow House Curb
Sequence: _____ Script Day: 1

Cast Members 2. Tim		
		Vehicles Suburban Car

Scene # 5		Date: _____
		Bkdown Page # 5
Script Page _____	Breakdown Sheet	EXT
Page Count 3/8		DAY

Scene Description: Woman stumbles into house. Mary gets cement block from car, marches back & throws it.
Setting: Yellow House/Lawn
Location: Yellow House
Sequence: _____ Script Day: 1

Cast Members		
1. Mary 3. Woman		
		Vehicles Suburban Car
Special Effects Prop Cement Block		

SCHEDULING

Scene # 6　　　　　　　　　　　　　　　　　　　　　　　　Date: _____
　　　　　　　　　　　　　　　　　　　　　　　　　　　　　Bkdown Page # 6
_____
Script Page _____　　　　　　　　　　　　　　　　　　　　　EXT
Page Count 2/8　　　　　　　Breakdown Sheet　　　　　　　　　DAY

Scene Description: Tim watches Mary get into car and sit in front seat. Mary laughs and puts glasses back on.
Setting: Car Curbside at Yellow House
Location: Yellow House Curb
Sequence: _____ Script Day: 1

Cast Members 1. Mary 2. Tim		**Props** 　Eyeglasses 　Ignition Key
		Vehicles 　Suburban Car

Scene # 7		Date:
		Bkdown Page # **14**
Script Page _____	Breakdown Sheet	EXT
Page Count 1/8		DAY

Scene Description: Car zooms off.
Setting: Neighborhood Street
Location: Neighborhood Street
Sequence: _____ Script Day: 1

Cast Members 1. Mary 2. Tim		
		Vehicles Suburban Car

SCHEDULING

Scene # 8

Script Page _____
Page Count 1/8

Breakdown Sheet

Date: _____
Bkdown Page # 8

INT
DAY

Scene Description: _Teenage Employee builds huge sundae._
Setting: _Ice Cream Parlor Counter_
Location: _Ice Cream Parlor_
Sequence: _____   Script Day: _1_

Cast Members		Props
4. Teenage Employee		Cherry
		Hot Fudge
		Ice cream Sundae
		Sprinkles
		Whipped Cream

Scene # 9   Date: _____
                                                              Bkdown Page # 9
Script Page _____   INT
                              Breakdown Sheet
Page Count 2/8   DAY

Scene Description: Mary fixes hair, relaxes and smiles at Tim.
Setting: Ice Cream Parlor Table
Location: Ice Cream Parlor
Sequence: _____   Script Day: 1

Cast Members		Props
1. Mary 2. Tim		Ice cream Sundae Small Compact Wet Napkin
Set Dressing Ice Cream Parlor Table		

Scene # 10
Script Page _____
Page Count 2/8

Breakdown Sheet

Date: _____
Bkdown Page # 10
INT
DAY

Scene Description: Tim eats sundae rapidly while Mary sees something out the parlor window on the street.
Setting: Ice Cream Parlor Table
Location: Ice Cream Parlor
Sequence: _____   Script Day: 1

Cast Members		Props
1. Mary 2. Tim		Big Spoon Ice cream Sundae
Set Dressing Ice Cream Parlor Table		

Scene # 11		Date:
		Bkdown Page # 11
Script Page	Breakdown Sheet	EXT
Page Count 3/8		DAY

Scene Description: Man and Blonde Woman walk hand-in-hand, get into Town Car and drive away.
Setting: Street Corner
Location: Street corner
Sequence: _____ Script Day: 1

Cast Members	Extras	
5. Blonde Woman 6. Man	5 People walking down street Town Car Driver	
		Vehicles Lincoln Town Car

SCHEDULING

Scene # 12

Script Page _____
Page Count 1/8

Breakdown Sheet

Date: _____
Bkdown Page # 12
INT
DAY

Scene Description: Mary is frozen while Tim eats sundae.
Setting: Ice Cream Parlor Table
Location: Ice Cream Parlor
Sequence: _____ Script Day: 1

Cast Members		Props
1. Mary		Big Spoon
2. Tim		Ice cream Sundae

Set Dressing		
Ice Cream Parlor Table		

Scene # 13

Script Page

Page Count 4/8

Date:

Bkdown Page # 13

INT

DAY

Breakdown Sheet

Scene Description: Mary asks Tim about Yellow House and he swallows a big gulp.

Setting: Ice Cream Parlor Table

Location: Ice Cream Parlor

Sequence: _____ Script Day: 1

Cast Members 1. Mary 2. Tim		**Props** Big Spoon Hot Fudge Ice cream Sundae Sprinkles Whipped Cream
	Costumes Tim's soiled shirt	
Set Dressing Ice Cream Parlor Table		

Now it's time to create the first pass of a production schedule utilizing specific scheduling principles to organize the scenes in the most cost-effective and rational way.

Scheduling Principles

Let's review the general strategies for film scheduling first. Many of these were discussed in Chapter 2 (*Script Breakdown*).

1. Generally, low-budget projects shoot 3-5 script pages per day with 12-hour days. The elements sheet includes the script page length information so the calculation can be made later on when scheduling.

2. In case of inclement weather, schedule exterior shoots early in the production schedule. This allows you to change the schedule and switch to a **cover set**—an interior location that is not affected by bad weather.

3. Schedule DAY scenes first and switch to NIGHT scenes later in the schedule. This way, if you need to move into night shooting, you'll wrap your final DAY shoot in the evening and then everyone will have that night and the entire next day off before having to arrive on set that evening for the first NIGHT shoot.

4. If at all possible, don't schedule a love scene or a very difficult scene for the first day of shooting. Put it later in the schedule when the cast and crew have gotten to know each other and are working well together before you tackle the more challenging scenes.

5. If possible, avoid shooting the opening scenes of the script on the first few days. The beginning of a film is the most critical section of a film—viewing audiences are trying to decide how they feel about your project. In order to have a strong start to your completed film it's best to shoot the opening scenes of a film later in the schedule. That way everyone is working well together, the actors are comfortable with their character work and the look of the film is established and consistent.

6. Don't shoot the last few scenes of the script on the first day, either. The ending is the next most important section of a film and all the issues above apply as well. Additionally, over the course of filming the screenwriter and director may make changes to final scenes of the script so it's best to shoot them later in the schedule.

7. Try to make the first day of shooting a relatively easy day, so you have a better chance of it going well. You want to keep up cast/crew morale and establish a sense of competency and momentum.

8. If possible, shoot out individual actors in as few days as possible. **Shooting out an actor** means that you group all their specific scenes together in the schedule which will save them time and save you money. If an actor only works in four scenes total, try to schedule them to be shot in one or two days so they don't need to be hired again.

9. When using elderly actors, or actors with limits to their stamina, try to keep their shoot days shorter.

10. When shooting with children, consult the labor laws for minors (children under 18 years old) in the U.S. state you are shooting in. Depending on the regulations, the children's ages will limit the amount of hours per day they can film on set. There may also be limits on which hours of the day they can work (perhaps no night shooting) and there may be a requirement for an on-set tutor for school study purposes during the academic year. Go to *www.ProducerToProducer.com* for more information.

11. When shooting any special effects (SFX), weapons, pyrotechnics, or choreography (fight or dance), consult with the SFX coordinator, weapons specialist, pyrotechnics person or choreographer to find out if they have any special needs that will impact the schedule.

12. The same goes for any scene that requires an animal. Consult the animal trainer or handler to find out what to expect and how it may impact the schedule.

13. In general, when scheduling the shooting order of specific shots for any scene, schedule the wide shot first, then medium shots, then close-ups. It helps with continuity.

14. Very rarely will you shoot a script in chronological order. Although it may be helpful or comforting to the director and/or actors to do so, it is almost never the most efficient or cost-effective way to shoot a project. Experienced film actors and crew expect this and know how to achieve continuity in their performances and across all the departments. Keep continuity with the assistance of a good script supervisor.

15. Keep company moves to a minimum because they reduce the amount of actual filming time in the schedule. A **company move** is when you have to pack up everything—cast, crew, equipment, props, etc., and move to another separate location. This is not the same as when you move from shooting in the bedroom to the living room in the same house location.

16. Remember to factor in any location specifics when creating the stripboard schedule, e.g., if you can't shoot on weekends or a certain location is only available during specific times.

Once you and the AD understand these scheduling principles, the AD can get started making the first pass at the schedule. Break out all the scenes at one location on the same day. If there are too many for one day, then put them on multiple days.

Once the AD has laid out a solid first draft of the schedule, they will send it first to the director, and then to the department heads, for comments and change requests. The AD will gather all the notes, adjust the schedule and issue the next—and improved—version of the shooting schedule.

This process is informed by the discussions the AD has with the director and department heads. After gathering all the specific details, they can adjust the schedule to accommodate each department's requirements. Here are some examples:

For the director and the DP—How many shots and setups are estimated for each scene. Will there be a need to set up a dolly or crane? Will a Steadicam be used? Any important (and time-consuming) setups for certain locations? Will windows need to be gelled? Any big lighting setups?

For the art department—Do they need to construct a set ahead of time for a specific scene? Do they have to get to a location the day before to set dress it?

For the hair/makeup department—How much time do they need at the beginning of each day to work on the actors? Is there specific SFX makeup that takes longer to apply? Does an actor need a haircut or makeup test before filming begins?

For the costume department—Are there particular costume issues that require extra time or prep? Will certain costumes only be available later in the shooting schedule so that day needs to be pushed back?

Which actors need to have costume fittings scheduled prior to principal photography?

The AD collates all of this info to finalize a good working shooting schedule.

Scheduling Steps

Creating a schedule is an important creative step for a producer and assistant director. This is where you pre-visualize what the production of the project will look and feel like. The schedule allows the production team to get their "arms around " all aspects of the project and begins a unification process that is vital to producing a great film. Each step in the scheduling process creates documents that the production team and key department heads use to make the film as easily and professionally as possible. Make sure to take these steps so you can lay out a strong and smart plan for the schedule.

After creating the script breakdown, use your software to create a "strip" for each Elements Breakdown sheet with all the pertinent information positioned on the strip. The software will automatically put each strip in the chronological order of the script to create a **stripboard**. The next step is to create the stripboard in *shooting order* based on myriad factors.

We'll go through the steps here and use the short film *Sundae* as the case study to illustrate them. I used the Movie Magic Scheduling software application so you'll see the software's paperwork and how it all fits together.

Here is the *Sundae* stripboard in chronological order:

SCHEDULING

CAST MEMBERS
1. Mary
2. Tim
3. Woman
4. Teenage Employee
5. Blonde Woman
6. Man

#	INT/EXT	Location	Set	Pages	Description
1	INT	Suburban Car	Car	2	Mary drives Tim around a neighborhood asking for directions.
2	EXT	Yellow House Curb	Car Curbside at Yellow House	2/8	Car pulls to the curb and Mary takes off glasses.
3	EXT	Yellow House	Yellow House/Lawn	2/8	Mary rings bell and fights with Woman at door.
4	EXT	Yellow House Curb	Car Curbside at Yellow House	1/8	Tim plays distractedly with car lock button.
5	EXT	Yellow House	Yellow House/Lawn	3/8	Woman stumbles into house. Mary gest cement block from car, marches back & throws at window.
6	EXT	Yellow House Curb	Car Curbside at Yellow House	2/8	Tim watches Mary get into car and sit in front seat. Mary laughs and puts glasses back on.
7	EXT	Neighborhood Street	Neighborhood Street	1/8	Car zooms off.
8	INT	Ice Cream Parlor	Ice Cream Parlor Counter	1/8	Teenage Employee builds huge sundae.
9	INT	Ice Cream Parlor	Ice Cream Parlor Table	2/8	Mary fixes hair, relaxes and smiles at Tim.
10	INT	Ice Cream Parlor	Ice Cream Parlor Table	2/8	Tim eats sundae rapidly while Mary sees something out the parlor window on the street.
11	EXT	Street corner	Street Corner	3/8	Man and Blonde Woman walk hand-in-hand, get into Town Car and drive away.
12	INT	Ice Cream Parlor	Ice Cream Parlor Table	1/8	Mary is frozen while Tim eats sundae.
13	INT	Ice Cream Parlor	Ice Cream Parlor Table	4/8	Mary asks Tim about Yellow House and he swallows a big gulp.

End Day # 1 Thursday, January 22, 2015 -- Total Pages: 5
End Day # 2 Friday, January 23, 2015 -- Total Pages:

Sundae Shooting Schedule Analysis

Before you create the shooting stripboard/schedule, analyze the elements sheets and production factors utilizing the scheduling principles discussed above. Here's an analysis of *Sundae*'s shooting schedule:

1. *Sundae* was technically a low-budget student film but the filmmakers put together a fully professional cast and crew. Everyone was donating his or her time and they wanted to keep the schedule tight, but doable.

2. The majority of the scenes were exterior or interior/exterior so weather factored into all scheduling decisions. It was filmed in Brooklyn, NY, in the winter, so snow or rain were possible and could have a big impact. The filmmakers decided to shoot rain or shine unless there was a snow blizzard and then they would postpone the entire shoot until the following weekend.

3. There were no night scenes but the days were short because of the winter light in the eastern United States. The AD checked for the sunrise and sunset times to maximize their use of whatever daylight was available.

4. The minor actor was 7 years old so the New York state child performer labor laws allow him to be on set for up to 8 hours a day, but he could only work for a total of 4 hours (out of the 8 hours) per day. A parent or guardian had to be with him on set the entire time. The AD knew that the shots with the minor actor might need a bit more time.

5. The first day of shooting was a doable day—most of the scenes were shot in the order of the script which is unusual. Day 2 had a few more emotional "beats" for the actors so that was helpful for the actors to ease into their roles.

6. The two lead actors played on both days. Any other actors or extras worked either Day 1 or Day 2 only.

7. For the fight choreography at the Yellow House, more time was given to rehearse and frame the shots so the actors could do the "punching and fighting" safely. For the stunt of throwing the cement block through the window, they scheduled more time so the actor could "fake it" while throwing a Styrofoam prop cement block properly. Camera framing was also critical for the stunt. The director knew this moment in the film was a key comedic beat and wanted enough time to get it right.

8. Prepping the Day 1 picture vehicle would require some time for pre-rigging the car mount for the camera.

Shooting Stripboard Creation

Once the analysis is complete, the shooting stripboard schedule can be created. This is one of my favorite steps in the filmmaking process. As an example, here's the shooting stripboard for *Sundae*:

CAST MEMBERS
1. Mary
2. Tim
3. Woman
4. Teenage Employee
5. Blonde Woman
6. Man

#	INT/EXT	Location	Set	Pages	Description
2	EXT	Yellow House Curb	Car Curbside at Yellow House	2/8	Car pulls to the curb and Mary takes off glasses.
4	EXT	Yellow House Curb	Car Curbside at Yellow House	1/8	Tim plays distractedly with car lock button.
6	EXT	Yellow House Curb	Car Curbside at Yellow House	2/8	Tim watches Mary get into car and sit in front seat. Mary laughs and puts glasses back on.
3	EXT	Yellow House	Yellow House/Lawn	2/8	Mary rings bell and fights with Woman at door.
5	EXT	Yellow House	Yellow House/Lawn	3/8	Woman stumbles into house. Mary gest cement block from car, marches back & throws it.
1	INT	Suburban Car	Car	2	Mary drives Tim around a neighborhood asking for directions.
7	EXT	Neighborhood Street	Neighborhood Street	1/8	Car zooms off.

End Day # 1 Thursday, January 22, 2015 -- Total Pages: 3 3/8

#	INT/EXT	Location	Set	Pages	Description
8	INT	Ice Cream Parlor	Ice Cream Parlor Counter	1/8	Teenage Employee builds huge sundae.
9	INT	Ice Cream Parlor	Ice Cream Parlor Table	2/8	Mary fixes hair, relaxes and smiles at Tim.
12	INT	Ice Cream Parlor	Ice Cream Parlor Table	1/8	Mary is frozen while Tim eats sundae.
11	EXT	Street corner	Street Corner	3/8	Man and Blonde Woman walk hand-in-hand, get into Town Car and drive away.
10	INT	Ice Cream Parlor	Ice Cream Parlor Table	2/8	Tim eats sundae rapidly while Mary sees something out the parlor window on the street.
13	INT	Ice Cream Parlor	Ice Cream Parlor Table	4/8	Mary asks Tim about Yellow House and he swallows a big gulp.

End Day # 2 Friday, January 23, 2015 -- Total Pages: 1 5/8

Day-Out-of-Days Schedule

Once the shooting schedule stripboard is created, the next step is to create the Day-Out-of-Days schedules to track the various production elements. This allows each department to plan its elements on a day-by-day basis. These are the elements: cast, background actors (extras), vehicles, props, wardrobe, hair/makeup, animals, locations, and set.

Each Day-Out-of-Days schedule focuses on one element only and tracks it for each shooting day of the production schedule. It comes in the form of a very stripped down calendar with a "shorthand" for when each element "starts and stops work" on the film. Each element or cast member is listed in the left-hand column. The rest of the columns refer to the shoot dates and work schedule.

SW—Start Work: The first day that the element or character works on the project

W—Work: Each day that the element or character works on the project

WF—Work Finish: The last day that the element or character works on the project

SWF—Start Work Finish: The first and last day that the element or character works on the project

Travel: The total number of travel days for the character

Work: The total number of work days for the element or character

Holiday: The total number of holidays for the character

Start: The date when the element or character begins work on the project

Finish: The date when the element or character finishes work on the project

Total—The total number of travel, work, and holidays the element or character has in the project's work schedule

Below are the DOOD schedules for the departments for *Sundae:*

Dec 8, 2016
11:24 AM   **Day Out of Days Report for Cast Members**

Month/Day	01/22	01/23	Co.						
Day of Week	Thu	Fri	Travel	Work	Hold	Holiday	Start	Finish	TOTAL
Shooting Day	1	2							
1. Mary	SW	WF		2			01/22	01/23	2
2. Tim	SW	WF		2			01/22	01/23	2
3. Woman	SWF			1			01/22	01/22	1
4. Blonde Woman		SWF		1			01/23	01/23	1
5. Man		SWF		1			01/23	01/23	1
Teenage Employee		SWF		1			01/23	01/23	1

Dec 8, 2016
11:25 AM   **Day Out of Days Report for Extras**

Month/Day	01/22	01/23	Co.						
Day of Week	Thu	Fri	Travel	Work	Hold	Holiday	Start	Finish	TOTAL
Shooting Day	1	2							
2 Young Kids	SWF			1			01/22	01/22	1
5 People walking down street		SWF		1			01/23	01/23	1
Middle-aged man	SWF			1			01/22	01/22	1
Town Car Driver		SWF		1			01/23	01/23	1

Dec 8, 2016
11:26 AM   **Day Out of Days Report for Vehicles**

Month/Day	01/22	01/23	Co.						
Day of Week	Thu	Fri	Travel	Work	Hold	Holiday	Start	Finish	TOTAL
Shooting Day	1	2							
Lincoln Town Car		SWF		1			01/23	01/23	1
Suburban Car	SWF			1			01/22	01/22	1

Dec 8, 2016
11:26 AM
Day Out of Days Report for Props

Page 1 of

Month/Day	01/22	01/23	Co.						
Day of Week	Thu	Fri	Travel	Work	Hold	Holiday	Start	Finish	TOTAL
Shooting Day	1	2							
Big Spoon		SWF		1			01/23	01/23	1
Cherry		SWF		1			01/23	01/23	1
Eyeglasses	SWF			1			01/22	01/22	1
Garbage Can	SWF			1			01/22	01/22	1
Hot Fudge		SWF		1			01/23	01/23	1
Ice cream Sundae		SWF		1			01/23	01/23	1
Ignition Key	SWF			1			01/22	01/22	1
Small Compact		SWF		1			01/23	01/23	1
Sprinkles		SWF		1			01/23	01/23	1
Wet Napkin		SWF		1			01/23	01/23	1
Whipped Cream		SWF		1			01/23	01/23	1

Dec 8, 2016
11:28 AM
Day Out of Days Report for Set Dressing

Page 1 of 1

Month/Day	01/22	01/23	Co.						
Day of Week	Thu	Fri	Travel	Work	Hold	Holiday	Start	Finish	TOTAL
Shooting Day	1	2							
Doorbell	SWF			1			01/22	01/22	1
Ice Cream Parlor Table		SWF		1			01/23	01/23	1

Dec 8, 2016
11:27 AM
Day Out of Days Report for Costumes

Page 1 of 1

Month/Day	01/22	01/23	Co.						
Day of Week	Thu	Fri	Travel	Work	Hold	Holiday	Start	Finish	TOTAL
Shooting Day	1	2							
Down Jacket	SWF			1			01/22	01/22	1
Tim's soiled shirt		SWF		1			01/23	01/23	1

Dec 8, 2016
11:27 AM
Day Out of Days Report for Special Effects

Page 1 of 1

Month/Day	01/22	01/23	Co.						
Day of Week	Thu	Fri	Travel	Work	Hold	Holiday	Start	Finish	TOTAL
Shooting Day	1	2							
Prop Cement Block	SWF			1			01/22	01/22	1

As you can see, all of this information is distilled from the initial elements sheets that were created for each scene. Inputting all the elements accurately is vital so the Assistant Director and key department heads can track each one, day by day and department by department. If done correctly, there shouldn't ever be a missing prop or a wrong vehicle for a particular setup on a specific shoot day.

Scheduling each shoot day—how do you know how long something will take to shoot?

Scheduling for a film is an art, not a science. Those who do it well have a unique combination of traits—an understanding of the big picture, the day-to-day arc of a production and the specific minutia that factor into the ever-evolving state of a film schedule.

To schedule a shoot day, there are many, many factors: the size of the crew, the number of company moves, the location or studio set-up time, how fast the crew can load in and set up, how fast the cast can get in and out of hair and makeup and wardrobe, and any other technical issues that could impact the schedule, e.g., setting up a crane or dolly shot.

When working on a low-budget shoot on location, I usually schedule two hours from the call time at the location before I expect to get the first shot off of the day. I put that on the schedule and know that it could be two and a half hours before we get the first shot. But that is a good rule of thumb. Then, depending on the shot list and the amount of setups, the AD schedules the rest of the day.

Feeding your crew every 6 hours and other union regulations that affect the day's schedule

There are several rules that are part of a union contract that directly impact how to create the day's schedule. For low-budget productions, it is often a combination of a non-union crew and a union cast. Some productions may work with a few unions but not all of them—maybe a union camera and grip/electric departments, but everyone else is non-union. If you are working under any union contract, you and the Assistant Director need to know the rules for meals and meal penalties, travel time, overtime, and the studio zone. Consult the union contract for the regulations. Here are many of the possible contract rules you'll need to understand:

Meal time—The first rule is to **feed the crew a hot meal every 6 hours.** If your call time is 7:00 a.m., then you have to break for lunch no later than 1:00 p.m. The lunch break has to be at least 30 minutes long and the "clock starts ticking" after all cast and crew have received their food. If you have a lunch line for a buffet meal, wait until each person has gotten a plate of food before the 30-minute countdown begins. Once the crew is back up and working, the clock resets and you have to provide another hot meal 6 hours later. This rule must be followed whether you are working with union or non-union crews—it is a matter of decency to feed the crew every six hours.

Meal penalty—**Meal penalties** are levied under a union contract when you don't feed the crew every six hours. The charge is usually added onto the hourly rate at 15-minute intervals (although this can vary with each union contract). So if you go past the lunch period by a half hour, you'll need to pay two times the meal penalty as stipulated in the contract for each union member.

Turnaround time—**Turnaround time** is the amount of time from the end of work on one shoot day to the call time for the next consecutive shoot day. It needs to be 12 hours for actors working under a union contract. For non-union cast and crew it should be at least 10 hours to make sure the cast/crew is working under safe conditions. Anything less than 10 hours is a very unsafe and untenable situation.

Overtime—Cast and crew are paid an hourly rate based on either an 8-hour, 10-hour, or 12-hour day. For SAG-AFTRA actors their rates are always based on an 8-hour day. Union contracts for crew are usually for a 10-hour day. Sometimes you can negotiate a rate based on 12 hours. The meal period is often "off the clock" so it's a "free" half hour. After the cast/crew work the entire day-rate period, an hourly overtime rate is calculated at 1.5 × for usually 2 or 4 hours, after which it goes up to 2 × the rate.

Studio Zone—This refers to the area around a major city that is considered "in the studio zone." So if the production location is inside the studio zone, the cast and crew are not paid for their travel time to the set/location. If you shoot outside of the studio zone, the cast and crew will be paid for the travel time between home (or a pickup location) and the set.

Travel time—Travel time refers to the time from when they leave home and get to the set and the same thing at the end of the day when traveling home; it is called "portal to portal." That means that the clock starts ticking from the time that they leave their homes to the time they arrive home—the travel time is "on the clock" and you have to calculate it accordingly. Sometimes you'll need to provide a van to transport cast/crew from a central meeting point and drive them to the location. In that case, the clock starts ticking from the time the van departs from the meeting point until the cast/crew is returned to the meeting point at the end of the day.

Portrait of a 1st Assistant Director

The 1st Assistant Director (1st AD or AD) is a very important and pivotal crew position on any project. Like the director and producer, they set the tone for how the production operates on a week-by-week, day-by-day and hour-by-hour basis. On rare occasions, I've worked with ADs who are tyrants and screamers. I have also worked with ADs who are the most competent humans on the planet. It's a tough position but for those who do it well, it's a revelation to watch them work. The best ADs operate and make decisions based on years of experience, intuition, split-second analysis, and mutual respect for others. They need to be master observers of human nature, be great negotiators (how do you get a diva starlet out of the Winnebago when she's having a tantrum?), have amazing stamina, and be able to move groups of people (sometimes very large ones) from one place to another quickly, efficiently and safely. In addition, they need a deep understanding of the director's film language and the ability to suggest shots or ways of getting a scene "in the can" when the sun is setting and you are losing light at the end of a long shoot day. It's a pretty tall order. But they are out there and when you find them and get to work with them, it's an awesome experience.

> ### *HOW BEST TO WORK WITH AN ASSISTANT DIRECTOR*
>
> ADs are the linchpins of the crew. They report to the producer and the director and it's important to keep the lines of communication clear. You need to keep them up to date on any schedule changes from the production side and they need to be reacting to the needs of the director at the same time. This can be a delicate balancing act. As producer, you want to get the director's vision on screen but you also want to stay on schedule and on budget. A good AD can help accomplish both.
>
> When we are shooting, I usually only communicate with the director through the AD. I don't want to distract the director and keeping all the communication through the AD allows the director to focus on their job properly. The AD is most intimately aware of what is happening on a minute-by-minute basis and can deliver the message at the right time to the director.
>
> Often I will only speak to the director at lunch. We'll spend some time doing a reality check about the day's schedule and discuss any other pressing matters. If we are behind schedule, lunchtime is when the director, AD, and producer can strategize and decide how best to get back on track. This may be the time to discuss dropping some shots or setups to make up time. It needs to be a gentle negotiation because no director wants to lose anything from the day's shot list. But you do need to walk away from the lunch table with a plan that everyone can live with. If you don't, the afternoon will devolve and the production will fall further behind and over budget.
>
> Consensus is key in the lunchtime discussion. As producer you will need to share your thoughts on how best to proceed for the rest of the day, but remember that it needs to be a conversation. The AD can be invaluable by helping to problem solve the situation.

Locking the Schedule

Locking the schedule at least a week before you start principal photography is essential so each department and all cast/crew know when/what to prepare for each scene. If you keep changing things around, it undermines the cast/crew's ability to fully prepare for each shoot day and will negatively impact everyone's ability to do the best job possible.

RECAP

1. Hire an AD several weeks before you begin principal photography to put together the final script breakdown and schedule.

2. Follow the scheduling principles outlined earlier when determining what is the best schedule for your project.

3. After all elements are entered into the elements sheets, you'll have a stripboard in script order. The next step is to move the strips around to create the schedule in shooting order.

4. Create day-out-of-days schedules for all production elements and departments.

5. Follow all union contract rules for overtime, meal penalties, and turnaround times.

6. Work in sync with the AD to maximize the efficiency of the production department.

CHAPTER 12
PRODUCTION

Now that you have completed all the tasks and steps discussed in Chapter 6, *Pre-Production*, you are now ready for the first day of principal photography. This is the moment you have been working toward for weeks/months. It is a great feeling finally to be *making* the project, instead of just *talking about* making the project. I've never gotten over the feeling of excitement and teamwork that occurs during this phase—it's a fascinating and fulfilling process. Finally, now is the time to take a leap into the deep end of the pool.

The Night Before Your First Day of Principal Photography

1. VISUALIZE THE DAY TO COME

As I mentioned in the *Pre-Production* chapter, pre-visualization is a key tool for me and I recommend it. Sit down and visualize the entire day to come, from the moment you awake until you go home, exhausted, after the shoot. No detail is too small to see in your mind's eye. I do this for every production I've been involved with, and it is

> *Caretake this moment. Immerse yourself in its particulars. Respond to this person, this challenge, this deed. Quit the evasions. Stop giving yourself needless trouble. It is time to really live; to fully inhabit the situation you happen to be in now.*
>
> —*Epictetus*

an absolutely indispensable tool. Though this might sound new age-y, I can't tell you how many times it has saved me, allowing me to catch an oversight the day before that would have adversely affected the next day's shoot.

I begin at the beginning: visualizing myself hearing the alarm clock, turning it off and getting up to take a shower. I figure out what I am going to wear, see myself having breakfast and packing up my computer, etc. Then I hear the doorbell ring as the PA arrives to pick me up and drive to set. We have a call time that falls within the rush hour, so I have researched where construction hot spots will be that morning—we avoid them and sail through to the location.

I visualize arriving on set at the same time as the AD and the craft service call. I make sure that we have the home phone and cell phone numbers for the stage manager of the studio (just in case she is a little late). The craft service person is setting up the coffee, and the AD and I have time to go over a few last-minute scheduling questions. Now it's time for the crew to arrive—in my mind, that is. Here we go—off to the races!

You get the idea. I do this for every moment of the day ... literally. While visualizing, I often "see" things that may become problems or that have been forgotten. Oops, I forgot to call the driver for the actor to let him know to pick up 15 minutes sooner. Or, we didn't tell the location manager that we have added another van to the production vehicle list. Or the production manager needs to remind the costume designer that we have switched to the blue dress for the lead actress to wear for the first scene. Since it is still the day before, I have time to address those issues. Once I have "seen" the entire day to come, I can relax. In my mind's eye, I have already done it all—tomorrow I will be doing it for the "second" time. And everything's easier the second time around!

2. CONFIRM ALL CALL TIMES AND PICK-UPS

No later than 6:00 p.m. the night before the shoot day, make sure that you check in with the person who has given out all the cast and crew call times (usually the AD or production manager) and confirm that they have heard back from everyone. If there are any outstanding confirmations, make sure this person calls/texts/emails again until they receive confirmation from every cast and crew person. For the drivers, remind them whom or what they will be picking up in the morning.

3. GO TO BED EARLY—AND MAKE SURE THE DIRECTOR DOES TOO
This is so important. Make sure you have taken care of everything ahead of time so you can get some good sleep the night before shooting begins. If you can, make sure the director gets enough sleep, as well. You'll both be running on adrenaline, but that will only get you so far. Film production is a marathon, not a sprint, so you need to pace yourself accordingly.

4. SET TWO SEPARATE, NON-ELECTRIC ALARMS
I can't tell you how many people have overslept for call times. Either the electrical power goes out overnight and their alarm clocks don't go off or they rely on wake-up calls from the front desk of a hotel and they never happen.

I strongly advise setting two separate wakeup alarms on two separate, non-electric devices. I use my cell phone and a cheap, battery-powered clock (they cost as little as $10). Set one for five minutes after the other, in case you fall back to sleep. Never rely on a wake-up call from the front desk of a hotel. The hotel's night staff can be unreliable and you shouldn't put your shoot day's fate in their hands. Many a time have I stood in a hotel lobby waiting for a crew person to come down for our departure in the van because they overslept. When shooting out of town, I usually travel with an extra alarm clock in case someone forgets to bring one along.

First Day of Principal Photography
The shooting period of a film or video with the main unit of crew and actors is called **principal photography**. Photography without the actors (establishing exterior shots or drive-by shots) is called **second unit photography**. This section will focus on production for principal photography. It's important that everything goes as smoothly as possible on the first day—you want to create momentum and win over the cast and crew.

Producer's To-Do list for the first day:
- *Leave your cell phone on.* From the moment you wake up until you go to sleep, keep your cell phone on so you are available to solve any last-minute issues.
- *Arrive on set ahead of time.* Watch how things start to unfold. Check in with the assistant director to make sure everyone arrives on set on time. The AD, the production staff, and the craft service person should have been on set 30 minutes before everyone else's call time. Having coffee, tea, and bagels set up for when the crew arrives is very important.
- *Pitch in.* It's good for the crew to see you as a hands-on producer—someone who is dedicated to making the production go well. Be sure

that all production personnel are organized and informed so they can support all that is going on with every department.
- *Set the proper tone.* It is crucial at this time to set a tone of mutual respect and support for the entire shoot. You want to instill the values of communication, collaboration, and *fun* from the very beginning. When I visit other producers' sets I can tell within 10 minutes if there's a good vibe or one of fear and resentment. Cast and crew pick up on the cues quickly so if you are respectful, supportive, communicative, and positive, the rest of the production will follow suit. As one of the leaders, be strong and steadfast.
- *Check in with the talent.* Find out if the actors are comfortable and happy, and let them know you are thinking of them and appreciate their contribution.
- *Check in with the director.* Is everything OK? Is she getting what she needs? Does she have the support she requires? Does she need to discuss any creative or logistical issues?
- *Watch the assistant director.* Is the AD keeping things moving? Is the AD communicating well with the cast and crew, and establishing the proper tone, as discussed above?
- *Get the first shot of the day off on time.* Remember in Chapter 11 (*Scheduling*) how we discussed starting with an "easy" setup on the morning of the first day? It's important to get that first shot off as close to the scheduled time as possible so you can build momentum. It is demoralizing to the cast and crew if you get to the lunch break and you haven't shot the first scene yet.
- *Serve a late-morning snack.* It's good to pass around a little snack, late-morning, if you can afford it. It makes people feel taken care of and gives them energy. But don't allow chocolate or candy out on the craft service table until *after* lunch, as the sugar highs and lows wreak havoc on cast/crew energy levels.
- *Keep everyone hydrated.* Make sure the PAs go around and offer water to cast and crew. The director, DP, and AD often don't have time to get more water if they run out. Hydration is a key to a healthy and productive crew.
- *Serve lunch on time* (no more than six hours after the first call time for cast/crew). Serving lunch late violates union rules and demonstrates a lack of caring and/or organization. Poll the crew ahead of time to find out if there are any food allergies or food specifications (like vegetarian or gluten-free).

- Personnel usually go through the food line in a certain order: 1) crew, 2) cast, 3) production staff. The 30-minute lunch period starts when the last person has gone through the line. Usually this works out to be about 40 or 45 minutes from the lunch call until the "back on set" call.
- *Maintain momentum after lunch.* The AD will give the "back on set" call. If you have served good, healthy food, people should be energized rather than sleepy. Getting cast/crew back to work quickly is key so you don't lose momentum.
- *Serve another snack later in the day.* It's great if you can have a little snack served a few hours after the lunch meal. Now is the time to put chocolate/candy out on the craft service table for people who want it. Also, having a fresh pot of coffee available is usually a good idea.
- *Watch out for problems.* Is the art department ready when it needs to be? Is the director consistently waiting on the costume department? Is the key grip able to keep his or her crew working together, or do they seem to be at cross purposes? Do the actors know their lines? Are they getting along with the director? Is the director getting all the planned shots or are we consistently falling behind in the schedule? What's the vibe?
- As the producer you need to be monitoring all of this so you can spot any potential issues that need to be resolved. It's best to keep your "finger on the pulse" so you can anticipate anything before it becomes a bigger issue. I also rely on the production manager to spot concerns ahead of time and I check in, often, throughout the day.
- *Make safety a priority.* Make sure everyone is working safely and properly all the time. You set the tone for the entire production and if everyone understands that safety is the most important concern, they will work accordingly.
- *Determine the next day's schedule.* Ideally the AD will have a first draft of the next day's call sheet (with call times, locations, and scene numbers) ready to discuss at lunch. If you are running behind, the AD may decide to try to add a scene to the next day (if you are on the same set or location) and shuffle the schedule a bit. Discuss and finalize this information together before it is locked at the end of the shoot day and distributed to the cast/crew by the AD department.
- *Call "wrap" on time.* **Wrap** is called by the AD when the last take of the last shot is completed and everyone is assured (usually by the AC) that the take is technically good or "clean." To wrap on time is important for all the reasons stated above. It gives the cast/crew confidence that the production knows how to schedule and produce a

well-planned day and execute it properly. Sometimes this is not possible and you'll have to start making plans for a second meal.

- *Make plans ahead of time if you need a second meal.* Order something that is healthy and hot: pizza is usually not acceptable and the crew will grumble. Discuss with the department heads whether they want a 30-minute sit-down meal or a walking meal. A **walking meal** means that they will all take about 10 minutes to grab some food when it arrives and then keep working. (If it looks like you'll be done with your shooting day within an hour of the meal call, often they will prefer a walking meal.) Note that cast and crew will not be "off the clock" for a walking meal (as they would be for a sit-down meal)—the walking meal will be computed as work time.
- *Stick to a 12-hour day and a 10- to 12-hour turnaround time.* As discussed previously, you do not want to go past a 12-hour day schedule. If you stick to 12-hour days you eliminate the need for a second meal and you can keep to a 10- to 12-hour turnaround time for all cast and crew. As discussed earlier, turnaround time allows the time for cast/crew to get enough sleep and is essential for the safety of your production.

WHO SAYS WHAT AND IN WHAT ORDER ON SET

PHRASE	WHO SAYS IT	WHY
"Quiet on set"	AD	To get everyone quiet and to let them know you are going for a take.
"Roll Sound"	AD	Asking for the Sound Recordist to start recording sound.
"Sound Rolling"	Sound Recordist	To let everyone know sound is recording properly.
"Roll Camera"	AD	Asking the Camera Department to start recording media.
"Camera Speed"	DP, Camera Operator, or AC	To let everyone know that the camera is on and recording properly.
"Background Action"	AD	To have the background action start their action, if required. *Note: if using union actors, only the AD can direct the background actors.*
"Action"	Director	To have everyone start the scene action.
"Cut"	Director	To let everyone know that the take is over.

Note: If the sound is being recorded in camera, there doesn't have to be "Roll Sound/Sound Rolling" cues.

Wrap Checklist

Once you call "Wrap!" there are several steps for the cast/crew to "wrap out the day" properly:

1. All actors need to change back into their street clothes and return their costumes to the wardrobe department. Never allow an actor to leave the set with a costume—they could forget a piece of it the next day, destroying continuity.

2. Leave the location in better shape than when you arrived. Make sure the cast and crew report any damage to the location to you or the production manager so it can be taken care of immediately.

3. Dispose of garbage properly. If you are on location, the location manager will know where to put the garbage. If in a studio, consult the studio manager and follow the proper procedures.

4. Confirm that each department has taken care of the required clean-up chores, like cleaning any necessary wardrobe overnight, finishing touches on a set piece, etc.

5. Confirm that the production manager has prepared the production report for the day. The **daily production report** will state all the wrap times, the amount of film or videotape shot (with roll numbers), and other pertinent information.

6. Make sure the cast/crew complete their post-wrap work and they leave set as soon as it is done. You want them "off the clock" as soon as possible so you avoid overtime.

7. Collect the visual media/shot material (organized by the AC and the DIT), the camera reports (with take numbers and tech notes), the recorded audio material, and the audio reports; create a purchase order (PO) that details how much/what kind of material is being sent to the post production facility. The PO will contain the written instructions on what will be done to the material (e.g., transcoding, dubbing, backing up, archiving, etc.) and when/how it needs to be delivered to the edit room.

8. Send a trusted PA to the post production facility. Remind the PA to go *directly* to the facility without any stop-offs. The material must never be left unattended in a vehicle, not even for a moment. Everyone in the business has heard the horror stories of PAs

stopping to get gas and having the film stolen out of the passenger side of the van.

9. Remember that there needs to be at least two different drives or cloud backups for all the acquired materials and they need to "live" in two separate, safe places. This will safeguard your project. A student of mine shot his film and put the hard drive and the backup hard drive in the home office of his parent's home while he went out of town to shoot another project. While he was away, the family home had a flood and he lost *all* of his material!

10. The script notes from the script supervisor should be sent to the editor, assistant editor, and producer. The editor will use these notes to create the assembly cut, looking for the takes the director has identified as the best.

11. If the director wants to look at **dailies** (the material that was shot a day or two before) each night after the shoot, create a workflow to accommodate the viewing. The director will decide if the DP, other key department heads, and/or actors will watch as well. Often this material is screened on the director's laptop or a computer monitor. If it's for a bigger group, you may need to rent a screening room.

12. Who watches dailies varies with each project. Usually it is the director, producer, and department heads that screen them together. They check to see how things are progressing in general, as well as the look of the film, how the performances are coming across, and so forth. Actors are usually not shown dailies during production. Discuss with the director what they prefer.

13. Get something good to eat. Go to sleep as early as you can. Get up and do it all over again.

Second Day Disasters

Beware of the Second Day Disasters phenomenon. I've been on many productions where everything goes like clockwork on the first day of shooting. Then the second day is an unmitigated disaster. The PA oversleeps and arrives 45 minutes late with the lead actor; the caterer gets lost and misses the lunch meal call time by half an hour; the assistant wardrobe person forgets the handbag that an actor needed in the third setup of the day, and so on.

Why? Because everyone was so busy gearing up for Day 1 they didn't prepare properly for Day 2. Day 1 went well because the adrenaline was pumping and everyone was so focused, but on Day 2 the adrenaline has been spent and people are now feeling how tired they really are. On the second day the crew is making mistakes and letting things fall through the cracks. This is not intentional—everyone wants to do a great job every day. But a film production is a marathon, not a sprint, and everyone has to pace themselves. Make sure to set up the production so it can sustain a high level of efficiency and professionalism from day to day, week after week.

I am often amazed at how well a shoot can go because every day could so easily be a disaster. There are so many little and big things that have to go right every minute of every day. So you need to be mindful and always watching to keep the production on track.

Enemy of the Production

There is another potential problem that you need to be aware of while you are in production. Veteran producer Richard Brick (*Sweet and Lowdown, Hangin' with the Homeboys*) referred to this problem as the Enemy of the Production (EOP) and you need to be on the lookout for him or her on the set. The **EOP** is the person who, for whatever reason, tries to sabotage the production in overt or covert ways.

It can be the person who complains about everything—the food, the pay, the long hours, etc., and starts to infect the work environment with a bad attitude. Or the person who tries to hijack the production by denigrating one of the key positions like the director or producer, undermining their leadership and trying to take control of the cast/crew. Or it can be an actor who battles with the director in front of everyone on set and tries to destroy the director's relationship and trust with the rest of the cast.

If you spot an EOP among your cast or crew, it is best to discuss your concerns about the person with the director before taking action. Once you and the director are on the same page, you need to act swiftly to take care of the problem. It's a two-step process. First, try to have an honest discussion with the EOP. State what you have witnessed and observed about their attitude, behavior, or work style and explain why you have grave concerns about its negative effects on the cast/crew. Then ask the EOP what they are thinking and feeling.

Make sure you really listen to what they are saying. Do they have legitimate complaints or it is coming from a place of malice and discontent that cannot be fixed through discussion and compromise? If you can, try to come to a mutual understanding about moving forward, working together. Then make it clear that you expect them to change their ways and treat the production with respect. If not, you'll need to terminate the person immediately.

Before you have this conversation make sure there is a back-up person for the EOP's crew position in case you have to replace them. It's not something any producer wants to do but the production will be better off without that person on the crew. In addition, it sends an immediate message to the rest of the crew about intolerance for that kind of behavior.

Now the only caveat to this rule is if the person is one of the actors already filmed for your production. Then it becomes a much more complicated issue that may not be resolved by termination but may only be dealt with by discussion and negotiation. It's best to discuss with the director before you contact the individual actor so you are both clear about how best to resolve the dilemma.

Actualized Budget

There are always three versions of a budget as you progress through a production. Your original *estimated* budget was "locked" when you started pre-production and approved by the financiers.

Then you take that budget and create a working budget that reflects the ongoing, changing reality as you move through pre-production and into production. For instance, in the estimated budget you may have originally budgeted $2,000 for the lighting/grip equipment rentals but you were able to get a deal and it only cost $1,750. At first you thought you'd need $3,000 for location fees but you end up spending $3,500 (and so on). Your working budget reflects the day-to-day budget reality.

Then, once invoices start coming in, you create the third and final version of the budget—the *actualized* budget where the actual numbers from the invoices are entered so you have a running tally of exactly what has been spent to date. We'll discuss this further in Chapter 14, *Wrap*.

Cigars and Fine Chocolates

Often it's the little things that can make all the difference with your production. It's about taking care of the people you work with and letting them know that you appreciate their assistance with the project.

This can be summed up by an experience a lighting designer (LD) friend had on a production a few summers ago in North Dakota. He was trying to get some important information from the director of the music festival so he could do his job of designing the lighting for the show. The festival director would not return phone calls or emails and generally ignored all requests for assistance during the pre-production phase. A few weeks later while on a location scout in North Dakota, the LD finally met the fest director. They got to talking and he found out that the fest director was a cigar smoker and he mentioned that he liked a certain cigar brand but they were too expensive, so he smoked this cheaper kind.

Two weeks later when the LD returned to North Dakota for the pre-light day, he presented the fest director with a box of luxury cigars that he had purchased from a shop in New York City. The festival director was clearly moved by the unexpected gesture—no one had ever done something like that for him before. That afternoon everything changed—the LD got everything he asked for and the gig went off without a hitch. A $250 box of cigars was the difference between success or failure.

This story illustrates how a small act of appreciation can go a long way to making a film production a smoother and nicer experience for all. Think about the different ways you can show your gratitude for those who are helpful and generous to your project.

> ### *DIRECTOR'S THROUGH-LINE*
>
> The collaboration between a producer and director is foundational for any project. My long-term working relationships with several highly talented directors have always been a source of great satisfaction to me. Each partnership is unique and requires specific strategies to help us work best together. As a producer, any insight into the director's psyche or personality can be incredibly helpful.
>
> Early in my career I realized that it would be advantageous if I could "predict" how a director would react to any given situation throughout the often stressful filmmaking process. I decided to use a technique that I was taught in a class called Directing the Actors in film school—analyzing a character's "spine" or "through-line." For actors, if you can figure out your character's spine then you could predict how he or she would react to any circumstance in the play or script. So I adapted this tool for collaborating with directors.
>
> Now when I start to work with a director I haven't worked with, I spend some time trying to figure out their through-line. Some of the ones I've worked with include—"to never be bored," "to always feel free and never boxed in," "to please others," "to always feel in control." Being able to anticipate a director's response under stress has made my life as a producer much easier and I highly recommend it!

RECAP

1. **Visualize the first day of principal photography at least one day before your shooting begins so you can make sure you have covered all the tasks that need to be accomplished.**

2. **Confirm all call times and pick-ups so everyone arrives on time and at the right location.**

3. **Go to bed early so you are well rested.**

4. **Set two separate alarms 5 minutes apart so you wake up on time for every shoot day.**

5. **Arrive on set early the first day and make sure all is running smoothly. Check in with all the key department heads and actors and troubleshoot any problems as they arise.**

6. **Set a good working tone of mutual respect.**

7. **Feed your crew every 6 hours.**

8. Call wrap no later than 12 hours from the call time. Make sure everyone has a 10- to 12-hour turnaround time (12-hour turnaround for union cast/crew) for the next day's production.

9. Leave the location better than when you arrived.

10. Avoid second day disasters and make sure all are prepared for the next day's shoot before they leave set.

11. Keep alert for EOPs (Enemy of the Production) and make sure to confront them as soon as they make themselves known. If necessary, fire them so they cannot "infect" the rest of the production.

12. Remember to demonstrate gratitude to those who help your production. Without everyone working together, you wouldn't be able to complete the project.

CHAPTER 13
SAFETY

OF ALL THE PRODUCER'S responsibilities on a project, the *most* important is the safety of all cast and crew. I can't emphasize this enough. You are making critical decisions every day that affect the lives, health, and safety of the cast and crew and protecting them is your solemn duty. And how you keep them safe is tied directly to how you protect equipment, locations, and other production elements.

> The way you do any thing is the way you do every thing.
>
> —Zen proverb, Tom Waits, and others

Safety for All

This chapter* is new to this edition and reflects the importance of safety for all, always. Safety is not an afterthought that gets in the way of a good shot, but rather a constant consideration and companion to every aspect of film production. Safety demonstrates your respect for each individual and component of the production and should be the pervasive culture. If you are not committed to the necessary safety principles of filmmaking, then quite simply, *don't*

---

* Special thanks to Jennifer Tromski, the director of Risk Management and Production Administration at Columbia University's Film program for sharing her insights and recommendations for this chapter.

be a producer. It's a crucial obligation and you must take it seriously and plan/execute it every day.

In this chapter we'll look at safety in the various aspects of prepping, shooting, and delivering a project.

Preparing for Safety in Pre-production

Running a safe set and working environment is a key role of the producer, production staff, and the 1st assistant director. This begins during the pre-production period when the research and planning is undertaken for every safety aspect of the project and continues day-by-day as production plans and elements evolve. Your responsibility to run a safe set and working environment ends only with the master delivery of the project. Depending on the ambition, location, and complexities of the production, these factors will change from project to project. While prepping for the production, keep in mind the following:

INSURANCE COVERAGE AND DEAL MEMOS

In Chapter 10 (*Insurance*) we discussed this topic in-depth, including the different types of insurance coverage, how and when to purchase, additional insurance riders, etc. Here I want to discuss the "why and how" insurance works regarding the safety of all hired personnel and volunteers.

Before anyone is hired to work or volunteer on your production you need to purchase production insurance (including general liability coverage) and accident insurance (it is called workers' compensation insurance in the United States.) This insurance needs to be in place in case someone has an accident—in the office or on set. If you plan to work with unpaid volunteers or interns you need to make sure your workers' compensation/accident policy will cover them. Some policies only cover paid personnel and this could affect your hiring plans. If filming internationally, research the laws for that country because they may require accident and disability insurance coverage for cast/crew members—each country has specific laws and regulations.

Deal memos need to be signed by everyone (paid or unpaid) who works on your production. As discussed in Chapter 12 (*Production*), a **deal memo** is a signed contract between the cast/crew member and the production company that states the work rules, salary and overtime rules, screen credit and arbitration rules, and gives the production company the "right" to the cast and crew members' work. A deal memo also codifies the hiring of each cast/crew member so they can be properly covered under the insurance policies.

THE IMPORTANCE OF THE 1ST ASSISTANT DIRECTOR

It's imperative to hire a safety-focused and experienced 1st Assistant Director for your production. Knowledgeable 1st ADs are aware of all safety rules and how to maintain proper working conditions. For any given situation, they will create the plan with other safety personnel and make sure every contingency is planned for, every rule is abided by, and every crew member is informed. They also discuss and obtain approval from the producer, who in turn will contact the insurance company if there are any questions or if additional insurance riders have to be purchased.

HIRING THE RIGHT PERSONNEL

For certain technical equipment, stunts, weapons, pyrotechnics, and more, you'll need to hire a highly trained expert to work safely and legally on set. It's imperative to hire the most highly competent, experienced and—in some cases—licensed experts to handle these jobs. You need to research to find the best and brightest, check their references, and meet with them before a hire is completed. During that process you'll be able to determine if they know what they are doing, but also if they put safety before all other considerations.

Following are the steps when planning for any stunt, fire, or gunshot, etc.:

1. Bring together all the relevant crew members to discuss the special task in minute detail. The director, DP, 1st AD, key grip, and other department heads need to be in the first conversations with the expert to make sure every aspect is discussed and considered. Scheduling, budgeting, and creative decisions will be a part of this discussion. The director may want a certain effect but the budget or schedule may not be able to accommodate it. Then the expert has to give other options—that are equally safe—and the conversation continues.

2. The producer and director will need to debrief to make certain decisions together about what is possible—especially for budget and schedule considerations. Once a general plan and budget has been approved, it will be time to let the rest of the team know so they can begin detailed prep.

3. The expert (in conjunction with the 1st AD and production staff) will do the following as part of their job:
- identify hazards
- hire qualified and competent personnel
- obtain proper permits
- meet with local authorities
- create and maintain required control measures on set
- establish the proper cueing system for the stunt
- set up and execute a rehearsal process
- communicate effectively with all cast and crew
- execute the stunt on the day of the shoot

4. If you ever have a question about a safety issue, bring it up immediately with the trained crew person. They should be able to answer any query so you are assured that all precautions have been taken care of.

Location Permissions and Planning

When shooting on location, precautions need to be taken to ensure safety for the cast/crew, equipment, and for protection of the location itself. Following is how to best plan for location shooting.

LOCATION ANALYSIS

While location scouting and during the tech scout, the producer, 1st AD, location manager, and key department heads need to analyze any possible location safety issues. For instance, if you are shooting in a remote area, a half-mile walk from the parking lot, how will you handle the logistics? How to get all the equipment safely into the woods—probably with carts and extra crew. How to make sure the cast/crew can walk that distance? Where will people go to the bathroom? (They can't just "go in the woods.") How to provide shade or warmth from extreme weather elements? Does the production have bug spray, sunscreen, water, and food? There are countless considerations that have to be discussed, planned for, and approved by the team and location owners.

LOCATION PERMISSIONS

Just because you completed successful negotiations to rent the location doesn't mean that's the end of the conversation. You need to make sure you go over all the plans for the shoot and get sign off from the owner on anything that might be safety related. Don't assume anything about the condition of the location. Ask about weight restrictions, electrical power needs, unsafe places on the location that need to be closed off so no one can wander into them by accident.

I filmed at a small horse stable in New Jersey once with a dirt back lot that looked perfect to park our trucks and RV. On our tech scout we showed the owner where we planned to park all the vehicles and they explained that the back lot was very "soft" and couldn't handle the weight. They pointed out a front area where we had to park every heavy vehicle so none of the trucks and vans got swallowed up and stuck in the dirt!

LOCATION PROTECTION

Protecting the location from damage is an important consideration. You might need to bring in a crew a day early to cover up certain furniture or move it into a garage to protect it from the film crew. There may be valuable artwork or collectibles that need to be locked away for safekeeping.

Or perhaps the location has a brand new hardwood floor and the key grip wants to put down dolly track. The owner will never give permission unless you have a clear and successful plan to discuss. You'll need to rent furniture blankets and purchase layout board to cover and protect the floors. No gaffer's tape can be put down on the floor because it will rip off the varnish when it's removed. (I know a filmmaker who did this and had to pay $5,000 to have wooden floors refinished.) You may need to tell the crew they must wear rubber-soled shoes for that shoot day. You get the idea—this all needs to be planned and approved prior to the shoot day.

As always, contact your insurance broker to find out what your production insurance covers and if you need to purchase an additional rider for your policy.

CALL SHEETS

Call sheets are an important way to communicate safety to all the cast and crew. Highlight any special conditions the cast/crew need to be aware of prior to the shoot day on the daily call sheet. Dress code—such as "closed-toe shoes only" or "long pants only." Or weather updates—such as "hot weather expected, make sure to hydrate properly," "very cold temperatures for exterior work, wear proper warm clothing and boots," "put on sunscreen for outside work."

All the important emergency information needs to be stated on the call sheet as well—nearest hospital, police and fire departments. If something happens, everyone needs to know where to go for immediate medical attention. (See additional information in Chapter 6, *Pre-Production*.)

WEATHER MONITORING

Extreme weather can have big consequences for film productions. The production staff need to monitor the weather forecast and research weather patterns for the time of year and places where filming will occur. For instance, each year August and September are peak months for hurricanes for the Caribbean Islands. Planning to produce a film during that time in that area of the world would have an elevated risk. Additionally, it may be very difficult or expensive to purchase production insurance for those same reasons.

With the changes and escalation in extreme weather, productions have to be more vigilant and strategic than ever before. Torrential rains, flooding, extreme heat, massive snow storms, hurricanes, tornadoes, and more are the kind of occurrences now causing productions to create weather contingencies more often. Educate yourself and the cast/crew so the production is prepared properly. The National Oceanic and Atmospheric Administration (*www.weather.noaa.gov*) and National Weather Service (*www.weather.gov*) have up-to-date weather information for any place in the world.

On-Set Precautions and Protocols

During principal photography, most of the focus is on all the work happening on set. It's a very complicated world: cast, crew, background actors, plus expensive equipment—cameras, lighting, grip, props, set dressing, set construction, costumes, special effects, and lots more! The production phase requires strict attention to all of these factors. See below how best to protect every one and every thing:

ON-SET SAFETY KITS AND PERSONNEL

Every set should have—at the very minimum—a first aid kit, sunscreen, and bug spray for use by cast and crew. The line producer should make sure that the unit production manager, the AD department and the production assistants all know where these elements are kept in case they are needed quickly.

Depending on what stunts or other factors are occurring on set, a medic, nurse or lifeguard may be needed.

CHAIN OF COMMAND

Keep in mind that film sets are run similarly to military operations; there is a chain of command within each department. For example, in the grip department it goes key grip, best boy grip, 3rd grip, 4th grip, etc. Each person reports up to their superior. Then the key grip reports to the DP and the 1st AD and ultimately to the producer and director. It is important for each person to know their relationship to each person in their department and how each department reports to the rest of the production.

UNION STEWARDS

All union/guild contracts require the designation of a **union steward** for every single day of pre-production, production, and wrap where union members are hired. Usually determined after a vote from the union members on set, this person is knowledgeable of all the rules and is the point person for any safety or working condition concerns. The 1st AD and the producer interact directly with the steward to address any issues immediately—this is a crucial relationship to ensure cast/crew safety.

SAFETY MEETING

At the beginning of each shoot day, a short safety meeting with the cast/crew should be given if there are any unusual safety issues that need to be addressed. There may be certain areas of the location that are "off limits" or "unsafe," certain conditions that need to be considered like "possible late morning thunderstorms," protocols that need to be followed for an on-set special effect; these need to be communicated to all.

As mentioned above, production should provide sunscreen, bug spray, a first aid kit, and water at the craft service table at all times. Production trailers, pop-up shelters, and other ways for cast/crew to shelter during exterior shoots should be provided when applicable.

Depending on the location of the shoot, there may be a need to hire security personnel for the cast/crew and equipment's safety. Nighttime exterior filming or unsafe neighborhoods may require such measures, so plan ahead.

TURNAROUND TIME AND COMPANY MOVES

As discussed in Chapter 12 (*Production*), overworking cast/crew without a proper turnaround time is one of the most dangerous violations on any production. Union contracts clearly state the 12-hour turnaround time for their members, but if you are not working under a union contract you still need to run your schedule by these rules. We all know the tragic consequences of crew personnel who died or were injured in accidents directly caused by fatigue or exhaustion due to lack of the proper amount of sleep.

Company moves (as discussed in Chapter 11) require the entire cast and crew to pack up all the equipment and production elements and drive to another location and set up everything there again. It takes a lot of time out of the daily shooting schedule but it also requires a lot of time and energy from the crew and wear and tear on the equipment and transportation vehicles. It's best to avoid company moves when possible and to minimize how many are scheduled in a day.

ANIMALS AND ANIMAL HANDLERS

Animals are sentient beings and need to be protected as much as any humans on set. Animals that are treated humanely and well are safer for humans on set and for general set safety. A scared animal in pain is one of the most dangerous and unpredictable on-set situations I can imagine.

As discussed in Chapter 12 (*Production*), if you have animals on your set for any period of time, you'll need to hire a trained animal handler. It can't just be a friend of yours who has a really sweet dog or cat and they plan to bring it on set. It has to be a professional animal handler with film credits and experience.

The animal handler needs to ensure that the animal is well-trained and socialized for work on a film set. They should be familiar with the species of animal and keep the animal safe, well rested, hydrated and fed when working with them. The handler will need to coordinate with the 1st AD and producer to understand the exact actions that will be required from the animal. They can break it down into doable actions for the animal and give feedback on what is and isn't possible. They will coordinate casting, pre-training, on-set work and off-set work with the animal. While on set, no one except the animal handler can interact with the animal. If an actor needs to work with an animal for a scene, the actor will only touch or work with the animal for the take and then the animal goes back to the handler between takes. This will ensure the safety of all cast and crew as well.

It is best to work with the American Humane Association (AHA) (*http://www.americanhumane.org*) whenever you hire animals for your project. This organization's mission is "to ensure the welfare, wellness and well-being of children and animals, and to unleash the full potential of the bond between humans and animals to the mutual benefit of both."

AHA created the *No Animals Were Harmed* certification program and logo for film productions. If you wish to receive the certification and be allowed to use the logo in your project's end credits, you'll need to register your production, have a Certified Animal Safety Representative (CASR) on set when animals are working, follow the AHA guidelines, and submit your final master to the AHA before you can be approved to do so. If you are working under a SAG-AFTRA agreement, there may be no charge or a discounted charge for the CASR.

Ethical considerations are always a part of any production. Before making a final decision to work with animals on set, consider if computer generated imagery (CGI) or animatronics are a better option. For many projects, it has become easier and cheaper to attain great post effects (without having to film with an actual animal) for any budget level.

Lastly, contact your insurance broker to find out what your production insurance covers and if you need to purchase an additional rider for your policy.

Speaking Up

What happens if you are on a set and feel unsafe, or witness unsafe practices or are subjected to unsafe conditions? You need to speak up. Contact the key department head and shop steward immediately. If you do not feel that your concerns were heeded, contact the assistant director and producer. If you feel that the conditions have not been addressed properly, then reach out to the Safety Hotlines below.

Cast and crew's health and safety may be at risk and it is up to each one of us to make sure filmmaking is a creative, but first and foremost, a *safe* endeavor, every day. *Remember—it's just a movie.* No one should ever be put in an unsafe situation when on a film project. There is always another way to get the shot done; you just need to work the problem to make sure it's safe.

If you have any concerns when on a film project, there are many ways to get help:

- Call the ICG (Local 600) Safety Hotline at 877-424-4685
- Call the DGA Safety Hotline at 800-342-3457
- Call the SAG Safety Hotline at 844-723-3773
- Download the free Set Safety app (available for free for iPhone and Android) which provides one-touch access to call safety hotlines, report excessive labor hours, submit proof of excessive hours, and read DGA bulletins that detail safety protocols and requirements across a wide variety of filming situations.

Security for Post Production and Deliverables

Protecting the project during post production is just as important as all the other elements we have discussed. In Chapter 12 (*Production*), we discussed backing up the acquired footage on multiple drives, on cloud computing sites, etc. When editing, saving the newest cut of the project must happen every day/night so none of the latest editorial work is lost.

Take every possible security measure to make sure your "system" can't be hacked from the outside. You don't want anyone to see your project until the final master is ready for public screening and piracy concerns are a big part of the film industry. Set up strict control and approval measures if you need to send out a work-in-progress cut to someone over the internet. There are many different ways to do this but you need to research how secure the website is. I've been on projects where a pen drive or hard drive is delivered to me in person so we don't take the chance on a possible hack. Plan out your security protocols for the editorial period and make sure all personnel and any outside post production facility follows your safety measures properly.

E&O INSURANCE

Once your project is delivered, if it will screen through a broadcast or distribution entity, you'll need to purchase Errors & Omissions (E&O) insurance. As discussed previously, the producer will have to fill out a signed questionnaire regarding the legal acquisition of all the "work" in the project to make sure it was properly done. Release forms, deal memos, licensing agreements, confidentiality agreements, etc., need to be provided as assurance that the project is protected from any potential lawsuits. The E&O insurance will provide money to pay for legal fees if someone decides to sue the production company or filmmakers.

Equipment Monitoring and Protection

Film equipment (cameras, lighting, grip equipment, dollies, cranes, walkie-talkies, trucks, vans, etc.) is *extremely* expensive. Protecting the equipment from damage and theft is a high priority for any producer. Follow the steps below:

EQUIPMENT DAMAGE

The best way to eliminate/control damage to the production equipment is to hire the most professional and experienced crew you can. Do the math—if you can't afford a professional assistant cameraperson and instead get a friend from film school to be the AC and then they damage a lens, the repair bill will be *much* more money than if you had spent the money to hire a professional in the first place.

Professional crew have been trained to take care of and use their equipment properly. They know what factors to watch out for, how to protect it, and how to manage any unforeseen circumstances or events. This also helps to ensure against technical problems for the production. Inexperienced crew may record at the wrong tech specs, or miss an important warning signal from a piece of equipment, thus causing very time-consuming and costly problems for post production.

CHECKING OUT EQUIPMENT

We discussed the importance of equipment checkouts in Chapter 6 (*Pre-Production*) and this is another way to insure against equipment problems. By having the assistant cameraperson and other technicians check out the equipment you are renting the day before the shoot, you make sure that it is all in good operating order. If a checkout is not done prior to taking the equipment out of the rental house, you'll be charged for any "broken" equipment that is returned afterwards, even if it was broken before you picked it up.

SECURITY AGAINST EQUIPMENT THEFT

As mentioned above, all the equipment used in film production is expensive. Consequently, it is imperative that it is kept in a safe, dry, and protected place at all times—before, during, and after a shoot day. When picking up equipment from a rental house, you'll need two production assistants in the van—one to stay in the locked vehicle and one to shuttle the equipment from the rental house to the van. The PAs have to have "eyes" on the equipment at all times and in a locked vehicle. If someone has to go to the bathroom, the other person must stay with the equipment. There are innumerable incidents of equipment stolen from cars and vans left unattended (if only for a few minutes).

On set, the same amount of vigilance must be kept at all times. Even in a studio, you need to make sure no one who is not a cast/crew member can just walk onto a set without permission or an escort. Some productions use "laminates" to make sure only authorized personnel are allowed in the location or venue. Security guards may be necessary, too. For exterior filming, the situation is even more complex. You may need to hire extra PAs to sit in locked vehicles with equipment or near equipment on set (often called "fire watch") to insure that no one can walk off with an expensive camera or lens case, etc.

Lastly, where and how you'll protect the vehicles and equipment overnight, when not shooting, is a key responsibility of the production team. Most of the time, productions rent spaces in 24-hour supervised and secured parking lots for all production/equipment vehicles. Every department will have a driver who will pick up and drop off the vehicle in the parking lot each day. The production team will need to research and sometimes make reservations so there is a safe and secure place for every prep, production, and wrap day of the schedule. In busy production centers and cities, reserve space ahead of time.

If you can't find a 24-hour supervised/secured parking lot, then you may need to bring all the equipment inside to a secure location/warehouse every day and night and even hire an overnight security guard. It's labor intensive but the alternative is the possibility of hundreds of thousands of dollars of equipment being stolen, which won't be covered by insurance. Production insurance policies specify that equipment needs to be stored safely and securely in order for an insurance company to pay out on a claim.

Contact your insurance broker to find out what your production insurance covers and if you need to purchase an additional rider for your policy.

WALKIE-TALKIES

Finally, a brief message about walkie-talkies. On most productions of a certain size, they are essential for effective communication on set. They are also surprisingly expensive! Even a missing walkie-talkie battery costs a few hundred dollars. Make sure you assign a competent production assistant to sign in and sign out walkie-talkies and batteries at the beginning and end of each day. Each crew person is responsible for their walkie-talkie and a sign in/sign out sheet is essential to keep track of the rental equipment.

EQUIPMENT AND ART DEPARTMENT RETURNS

I can't overstate how important it is to plan as carefully for the equipment returns as you did for the pickup days. Often, producers are so fixated on the prep and production phases that they forget to plan for how to wrap and return all the rental equipment and production design elements. The potential for theft and/or damage is elevated when you have an exhausted crew member or not enough people to secure, protect, and return the valuable rental equipment.

Make sure you have enough crew to do the returns. If the production PAs are sleep-deprived, bring in a fresh crew to execute the returns for the production. Go back to your original pickup list and make sure you account for every piece of equipment. A smart and careful returns schedule will help you accomplish this. As before, hire two people for each van/truck that has to drop off equipment or props/set dressing so there is always one person staying with the vehicle that is loaded up with expensive cargo.

Plan to keep the equipment/props in a 24-hour supervised parking lot if any of it needs to be stored overnight. The production is responsible until all the rentals are returned, checked back in and are confirmed to have no damage. The better planned the returns process, the less missing/damaged charges you will incur.

Safety Protocols for Equipment and Special Conditions

Film production utilizes lots of technically advanced and expensive equipment to create the cinemagraphic magic on screen. Consequently, you'll need to be very careful when working with any of the equipment listed below. Make sure you rent from a reputable vendor, hire expert operators, and follow all of the safety protocols.

PROCESS TRAILERS

Process Trailers or Camera Cars are used often when shooting footage of actors talking while driving picture vehicles. When using a process trailer, the picture vehicle is attached to the back of the trailer (the picture vehicle's wheels don't touch the ground) and the actor does not actively drive because the process trailer operator does the actual driving. The process trailer has an open back with space to place a camera, lighting, grip equipment, and several crew members—often the director, camera operator, sound recordist, and 1st AD.

But process trailers are not without their own risks. There have been accidents, especially when making turns on the road. This is serious business and crew people can't just hop on the back of a process trailer because it seems like "fun."

To address any safety issues, the trailer should be operated by an experienced driver who understands how much camera, lighting, and grip equipment and crew members can be put safely into the back of the trailer. All proper filming permits need to be procured. Prior to shooting, the local police/sheriff's department needs to be contacted and plans need to be discussed and approved before you can do any filming.

Driving on open public roads is dangerous and it is always safer if you can "lock down" a street so you have full control over the roadway. These and other plans need to be coordinated in detail with the 1st AD, local authorities, local film commission, and cast/crew. Depending on the locale, you'll need to hire police and/or fire department personnel and you may need to purchase additional insurance.

HELICOPTERS

Shooting aerial footage from helicopters is another area of potential safety risks. There are single-engine and double-engine helicopters and I always suggest that production companies only hire double-engine helicopters for aerial photography. I won't go up in a single-engine copter myself because there is no backup if that one engine fails.

Contact reputable aerial photography companies/operators and make sure all the plans are in place to secure the camera and personnel during the install of the equipment and shooting of the footage. It's critical that all equipment and crew are strapped in securely before takeoff! Contact your insurance broker to find out what your production insurance covers and if you need to purchase an additional rider for your policy.

UNMANNED AERIAL VEHICLES AND DRONES

Unmanned Aerial Vehicles (UAVs) are a relatively new technology and their use on productions and the regulations that govern their operation will continue to evolve. Drones are a category of this technology and the one that we hear about most in film production. Researching the local laws and ordinances that pertain to their use in the production location is the first step in the process. If drone operation is allowed, you'll need to hire an experienced operator and coordinate with the municipality to make sure you are following all the legal protocols and rules.

There may be different rules state by state, country by country, and urban vs. rural areas for drone operation. Contact the local film commission and/or the relevant city/state governing bodies to find out the latest information before you plan for a drone shoot. Double check that research close to your shoot dates. The regulations are changing very quickly and you can't rely solely on the drone operator to have all the latest information.

Contact your insurance broker to find out what your production insurance covers and if you need to purchase an additional rider for your policy.

CRANES/JIBS/OVERHEAD CAMERAS

Cranes and jibs require experienced operators to maintain safety for the cast/crew and equipment itself. The 1st AD will coordinate the production plan with the crane/jib technicians, the grip department, the DP, and any other relevant crew members. Working with the location manager, the 1st AD needs to make sure that such a large piece of equipment is allowed to work on the premises and that the weight of the equipment can be supported by the location floor. Additional safety protocols need to be in place for the operation of the equipment when it moves through a space (it can take up large amounts of space) and any use of lead weights that are often placed on the back of a crane as a counterweight.

Overhead cameras require cables to glide/fly over a space. These are often used during sporting events and concerts but can also be used in spaces with very high ceilings. The same approval protocols are required and *double* safety cords are necessary to make sure that the glide cable can't break and fall on anybody or anything below.

Contact your insurance broker to find out what your production insurance covers and if you need to purchase an additional rider for your policy.

STUNTS

For any stunt, from an actor "punching" another actor to crashing a car on the San Diego Freeway, you'll need to hire a stunt coordinator and stunt performers. Each stunt will need to be fully planned and vetted by the stunt coordinator in consultation with the 1st AD. Precise discussions with the DP will allow all to figure out which camera angle will work best for each shot in sequence for a stunt. Detailed storyboards map how each shot will be accomplished to keep the stunt performers safe and capture the footage necessary for the project. Stunt performers may be working with animals, fire, explosions, falls, crashes, fights, driving, water, and wires. Hiring the best stunt team for each kind of stunt is critical.

If working under a SAG-AFTRA agreement, stunt coordinators and stunt performers are covered under the guild agreement, so make sure to research the work rules and salary rates.

Contact your insurance broker to find out what your production insurance covers and if you need to purchase an additional rider for your policy.

PROP WEAPONS

Prop weapons include anything that could potentially harm anyone for any reason—scissors, knives, baseball bats, ice picks, swords, handguns, rifles, bombs, etc. These are rubber and plastic versions of the real thing—they look real but are non-working, non-firing. Prop weapons rental houses rent to productions, usually on a weekly rate. There should be a designated crew person in charge of the prop weapon. In some cases it may be used in a fight, in which case the stunt coordinator will have possession of the prop on set.

Any time a *firing* prop weapon or a dulled real blade (like a real machete that has been dulled) is used on a film set, you need to hire a weaponer/armorer/weapons specialist. Included in this category would be any prop weapon involved in a stunt or other kind of intensive weapon play.

The weaponer trains the actor and confirms that they can use it properly before handing it over to them for use on set. As soon as the take is over, the prop weapon is immediately given back to the weaponer for reloading or safekeeping until it is time for the next take. *Never is an actor or other crew member allowed to touch or have possession of the prop weapon at any other time!*

Weaponers also create and implement **squibs,** which are special effects devices that mimic what a bullet does when it hits a surface, like skin, clothing, or glass. It's the pouch that spurts "blood" when an actor is "shot" in the arm.

When guns need to be "fired" on set, this is done with blank cartridges. **Blanks** are empty shell casings (no bullets) that contain a small amount of gun powder to create the sound and flash of a gunshot. They also provide sufficient recoil to eject the fired shell casing from a semi-automatic firearm, simulating actual functioning. Consequently, blanks can and have killed actors because they weren't used properly. Only a professional weaponer can set up and handle a prop gun and blanks because only they know the distance that must be maintained to render the blank cartridges "safe."

If a blank is fired against or close to an actor's skull, chest, or other body part, it can be lethal. Over the years, there have been tragic incidents of blanks killing/injuring actors because the proper protocols and firing distance were not followed. I've seen dramatic demos of a blank being fired into an apple at close range and you can see how dangerous these "props" can be. Educate yourself, hire the best professionals, and plan carefully if working with any prop weapons on set.

Weaponer/Armorers can also give you advice on how best to achieve a particular special effect regarding weapons and come up with the safest and easiest solutions. With incredible computer special effects, it's possible to create a lot of the sound and flash in post production now, reducing risk on set even more.

Contact your insurance broker to find out what your production insurance covers and if you need to purchase an additional rider for your policy.

FILMING EXTERIORS WITH PROP WEAPONS OR STUNTS

Filming outside, where anyone from the public can see a prop weapon or stunt, is automatically a dangerous situation. Any uninformed passerby can mistake the fake gunshot for a real one and call the local police department, who then arrive with guns drawn, thinking it is a real situation! Unfortunately this potentially lethal situation can occur when safety isn't valued by inept producers and directors.

A few years ago, a film crew staged a fake holdup in a convenience store on Long Island for an independent film. A passerby called 911 and the police arrived with loaded guns pointed at an actor with a fake prop weapon during a scripted scene from a film shoot. Don't ever do this—make sure to contact the local film commissions and police department to find out what is allowed. If possible, spend the time and resources necessary to cover up the set so the public can't see into the space. Lastly, have a plan in place to notify passersby that filming is taking place so they don't assume it is a real crime occurring.

If you rent a prop weapon, check with the prop house regarding how/where you can transport the prop gun, etc. In New York, you can't carry a prop weapon on the subway, so you'll need to drive it to set. There are also protocols for when you ship a prop weapon or fly with one. Ask the weapon house about these details and fill out the proper paperwork so you are in compliance with all local and federal laws.

PYROTECHNICS

If you plan to set something/someone on fire, blow up a building, create a smoke effect, or light fireworks for a scene, you'll need to hire a licensed pyrotechnician. The only exceptions to the list would be if the fire is in a fireplace, barbecue grill, or a sanctioned campfire location. Squibs (see the Prop Weapons section above) may also fall under the purview of a pyrotechnician because of the ignition aspect of the special effect. If you would like to make a controlled fire outside *anywhere* you will need to contact the local fire department. Certain neighborhoods, areas and regions prohibit any pyrotechnic of any kind because of dry conditions where a fire could become uncontrollable and unstoppable.

Each state has their own rules for pyrotechnics so make sure the people you hire have the correct license for the state you are filming in. The expert will create the safety plan, work on storyboards, hire the proper personnel, and coordinate with the 1st AD and producer as outlined above.

Contact your insurance broker to find out what your production insurance covers and if you need to purchase an additional rider for your policy.

RAILROAD TRACKS

I've included railroad tracks in this chapter because filming on tracks of any kind (active or inactive) is always a potentially dangerous situation. Even inactive tracks may be capable of carrying railcars and such remote possibilities need to be considered and planned for.

If you wish to shoot on or near railroad tracks, you'll need to find out who owns the tracks—private, city, state, or federal—and contact them for permission and sign a legal contract allowing you to film on the tracks. You must have a safety plan and work in coordination with the track authority to make sure that no train could possibly run on the track while your cast/crew is on site.

There was a fatal incident on a film set while shooting on railroad tracks a few years ago and assistant cameraperson Sarah Jones was killed. Her family created a foundation, Safety for Sarah (*http://www.safetyforsarah.com*), and has worked tirelessly to promote safety on film sets. Check out the website for more information.

Global Safety Issues

When putting together a production, there are always myriad factors that can affect your safety plans and it is the production staff's job to keep up on any factor that could have a negative impact.

HEALTH ADVISORY

Monitoring health advisories is also a part of the production team's job. Agencies like the World Health Organization (*www.who.int*) and the Centers for Disease Control and Prevention (*www.cdc.gov*) monitor virus outbreaks, pandemics, and other health emergencies. Consult the websites to determine if there are any advisories for the area of the world you'll be shooting in.

GLOBAL EVENTS

Global events and crises can impact a production as well. If there is an attack or civil unrest in a city or region it may not be safe to shoot there and your insurance company may not extend coverage for a period of time. Consult the U.S. Dept. of State (*travel.state.gov*) for any Travel Warnings (domestic and international) issued by the U.S. government. Insurance companies consult this website as well and may change your coverage based on updated advisories. Stay informed about global events that could impact your production.

RECAP

1. **A producer's No. 1 priority is the health and safety of all cast and crew. Good planning and vigilance is important from day one until master delivery. The 1st AD, key department heads, special effects personnel, and the production team need to work together to map out a safe plan ahead of time for any stunt or special effect on set.**

2. **Protecting animals on set requires a properly trained animal handler. If you wish to use the logo *No Animals Were Harmed®* in your project's end credits, you'll need to contact the American Humane Association and follow their program.**

3. **Remember to research each location ahead of time to plan and implement safety systems to protect it properly.**

4. **Film equipment is extremely expensive. The production team needs to plan for its safety from the time it is picked up from a rental house until its return to protect it from theft and damage.**

5. All acquired footage, various editorial cuts, and all processes during post production need to be protected from hacks or other kinds of loss through backups, cloud computing, and other online protections.

6. Hire the proper personnel (e.g., stunt coordinator, drone operator, weaponer, crane operator, pyrotechnics expert, etc.) whenever working with specialized equipment.

7. Extreme weather and travel warnings need to be factored into any production decisions when planning and scheduling a project. Research weather and the socio-political situations in the area of the world you are filming to protect everyone and everything.

CHAPTER 14
WRAP

CALLING "WRAP" FOR THE last time on the last day of principal photography is a joyous moment. Congratulations! You have pulled off a minor miracle and you should be proud of yourself and the rest of your cast and crew. Enjoy the sensation, but not for too long, because you, the production staff and crew have to spend the next few days "wrapping out the job."

Wrapping Out

Wrapping out is almost like doing everything you did leading up to the shoot but now in reverse order. Equipment, sets, props, costumes, etc., need to be packed up and returned to where they came from. Things that were rented will be sent back to the rental houses and purchased materials will be stored, sold, recycled, or donated.

While you were shooting, each department was making returns when possible but most things had to be kept until the last day of shooting, so now there is a lot to do. The production department oversees the wrap out—checking in with each individual department to make sure all is done properly and in a timely manner.

If one advances confidently in the direction of his dreams, and endeavors to live the life he has imagined, he will meet with a success unexpected in common hours.

—Henry David Thoreau

Some guidelines for wrapping out:
1. Most rentals need to be returned the day after the last day of shooting *by a certain time* or else the production will be charged an additional rental day.
2. Rental costumes need to be dry cleaned before being returned (unless the rental company has a different policy).
3. Certain rental and purchased wardrobe, set construction pieces, and purchased props may need to be rented/stored until it is determined there will be no re-shoots.
4. Anything that was purchased and can be used again should be given back to the production company from each department head. This can include expendables (gaffer's tape, gels), camera accessories, wardrobe, props, furniture, and office supplies.
5. Anything that can't be put to good use can be donated to thrift stores—it keeps it out of the landfill and the production company could obtain a tax deduction. There are other organizations geared toward artists or film productions in certain cities that recycle the materials you donate for use by other artists and films. Go to *www.ProducerToProducer.com* for more information.

Loss & Damaged/Missing & Damaged

L&D or M&D refers to loss, missing, and damaged. These are dreaded words for any producer. You work so hard to come in under budget and it could all be blown away when a crew person loses an expensive walkie-talkie or someone breaks a piece of expensive equipment while shooting. The production will have to pay to replace the items or to have them repaired so it's necessary to budget for these costs in the estimated budget. Hiring professional and responsible crew is the best way to minimize losses and damages.

Deposit Checks and Credit Card Authorizations

As discussed in Chapter 6 (*Pre-Production*), most equipment, prop, and costume rental houses will require the production to put down a credit card deposit to secure the transaction. When making their returns, the production department will want to make sure to get the deposit amount back and confirmation paperwork to reflect the credit. Usually the rental house will comply after they have checked all the rentals back in and nothing is missing or damaged (M&D).

Actualized Budget

The **actualized budget** contains all the actual invoices, petty cash, and payroll that has been paid or will be paid to produce the film. These numbers will be entered and totaled up in the Actual column of the budget, which is located to the right of the Estimated column (sometimes the working budget is in between these two columns).

To create an actualized budget you will need to create a purchase order for each invoice. A **purchase order** is a binding document that signifies that the production company agrees to pay the vendor the amount stated on the order according to a specific payment schedule (usually within 30 days of invoice date). Purchase orders are listed by consecutive PO numbers and contain the following info: vendor address, phone, email address, invoice #, invoice date, company tax ID #, what was purchased, invoice amount, budget line item #, payment method (on account, check #, or credit card payment) and payment due date.

Once you have entered this information onto the purchase order you will transfer some of the key details to the purchase order log. This log will utilize one line for each PO. You'll enter the Budget line item #, date, PO #, vendor name, amount, payment status (paid or unpaid) and payment method. If you are using the budget template downloaded from *www.ProducerToProducer.com* or other budget computer software, you can enter the information within the budget template, push a "send actuals" button and all the numbers are automatically transferred and totaled in the Actual column of the budget.

As you move through the production, you will keep adding to the list of invoices to be paid and entering them in the Actual column. It's important to track the estimated and actual columns of each line item so you can anticipate any overages and figure out ways to mitigate them by saving money in other budget areas. The goal is to always come in under budget.

Petty Cash

Petty cash refers to the money that is paid out in cash for purchases and expenses. Each purchase must have a written receipt so you can track where all the cash outlay has been spent. Similarly to the Purchase Order log, all the pertinent info will be entered into a Petty Cash log and the amounts are sent to the proper line item's Actual column. Some producers like to give out pre-loaded debit cards for petty cash use instead of cash. It allows the production to track every purchase and limit the amount that any crew member or department is given to spend.

Regarding our case study film *Sundae*, the original estimated budget was $12,008 and the final actualized number came to $8,727. You can see the side-by-side comparison of estimated vs. actual—they came in *under* budget by $3,281—27% less than originally budgeted!

Here is the *Sundae* actualized budget.

Producer To Producer Budget Template

Title	SUNDAE		
Length	5:00		
Client			
Production Co.			
Address			
Address			
Telephone			
Cel			
Email			
Job #			
Exec. Producer			
Director	Sonya Goddy		
Producer	Kristin Frost/Co-producer-Birgit Gernboeck		
DP	Andrew Ellmaker		
Editor			
Pre-Prod. Days			
Pre-Lite Days			
Studio Days			
Location Days	2		
Location(s)	Brooklyn, NY		
Format	RED Dragon		
Shoot Date(s)	January 22-23		
	SUMMARY	ESTIMATED	ACTUAL
1	Pre-Production and wrap costs (Totals A & C)	700	500
2	Shooting Crew Labor (Total B)	1,000	1,000
3	Location and travel expenses (Total D)	2,618	2,350
4	Props. Wardrobe and animals (Total E)	1,150	330
5	Studio & set construction costs (Total F/G/H)	0	0
6	Equipment costs (Total I)	2,650	2,291
7	Media/Storage costs (Total J)	300	957
8	Miscellaneous Costs (Total K)	230	230
9	Talent costs and expenses (Total M & N)	360	195
10	Post Production costs (Total O-T)	3,000	600
	SUBTOTAL	12,008	8,453
11	Insurance	0	169
	SUBTOTAL Direct Costs	12,008	8,622
12	Director/Creative Fees (Total L-Not including Direct Costs)	0	0
13	Production Fee		
14	Contingency		
15	Weather Day		
	GRAND TOTAL	12,008	8,622

COMMENTS

Budget for 2 day shoot in Brooklyn, NY.
DP will work for free – will rent his camera.
SAG-AFTRA actors will work under the Student Film contract.
Music licensing will be free.

Producer to Producer Budget Template

A PRE-PROD & WRAP LABOR	Days	Rate	OT (1.5)	OT sub	OT (2.0)	OT sub	ESTIMATED	ACTUAL
1 Producer				0		0	0	0
2 1st Assistant Director				0		0	0	0
3 Director of Photography				0		0	0	0
4 Camera Operator(s)				0		0	0	0
5 2nd Assistant Director				0		0	0	0
6 Assistant Camera				0		0	0	0
7 Loader				0		0	0	0
8 Production Designer				0		0	0	0
9 Art Director				0		0	0	0
10 Set Decorator				0		0	0	0
11 Props				0		0	0	0
12 Props Assistant				0		0	0	0
13 Gaffer				0		0	0	0
14 Best Boy Electrician				0		0	0	0
15 Electrician				0		0	0	0
16 Key Grip				0		0	0	0
17 Best Boy Grip				0		0	0	0
18 Grip				0		0	0	0
19 DIT				0		0	0	0
20 Swing				0		0	0	0
21 Sound Recordist				0		0	0	0
22 Boom Operator				0		0	0	0
23 Key Hair/Makeup				0		0	0	0
24 Hair/Makeup Assistant				0		0	0	0
25 Hair/Makeup Assistant				0		0	0	0
26 Stylist				0		0	0	0
27 Costume Designer				0		0	0	0
28 Wardrobe Supervisor				0		0	0	0
29 Wardrobe Assistant				0		0	0	0
30 Script Supervisor				0		0	0	0
31 Food Stylist				0		0	0	0
32 Assistant Food Stylist				0		0	0	0
33 Video Engineer				0		0	0	0
34 Line Producer				0		0	0	0
35 Production Manager				0		0	0	0
36 Production Coordinator				0		0	0	0
37 Location Manager				0		0	0	0
38 Location Scout				0		0	0	0
39 Police				0		0	0	0
40 Fire				0		0	0	0
41 On Set Tutor				0		0	0	0
42 Motorhome Driver				0		0	0	0
43 Craft Service				0		0	0	0
44 Still Photographer				0		0	0	0
45 Weaponer/Pyrotechnics				0		0	0	0
46 Key PA				0		0	0	0
47 Production Assistant				0		0	0	0
48 Production Assistant				0		0	0	0
49 Production Assistant				0		0	0	0
50 Production Assistant				0		0	0	0
TOTAL A				0		0	0	0

Producer To Producer Budget Template

B	SHOOTING LABOR	Days	Rate	OT (1.5)	OT sub	OT (2.0)	OT sub	ESTIMATED	ACTUAL
51	Producer				0		0	0	0
52	1st Assistant Director				0		0	0	0
53	Director of Photography				0		0	0	0
54	Camera Operator(s)				0		0	0	0
55	2nd Assistant Director				0		0	0	0
56	Assistant Camera				0		0	0	0
57	Loader				0		0	0	0
58	Production Designer				0		0	0	0
59	Art Director				0		0	0	0
60	Set Decorator				0		0	0	0
61	Props				0		0	0	0
62	Props Assistant				0		0	0	0
63	Gaffer				0		0	0	200
64	Best Boy Electrician				0		0	0	0
65	Electrician				0		0	0	0
66	Key Grip	2	100		0		0	200	400
67	Best Boy Grip	1	100		0		0	100	100
68	Grip				0		0	0	0
69	DIT				0		0	0	0
70	Swing				0		0	0	0
71	Sound Recordist	2	150		0		0	300	300
72	Boom Operator				0		0	0	0
73	Key Hair/Makeup	2	100		0		0	200	0
74	Hair/Makeup Assistant				0		0	0	0
75	Hair/Makeup Assistant				0		0	0	0
76	Stylist				0		0	0	0
77	Costume Designer				0		0	0	0
78	Wardrobe Supervisor				0		0	0	0
79	Wardrobe Assistant				0		0	0	0
80	Script Supervisor				0		0	0	0
81	Food Stylist				0		0	0	0
82	Assistant Food Stylist				0		0	0	0
83	Video Engineer				0		0	0	0
84	Line Producer				0		0	0	0
85	Production Manager				0		0	0	0
86	Production Coordinator				0		0	0	0
87	Location Manager				0		0	0	0
88	Location Scout				0		0	0	0
89	Police				0		0	0	0
90	Fire				0		0	0	0
91	On Set Tutor				0		0	0	0
92	Motorhome Driver				0		0	0	0
93	Craft Service				0		0	0	0
94	Still Photographer				0		0	0	0
95	Weaponer/Pyrotechnics	2	100		0		0	200	0
96	Key PA				0		0	0	0
97	Production Assistant				0		0	0	0
98	Production Assistant				0		0	0	0
99	Production Assistant				0		0	0	0
100	Production Assistant				0		0	0	0
	TOTAL B				0		0	1000	1000

Producer To Producer Budget Template

	C PRE-PROD./WRAP EXPENSES		Amount	Rate	x	ESTIMATED	ACTUAL
101	Hotel(s)					0	0
102	Airfare(s)					0	0
103	Per Diem					0	0
104	Auto Rental(s)					0	0
105	Messengers					0	0
106	Office Rental					0	0
107	Taxis					0	0
108	Office Supplies					0	0
109	Copies						
110	Phones/Cel					0	0
111	Casting Director	flat fee	1	500	1	500	500
112	Casting Expenses					0	0
113	Working Meals		1	200	1	200	0
	TOTAL C					700	500

	D LOCATION/TRAVEL EXPENSES		Amount	Rate	x	ESTIMATED	ACTUAL
114	Location Fees	Ice cream parlor	1	400	1	400	100
115	Permits		1	300	1	300	300
116	Auto Rental(s)					0	0
117	Van Rental(s)		1	190	1	190	340
118	RV/Winnebago Rental					0	0
119	Parking, Tolls & Gas	prod. & picture vehicles	1	200	1	200	200
120	Truck Rental(s)					0	0
121	Other Vehicles					0	0
122	Other Trucking					0	0
123	Hotel(s)					0	0
124	Airfare(s)					0	700
125	Per Diem					0	0
126	Train fare(s)					0	0
127	Airport Transfers					0	0
128	Breakfast	20 people	2	7	20	280	208
129	Lunch	22 people	2	8	22	352	343
130	Dinner	22 people	2	9	22	396	0
131	Craft Service		2	100	1	200	159
132	Taxis & Other Transport	cast transport	1	175	1	175	0
133	Kit Rental(s)	crew transport	1	125	1	125	0
134	Cel phone(s)					0	0
135	Gratuities					0	0
136	Table & Chair rental					0	0
137						0	0
	TOTAL D					2618	2350

	E PROPS/RELATED EXPENSES		Amount	Rate	x	ESTIMATED	ACTUAL
138	Prop Rental					0	0
139	Prop Purchase		1	150	1	150	75
140	Wardrobe Rental					0	0
141	Wardrobe Purchase		1	150	1	150	0
142	Wardrobe Cleaning						
143	Picture Vehicles	2 picture vehicles/1 day each	1	375	2	750	255
144	Animals & Handlers					0	0
145	Hair/Makeup Expenses		1	100	1	100	0
146	Weapons Rentals					0	0
147	SFX Expenses					0	0
148							
149							
150							
	TOTAL E					1150	330

Producer To Producer Budget Template

F	STUDIO RENTAL & EXPENSES	Amount	Rate	x	ESTIMATED	ACTUAL
151	Build Day Rental				0	0
152	Build Day OT				0	0
153	Pre-Lite Day Rental				0	0
154	Pre-Lite Day OT				0	0
155	Shoot Day Rental				0	0
156	Shoot Day OT				0	0
157	Strike Day Rental				0	0
158	Strike Day OT				0	0
159	Electricity/Power Charges				0	0
160	Hair/MU/Wardrobe/Green Room				0	0
161	Studio Parking				0	0
162	Studio Manager				0	0
163	Phone/Internet/Copies				0	0
164	Cartage/Dumpster Rental				0	0
165	Miscellaneous Equipment				0	0
166	Studio Painting				0	0
167	Trash Removal				0	0
	TOTAL F				0	0

G	SET CONSTRUCTION LABOR	Amount	Rate	x	ESTIMATED	ACTUAL
168	Set Designer				0	0
169	Art Department Coordinator				0	0
170	Set Decorator				0	0
171	Lead Person				0	0
172	Set Dresser(s)				0	0
173	Greensperson				0	0
174	Draftsperson				0	0
175	Lead Scenic				0	0
176	Scenics				0	0
177	Painters				0	0
178	Construction Coordinator				0	0
179	Carpenter(s)				0	0
180	Grip(s)				0	0
181	Strike Crew				0	0
182	Art Production Assistant(s)				0	0
	TOTAL G				0	0

H	SET CONSTRUCTION MATERIALS	Amount	Rate	x	ESTIMATED	ACTUAL
183	Set Dressing/Props Rentals				0	0
184	Set Dressing/Props Purchases				0	0
185	Lumber				0	0
186	Paint				0	0
187	Hardware				0	0
188	Special Effects				0	0
189	Construction Materials/Rentals				0	0
190	Art Trucking				0	0
191	Meals, Parking				0	0
192					0	0
	TOTAL H				0	0

Producer To Producer Budget Template

I	EQUIPMENT/EXPENSES		Amount	Rate	x	ESTIMATED	ACTUAL
193	Camera Rental	flat	1	500	1	500	500
194	Sound Rental					0	0
195	Lighting Rental					0	0
196	Grip Rental	flat	1	1000	1	1000	1550
197	Generator Rental					0	0
198	Camera Lens Rental	flat	1	200	1	200	114
199	Camera Accessories Rental					0	0
200	DIT Equipment Rental					0	0
201	Walkie Talkie Rental	flat	1	100	1	100	0
202	Dolly Rental + Accessories					0	0
203	Crane/Jib Rental					0	0
204	Drone Rental					0	0
205	Production Supplies		1	150	1	150	127
206	Expendables		1	200	1	200	0
207	Aerial Photography					0	0
208	Green Screen Rental					0	0
209	Underwater Housing Rental					0	0
210	Missing & Damaged		1	500	1	500	0
	TOTAL I					2650	2291
J	MEDIA/STORAGE		Amount	Rate	x	ESTIMATED	ACTUAL
211	Digital storage purchase	2 hard drives	1	150	2	300	957
212	Film Stock Purchase					0	0
213	Film stock Prep & Process					0	0
214	Telecine/Film to Digital Transfer					0	0
215	Videotape/Audiotape Stock					0	0
216						0	0
	TOTAL J					300	957
K	MISCELLANEOUS COSTS		Amount	Rate	x	ESTIMATED	ACTUAL
217	Rights purchase					0	0
218	Air Shipping					0	0
219	Accounting Fees					0	0
220	Bank Charges					0	0
221	Production Insurance	school rate/workers comp	1	230	1	230	230
222	E & O Insurance					0	0
223	Legal Fees					0	0
224	Business License/Taxes					0	0
225	Film Festival Fees/Expenses					0	0
226	Publicity/Marketing					0	0
	TOTAL K					230	230
L	CREATIVE FEES		Amount	Rate	x	ESTIMATED	ACTUAL
227	Writer Fee					0	0
228	Director Fee – Prep					0	0
229	Director Fee – Travel					0	0
230	Director Fee – Shoot					0	0
231	Director Fee – Post					0	0
232	Fringes for Labor Costs					0	0
233						0	0
	TOTAL L					0	0

Producer To Producer Budget Template

M	TALENT LABOR	Days	Rate	OT (1.5)	OT sub	OT (2.0)	OT sub	ESTIMATED	ACTUAL
234	O/C Principal				0		0	0	0
235	O/C Principal				0		0	0	0
236	O/C Principal				0		0	0	0
237	O/C Principal				0		0	0	0
238	O/C Principal				0		0	0	0
239	O/C Principal				0		0	0	0
240	O/C Principal				0		0	0	0
241	O/C Principal				0		0	0	0
242	O/C Principal				0		0	0	0
243	O/C Principal				0		0	0	0
244					0		0	0	0
245	Day Player				0		0	0	0
246	Day Player				0		0	0	0
247	Day Player				0		0	0	0
248	Day Player				0		0	0	0
249					0		0	0	0
250	Background Actor				0		0	0	0
251	Background Actor				0		0	0	0
252	Background Actor				0		0	0	0
253	Voice Over Talent				0		0	0	0
254	Voice Over Talent				0		0	0	0
255	Dialect Coach				0		0	0	0
256	Choreographer				0		0	0	0
257	Stunt Coordinator	1	150		0		0	150	150
258	Stunt Player(s)				0		0	0	0
259	Fitting Fee				0		0	0	0
260	Rehearsal Fee				0		0	0	0
261					0		0	0	0
262	Pension & Welfare				0		0	0	0
	TOTAL M							150	150

N	TALENT EXPENSES	Days	Rate	OT (1.5)	OT sub	OT (2.0)	OT sub	ESTIMATED	ACTUAL
263	Airfare(s)				0		0	0	0
264	Hotel(s)				0		0	0	0
265	Per Diem	2	30		0		0	60	0
266	Cabs and Transportation	1	150		0		0	150	45
267	Extras Casting Director				0		0	0	0
268	Work Visa Fees				0		0	0	0
269					0		0	0	0
270	Talent Agency Fee (10%)				0		0	0	0
271					0		0	0	0
272					0		0	0	0
273					0		0	0	0
274					0		0	0	0
275					0		0	0	0
276					0		0	0	0
	TOTAL N							210	45

Producer To Producer Budget Template

O	EDITORIAL	Amount	Rate	X	ESTIMATED	ACTUAL
277	Editor				0	0
278	Assistant Editor				0	0
279	Post Production Supervisor				0	0
280	Editing Room Rental				0	0
281	Editing System Rental				0	0
282	Transcription				0	0
283	Online Edit/Conform				0	0
284	Screening Room Rental				0	0
	TOTAL O				0	0

P	MUSIC	Amount	Rate	X	ESTIMATED	ACTUAL
285	Music Composition				0	0
286	Music Licensing/Clearance				0	0
287	Music Recording				0	0
288	Recording Expenses/Rentals				0	0
289	Music Supervisor				0	0
290	Audiotape Stock/Files				0	0
	TOTAL P				0	0

Q	POST PRODUCTION SOUND	Amount	Rate	X	ESTIMATED	ACTUAL
292	Sound Editor				0	0
293	Assistant Sound Editor				0	0
294	Music Editor				0	0
295	ADR				0	0
296	Foley Stage/Editor				0	0
297	Foley Artists				0	0
298	Narration Recording				0	0
299	Audio Mix	1	1500	1	1500	0
300	Audio Layback				0	0
301	Dolby/DTS License				0	0
	TOTAL Q				1500	0

R	DIGITAL INTERMEDIATE	Amount	Rate	X	ESTIMATED	ACTUAL
302	Color Grading/Digital Intermediate	1	1500	1	1500	600
303	Hard Drive Purchase(s)/Storage				0	0
	TOTAL R				1500	600

S	POST PRODUCTION-DIGITAL/FILM	Amount	Rate	X	ESTIMATED	ACTUAL
304	Archival Footage/Photos				0	0
305	Archival Researcher				0	0
306	Clearance Supervisor				0	0
307	Screeners				0	0
308	Film Prints				0	0
309	Masters/Clones				0	0
310					0	0
	TOTAL S				0	0

T	TITLING/GRAPHICS/ANIMATION	Amount	Rate	X	ESTIMATED	ACTUAL
311	Titling				0	0
312	Graphic Designer				0	0
313	Visual Effects (VHX)				0	0
314	Animation				0	0
315	Motion Control				0	0
316	Closed Captioning				0	0
317	Subtitling				0	0
	TOTAL T				0	0

U	MISCELLANEOUS	Amount	Rate	X	ESTIMATED	ACTUAL
318	Shipping				0	0
319	Messengers				0	0
320	Post Working Meals				0	0
	TOTAL T				0	0
	TOTAL POST PRODUCTION				3000	600

Budget Analysis

It's incredibly helpful and necessary to analyze the budget, line by line, after you have finalized it. You've collected a treasure trove of information that can inform your future productions. With an actualized budget, you have the final answers to the questions you posed to yourself when you first created the estimated budget months or years before.

For *Sundae* the "underage" came from a few places. Labor costs were pretty much on target. They saved money on the location fees—a family friend let them shoot at her home for the Yellow House, and the Ice Cream Parlor didn't have to close and let them shoot on a quiet day. The production paid for all the ice cream, etc. that they used for the shoot.

They came in under on cast/crew food costs by eating at two local restaurants and saved on the picture vehicle costs because a local rental company had cheap black town cars. They spent more money on hard drives because the RED Dragon media took up more memory space than anticipated. The only unanticipated cost was the director's airfare to Paris to work with a talented editor who could also get the audio mix for free, which helped save money in the post budget. Their color correct was less expensive than originally budgeted.

Overall, their estimated budget was a solid, realistic one and they had a production without any mishaps. Through friends, favors, and other smart decision making, they were able to create an award-winning short film for about $8,000—a very impressive feat.

For your own productions, actualized budgets become your own budgetary database that allows you to estimate future budgets with greater clarity and accuracy. Make sure to keep accurate accounting so your actuals are correct and save them for future reference. Then when you go to budget for another project, you can use a past budget as a template and then scale it up or down for the new project.

Wrap Paperwork

To wrap out the production there is much paperwork that needs to be finalized and archived. Many of these documents will be required for the Deliverables for the project (see Chapter 15, *Post Production*):

Cast Contracts—All SAG-AFTRA or non-union contracts for the cast. If you registered the production with a guild, you'll need to send them all signed required documents to close out your production and have your bond returned. Always keep copies for your files.

Crew Deal Memos—All deal memos for each crew member.

Location Contracts and Release Forms—All contracts and signed location release forms for each location used.

Actualized Budget—The final budget as discussed above including Purchase Orders, PO Log, Petty Cash Log, Payroll Log, Sales Log and Check Log.

Payment Paperwork—A copy of all payment documentation for cast, crew, and paid invoices.

Music Contracts—All negotiated and signed music licensing contracts including master license and synchronization documents. (See Chapter 17, *Music*.)

Daily Call Sheets—A copy of each call sheet for every day of principal photography.

Daily Production Reports—A copy of each production report for every day of principal photography.

Production Book—The production book, including all contact info for cast and crew, vendor contact info, and any other production-related information.

Insurance Coverage Documents and Certificates—A copy of the insurance policy/coverage and any insurance certificates issued during the production.

Wrap Party

It's always nice to have a party for the cast and crew after you have wrapped production. Your budget will dictate what you can afford but it's a fun way for everyone to get closure (you've been through a lot together) and to thank all for their hard work and talent. On low-budget projects, you can set it up at a bar or restaurant where the cast/crew can gather at a certain time and share in the sense of accomplishment and collaboration. If you can pay for the first round of drinks it is always a generous and appreciated gesture.

For me, making a film is always an awe-inspiring feat no matter what the circumstances. I'm always uniquely aware of how impossible the odds are, so when you can pull it off, it feels like a small miracle! Yet the miracle is one manifested by every single person who put his or her efforts and talent to realize the vision. Without the collective will of the cast and crew, the project wouldn't exist.

RECAP

1. All departments return rentals promptly after the wrap so the production is not charged for additional rental days.

2. Assess any lost, damaged, or missing equipment and take care of the paperwork and payment promptly.

3. Retrieve credit card authorizations and deposit checks.

4. Actualize the budget by entering and adding up all invoices and expenses through a PO log and a petty cash log.

5. Take some time to analyze the variance between the estimated budget and the actual one so you can accurately plan for future projects.

6. Create a binder and keep copies of all wrap paperwork on file. You'll need it for when you deliver the project.

7. A wrap party for all cast and crew is a nice way to thank everyone and let them know how much you appreciate their hard work and talent.

CHAPTER 15
POST PRODUCTION

ALTHOUGH IT'S CALLED POST production, the work actually begins during pre-production.* You need to plan all the steps for the finishing of the project while you are planning all the steps for the *beginning* of the project—this is called **workflow.**

Workflow

To create the workflow, answer the following questions:

1. What is the highest quality that you can afford to shoot on and master to?

2. What media format best suits the aesthetics of your project?

3. Will you need to transcode any material?

4. How much digital storage space will your project require? How much "throughput" or speed of processing and connectivity speed will you need in your hard drive purchases?

In many ways, a director's job is how he uses all his second chances.

—*Twyla Tharp*

---

* *Special thanks to Director of Photography/Lighting Designer Rick Siegel (www.ricksiegel.net) for his technical expertise, which was a great help to me in writing this section.*

5. How will you "back up" the acquired and edited materials to guard against loss, theft, or damage?

6. Whom do you need to consult to make and implement these choices and decisions? When do they need to be brought into the process?

7. Where will your project be shown? Film festivals, television/cable, theaters, digital streaming, DVD, VOD, mobile, internet, social media, and any media yet to be invented?

8. What are the technical requirements for the project's audio and video masters?

9. What are the required deliverables?

Picking a Format

These days most projects are usually shot in digital video, although some are shot in film (35mm or Super 16mm). New formats and technologies emerge frequently. It's best to discuss format choices with the project's director and DP. You can find the latest tech information by reading trade publications and manufacturers' websites and going to technology conventions. At the beginning of pre-production, the director, DP, editor, and post production supervisor will discuss tech decisions. Below is a list of the tech aspects to understand and consider:

SENSORS AND PIXELS

Different camera manufacturers have different size sensors which present different qualities or looks and come in different megapixel counts. If you use insufficient **pixels** (picture elements) for your filming situation, the image will look fuzzy or blocky. A sufficient number of pixels for the end use of the project—say, projection in a theater—and the human eye won't even see that there are pixels. It's best to figure out where your project will screen and then decide which sensor is right for the job.

FRAME SIZE

Frame size is determined by the number of pixels and scan lines that make up the digital image. When we say "definition" we are talking about the amount of detail in the image. High definition (HD) has two basic sizes, both in 16:9 aspect ratio—**720** and **1080**. 720 is also known as 1280 × 720, meaning there are 720 lines of 1280 pixels per line. 1080 is also known as 1920 × 1080—1080 lines of 1920 pixels per line. 2K, 4K, 5K, 8K (more Ks in the future?) have scan lines that exceed 2000, 4000,

5000, and 8000 horizontal lines respectively. Ultra high definition (UHD) is 3840 × 2160 and is the latest pixel resolution. Your delivery requirements will determine your selection of frame size.

ASPECT RATIO

Aspect ratio is the ratio of width to height of a video image. Projects viewed on smaller screens (e.g., TV, mobile, computer) are usually 16:9 or 1.77:1, (which equals 16 divided by 9). Theatrical films can be 1.85:1 and go up to 2.35:1 (widescreen). The director and DP will have strong opinions about what aspect ratio is best for the project.

If shooting film, make sure the assistant cameraperson sets the viewfinder masking on the camera to whatever aspect ratio has been chosen.

FRAME RATE

Frame rate refers to the number of images that are recorded or displayed per second. Don't confuse it with shutter speed, which is the amount of time that light hits the sensor as each frame is captured. Common frame rates are 23.97 frames per second (fps), 24 fps, 29.97 fps or 30 fps. The director, DP, and editor will want to decide the frame rate based on aesthetics and delivery requirements.

PULL DOWN/PULL UP

Pull down/pull up occurs when you need to convert your digital material from one frame rate to another. If you shoot at one frame rate but need to deliver your master at another frame rate, you'll need to do a pull down/pull up. Prior to filming, make sure the post production supervisor is part of this discussion before the frame rate decision is finalized.

CODEC/COMPRESSION

Codec (**co**mpression/**dec**ompression) is a compression scheme for recording video. Video and audio signals are usually compressed during storage and transmission and then the signals are decompressed when you master your project. Codecs come into play when you record or transcode the material. **Transcoding** is the process of converting digital material from one codec to another. This is often done so the original digital files can be compressed and loaded into the editing system—that way it takes up less media storage space.

Some cameras can output **RAW**, which is picture information directly from the sensor without any signal processing whatsoever. This will take up much, much more digital storage space and could cost more time and money in post production. Figure out if your project requires RAW digital files and whether the budget can support the added costs. Remember to factor in throughput speed and storage space requirements for the massive amount of digital information that RAW files need.

BIT DEPTH

Bit depth is a measure of light sample size or shades of gray, or color representation. It is expressed as a number—usually as either 8 bit or 10 bit—but it can go higher. There are more "steps" in 10 bit than in 8 bit and 10 bit gives the video more markers and precision which allows for rendering and manipulation with more detail in post production. Depending on what you are filming (like green screen or material for visual effects) and how the final master will be seen (like cinema vs. mobile phones), you can decide what bit depth is needed.

CAMERA SENSOR AND DYNAMIC RANGE

Each camera model has a specific sensor and dynamic range, although most digital cameras and 35mm film have 12–14 exposure stops of dynamic range. Most monitors and theatrical projectors allow our eyes to see only five exposure stops of dynamic range so each digital camera manufacturer has created a logarithmic formula to maximize the full dynamic range on a five-exposure stop display device. Some of these formulas have names—Sony has S-Log, Arri has C-Log, and RED has their own formula. Keep in mind that new HDR (High Dynamic Range) monitors are able to show full dynamic range and over time will become more affordable and access will increase.

LUT

A **Look Up Table (LUT)** is a computer application that affects the way you see full dynamic range video out of the camera and on monitors on a film set or in the edit room. A LUT is "non-destructive" and does not actually change the raw footage logarithmically to the off-board recorder. The default LUTs are "Rec 709" and "Rec 2020," which were created to conform to the five exposure stops of dynamic range that display devices can show (see above). Consult with the DP to find out if she has a different LUT they want to use for the project or go with Rec 709 or Rec 2020.

COLOR SAMPLING

Color sampling is made up of *luminance,* which measures brightness and *chrominance,* which measures color. To keep it simple—color resolution is expressed by 3 or 4 numbers, most commonly as 4:2:2 and 4:4:4. The higher each number, the higher the color resolution of the image. If color resolution is critical for your project (i.e., green screen or visual effects), try to work with a camera and recording CODEC that allows for the higher color resolution, like 4:4:4.

Camera Test/Workflow Test

Before finalizing the format choice for your project, the DP will need to perform a camera test on the formats being considered for the project. Different cameras have different tech specs and "looks." Testing various lenses, filters, and the innumerable menu settings on a camera will produce varied cinematic results.

When doing a camera test, try to re-create the lighting that is planned for the project so the results will reflect the final look as much as possible. Once you have found the look you like best, make sure to keep detailed notes and save the menu settings to a memory drive so they can be replicated when you shoot the project.

After the camera test, the next step is to test the post production workflow. You'll start with the acquired material, load it into the planned edit system, then color correct and create a final master at whatever post facility you plan to use. This way everyone really understands every step in the process and can see how it works and affects the final master. You'll want to know where/how the project will be seen after completion—screening in a cinema is far different than a project that plays exclusively on laptops and mobile devices.

Tech Specs Sheet

After the workflow and tech aspects are decided, the producer or post production supervisor should write up a **Tech Specs sheet** to codify all of the tech requirements for the cameraperson, digital imaging technician (DIT), and sound recordist into one document. It should be sent to each crew person when they are hired so they are aware of the requirements and can ask questions ahead of time. In some cases they may need to adjust their equipment order to meet certain requirements. If you are working with different people for each of these job positions (like shooting in multiple cities and picking up different crew people in each one) it is even more critical to make sure everyone is on the same page technically. Any mistakes or variations made "in the field" will disrupt the post production phase and could add time and money to the budget/schedule.

How to Put Together a Post Production Team

As the producer you'll need to put together a good post production team to create and deliver a great project. Below is a list of the key team members, what they do and when they work. Depending on the project itself and budget, your team may not include all of these crew positions. Here's a breakdown:

Post Production Supervisor—hires key post production personnel, creates and maintains the post production schedule, and creates/completes the deliverable requirements. Consults during prep and then comes onto the project during post production.

Post Production Coordinator—assists the Supervisor with scheduling, coordinating, and paperwork requirements.

Editor—edits the film during and after principal photography.

Assistant Editor—assists the editor, loads and logs all media into editing system, organizes the edit, constantly and consistently backs up all media and Edit Decision Lists (EDLs).

Sound Editor—adds sound effects, edits audio tracks, and organizes the tracks in preparation for the audio mix. Works mostly after "picture lock."

Foley Artist—creates sound effects in a foley studio that can't be found in a sound effects library or from wild sound tracks. Usually works after picture lock.

Sound Mixer—mixes the audio tracks, masters the soundtrack, and lays it back to the project's final visual master file.

Music Supervisor—collaborates with the director and the editor to find pieces of music for the film's soundtrack.

Music Composer—composes an original soundtrack for the project.

Archivist/Researcher—researches and finds archival material (photographs, film or video, newspaper articles) related to the project's narrative. Starts work during pre-production.

Online Editor—re-creates the project with higher resolution materials from the editor's Edit Decision List (EDL).

Colorist—color corrects the final master in consultation with the director and director of photography to achieve the final desired cinematic look.

Transcriber—transcribes any audio material (usually interviews) to allow the editor and director to choose appropriate clips for the edit.

Graphics—creates any graphics or screen titles for the project during post production.

Visual effects—creates any visual effects (VFX) for the project. Often starts planning during pre-production, is on set during filming, and then works throughout post production to complete the VFX work.

Hiring the post production supervisor is a critical decision—this position is similar to the assistant director during the production phase of the filmmaking. **Post production supervisors** oversee the teams, create schedules, coordinate vendor bids and budgets, and keep track of all the tech specs and deliverable requirements. They should be knowledgeable about the latest post tech information and have relationships with post facilities to make for the best finishing outcomes for the project. If you can't hire a post supervisor, you will need to learn/know this important information and take on this role in post production.

Planning for Post

Once you have a general plan for finishing your project, set up a meeting with the post production supervisor at whatever post production facilities you plan to use. Often there will be several places—one for audio work, another for digital intermediate (DI)/online work, and another for the color correct. You'll need to set up meetings at each place and coordinate between the three facilities. The earlier you have these meetings the better so that the post production supervisor and editor can set the master plan/schedule and put time "on hold" at each facility. This will keep everyone on track and on budget.

When creating the calendar, don't schedule each step of the process back to back. It may look like it all fits perfectly on the paper calendar but there are inevitable glitches, equipment failures, time overruns, etc., so it is always good to give a day or two extra for each process, e.g., audio mix, color correct, online edit, DI, mastering, etc. For a low-budget narrative feature film, 14–16 weeks is a good rule of thumb for editing and finishing. Feature documentaries often take longer to edit, depending on the amount of footage and what the project requires.

Digital Workflow Example

Most independent productions shoot digitally and finish digitally these days. Some may shoot in film and a few may release on film (although it is fairly rare now.) The information below will be geared toward the digital/digital model but I'll cover information about film when appropriate and helpful. Below is a sample workflow for a project that is shot digitally and mastered to a digital format:

WORKFLOW EXAMPLE
Acquisition format: High definition (HD) Digital
Release/Delivery format: 1080i Digital file and DCP master

Step-by-step workflow:

1. Acquire HD digital media

As discussed earlier in this chapter there is a long list of technical and aesthetic factors that need to be discussed and decided before choosing a camera and post workflow. Then, once on the film set, the DP, camera operator and assistant cameraperson will ensure the material is captured properly—in focus and well exposed. The Digital Imaging Technician (DIT) will work with them to record all material properly onto media cards, hard drives, and backed up properly so there is no loss of any material.

Protocols will have been set up ahead of time with the producer, post production supervisor, and editor, and a tech specs sheet sent to the DIT ahead of the job. The DIT will transcode, back up material, compile the audio files, and make sure the day's media is delivered daily to the edit room or some other secure location.

2. Edit the project

The assistant editor (AE) (or editor if you don't have an AE) will connect the media drives to the editing system. If media needs to be transcoded, the AE will do that work to prep the material prior to editing. Refer to the earlier *Picking a Format* section to make sure the material in the edit system is all in the same and correct CODEC. If not, it could compromise the technological quality of the footage, causing inconsistencies with audio sync, shifts in time code, and other problems that could affect the accuracy of your EDL.

Popular editing systems include Final Cut Pro (FCP), Avid, and Adobe Media Composer. Hard drives with all the digital material will connect to the editing system so the editor can cut the project. While filming takes place, the editor often cuts quickly utilizing the script supervisor's notes to create an assembly or "string out" of the project so the director can see how the scenes are cutting together while they are still shooting. Giving the director immediate feedback on performance and production allows the director to adjust quickly and easily. Once principal photography is completed, the editor usually works in tandem with the director. Each director and editor team will decide how best to work together.

The editor will cut the picture and audio and create separate audio tracks for sync sound (usually actors' voices) and for music and sound effects. Remember throughout the editing period to *backup* all materials, editing timelines, and whatever else is important, in case the computer crashes. Often separate hard drives are used for backup or cloud computing storage or both.

3. Decide on music
Choosing music is an important step in the process. The soundtrack may include existing musical recordings and/or new compositions recorded specifically for the project. Music supervisors facilitate music selection and are a real asset to the director and editor during the process. Temp music may be used initially in the edit room while licensing deals are made and music is composed and recorded. (See Chapter 17, *Music*.)

4. Graphics/Titles
Any graphics or screen titles (opening credits, end credits, and lower thirds) will need to be created and added to the project before locking picture.

5. Visual Effects
Visual effects will be added throughout the editing process as they become available in various stages of completion. Ideally the final VFX will be integrated into the final project before picture lock.

6. Schedule work-in-progress screenings
Make sure to screen the project for audiences in as big a screening room as the budget will allow before the project is finalized to get invaluable audience feedback (see *Work-in-Progress Screenings* section later in this chapter.)

7. Lock picture
Locking picture is a big moment in the life of a project. This is when picture editing stops and there will be no more changes! Now the final stages of finishing will begin.

8. Sound editing

Utilizing a computer system with audio mixing software like ProTools allows the sound editor to create and edit all the sounds needed for the project. Every piece of audio—actor dialogue, music, sound effects, narration, etc.—that is heard at the same moment in the soundtrack will need to be placed on a separate track. This allows the sound editor to put each track at a different volume level for later use by the audio mixer. (See Chapter 16, *Audio*.)

9. Record automated dialogue replacement (ADR) if necessary.

ADR refers to the process of recording actors' dialogue during the post production phase. This is done to replace inaudible original dialogue or to add lines where none existed before. ADR is usually done at an audio recording facility with a recording booth for the actors so they can watch video playback and lip sync to the section they are replacing or adding to. Keep in mind that if you are adding lines, it is sometimes a better audio match if you can re-record at a location similar to the place where the scene was originally recorded. If at all possible, it's best to use the same brand/model/type of microphone so it records a similar sound quality.

10. Record foley sounds, if necessary

Foley is the creation of additional everyday sound effects to match specific action in a film. A foley session will utilize foley artists to create the sound of actions or circumstances on screen like footsteps, a car door closing, clothes rustling, or the background murmur of a busy restaurant.

11. Audio mix

Once all the tracks are properly laid out, the sound editor will hand off the project to the sound mixer who will mix the tracks so they are heard in proper relationship to each other on the soundtrack. For instance, there may be a scene with a couple walking along the street in Times Square on a busy summer evening. The tracks will include 1) Actor A's voice, 2) Actor B's voice 3) foley sounds of Actor A's footsteps on the pavement 4) foley sounds of Actor B's footsteps 5) wild sound of Times Square recorded on the shoot day 6) sound effect of a bus driving by 7) sound effect of a cab horn honking, and 8/9) the stereo tracks of the music composition. And that's a fairly simple scene!

Once the sound mixer has mixed all the tracks throughout the project, the levels are saved on the computer as the multi-track recording. The next step will be a "mix down" to four final tracks—tracks 1 and 2 for voice and tracks 3 and 4 for music and effects (M&E). (See Chapter 16, *Audio,* for more details.)

12. Finalize licensing

During the finishing stage of your project, there are several steps going on at once. There may be several kinds of licensing that will need to be finalized—music licensing (for any recorded music on the soundtrack), archival licensing (for film/video clips, photographs, graphic images) and Dolby or DTS licensing (for proprietary audio technology.) Keep signed copies of the documents to include in the paper deliverables. See chapters 16 *(Audio),* 17 *(Music),* and 18 *(Archive Materials)* for more details.

13. Online Edit/Conform

Depending on the post production schedule, this step can happen at the same time as the audio work and mixing.

Based on the workflow, budget, and deliverables, you may decide to finish the project on the computer editing system entirely. From a technical perspective, you can lock picture and do any of the finishing work like audio mix, titling, and color grading on the same computer editing system and then output a master digital file.

Although you can finish your project in your computer editing system, it won't be as technically sophisticated as if you go to a post facility and do an online edit/conform of your project. For this step, you'll take the EDL, project file, and reference cut and replace all of the low resolution (low res) materials with the exact same frames from the high res (uncompressed) materials from the camera originals (or telecined masters). During this process the hi res visual effects, graphics, and stock footage will be integrated too. The conform is usually a combination of automated reassembling and the hands-on work of the online editor and assistant.

14. Color grading and Digital Intermediate (DI)

After the conform, there will be color grading and then final output to a digital intermediate (DI). **Color grading** is the digital process whereby you can manipulate all photographic screen elements, including luminance (light and shadow) and chrominance (color and hue) levels to create the desired final look for the project.

The director and the DP attend the color grading (or color correct) sessions. This is essential because the material was shot in a specific way with a plan on how it would be finished in the color grading session to realize the full cinemagraphic potency of the images. The producer or post supervisor should be there as well to make sure everyone stays on budget and schedule.

If you have not experienced a color correct session, I suggest you contact a post facility and ask to sit in and watch one. It really helps to see the process in action to better understand the information discussed above. The **DI** is the final output file after all of the picture finishing work is completed.

15. Do the audio layback

Once you have the DI and the final audio mix, it's time to marry them together to create your final master. At the **audio layback** the beginning of the mixed soundtrack is synced to the beginning of the final visual master and now you have the final master of your project!

16. Create the deliverables

Once you have completed the final master digital file, the deliverables can be created. Store multiple backups of the master in several different physical spaces—on hard drives and on a cloud computing storage space. **Deliverables** (discussed in greater detail later in this chapter) refers to the list of masters in multiple formats and other tech requirements needed by a distributor, network, or film festival.

Post Finishing Information (film only)

If your project has been shot on film there will be two additional steps before the editor can connect the digital files to the editing system and start the process outlined above. The exposed film stock will need to be processed, prepped, and transferred to digital files.

PROCESS AND PREP EXPOSED FILM STOCK

At the end of each shooting day the Assistant Cameraperson will take all of the exposed film stock and attach camera reports to each film can with a purchase order for the total amount of film stock and instructions for the processing and telecine. The production team will send a production assistant to the film lab or they will pack up the film stock and ship it out to the film lab.

At the film lab, the technicians will develop/process the film and prep the film reels for the next step. The processing and prep is charged on the amount of exposed film stock on a "per foot" basis.

FILM-TO-DIGITAL TRANSFER OR TELECINE:
The next step is to have a post facility transfer all the film to digital files. This is called the **telecine**. It can be done several different ways—each one takes a different amount of time and is priced accordingly. Here they are in ascending order of cost:

One-light/Unsupervised—The least expensive and least time-consuming telecine is a **one-light or unsupervised** transfer. For this kind of transfer, the colorist sets a general look for each lighting setup and then lets the film go through the telecine machine until the film shows a new lighting/location setup. Then the technician re-adjusts the machine and lets the film go on through the process. Before the session, the colorist will often have a brief discussion with the DP and/or the director to get general notes. Otherwise there is no input into the process and it is done by the colorist alone. This type of transfer is often charged on a "per foot" basis.

If you choose an unsupervised telecine you may decide later to re-transfer the **selects** (final sections of the film that end up in the final cut) at a supervised transfer (see below) at the end of the editing process. It is more cost effective because you'll do the supervised transfer on a much smaller amount of film footage.

Best Light—A **best light** transfer is the next step up from a one-light. This allows for more interaction and discussion with the colorist and more time for adjustment throughout the transfer process.

Supervised—A **supervised** transfer is the most expensive telecine and it allows for the DP, director, and/or producer to be in the session the entire time. The colorist works in tandem with the DP and/or director on every frame of the film to make it look exactly as it should, to complete the total aesthetic look of the film. This is a very dynamic process and the more experienced the colorist, the more expensive the session. This kind of session is billed on a "per hour" basis. I usually budget triple the running time of the footage as a gauge of how much time and money a supervised transfer will take.

Film Negative and Match Back (film only)

Sometimes you may need to go back to the film footage originals for either a re-transfer or to cut the negative (a very rare occurrence these days). First you need to understand time code and keykode:

TIME CODE/EDGE NUMBERS/KEYKODE

SMPTE (Society of Motion Picture and Television Engineers) **time code** is a standard created by the society to label individual video frames. **Edge numbers** and **keykode** are numbers that are placed on each film stock frame in consecutive order. Make sure, during the telecine session, that the edge numbers/keykode and time code information are placed either on screen (lower left, right or center of frame) or in another area of the frame so it can be read by the editor but not seen on the television monitor.

You'll need the edge numbers/keykode info if you end up having to go back to the film negative and need to "match back," so you can find the exact film frame that corresponds to the exact frame of video. The time code is needed so that your edit decision list (EDL) can properly record each edit and keep track of it in your editing system.

MATCHING BACK TO YOUR ORIGINAL FILM NEGATIVE

As discussed above in the telecine section, if you need to match back to the negative you will use the keykode numbers to locate the particular film frames from the original film negative to re-transfer the "selects." The colorist will go to the film negative reels and put up only the sections of the negative that are in the final master of the film. Once these are re-transferred and color corrected, you'll need to re-edit or "auto conform" the new re-transferred bits of film according to the EDL.

Deliverables

All the materials (paper and tech) that are required when you deliver a project to a distributor, broadcaster, or other media outlet are called **deliverables**. There are general certain deliverable requirements but each distributor/broadcaster will have their own specific deliverables list. Time-consuming and expensive to produce, tech deliverables have strict technical requirements. The paper deliverables list is comprised of the legal and financial document requirements such as deal memos, contracts, licenses, insurance, and budget actuals.

Usually the last payment from a distributor or broadcaster is tied to the master delivery and completion of all deliverables. The quality control engineers will go through all the tech deliverables to make sure they are correct before the last payment is released. Creating all the deliverables is usually costly; work out your cash flow so that you have enough capital to pay for the delivery work before you receive your last payment.

Here's a sample deliverables list:

SAMPLE DELIVERABLES LIST FOR NON-THEATRICAL DISTRIBUTION

DIGITAL CINEMA MASTERS
Digital Cinema Package (DCP) encrypted with a Digital Cinema Distribution Master (DCDM) on hard drive

VIDEOTAPE MASTERS
HDCamSR digital master 16 × 9 full frame (1.77:1) Texted

HDCamSR digital master 16 × 9 full frame (1.77:1) Textless

HDCamSR digital master 16 × 9 letterbox (1.85:1 or 2.35:1) Texted

HDCamSR digital master 4 × 3 full frame (1.33:1) Texted

Apple ProRes file—2K (2.35:1) ProRes 444 file type

DVD screening disc with copyright on-screen

SOUND ELEMENTS
Master Stems for Dialogue tracks, Music tracks and Sound Effects tracks

6-track Printmaster

2-track Printmaster

6-track Music and Effects tracks

6-track (4 + 2) Music and Effects tracks

2-track Music and Effects Printmaster (LT/RT)

6-track Stereo Split-Track Master (D/M/E)

Source Music & Composer's Score

GENERAL DOCUMENTS
Dialogue script in English

Combined Dialogue/Continuity Spotting list

Closed caption & Video description files

Stock Footage licenses

Written credit list for all crew and cast

All cast and crew contracts, deal memos, release forms and confidentiality agreements

Advertising Key Artwork

Paid Advertising statement

Laboratory Access letter
Union contracts
Non-union contracts
E&O insurance
Chain of Title documents
Certificate of Origin & Certificate of Authorship
Title Report
Dubbing and Editing restrictions
MPAA registration
US Form PA Copyright Registration certificate
List of any residual payments

MUSIC DOCUMENTS
Music cue sheet
Music contracts
Music licenses
Dolby or DTS license

PUBLICITY MATERIALS
Press Kit with log line, short and long synopsis, above-the-line bios, director's statement, and production notes
100 hi-resolution (300 dpi or higher) digital still publicity photographs
"Making of" or Electronic Press Kit (EPK) video
HD video film trailer
Website

Editorial Notes

As producer, one of your key responsibilities is giving notes on the various cuts of the project as it goes through the editorial process. You will also schedule and coordinate work-in-progress screenings for audiences during critical times in the edit process.

How you give notes is just as important as the content and quality of your notes. I always start with what is positive about the cut and what is "working." It may sound obvious but I have seen people launch into a litany of needed changes and what isn't working first—without saying the positive—and even the most seasoned editors have a hard time "hearing" the notes.

Obviously the editor and director think what they have done is best, so if you have a different opinion you'll need to advocate and explain your thoughts carefully. A blanket comment like "The first act isn't working, you'll need to fix that" isn't constructive. If you think the first act isn't working, you should cite specific places where there are problems and offer suggestions as to how it might be fixed. Notes are not edicts—they should be the beginning of a dialogue about what can be done *with* the editor and director. That way you are working together to solve issues.

If you disagree on a key point in the project, then it will require a more in-depth discussion. You'll need to be able to speak freely and talk things through to resolve issues. Work-in-progress screenings can be helpful so that the director and editor can hear the opinions of more objective viewers.

Work-in-Progress Screenings

A **work-in-progress screening** is a viewing of the latest cut for a group of people to give feedback on what is and is not working with the project. The project should be in at least a good rough-cut form and in a good enough technical state (i.e., all the dialogue is audible and temporary music has been placed in the soundtrack) so the audience will not have trouble watching/hearing it. Rent or borrow a screening room with adequate seating for the amount of people who will attend. Ideally it is a small screening room with nice seats, clear sight lines, good audio, and a big screen. Do a tech test ahead of the screening so there won't be any technical problems. If you can't afford to rent a space, you might be able to use someone's living room if there are enough seats and a big enough screen with good sound.

Once you have a room reserved, contact your invitees at least two weeks before the event with time, date, location and the general rundown of the schedule—first the screening, a short break, and then a question and answer session—so they know how much time to allow. I usually invite almost twice as many people as I can accommodate so I'm assured of a full house.

After the screening, ask the audience to fill out a brief questionnaire and then do a 30-minute Q&A to get consensus and discussion from the audience. Remember, they are giving you approximately three hours of their personal time to watch and comment on your project, so make sure you are considerate of their generosity. Start on time, serve beverages and snacks (if you can afford it), and keep to the schedule so people get out on time.

Spend time in creating the questionnaire so it reflects the kind of information you need for the continuing editorial process. Good sample questions include:

1. Total running time—too long or short?

2. Pacing—too slow or too fast?

3. Lead actors' performances—great, good, OK, not so good?

4. Anything not understandable?

5. Anything overstated or too expositional?

6. Any scenes that should definitely be cut or definitely kept?

7. Would you recommend to other people to watch—if so, what demographic would enjoy it most?

8. Whatever else the viewer wants to share.

Once the audience has completed the survey, lead a 30-minute discussion about key questions you want to focus on with the group. It's helpful to let everyone know that you really want to hear *constructive* criticism and not only positive encouragement. You may know many of the audience members personally and it's human nature to not be overtly critical, but you are relying on them to state problems and concerns constructively so you understand what you need to improve to make a better film. Breaking the ice at the beginning of the discussion by positing a criticism can be useful—like, "Some people think the cut is too long—do you agree?" or, "There's a scene in the middle with the father that some people think should be cut out—what do you think?"

Make sure everyone gets to speak a bit at the beginning. If one or two people monopolize the session it won't be an effective session. If you start to get consensus around an opinion, ask everyone if they agree or disagree with a show of hands, then pick someone who disagrees to state the opposite view so you can test it out.

Lastly, there will come a point (usually around 30 minutes) where the conversation devolves into "nit-picking" and then it's time to end it. After that point the constructiveness is depleted and the notes are no longer useful. Thank everyone and collect the questionnaires and then get to work with the director and editor on making the next cut better.

RECAP

1. Consider the myriad technical issues, deliverables, and distribution streams when deciding what format to shoot for your production. Research these factors and do tests before making the final decision.

2. Put together a strong team starting with a knowledgeable and experienced post production supervisor and editor.

3. Create a workflow for the entire post production/finishing process. Create Tech Specs sheets so all the technicians on set know what to do to capture the proper materials and files.

4. Know the deliverables list and tech requirements before you finalize the budget/schedule for post production.

5. Give specific editorial notes periodically throughout the post process. Consult the director and editor on how best to communicate the notes and set up a schedule for such screenings.

6. Arrange for work-in-progress screenings after the project is at the rough-cut stage to get objective feedback and notes.

CHAPTER 16
AUDIO

Sound Recording During Principal Photography*

THE AUDIO WORK ON your project begins with the recording of the sound on set during principal photography. The sound recordist/production mixer is a key member of the crew and your project will be greatly impacted by how well your sound is recorded "in the field." Low-budget projects are notorious for not having the best sound and the films suffer for it. If you don't invest wisely in professional audio recording, you'll be throwing good money after bad to try to fix things that weren't recorded properly the first time around. It's always more expensive to fix something in post production than to do it properly at the time of recording.

As with all key crew department heads, interview your top candidates and check two references of your final choice for the position of sound recordist. Then on the first day of shooting, if you haven't worked with the recordist before, take the time to listen on headphones to the first

> *Habitually creative people are prepared to be lucky.*
>
> —E. B. White

---

* I've been expertly assisted in this chapter by the talented sound designer Zach Seivers of Snap Sound in Los Angeles, CA (*www.SnapSound.tv*).

couple of takes after you have begun shooting. Make sure it sounds technically correct to you—no over modulation, no hissing, etc.—good, clean sound. If it doesn't sound good, you should discuss your concerns discreetly with the director and sound recordist, immediately, until you are satisfied that the problem has been corrected and that you have confidence in the recordist's abilities. If you do not, then replace him or her immediately.

I had a situation like this on a film I coproduced a few years ago. It was a very low-budget film, so I couldn't hire the sound recordist I usually work with. I hired someone who was recommended to me but he was just starting out and didn't have a lot of work experience. Unfortunately, we realized after listening to the first few takes on set that our new recordist wasn't up to the professional standard we needed. We called our backup sound recordist (who was a bit more expensive) immediately and brought him in for the next day's shoot. It was a bit awkward, but it was imperative to get the best sound for the production.

How to Get the Best Sound on Set

As producer, your first job is to hire the best recordist/mixer you can. The next thing you need to do is *listen* to what the sound recordist tells you when you are shooting on set. In the hierarchy of production, the visual elements always seem to take precedence over the aural ones. But you should resist this urge to dismiss audio concerns raised by the sound recordist when on a tech scout or while shooting. You only have one shot at getting good, clean, well-recorded sound. If you don't get it in the field, whatever you do in post will never be as good as what was really happening on set that day and it will always cost more time and money.

Tech Scouts

In the *Pre-Production* chapter I outlined the key department heads that need to attend the tech scout and it included the sound recordist. It's important to have the recordist there so they can listen for any red flags or audio concerns and bring it to the producer's attention ahead of the production. This will save you headaches on the shoot day, so it's critical to listen to the space and to the recordist's recommendations. If you can't bring the sound recordist on the tech scout, someone on the production team should be listening for any problems. Below is a list of red flags:

> **AURAL RED FLAGS ON TECH SCOUTS AND SHOOT DAYS**
>
> Refrigerator (put your car keys in the fridge or put a big reminder note by the video monitor so you don't forget to turn it back on!)
> Telephones/cell phones
> Electric generators/electric transformers
> Airplanes/airports
> Buses
> Trains/subways
> Construction
> Landscaping work—lawn mowers and leaf blowers
> Air conditioners
> Muzak (in elevators and retail stores)
> Barking dogs
> Paper thin floors, ceilings, and walls in apartments
> Beach waves
> Road traffic
> Elevator shaft noise
> Local parades or street fairs

As discussed in Chapter 15 (*Post Production*), discussing and testing the workflow for the audio recording, mixing, and finishing is essential to ensure a good technical audio outcome for the project. The sound recordist and the post production sound designer should talk and test the audio workflow before principal photography begins. Establishing this line of communication has many rewards, saving lots of time and money and avoiding costly mistakes.

Room Tone

Room tone is the recording of the sound of the room you were filming in without anyone talking or making noise for at least 30 seconds. It is used in post production by the editor/sound editor to fill in "gaps" in the aural environment when an edit/cut occurs and the audio "drops" or changes. Room tone is usually recorded before you move on to another setup in a different audio environment. Keep the actors in their places on set in the way they were for the scenes you just recorded. Often they will be wearing **lavaliere** microphones—small mikes that can be clipped under a person's clothing—so sound will be recorded through those mikes, as well as through the boom microphone. The assistant director or sound recordist will ask for "quiet on set" and then say "recording room tone." The recordist will capture the sound of the room through all of the microphones for at least 30 seconds. If you are recording audio into the camera as well, the camera operator will often record a shot of a microphone so it is clear that this section is room tone and not sync sound.

There is a caveat to the issue of room tone. Some editors and sound designers do not use it. They use the recorded silence between dialogue from the production footage to fill the aural gap in post production. Consult the editor and sound designer before you begin principal photography to decide if you need to record room tone.

Wild Sound
Wild sound is any recorded audio that is not part of the sync sound recording while the camera is rolling. Examples include the sounds of birds chirping in a park or the sound of a flag flapping in the wind.

The director, in consultation with the editor and the sound recordist, should create a list of wild sounds they want recorded during the shooting period. Wild sound is a great benefit because it is real sound recorded in the field specifically for your production. It can help to fill out the sound design for your project and reduce the need to purchase audio from a sound effects library.

Audio Post Production
The audio recorded in the field will be used during the editing of the film. As discussed in Chapter 15 (*Post Production*), there are several different steps in audio post production: 1) building the various audio tracks; 2) adding sound effects; 3) recording Automated Dialogue Replacement or looping; 4) creating and recording foley work; 5) laying in music tracks; 6) sound editing; 7) sound mixing; 8) audio layback.

Building Audio Tracks/Sound Design
Throughout the editorial process, the project's soundtrack will be comprised of multiple audio tracks. By isolating each sound on its own track, the sound mixer can adjust each one separately for the overall audio mix. In a particular scene an actor's voice will be set at a different volume level than ambient background sounds. The music soundtrack may be mixed low when heard under dialogue but may come up full when played during a montage scene without dialogue. By putting each piece of audio on a separate track, the audio mixer can make the adjustments and set the levels individually to create the final mix. As a general rule, dialogue

is put on certain numbered tracks, sound effects on others, music on others, etc. Usually, the picture editor will do a rough version of what a sound designer will do later in the post production process.

Adding Sound Effects

A sound editor fills in the soundscape of the film with the audio elements to make each scene work. The sound editor uses elements from many places—the production wild sound, sound effects libraries, and audio from foley work.

Creating and Recording Foley

Foley is the craft of creating and adding sound that specifically matches action happening on screen, e.g., the rustle of someone's coat when put on, or footsteps as an actor climbs the stairs, or the clink of a glass when someone gives a celebratory toast in a restaurant. The craft is named after Jack Foley, the sound effects pioneer who virtually invented the process when working on films in the early days at Universal Studios.

A foley artist works in a recording studio, watches the film and simultaneously creates the appropriate sound to match the action on screen. They often create sounds from things that have absolutely nothing to do with the unique action on screen, like coconut shells with padding for horse hoofbeats, or a heavy metal stapler for gun shots, or corn starch in a leather pouch for snow crunches. If you ever get a chance to watch a foley session, make sure you go ... it's *so* entertaining.

In an ideal world, all added sound effects would be created by a foley artist. For low-budget productions, it is often not affordable and sound effects have to be created from libraries and recorded sound exclusively.

Recording ADR

Automated Dialogue Replacement (ADR) or "looping" is when an actor records or re-records dialogue to replace or add to the original audio in a scene. This can be needed for several reasons. If an actor didn't have the proper accent during the original recording, she can work with a dialogue coach and re-record the proper-sounding accent to make it work. Or if a scene took place at a very noisy place, like a beach or on a busy street, the original dialogue recording would be inaudible and all the dialogue would be looped. ADR can be used to change or add to dialogue. If the shot is far enough away from the actor's face or the back of their head, you can record and replace new dialogue easily.

Laying in Music Tracks

The project's music will consist of licensed music, composed music, or both. The director will meet with the composer, music supervisor, and sound editor to "spot" the project with them. **Spotting** is when they all watch and listen to the edited cut and make notes on where/how/what kind of music needs to be placed in specific places throughout the film. The director will describe the kind of mood, emotions, and feelings that should happen in each scene and cite audio references to give examples of what they might like to hear at each place in the soundtrack. The rest of the music team will give their feedback and ideas and a creative plan and schedule will be put together.

Sound Mixing

A **sound mixer** takes all the separated tracks laid out by the sound editor and puts them in the right aural relationship to each other in the full soundtrack. Working with the director and editor, the sound editor mixes it all together based on previous discussions. One section may be all dialogue with ambient sound in the deep background and no music. Another section may have an emphasis on the music, with no dialogue and minimal ambient sound. The mix will reflect the director's overall vision.

The sound mix takes place in a recording studio and the director, editor, and producer are usually in attendance. The mixer mixes the tracks and then plays it back for all to hear, then the director gives notes, the mixer makes adjustments, and they listen to it all over again. The entire mix is done this way until its completion.

Recording studios are fitted out with fantastic sounding stereo audio speakers which allow you to listen to the project in one of the best sounding audio environments you'll ever experience. But don't be completely seduced by the awesome sonic technology. Your film will be watched in many different ways and places with differing levels of technological sophistication. It will be played in state-of-the-art cinemas, in fancy home theaters with surround sound speakers, on laptops, cell phones, and old television monitors. Keep this in mind as you mix your film and always ask to listen to the mix on the TV speakers at some point while you are in the mixing studio. **TV speakers** replicate the worst-case audio scenario and let you hear how the mix sounds on not-so-great speakers. It can be a revelation—the fantastic music mix now drowns out the dialogue of your lead actor in the restaurant scene. Or the ambient track is too low in the mix and you can't hear the birds while your actors are walking through a park. Once the entire soundtrack is mixed and locked, the next step will be the layback.

Layback

Layback is when the soundtrack is put in sync at the very beginning on the project and then "laid down" or "laid back" to match the picture frame by frame. By matching the time code at the head of the master, the audio should be completely in sync from start to finish. If you are creating a 16mm or 35mm film print, the final soundtrack will be converted to a magnetic optical track and married to the visual film track to create the final film print. After the layback (and the color correct is completed), you will now have your final master!

Dolby Digital, DTS, and THX

Often a soundtrack will be mixed with trademarked technology (either Dolby or DTS) that is used to reduce audio "noise." If your 35mm film print or digital master will be played in Dolby/DTS-enabled theaters then you'll need to use this technology. If you wish to use Dolby or DTS you'll need to pay for a usage license and have a company consultant attend the audio layback to certify that it meets the technical standards of the proprietary technology. License prices depend on the usage. A film-festival-only license is a lower rate than a theatrical rate.

THX is a certification process for cinemas. Created by Lucasfilm, it requires movie theaters to follow strict technical specifications for their screen projection and audio systems to receive the certification.

RECAP

1. Hiring a sound recordist/production mixer for principal photography is very important. Research references and choose the best person you can afford.

2. Facilitate communication between the recordist and the sound designer so they can plan ahead for audio post production while in pre-production.

3. Check with the sound editor/designer to decide if room tone should be recorded at each location for use in the post production.

4. Sound editing includes the laying out of multiple audio tracks, ADR, sound effects, and foley work to create a full and proper audio landscape for your film.

5. Sound mixing is a collaboration between the director and the mixer to achieve the final mix to maximize the aural experience of the film.

6. Depending on where your film will be screened, you may need to license proprietary audio technology (Dolby Digital or DTS) for your mix.

7. An audio layback occurs when you match the audio track to the final visual master of your project.

CHAPTER 17
MUSIC

Obtaining Music Rights

A MUSIC SOUNDTRACK USUALLY CONSISTS of music that was previously produced and is commercially available and/or music composed specifically for the project by a composer. Either way, you'll need to obtain the music rights.

Music rights consist of two kinds of rights for each piece of music—the Master Recording License and the Synchronization (Sync) License. A **master recording license** refers to the rights for the performance of a piece of music. These rights are usually obtained through the record label that made the recording. The **synchronization (sync) license** pertains to the rights for the song itself and is usually held by a publishing company that represents the person who wrote the song.

To give an example let's use Bruce Springsteen's recording of *Santa Claus Is Coming to Town*. The master recording license will need to be negotiated with Columbia Records, a subsidiary of Sony Music Entertainment. The writers of the song *Santa Claus Is Coming to Town* are J. Fred Coots and Haven Gillespie and on the *ASCAP.com* website their

> *Everything should be as simple as it is, but not simpler.*
>
> —Albert Einstein

publishing companies are listed as EMI Feist Catalog, Inc. and Haven Gillespie Music Publishing Company respectively. While researching this information, I found out that the J. Fred Coots estate has sought to terminate the publishing rights deal with EMI Feist, so future negotiations for those rights may change. This is a great example of how important it is to do thorough research in the complicated world of music licensing.

To negotiate the master recording license, contact the record company and ask for the licensing department. You can often find this information from an internet search or, if you have a CD of the song, you can get the information from the back cover. To research the publisher for the sync license you can search the websites of the three major publishing groups—*www.BMI.com*, *www.ASCAP.com* and *www.SESAC.com*. As the producer, contact each company—Columbia Records, EMI Feist, and Haven Gillespie and request the rights you require for your project. This process is called **clearing the rights** to a song.

What Rights Do You Need?

Once you have the contact information for the music companies, figure out what rights and what length of time you need each license. Here are the rights generally available for any piece of music:

- U.S. theatrical
- U.S. network television
- U.S. cable television
- U.S. DVD
- U.S. VOD (Video on Demand)
- U.S. digital streaming
- International theatrical
- International network television
- International cable television
- International DVD
- International VOD (Video on Demand)
- International digital streaming
- Internet/Web
- Film festivals
- Educational

For international rights, they can be sold per region or per country, e.g., UK/Ireland, Spain, France, etc. If you can afford it, the best rights level to ask for is *all* of the above. That is usually referred to as "all media worldwide." The other consideration is the length of time you own the rights. The longest time period is usually referred to as "in perpetuity." If you can afford "all media worldwide, in perpetuity," then you are covered for every scenario forever.

Whether a license is "exclusive" or "non-exclusive" is another deal point to consider. Usually "non-exclusive" is enough for a film soundtrack and it allows the rights holder to license the same song to others for other purposes. "Exclusive" would mean the publisher and the recording artist couldn't license to other entities for other uses. Decide what you need before you contact publishers and record labels.

Depending on the artist, the song, the record label, and the publisher, you may not be able to afford all the rights you want or need. That's when negotiation comes into play. The publisher may be willing to give you the sync license for all media worldwide, in perpetuity, for a reasonable sum but you can't afford the rights for the specific performance on the record.

Regarding the Bruce Springsteen example, you might be able to obtain an affordable price for the sync license but Springsteen's record label will require a fee that is well beyond what you can afford to pay. You could decide to record your own version of the song with a singer that would be an affordable alternate. Then you would do a "buyout" with that vocalist so you had the rights for all media worldwide, in perpetuity. Or you may decide you *have* to use Springsteen's version, but can only afford the film festival rights for two years. But if you decide to license for film festivals only, you might be taking a big gamble.

If the project does well at film festivals and a company wants to distribute it, you may not be able to purchase all the music rights in order to take the deal. Then you'll have to face a hard decision to either turn down the distribution deal, re-record the song with a different artist, or replace the song completely. If you re-record or replace, you'll need to check with the distribution company to make sure they still want to buy your project with a different soundtrack.

My advice is to *not* take that gamble. Always plan for the success of your film and lock down all the rights you need for all markets, domestic and internationally. If this is not possible, then purchase film festival music rights only and *pre-negotiate* all rights in case you need to license the music to include additional rights after a sale. That way you'll know what your music licensing costs will be and what you'll need to get for a distribution fee if you sell the project in order to cover the music licensing costs.

Putting in the License Request

Now that you understand master recording and sync licenses, there is a timeline for licensing requests to music companies. If the song is sung or heard as diegetic sound in the film, then you need to obtain the rights *before* you shoot the scene during production.

For example, if you have a scene with a character singing a lullaby to her baby, you'll need to obtain the sync rights from the song's publisher and written permission from the actress for her performance, all *before* you shoot that scene on set. If a band is performing a song on a stage while actors dance, you'll need to obtain both the master recording rights to the performance and the sync rights for the song the band performs. This needs to happen *before* you film the scene. For this usage you'll need to secure *all* rights for *all* territories so you are assured of being able to use the footage no matter what sales you receive for the project. You can't take the risk because the performance of the actors is tied to that specific song/performance.

If you shot the scene without the rights and find out later that you can't afford them, you'd have to find another song with the same tempo and try to re-cut the scene, thus avoiding any close-up shots of the band. It would be incredibly difficult—perhaps impossible—and a huge waste of time and energy in post production. It would be much smarter to get the rights before you plan to shoot the performance of the song on-camera.

For music that will end up in the project's soundtrack, contact the record labels and publishers early enough so there is enough time to get an answer before you lock picture. If you find that you can't afford the rights to a song, you have time to replace it with another piece of music. You don't want to waste time on negotiating rights to music that ends up on the cutting room floor, so try to figure out what music has a good chance of ending up in the final soundtrack and begin contacting the appropriate entities. Lastly, if you have several recordings that are on the same record label, it may help to negotiate a better deal by waiting until you have the list of everything on that one label before sending in your request.

The timing on getting rights is tricky because it can take many months to successfully negotiate a license. Start at least three to five months ahead of time for major record labels. They have more requests and bureaucracy so you need a longer lead time.

Music Rights Request Letter Format

Finding out who owns the master recording rights and the sync rights to any given piece of music can require a bit of detective work. As discussed earlier, if you have a CD, the info will be on the cover art or disc. Otherwise do a search at the top performing rights society websites—*www.BMI.com* (Broadcast Music, Inc.), *www.ASCAP.com* (American Society of Composers, Authors and Publishers) and *www.SESAC.com* (Society of European Stage Authors & Composers)—they collect the fees and distribute the royalties to the songwriters and publishers. Each has fairly powerful search engines that allow you to type in the name of the song to track down the publishing information and other relevant contact information.

Once you have the contact info for the publisher and the record label, call them and ask for the music rights person. You will be given the correct name and email address. Your written request should include the following information:

1. Title of recording/composition

2. Album title

3. Artist/band/orchestra name

4. Usage you require, e.g., background music under pictures, sung by the lead character. Also describe what is seen on the screen when the music is heard, e.g., someone being shot or a family driving in a car on a highway.

5. Short description of your film.

6. Time length of usage, specify minutes and seconds and if it is repeated later in the film, state the time length for the additional usage.

7. What territories you are requesting e.g., all media, worldwide, in perpetuity.

8. Exclusive or non-exclusive use.

9. What you can afford to pay for the rights (or gratis) and if you have already made deals for the same amount of money to other publishers/record labels.

Negotiating for the Music Rights

The music rights owners (record label or publisher) will always want to charge as much as possible and you will want to pay as little as possible. Therein lies the negotiation process.

Use the sales skills that you perfected throughout the making of your film. Explain how your project will give exposure to the songwriter or performer if included on the soundtrack and where you expect your project to be seen, e.g., film festivals, VOD, television, DVD, digital streaming, etc. This kind of exposure could be of real value for an up-and-coming music artist.

To increase your chances of a successful negotiation try to find a mutual friend or contact who can bring your request directly to the artist or songwriter. As we discussed in Chapter 5 (*Casting*), when you were attaching talent to your film, getting in direct contact can help make a much stronger case for your request. If you go through the label or the manager, you could get a "no" without the artist even knowing about it because the manager deemed the monetary offer too small. But if you can send the artist a copy of your project with a beautiful handwritten note from the director explaining why the song is brilliant and essential to the film, you might get a wholly different answer. I've had this happen many times and I call it the "director's magic letter"—we get a quick "no" from a manager and then send a copy of the film and a persuasive letter to the artist directly. They read it and then we get the rights for an affordable sum. Don't underestimate the connection between two artists when creating art!

Writer/director/producer Paul Cotter (*Bomber, Vera*) has some advice regarding music soundtracks for low-budget films:

"If you've got a tight budget, it's great to be flexible about the music and who you get on the soundtrack. The basic rule I follow is 'like attracts like.' If you've got no money, find bands who have no money. You're then on a level playing field and they're usually cool, understand your predicament, and are willing to play along. Just be honest and upfront with them, which is something you should be with everybody (honesty goes a long, long way in low-budget filmmaking). Also, they need the publicity you can give them. Don't go for Lionel Ritchie. He's loaded and doesn't have time for "riff raff" like us."

Most Favored Nation

The term **most favored nation (MFN)** refers to the concept in the film industry of paying everyone the same amount of money for the same thing. The concept is commonly used in international trade agreements where each country signed to an agreement has the same terms as every other country. We discussed this in Chapter 6 (*Pre-production*) regarding how to pay crew members and keep pay rates consistent across salary levels. Music rights negotiation uses the concept of *most favored nation*, as well. It is the industry practice to pay the publisher (sync rights) the same amount as is paid to the record label (master recording rights). Additionally you usually pay the same amount for each piece of music—so if you are paying $500 for sync rights and $500 for master recording rights for one song, you will do that same deal for all of the other songs on the soundtrack. The only exception might be for a song by a very famous band that would require a vastly higher number and would not be part of the MFN pricing system.

The best negotiating strategy is to go to the entity (publisher or label) you think will give you the best deal first. If the song is a well-known composition being sung by an unknown performer, go to the record label first to make a deal. Once you have an affordable negotiated rate in writing, then you go to the publisher for that song. Inform them of the master recording rate you just negotiated and ask if they would be willing to accept the same amount for the sync rights.

This will be the process for all the music rights you need to "clear" for the soundtrack. Let's say you have seven pieces of music you wish to clear—start with the five songs that will be the easiest and most affordable first. Then go to the last two and let them know the license amount you have already negotiated for most of your soundtrack and ask them to take the same deal for their music.

If they agree to it, send out the paperwork for signature. If not, you may have to agree to a higher amount for the last two songs to make the deal. If this happens, because you are working on a MFN basis, you'll have to pay the higher amount to the first five publisher/labels, as well. It's like the tide in the ocean—it raises or lowers all boats equally.

If the higher amount for each composition proves to be too expensive, you may decide to replace the expensive songs with songs that will accept the lower MFN rate so you can keep to your music budget.

Out-of-Copyright/Public Domain Music

Copyright law in the U.S. has specific rules that cover the length of the copyright for the creator of the material. After the copyright expires the work is considered in the **public domain (PD)** and you do not need to purchase a license. Always consult an attorney to confirm a piece of music is in the public domain. Here are the general guidelines:

For works created after Jan. 1, 1978—under copyright for at least the life of the longest surviving author plus 70 years—earliest possible PD date is 1/1/2048

For works registered before Jan. 1, 1978—under copyright for 95 years from the date copyright was secured.

For works registered before Jan. 1, 1923—copyright protection of 75 years has expired and these works are in the public domain.

For a piece of music composed by Wolfgang Amadeus Mozart in 1777 there is no copyright on the material and there are no synch rights for the composition. But you will need to acquire the master recording license for the performance recording by a specific orchestra on a specific album. When you pick a recording of a classical piece of music it is wise to choose a smaller record label because you'll have a greater chance of negotiating an affordable price than if you go after the rights to the New York Philharmonic recorded at Carnegie Hall for a major record label. The great thing about classical music is that there are often numerous recordings of the same piece of music and you can choose to edit with the most affordable recording of that composition.

Fair Use

Fair use is discussed fully in Chapter 9 (*Legal*). Please go there for a more in-depth explanation of the concept and its use. Two good websites for more information are at *www.fairuse.stanford.edu* and *www.centerforsocialmedia.org*.

Fair Use is an important concept that pertains to usage of various copyrighted materials such as books, archival footage—and music too. This is a definition from the Stanford website—"fair use is a copyright principle based on the belief that the public is entitled to freely use portions of copyrighted materials for purposes of commentary and criticism. For example, if you wish to criticize a novelist, you should have the freedom to quote a portion of the novelist's work without asking permission. Absent this freedom, copyright owners could stifle any negative comments about their work." At the American University's Center for Social Media there is a downloadable *Documentary Filmmakers' Statement of Best Practices in Fair Use* handbook that is very helpful.

E&O Insurance

As discussed in the *Insurance* chapter, if you need to purchase E&O insurance, you'll be required to demonstrate that you have all the pertinent music licensing completed for the project. Proper music clearance will be necessary in case there is ever a claim filed against the project.

Blanket TV Agreements

The term "blanket" music rights agreement refers to certain agreements that major broadcast television and radio networks obtain from the music performing rights societies (BMI, ASCAP, and SESAC). Networks like PBS, BBC, VH1, and MTV have these agreements because of the sheer volume of the music they use in their programming. The agreements grant them permission to use songs in catalogs represented by the society. The rates are based on the volume of music used and the type of usage and allow the broadcaster to pay for the music fees for your project when it airs on their network.

If you sell your project to a network with such an agreement, it is important to find out what it does and does not cover. It can save you from having to clear your music for certain markets (e.g., U.S. television only) or all markets, depending on the agreement they have in place.

Music Cue Sheet

A **music cue sheet** is a standard form that lists information about each piece of music included in your project's soundtrack. The cue sheet is then filed with the performing rights societies prior to a theatrical release or television broadcast so they can track payments due to the music publishers. There is an example at *www.ProducerToProducer.com*. It lists each piece of music, the publisher, the record label, usage length (minutes and seconds) and its use (e.g., background music, song performed by an actor, opening title music). Music cue sheets are a key paperwork deliverable so you need to keep track of this information throughout the post production process.

Cease and Desist

If you screen or distribute your project publicly without properly clearing the music materials you will be in violation of copyright law and there are legal ramifications. Additionally, if your film gets into a film festival, often you'll be required to sign a document stating that you have all the rights to the material in the film. If you sign this form without the proper rights, you are violating the agreement and are at risk for legal action if you are caught.

If this occurs, you most likely will be sent a **cease and desist letter** from the copyright holder citing your alleged violation and requiring you to immediately stop showing the project publicly (e.g., film festivals, digital, television, theaters). If their allegations are true, you then have two options after you stop showing the project. You can: 1) immediately try to negotiate a deal for the rights (and they will probably be more expensive than if you had negotiated properly in the first place), or; 2) remove the music and create/record a new soundtrack with different, cleared music. After the music licensing paperwork is signed, you can go back to showing your project.

Don't take this risk. Make sure you have the proper rights to material before you screen or broadcast it publicly.

What Happens if You Can't Find the Copyright Holder?

Sometimes, no matter how much research you do, you won't be able to find the copyright holders for a given piece of music. In that case, document your attempts to find and contact the copyright holders by keeping a phone call/email log of all your attempts to contact them. If the copyright owner comes forward at a later date, you can prove that you made best efforts to find and contact them. You'll still need to negotiate at that time for the rights, but your log will demonstrate that you did not willfully ignore the copyright law.

Music Rights Clearance Person/Company

By now you may have decided *not* to use any music because the prospect of clearing the rights yourself sounds a bit daunting. After reading this chapter, you may decide that you will pay any amount of money to not have to go through the steps I have outlined! Have no fear, there are several companies and individuals that are in the business of clearing music rights for productions.

Clearance companies/individuals charge fees on a per song, per project, or hourly basis. Music clearance people or music supervisors have long-standing relationships with all the record labels, which comes in handy when dealing with a well-known artist or with a particularly difficult negotiation. On a film I produced several years ago, a few of the songs in the soundtrack were performed by a very well-known musician on a big record label. I tried to get the rights on my own for a low price and was turned down. Because we really needed to procure the rights on a deadline, we hired an experienced music clearance company to try to procure the rights on our behalf. They got the deal done within two weeks and we made our deadline!

Original Music Compositions for Your Project

Another option for your soundtrack is to hire a composer to create original music compositions. Depending on the composer, the length of your film, and how many pieces need to be composed, this may be the best option. It allows you to customize the music to fit your visual material—down to the second—and at the outset you can negotiate a composition fee for all the rights, in perpetuity, worldwide, or whatever licensing requirements you need.

A music composition license is specific for each project, but remember to consider the category of "exclusive" or "non-exclusive" rights. Exclusive means that only your project can use the particular compositions for the territories and time period stated in the contract. "Non-exclusive" allows the composer to license the same music to other entities for the time period and territories stated in the contract. Non-exclusive is usually a cheaper rate than exclusive, so consider what you really need before deciding.

If you plan to create a CD/downloadable music of the film's soundtrack, make sure to license all the music for that purpose. It will probably be more expensive and include a profit-sharing arrangement with the composer based on sales.

Finding a composer is much like hiring any other key department head. You should look up screen credits for films you really like and think will be appropriate for your project and talk to other filmmakers to get recommendations. If you have a no/low-budget, go to music programs at local universities and find out if there are music students who would want to create a soundtrack for your project.

Music Libraries and Royalty-Free Music

Using music libraries can be a cost-effective way to license music; many have a wide range of music genres to fulfill your particular need. Music library websites allow you to search, listen to, and try out virtually unlimited music samples. Some libraries focus on a certain genre of music while others are exclusive to one composer's work. Once you decide to use the music in your soundtrack, you can choose the kind of license (and length of time) you need and pay for it online with a credit card—very easy and straightforward.

"Royalty-free" music allows you to purchase the music for a particular usage in your project and never need to renew the license for the life of the project. For all music in your soundtrack—wherever it is acquired from—you still need to fill out a Music Cue Sheet.

Music Supervisors

Music supervisors are hired to consult and create music soundtracks. They are experts at making recommendations about what song or composition would work well for your particular project. They get pitched a lot of music from artists who want to be included on soundtracks and their job is to know what bands and artists would be right for your film. If you have a tight budget it may make sense to hire a music supervisor because they would know where to get good deals from various artists. Music supervisors also license music and their relationships with music creators allow them to negotiate affordable and appropriate licenses that match your budget. Look at screen credits on projects that you admire for music supervisors who would be right for your project.

RECAP

1. **When licensing music for your film, you'll need to purchase the master recording license from the record label and the synchronization (sync) rights from the publisher.**
2. **The preference is to acquire the rights to "all media, worldwide, in perpetuity."**

3. Research the rights holders and submit a licensing request form via email far in advance of your deadline.

4. Negotiate the music rights with the entity that will be least expensive first. Then use the "most favored nation" principle to get the other entities to agree to the same licensing fee.

5. In the United States, for music copyrighted after 1978, the copyright remains in effect for at least 70 years after the death of the composer. Public domain music does not require a sync licensing fee.

6. Some radio and television broadcast networks have blanket license agreements with performing rights societies whereby they pay performance royalties to the society for the song's writers.

7. Music cue sheets are used to track payments to the music publishers.

8. Make sure you clear all your music before your project is screened publicly.

9. If you can't find the copyright holder, keep written documentation of your attempts to find and contact the music's composer and record label.

10. A music rights clearance person is a professional who can assist you in acquiring and negotiating music licenses.

11. Look at screen credits and ask for recommendations for music composers if you wish to hire someone to create a music soundtrack for your film.

12. Music supervisors recommend music for inclusion in your soundtrack. Their relationships with music creators can be invaluable in putting together a good soundtrack.

CHAPTER 18
ARCHIVE MATERIALS

Archive and Research

RESEARCH AND ACQUISITION OF archive materials may be a part of your project. While its usage is most common in documentaries, archival materials may be needed in narrative projects as well. For example, a film may include a scene where a character watches television or listens to a car radio or looks at specific archival photos in a photo album. All of those archival materials will require research, acquisition, and licensing so you can use them.

To begin archival research, you'll want to locate the online and physical locations that contain your required subject matter and materials. There are many archival websites that allow you to view clips/photos online, while others require an in-person visit to view the material. For those requiring an in-person visit, you can arrange to have someone from your production travel to the archive or hire a local researcher who can make the trip on your behalf.

Once clips/photos of merit are located at an archive, you'll need to request a screener. A **screener** is a low-quality/low-resolution copy of the original material, usually with burn in time code (BITC) and a watermark

Do, or do not. There is no "try."

—Yoda, from The Empire Strikes Back

added to the video frame. Archives charge nominal fees to cover the research, dubbing, and shipping costs of screeners and these fees can add up over time. Your editor will use the low-res screener during editorial. Once the material is licensed, the reference time code numbers will be sent to the archive and they will send back a digital file (of the highest technical quality without the time code) to be included in the completion of the project.

Steps to Acquire and Use Archive Materials in Your Project

There are several steps required to obtain and utilize archive materials for your film:

1. Research and find the needed material
2. Contact the rights holder and acquire a copy of the photo or a screener of the material
3. Edit the film utilizing the archive materials
4. Lock picture and create a list of all the archive materials needed for the final cut of the film
5. Contact the rights holder and negotiate a licensing fee for the rights you require
6. Obtain a copy of the highest quality version of the material to re-edit into the final film
7. Sign paperwork and pay for the licensing fee

Archive Researcher

Depending on the project, you may need to hire an archive researcher to do the work—it can be a complex and time-consuming job. In some cases the archive materials may come from the people who are the subject of your film and you will not need to go to an archive library. That will reduce or eliminate the research phase of the process but you will still need to take all the other steps outlined above. Archive research requires a good understanding of where to go and how to sniff out the places that might have the right material for your film. Researchers know all the various libraries and archives and will log, track, and organize the material. They have relationships with many of the big archive libraries and can be helpful in brokering a deal to get the licenses for your film.

Archive Libraries

There are many archive libraries and most of them can be searched online. Check out *www.ProducerToProducer.com* to find out which ones may have the material you are searching for. Here's a list of the kind of places that will have material:

- Photo and film/video libraries
- National and international television news companies
- Local newscasts
- Historical museums and institutions—national, local, and university
- The U.S. National Archives
- Individual archives owned by a person or estate

Once you have found material at an institution you'll need to get a low-quality copy so you can work with it in the editing of your film. This is usually done by purchasing a screener copy. For photos, you'd be sent a low-resolution copy of the photo. There will be a watermark on the photo or a running time code on the video that matches back to the original, higher-quality master for the video/film. You'll cut in the material you want for your film from the screener and decide if it belongs in the final cut of the film. Once you know all the elements that will be a part of the film, create a master list of the archive name, the time code numbers for the beginning and end of the clip, the length of the clip and a brief description of what is happening on screen. Once you have every photo or clip in a master list, you should collate it by archive name.

The next step will be to contact each archive and negotiate for the licensing of the clip/photo. Although you have locked picture on your film, you should not completely finish the film until you know you have successfully negotiated the rights for each archival element. If you can't afford a certain clip, you may need to alter your film by removing the archival material and changing the final cut.

National Archives and Records Administration

The United States government maintains the National Archives and Records Administration (NARA) in College Park, MD. It was established in 1934 by President Franklin Roosevelt but has holdings that date back to 1775. It contains copies of the Declaration of Independence, the U.S. Constitution, and the Bill of Rights. More than 365,000 reels of film and 110,000 videotapes reside in the archives. Many of the films and videos are listed online, but usually you need to go to the archives or hire a researcher to see what holdings might be useful for your film. Go to *www.archives.gov* for more information about how to research and obtain reproduction copies of their materials. Usually you will need to pay for reproduction costs (which may include a digital intermediate copy for the archive itself, as well) at an approved vendor.

The archives were created by employees or agents of the U.S. government, so most of the records in the custody of the NARA are in the public domain. But some of the documentary materials may be protected by copyright. In that case, you'll need to contact the rights holder to get permission and perhaps pay a licensing fee.

Fair Use

Fair use is discussed fully in Chapter 9, *Legal*. Please go there for a more in-depth explanation of the concept and its use. Two good websites offering more information are *www.fairuse.stanford.edu* and *www.centerforsocialmedia.org*. This is a definition from the Stanford website: "Fair use is a copyright principle based on the belief that the public is entitled to freely use portions of copyrighted materials for purposes of commentary and criticism. For example, if you wish to criticize a novelist, you should have the freedom to quote a portion of the novelist's work without asking permission. Absent this freedom, copyright owners could stifle any negative comments about their work." At the American University's Center for Social Media there is a downloadable handbook, *Documentary Filmmakers' Statement of Best Practices in Fair Use*, that is very helpful.

If you use material in your film and you think it falls under one of the guidelines for fair use, you should consult an attorney to make sure you are on solid legal ground. Once you feel certain you are in compliance, use it in your film with confidence and you will not need to pay a license fee.

Archival Usage and Negotiation

To negotiate the rights for the archival material you require you'll need to know a few things:

1. The archive's identification number for the photo or clip.

2. The name and contact details for the archive.

3. For a clip, the required length (measured by # of seconds) and the number of times it is used in the film.

4. The rights you require (e.g., all rights worldwide, in perpetuity, or U.S. television and theatrical only, etc.).

5. Are there any other photos or clips you need from the same archive?

Once you have all of these details you can contact the archive and begin the negotiation.

Each archive will have a price list based on the rights requested. The most expensive will be all rights worldwide, in perpetuity, and the least expensive will probably be for film festival only. For moving image clips, the rates will be based on a per-second charge and there is usually a minimum required—often 30 seconds. If you only need 15 seconds, you will still be charged for 30 seconds regardless, so it is important to group your material by archive. Sometimes multiple archives have the same photo or clip and you can group your archival purchases to one archive so your total clip requests are over the minimum and you save money. If you have one 10-second clip, one 15-second clip, and another 5-second clip (which add up to 30 seconds), you'll get more material for the same cost.

Everything is open to negotiation. If you are purchasing a lot of material from one or two archives you have some leverage. Each archive will give you the standard charge as the first price but it's always a good idea to go back to your contact person to ask for a discount if your budget is tight.

License Paperwork

Once you have negotiated a price, ask each archive for the license agreement for the photos or footage. It is best to run it by your attorney to make sure that it covers the proper rights and usage you require. Confirm that the document proves that the archive has full ownership of the material so they are legally allowed to grant you the rights.

All of the archival licensing agreements will be needed when you apply for Errors & Omissions (E&O) insurance (see Chapter 10, *Insurance*). The insurance company may request copies when you submit the E&O application to prove that the production has all the rights required. The licensing agreements are an essential part of the legal paperwork/deliverables for your project.

Cease and Desist

If you screen or distribute your project publicly without properly clearing the archival materials, you will be in violation of copyright law and there are legal ramifications. Additionally, if your film gets into a film festival, often you'll be required to sign a document stating that you have all the rights to the material in the film. If you sign this form without the proper rights, you are violating the agreement and are at risk for legal action if you are caught.

If this occurs, you most likely will be sent a *cease and desist* letter from the copyright holder citing your alleged violation and requiring you to immediately stop showing the project publicly (e.g., film festivals, digital, television, theaters). If their allegations are true, you then have two options after you stop showing the project. You can: 1) immediately try to negotiate a deal for the rights (and they will probably be more expensive than if you had negotiated properly in the first place), or; 2) remove the material from the project and re-edit.

Don't take this risk. Make sure you have the proper rights to material before you screen or broadcast it publicly.

RECAP

1. **Use photo and moving image archives when you need to acquire historical material for your project.**

2. **Archive researchers are knowledgeable about archive resources and can find and procure the materials you need.**

3. **Negotiate for the rights you require for the project—"all media worldwide, in perpetuity" is best.**

4. **If you think your usage falls under the fair use criteria, consult an attorney to make sure you are correct and don't need to pay a license fee.**

5. **For moving-image material, the licensing fee is usually charged by the second and there is often a 30-second minimum. Group archive clips from the same archive together to save money.**

6. **You may need to submit the archive license agreements when you apply for the E&O insurance policy.**

7. **If you don't clear all the archival materials, the copyright holder could send a cease and desist letter to stop screening/distribution of the project.**

CHAPTER 19
MARKETING/PUBLICITY

MARKETING AND PUBLICITY ARE an important part of making your project. **Marketing** refers to how you brand, promote, and sell your project to sales agents, distributors, and audiences. **Publicity** refers to the dissemination of promotional materials to make sales agents, distributors, and the public aware of your film and generate sales. The two areas go hand in hand and overlap. Audience engagement is a key part as well.

A critical aspect of making your project—the marketing/publicity plan and materials should be discussed and planned for at the very *beginning* of the development of your project (see Chapter 1, *Development*). In fact, it should be considered an integral part of the development process. So often I see filmmakers go off and make their passion project with no consideration if there is even an audience or sales potential for it. That's fine if you only want a few people ultimately seeing your work, but I think most filmmakers want their work to be seen by as many people as possible. The "commercial" considerations don't have to drive the creative, but they must be

> *Recognize and tell the truth. The truth is the most attractive thing of all, but it requires skills and awareness.*
>
> —Thomas Leonard

considered in the context of what kind of success (i.e. distribution, sales, and audience) you are striving for.

Questions to contemplate for Marketing/Publicity/Audience Engagement:

- Where do you see your project screening? Film festivals? Theaters? Television? Streaming? Online? DVD? Free? Paid?
- Who is your audience? What demographic? What niche?
- How do you reach your audience? Physical materials? Online? Social media?
- What is the progression? Do you start with one format for distribution and then roll it out to others? If so, what is the order and how do you reach each different audience as you go?
- Who is creating and implementing the marketing and publicity? Is it all done by the filmmakers? Will professional publicists be hired? If so, when?
- What is the social media campaign and who is managing it?
- Who is creating the website for the project? When will it go online and how will it be updated?
- Will there be a social action campaign? If so, who is making the materials and who is paying for them?

Producer of Marketing and Distribution

There is a lot to think about, create, and plan. It's a full time job *in addition* to making the project so you have to figure out how all that work will be covered while producing the project. Consequently a new job position has been created with the title *Producer of Marketing and Distribution*. Promulgated by director/producer Jon Reiss (*www.JonReiss.com*), the PMD is "the person on a filmmaking team who takes charge of and directs the marketing and distribution process for that film to achieve the filmmaking team's goals. It is preferable for a PMD to start as early as possible in the filmmaking process." Below are the many different pieces of the puzzle to consider and create—with or without a PMD—as you make your project.

Social Media

Once it's clear that you will be producing a project, the probable first step in audience engagement will be setting up a Facebook page, Twitter account, Instagram account, or whatever other future social media sites and apps are most appropriate for your audience. I'll use the current sites/apps for the discussion here but with the understanding that technology evolves very quickly. There may be different names/forms in the future but the general ideas will be consistent.

Setting up a Facebook page is fast and easy and gives your project a place to engage with your audience through all the stages of producing—development, financing, filmmaking, post production and distribution. Updates can be easily added, along with screening dates, blog posts, photos, videos, website, crowdfunding and purchasing information, etc. You can decide how often to update the page as your project progresses. Adding Facebook Friends allows you to grow your audience before the first day of principal photography and take them along with you through the marketing and distribution phases.

Twitter is another social media tool that allows you to send out short updates to all Twitter followers so you continue to build audience engagement. Instagram allows you to post photos throughout the producing process as well. All of these are free and are excellent tools for publicity about your project.

Website

Depending on your project, creating a website may be your next step. Before setting up the website, you'll need to acquire a URL for the site—often people choose the title of the film followed by "the movie" or "the film." After registering your URL, you'll need to pay for a web hosting service and then set up your site. You can hire a web designer or do it yourself—there are many content management systems (CMS) that are very easy to use for people who don't know how to code. Do research online to decide what is the best solution for you.

Once your website is technically working, you'll need to design the elements. Here is a list of possible components:

1. Home page—film title, graphic, short synopsis, and general facts about the film. This is also the place to put any "laurels" from film festival screenings or awards.
2. Blog—the place to add informational updates as the film progresses. It's easy to embed photos and videos on the blog and it can be linked to your social media outlets as they are updated simultaneously when you post.
3. Press Kit—available for download for publicity purposes.
4. Trailer—a short trailer of your film.
5. Publicity photos—in a high-resolution (300 dpi) format that the press and others can use for articles and other publicity. Production stills should include lead cast members in the film, the director

working on set, and any other key personnel and features of the film you want to illustrate.

6. Schedule—an updated list of festival screenings, theatrical runs, broadcast dates, and DVD release dates in the coming months. Keep it current.

7. Awards list—an updated list of any awards the film has won.

8. Links—to press articles online, to your social media outlets tied to the film, crowdfunding campaigns and any other pertinent material.

Press Kit

A press kit is an essential building block in the marketing of your film. Some of the material created in the investment plan (see Chapter 1, *Development*) can be re-used or amended for the press kit now. The following elements make up a press kit:

1. Title Page—The first page should have the project's title, a strong image from the film, and the publicity contact info with email address, social media names, and cell phone number.

2. Log Line—see the *Development* chapter.

3. Synopsis—see the *Development* chapter.

4. Director's Bio & Statement—the director's biographical details and their inspiration, working philosophy, and vision for the project.

5. Cast Bios—the key cast's biographical information and filmographies.

6. Key Personnel Bios (producer, cinematographer, editor)—the key personnel biographical information and filmographies.

7. Press Clippings with Links—any good reviews or articles about the project with the URLs for quick online reading.

8. Complete Screen Credit List—the entire list of screen credits with proper spelling and titles—the press will refer to this list for accuracy.

9. Production Stills/Publicity Photos—in hi-resolution formats for press usage.

10. Director's Filmography—a list of the director's past projects including dates.

11. The press kit is usually posted on the website as a PDF document so it can't be changed or amended by anyone other than the production/publicity team.

Here is the *Sundae* press kit.

SUNDAE
A SHORT FILM BY SONYA GODDY

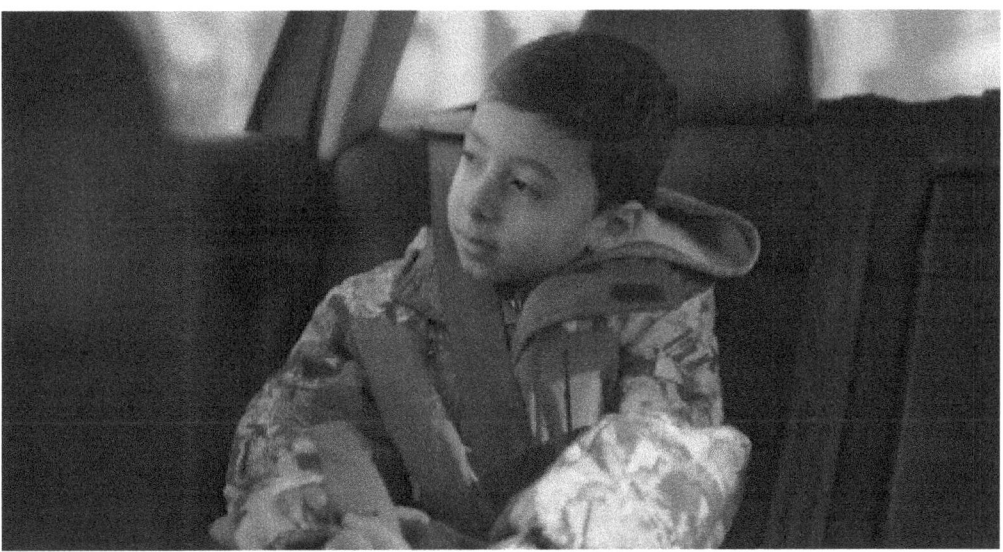

For press inquiries, please contact Sonya Goddy at www.sonyagoddy.com

SYNOPSIS

An irritated mother bribes her young son with ice cream in exchange for vital information.

CREDITS

Directed by
Sonya Goddy

Written by
Sonya Goddy

Starring
Julian Antonio de Leon
Finnerty Steeves

Produced by
Kristin Frost

Co-produced by
Birgit Gernböck

Cinematography by
Andrew Ellmaker

Film Editing by
Souliman Schelfout

Casting By
Judy Bowman

Production Management
Giovanni Ferrari

Assistant Director
Connor Gaffey

SELECTED AWARDS

Winner, Faculty Selects, Columbia University Film Festival 2015

Winner, Best Female Director Award, Columbia University Film Festival 2015

Official Selection, New York Film Festival 2015

Official Selection, Leeds International Film Festival 2015

Official Selection, Atlanta Film Festival 2016

SELECTED PRESS

"Sonya Goddy, a freshly minted Columbia MFA graduate, shows you how it's done. [Sundae]'s originality tops even Pixar's streamlined seven-minute animation short (Sanja's SuperTeam)… Goddy's on her way."

—Kurt Brokaw of Independent Magazine

(http://independent-magazine.org/2015/09/nyff-2015-critic-picks/)

"A seven-minute cherry-topped treat that packs a big punch and a sweet kicker… the biggest crowd pleaser of the Columbia University Film Festival, [with] the smallest budget."

—Paul Hond, Columbia Magazine

(http://magazine.columbia.edu/college-walk/fall-2015/producers-chair)

Sundae
(Sonya Goddy, 2015, USA, 7 min.)

Short subjects with a true conceptual twist are a rarity. Adding a coda ending that makes you rethink everything you've watched almost never happens. Sonya Goddy, a freshly minted Columbia MFA graduate, shows you how it's done.

We're behind the wheel cruising a residential neighborhood of old homes, with a mom (Finnerty Steeves) and her bright 5-year-old (Julian Antonio de Leon) looking for what the boy remembers as a large yellow house. Why? We don't know. But the distraught mother promises her son a sundae with all the fixin's if he recognizes the house.

A big yellow home pulls into view. The child signals that's the one. Mom turns off the ignition, marches up to the door and rings the bell. An attractive woman opens the door. Mom wallops the woman with the hardest punch she can throw. Then she hurries back to the car, takes out a large red brick and hurls it through the picture window. She and her son drive off—and discover a scene not too far away that instantly clarifies the woman's anger and rage.

The boy quietly spoons in his mammoth sundae. But then he tells mom something she (and we) never expected to hear—the coda closer. This all happens in a neat-as-a-pin seven minutes. Goddy's short has already won the Adrienne Shelly Foundation award for best female director. Its originality tops even Pixar's streamlined seven-minute animation short Sanjay's Super Team that probably cost a zillion times more. Goddy's on her way.

Sundae is part of **Shorts Program #4 ("New York")**.

FILMMAKER BIOS

SONYA GODDY was born in 1984 in Manhattan, was raised in Flatbush, Brooklyn and is a recent graduate of Columbia's MFA Film Program. Kurt Brokaw of Independent Magazine singled out her short film SUNDAE as one of the highlights of the 2015 New York Film Festival (link). In 2015, she received the Adrienne Shelly Award for Best Female Director and the Zaki Gordon Award for Excellence in Screenwriting. In addition to NYFF, her short films have played at Leeds International Film Festival, BAMCinemaFest, Woodstock Film Festival and Palm Springs Shortfest, and have been distributed by Shorts International. She also wrote and co-produced THE YOUNG HOUSEFLY starring Alex Karpovsky, about a housefly who falls in love with a suburban teenager, which was made for under $1,000 and nominated for a Student Academy Award.
Her first feature film, HOLY NEW YORK, is in pre-production and her second feature, BEFORE/DURING/AFTER, written by and starring SUNDAE star Finnerty Steeves, is slated to shoot in the fall.

KRISTIN FROST (PRODUCER) worked in development, PR and production at the Darden School of Business and the International Rescue Committee before pursuing her MFA in Creative Producing at Columbia University, where she was the recipient of the 2015 HBO Young Producers Development Award, the 2014 Katharina Otto-Bernstein Development Award, as well as the 2014 Sound Lounge Sound and Design Award.

MARKETING/PUBLICITY

BIRGIT "BITZ" GERNBOECK (CO-PRODUCER) is an international producer who had already worked on more than 30 television movies for German broadcasters when she moved to New York to pursue an MFA at Columbia University in Creative Producing. She also produced films in Italy, Austria, the UK, Spain, Tunisia and South Africa for the German production company U5 Filmproduktion. Recently, she production-managed the narrative feature *Doktorspiele* for 20th Century Fox Germany, and raised development funds for the feature documentary *Stair Cases* by award-winning writer/director Oliver Husain. While at Columbia she has been the recipient of several producing awards, and co- produced Sonya Goddy's award-winning short *Sundae*.

ANDREW ELLMAKER (DIRECTOR OF PHOTOGRAPHY) is a filmmaker and cinematographer born in Portland, Oregon. After studying film and painting at the School of the Museum of Fine Art, Boston, he showed video work in the Oregon Biennial and two short films at the SXSW Film Festival. He spent a few years in the commercial world directing web content for Wieden + Kennedy and producing NBA videos for Adidas before going back to school to get an MFA in Directing at Columbia. His short film *Total Freak* was awarded the 20th Century Fox Outstanding Achievement in Comedy in 2013. He has since shot over a dozen narrative short films.

Production Stills and Publicity Photos

Capturing good production stills and publicity photos is an essential part of a good press kit, yet most independent filmmakers don't invest the time and energy to acquire strong and useful images.

For production stills you'll need to have a good set photographer on your shoot for at least 1–2 days to get photos of the director, actors, and key personnel working on set. For example, there is the classic shot of the director pointing at something with the DP or other key department head looking on and nodding. This may seem trite, but how else can you capture an image of what a director *does* on set? Make sure to get this kind of photo and any others that exemplify people directing, acting, producing, and making the project.

Usually it's smart to have the still photographer on set on the days production is doing something that is visually compelling. If you have a car crash day or a fun special effects day, schedule the photographer on set to capture the exciting production values. Keep in mind that set photography is not as easy as it looks, so check references and look over the still photographers' portfolios before making the hire for your project.

Many directors I have worked with are rather shy and publicity adverse and don't like their picture being taken. As the producer, you'll need to figure out a way for them to feel comfortable with a still photographer on set for a short amount of time. Remember, this is one of the elements on the Deliverables list (see Chapter 15, *Post Production*) so you have to get some hi-res photos in order to complete your contractual obligations.

Regarding publicity photos of the project, people often plan to take "freeze frames" for the final master for these types of images. It usually works fine if you are shooting high enough resolution, but it's always best to have the still photographer take some shots during rehearsals from the same perspective as the shooting camera so you can use those photos without having to pull them from the project's digital master.

Crowdfunding

We discussed crowdfunding to help finance your project in Chapter 4, *Funding*, but sometimes it is used to raise funds for post production or marketing/publicity costs. Sometimes filmmakers will have enough money to shoot and edit their project, then apply to film festivals. Once they get accepted, they start a crowdfunding campaign to raise the money to master/finish their project and pay for travel and publicity costs.

As with all crowdfunding campaigns, it affords the filmmakers the opportunity to promote their project and increase audience awareness for their film. By linking your website and social media outlets to your crowdfunding page, you can get the word out about your project in another way.

IMDb.com

The **Internet Movie Database (www IMDb.com)** is the go-to website to look up credits for any film, television show, actor, filmmaker, and crew personnel over the last several decades. When your film meets the IMDb criteria you can create an entry for it. As the producer, make sure that whoever posts the names and titles does so accurately. It's a public record of your film's screen credits and you want it to be correct.

The database also compiles profiles for anyone who has at least one screen credit so it also serves as a kind of online résumé for anyone to see. It's important to confirm your credits are correct and up to date whenever a film you have worked on is added to the database. If you find your credit missing or an incorrect attribution for your name, contact the producers of the film and ask them to correct it. In the film industry it is common practice to look up people on IMDb to get some sense of a person's background before a meeting or an introduction. It's an indispensible tool.

Screeners

Screeners are copies of your final master that are sent out to people who want to see your film—press, sales agents, distributors, acquisitions people, etc. They are also required for any film festival or awards applications. Screeners need to be watermarked to prevent theft, illegal duplication, or use by someone who is not authorized to view it. They should never be used for public screenings—thus the importance of the watermark. **Watermarks** can be the name of your company on the lower part of the image, or a phrase like "Not for duplication." Watermarks can stay on the screen throughout the entire film or dissolve on and off the screen every three to five minutes. You decide how you want to do it, but make sure it is on every screener you send out.

Screener formats are either DVD or a password-protected digital file posted online. Digital files are the industry standard now and there are many websites that allow various layers of security and tracking. Some allow you to set it up so that the file is only available to the invited viewer (or it can be shared) for a certain amount of time (e.g., ten days or two months) and you are notified when the viewer watches it. Others allow you to change the password at anytime so you can control who sees the project. DVDs are still used for awards applications but this is changing too.

Piracy is a big problem in the film industry so use whatever new technology is available to protect your project. Once it is "out there" in the public domain you can't get it back.

Social Action Campaigns (SAC)

For certain documentaries and for narrative films that are tied closely to a specific societal topic, social action campaigns are a great way to drive awareness about your film and get it out to larger audiences that will appreciate its message. **Social Action Campaigns** usually incorporate several components—a social media strategy, educational materials, grassroots screenings, and partnership development. Your campaign plan will be dictated by the project itself, the topic, and the audience you want to reach.

Social media can be utilized to maximize awareness of the topic and/or a particular screening or broadcast date. It's always best to coordinate a social media campaign with the film's distributor(s) and/or partner organizations to maximize its impact and message.

Educational materials may be geared toward school curriculums, non-profit organizations, or a general public audience. Through research, the written and online materials can be honed, created, and distributed to empower awareness and effect social change.

Grassroots screenings are a great way to get your project seen by the communities interested in the content/message. Through your partnership organization research you'll know the groups and non-profit organizations interested in the project's topic and can contact them to schedule a screening. They may want to plan a Q&A/panel discussion afterwards as well. There are many event management websites that enable event coordination and a few that allow you to set up screenings at local film venues with a minimum requirement for the number of ticket purchasers.

Partnership development will be ongoing as you produce your project. Once the project is completed, those organizations and communities can leverage their communications formats to send out press releases, create blog posts, and use social media to get out the word to a larger audience that cares.

Some non-profit foundations provide grants to filmmakers to create and implement SACs around their projects' topics. If you receive a grant, it can pay for the research, outreach, and sometimes travel expenses to support a social action campaign.

Key Artwork

While you are making your project you'll be creating images that can be used for marketing. Now is the time to finalize how to present your film visually to audiences and distributors. You'll want to create a poster and images that will "brand" the project for audiences—in the online and physical worlds.

Depending on your resources you may hire a graphics person to do the work or you may pull images from your final master or from the still photographer's work. Look at other successful ad campaigns and analyze why they were effective. This image will be used over and over again on posters, postcards, in film festival guides, in advertisements, online ads, VOD menus, distribution catalogs, etc.

How to Hire a Publicist

With a plethora of film festivals, distribution outlets, and so much other media vying for an audience's attention, it's vital to work on marketing and publicity throughout the filmmaking process so you can support your project in the best possible way. Hiring a publicist may be a good choice for your project.

Publicists have long-standing relationships with press, magazines, news organizations, online outlets, and other places that are interested in the news about your film. They have email lists of all the people who write for print and online media and will send out press releases regarding your project. Publicists will determine what is newsworthy about your film and pitch story ideas for articles to try to get journalists and bloggers to write about your film.

Depending on your funds and marketing strategy, hiring a publicist for your film can be a good investment. If your film appeals to mainstream media then you'll want a publicist with those connections. If your film's audience is more orientated to online outlets and blogs, you'll want a publicist who is an expert in that media.

Track which films were well publicized in the independent or digital worlds over the last year. Find out who the publicist was and contact her to see if she would be interested in your project and what rates she charges. Local film organizations can be a good place to get referrals for publicists, as well.

RECAP

1. Marketing and publicity are vital to getting out information to the press and the public about your film when it is ready to premiere.

2. As soon as you know your project is going to move forward, create social media outlets and a website for it.

3. Marketing tools include a press kit, screeners, website, social media, blogs, and social action campaigns.

4. IMDb.com (International Movie Database) is used by the film industry as an online résumé for everyone who has ever had a screen credit on a film.

5. When creating and disseminating screeners, protect them with passwords and watermarks to deter piracy.

6. Hiring a publicist may be an option if you have the budget and it makes sense for your project.

CHAPTER 20
FILM FESTIVALS

THERE ARE FILM FESTIVALS all over the world, in countless cities and towns, throughout the year, for every genre, niche, and format. If you want to apply to film festivals, you'll need to do some research and figure out what festivals are the best fit for your project. Festivals are a great way to get your film seen by audiences, distributors, talent agencies, sales agents, and scouts for other film festivals. If you haven't sold your project yet, screening it at film festivals can be very helpful in making a sale—the film gets exposure, critical reviews, press, and has the potential to win awards.

If you already have sold your project to a distributor, broadcaster, or some other distribution format, look at your contracts to make sure you are allowed to screen it at festivals prior to the transmission or release of the project. Some contracts have a "hold back" period that prevents you from having any public screenings (including film festivals.) If your contract has such a stipulation, it doesn't stop you from asking for permission to screen at a film festival. Often it

Art first. All else will follow.

—*Jerry Saltz*

can be helpful to a broadcast premiere and the entity will be very supportive of film festival participation.

If you decide you want to apply to film festivals, there are thousands of them around the globe. It can be a bit overwhelming and expensive (most applications require an application fee), so it's important to do research on the various film festivals to figure out which ones are right for your project.

There are several clearinghouses for submission information about film festivals, including *www.withoutabox.com* and *www.filmfreeway.com*. These websites have in-depth databases you can search for festivals that fit your criteria—narrative features, web series, documentaries, experimental, horror, comedy, short films, music videos, etc. Through these kinds of websites you pay a fee to register your film online, upload your digital master and use the website to apply to film festivals. It saves tons of time and after registering your project, it allows you to apply to multiple film festivals with a couple of clicks.

Registering your project requires a lot of information—title, running time, short synopsis, aspect ratio, shooting format, genre, website, twitter, Facebook, key creative/cast names and credit lists, contact info, past screenings/awards, distribution info, filmographies, and press kit. Submission fees are determined by each film festival and there are usually several application deadlines—Earlybird, Regular, and Late. The earlier you send in the application, the less expensive the submission fee. Some festivals don't have entry fees but that happens more often in Europe than in the United States. When you register your project you can upload your digital master as well.

Fee Waivers and Screening Fees

Those film festival submission fees can really add up. Requesting fee waivers and screening fees is a way to mitigate some of the expense. Depending on your film and your past relationship with the festival, you can sometimes request a fee waiver to eliminate or discount the entry fee. You'll still need to submit an application, but you can put in a fee waiver code so you are not charged the fee. If you are a first-time filmmaker without a track record, chances are you won't be given a fee waiver. Fee waivers are usually given if your previous film played at that festival, if the festival programmer saw and liked your project at another festival, or if your film won a top award at another festival. If you are a student filmmaker, some film festivals will extend a fee waiver or discount if you ask nicely.

The screening fee is another little-known aspect of the film festival circuit. Some festivals pay screening fees to certain films that they program. After all, festivals sell tickets to screenings and it makes sense that filmmakers should share some of the income. It's a good idea to ask about screening fees when you receive an acceptance notification from the festival as each one has a different policy. Many festivals don't have a budget for screening fees but often can offer a travel stipend or hotel for one of the filmmakers.

Film Festival Strategy—A, B, C and Niche

With the proliferation of domestic and international film festivals there are more and more opportunities for your project to screen publicly. Just as there has been a rise in the number of festivals, there has been a tsunami of film production; getting into a top film festival is incredibly competitive.

Having a cogent festival submission strategy increases the chances for success for you and your project and keeps your submission fee budget to a minimum. Consider the following questions:

1. Think about your project *objectively*. What genre is it? Is there a specific target audience? Does it have well-known actors? Is it topical?

2. What kind of festival would be interested in your project? Is it similar in type to past films? If so, where did those projects screen?

3. What do you want to accomplish with your project? Fame, Fortune or Change the World?

4. Where do you want to have the world premiere for your film? U.S., International, Regional, Local?

5. Is Oscar eligibility important to you? (See below.)

6. Do you plan to travel and attend the festivals to network and meet filmmakers and programmers?

7. Do you want to attend workshops and seminars as part of the festival experience?

8. If you are trying to sell your project, do you need a market attached to the festival?

Now that you have answered the above questions, you can create a strategy based on two criteria. I call it **A, B, C Plus Niche**—it's not an exact science but it really helps to finalize a plan.

- **A, B, C**—refers to the level of the film festival itself. **A** are the top festivals around the world. **B** are the next level of festivals with strong reputations. **C** are good regional and local festivals that are not as well known but are good opportunities for your project. If you shot your project in that region or if you come from the area, it's a great way to show your film to the local audience.
- **A** festival examples would include Cannes, Sundance, Toronto, Berlin, Venice, New York, and Telluride.
- **B** festival examples would include a very wide swath (one could even give B+, B, and B- within this level)—San Sebastián, Woodstock, Los Angeles (LA), Hamptons, Savannah, SXSW, Rotterdam, Tribeca, Karlovy Vary, AFI, Palm Springs, Dubai, Busan, London, Nashville, Chicago, San Francisco, Austin, Mill Valley, etc.
- **C** festival examples would include Rhode Island, Portland, Brooklyn, Montclair, Long Beach, Woods Hole, etc.
- **Niche**—refers to what kind of project you've produced and what festivals fit that niche.
- Niche examples include Horror, Comedy, LGBTQ, Jewish, Sci-fi, Asian-American, African-American, Shorts, Documentary, Spiritual, Human Rights, Women, Web series, etc. Analyze your project and figure out what niches are a good fit based on the film's elements and themes.
- To create a good strategy for your project (and to avoid bankruptcy paying for all the application fees), pick a few festivals from each category and apply simultaneously. That way if you don't get into an A festival, you can have your film premiere at a B festival and start a festival tour. I've seen too many filmmakers who only apply to Sundance and when they don't get in, half the festival "year" is over and they need to start applying all over again. Don't waste time; apply to several different levels and niches at the same time.
- Festival programmers go to other festivals earlier in the year to scout for good material and often will invite favorite films to their festival (and give a fee waiver). So getting your project out there at festivals often helps it screen elsewhere.

Film Markets

Markets are where film buyers and film sellers (the filmmakers) meet to do the business of buying and selling and making deals. Cannes, Toronto, Berlin and LA have markets attached to their festivals and Sundance is where all the buyers go each January. If you are looking to sell your project, it's most advantageous to have your film play at one of these festivals where the distributors are going to buy projects.

Film Festival Premieres

As mentioned earlier, for feature films, where your project screens for the first time is considered its world premiere. It's a coveted event for a film festival to have your film's world premiere. (For shorts it is not as much of an issue.) It adds cachet to their festival and, depending on their selectivity criteria, it may be factored in your application. You can only have *one* world premiere for your film so it's really important to plan carefully. The descending order of domestic premiere designations are World premiere, North American premiere, U.S. premiere, and U.S. regional premiere. For international film festivals, it's based on geographical region (e.g., European, Middle Eastern, Asian, African) or a country premiere. These classifications matter for festivals, so keep track of your project's premiere status as it moves through the festival circuit.

So if your film is screened for the first time publicly at the Toronto International Film Festival and you are a U.S. filmmaker, that screening will be considered the World and North American premiere. If it next plays at the New York Film Festival, that screening will be considered the U.S. premiere. If it plays next at the Los Angeles Film Festival, it can be considered the West Coast premiere, and if it plays later at the Berlin Film Festival it will be considered its European premiere.

Festivals don't usually have the same rules about premieres for short films. Check to make sure, but most film festivals will take your short project even if it has premiered at other festivals.

Oscar Eligibility

Many filmmakers dream of winning an Academy Award. The competition is fierce and the odds of getting a nomination are akin to winning the lottery, but it can happen. The Academy of Motion Picture Arts and Sciences (AMPAS) has specific categories for eligibility: narrative feature films, live-action shorts, animated feature films, animated shorts, documentary features, and documentary shorts. Go to *www.oscars.org* to read about the specific rules and regulations for the eligibility requirements. For feature films, there are theatrical distribution requirements. For short films, there is a list of qualifying film festivals. If your film wins certain awards at one of the AMPAS-qualifying festivals, then your short film becomes eligible for a nomination in a live-action, animated, or documentary category.

The Student Academy Awards is a different awards program for students in domestic and international film schools. The awards are given in three categories—narrative, experimental, and documentary and the awards ceremony takes place in Los Angeles. Check out *www.oscars.org* for more information.

Other Awards

There are almost as many awards shows as there are film festivals. The Independent Spirit Awards (given out by Film Independent) and the Gotham Awards (given out by Independent Feature Project) are two of the best known for independent films, but there are many others that are geared toward specific genres and indie categories. Research online for awards that your film may be eligible for.

In or Out of Competition

Film festivals often have several "programs" within the festival. Some of the programs are considered "in competition" and some are deemed to be "out of competition." If your project is "in competition," it usually means it is eligible for prizes. Each festival decides which films are in competition; often the criteria is based on how "new" the film is to the festival circuit. After a film has played at many festivals, it is no longer eligible for "in competition" status or prizes. Other times, the festival is so large that only a small number of the films can be viewed by the jury and that limits how many films are eligible to be in competition. Check each festival's individual website to find out the specific application rules for each program and the competition requirements for your film.

Jury and Audience Awards

Most film festivals give out awards. They fall into two categories, 1) Jury prizes and 2) Audience awards. Jury prizes are usually decided by a panel of judges who watch all the films in competition at the festival. Often there are a few different panels that are devoted to a certain type of film, e.g., documentary, narrative features, short films. Audience awards are voted on by the audiences that attend the screenings. Utilizing a ballot system after each screening, the festival organizers tally the votes to determine the audience award winners.

Awards may or may not have cash or gifts attached. If you win an award, congrats! If you don't, no worries. But if you do, use it to your advantage—send out a press release, announce it on your website, and post it on social media. Also put notice of the award on your marketing materials by using the "laurels" logo from that particular festival.

What to Expect from a Film Festival

By screening and publicizing new films (with or without distribution), fostering film industry networking and introducing filmmakers to critics and tastemakers, festivals play an important role for independent projects. Meeting and connecting with film programmers is very helpful as well. Programmers often move from one festival to another over time. You may have met a programmer at a small festival, but by the time your next project is ready, they have moved on to a larger film festival and your network expands.

Festivals are often filled with panel discussions where industry professionals speak about current issues in the film business. Learning about cutting-edge technologies and meeting experts can be incredibly helpful, too.

Festivals want the filmmakers to be present for post-screening Q&A sessions so the audience can meet and discuss the film with the creators. Often festival organizers will offer roundtrip airfare and hotel accommodations for filmmakers. Usually the airfare/hotel is offered to the directors of the projects but, if they are not available, the producers or other key creatives on the film may be able to attend instead. Once your film is accepted, the festival's hospitality department will coordinate these details.

Getting a festival pass is also an important perk for the filmmaker. Usually your film will be offered at least one pass that allows access to all screenings and panel discussions. If more than one person from the film is attending you can request more passes and tickets to your screenings. Each festival has its own policies about passes and tickets. Take advantage of all that the film festivals and markets offer so you can maximize your time and expense money while you are there.

Posters, Postcards, and Photos

When your project is accepted at a film festival, you will be asked to send the festival organizers several things—the film master (in the highest-quality format that the venue can project), a press kit (see Chapter 19,

Marketing/Publicity), posters and/or postcards, digital still photos, and a personal photo for a festival ID badge.

Most festivals will request several posters for use during the festival. You'll need postcards to put out on the tables around the festival lounges and venues and hand out to publicize your project. Uploading your digital publicity images to a low-cost online printer will help keep costs down.

Technical Issues at Festivals

Getting your project's master digital file or digital cinema package (DCP) to and from the film festival is usually coordinated by the traffic department. They will contact you several weeks before your film is due to screen and ask for the tech specifications (i.e., screening format, aspect ratio, frames per second, audio format, running time) for your film. Getting that information back to them as soon as possible is important so you can confirm the tech specs for their projection system. Each festival is different and for international festivals it's even more important to make sure your master is compatible with their projectors. Frame rates could be different and you'll need extra time and money to get your master converted.

Tech Test

You've worked hard to make your project the best it can be, so you want to make sure it has the best technical presentation possible at every festival. To that end, request a tech test before it screens for the first time at a festival theater. A **tech test** is a screening of the first few minutes of your film by the projectionist right before the doors of the theater are opened to the public. This is a courtesy that most festivals extend to filmmakers who ask for it ahead of time and who can show up promptly at the theater. Check for the following: aspect ratio (is the frame cropped in any way?); audio volume (is it too loud, too low, or non-existent?); brightness (is it bright enough?); focus; contrast ratio; and frame-rate speed (is it running too fast or too slow?). You know your film best and within a few seconds you'll be able to tell if all the technical aspects are correct for the best possible viewing experience in that theater.

Before the screening of a feature film I had produced at a well-known international film festival, I asked to do a tech test. I was reassured that the projectionist had already done a tech test and everything was fine. I acquiesced and settled into my seat next to the director and director of photography (DP). The audience arrived, then the lights went down and the film started. The aspect ratio was completely wrong and the audio volume was too low! It was devastating because although we could get the projectionist to raise the volume, we couldn't change the aspect ratio unless we stopped the screening to correct it. So we watched the whole film that way! Make the effort to get a tech test done in the few minutes after one film finishes and your film starts—it can make all the difference.

RECAP

1. **Film festivals are a vital part of any release plan for an independent project.**

2. **Create a film festival strategy based on "A, B, C and Niche." Research which festivals are best for your project through online festival databases and application websites.**

3. **Decide where you'd like to have the world premiere for your film. Be mindful of how best to exploit the various regional premieres at different film festivals.**

4. **Go to *www.oscars.org* to research the rules for Academy Award eligibility.**

5. **Film markets are focused on bringing sales agents and distributors together in pursuit of film acquisitions.**

6. **If your film is "in competition" it is usually eligible for various jury awards and special prizes.**

7. **Coordinate travel/accommodations with the festival hospitality department and send the film master to the festival traffic department.**

8. **Request a tech test with the festival projectionist before your first screening to make sure your project will be properly projected.**

CHAPTER 21

DISTRIBUTION/ SALES

PRODUCING AND COMPLETING YOUR project is a tremendous accomplishment. But that is only the first half of the process. Selling your project and getting it distributed is, in some ways, *the* most important part of making the film. You need to pay back your investors and make sure your project is seen by as many people as possible. By providing a return on investment (ROI), hopefully you can go out and do it all again. If not, no matter how impressive and brilliant your film, it is not a sustainable business model.

There are more options for selling your project and getting it seen than ever before. But getting sales that pay you and your investors "enough" is a more complicated question. For this chapter I will outline the general principles and steps necessary to sell and distribute a project. Beyond that I will leave it up to you to keep up with the latest industry information to figure out how best to sell your project in the constantly changing technologies and business models.

Producers produce.

—*Ira Deutchman*

Sales Agents

Sales agents are representatives of your project in the marketplace. They have contacts and relationships with distribution entities and work to sell your film for you. Sales agents usually delineate between North American and international sales markets. Some agents cover world rights but it is common for them to concentrate on either domestic or international because they are very different markets with different companies and countries in each one. Agents also can leverage the other films they represent so that your project is included for consideration when they make a pitch to a company for distribution. If they have several films that distributors are interested in, it can help get them to watch your project for possible acquisition, as well.

Sales agents charge a fee based on a percentage of the sales they get for your film. In addition, there are often expenses that get charged to cover the costs of travel to film festivals and meetings, as well as overhead costs for their offices and support staffs. Negotiating a cap on expenses is wise so you don't lose revenue to lots of agent expenses. Make sure to read your contract carefully and consult with your lawyer before signing a sales agent agreement. Your lawyer will want to examine the representation time period and how long an agent can collect fees for deals that began during the time period but are concluded afterwards.

Finding a good sales agent when it's a low-budget production and/or you are starting out in your career can be a challenge. The best time to find one is when you have just gotten into a prominent film festival. Once the participating films are announced, sales agents may contact you to see your film and decide if they wish to represent it. If not, it's the best time for you to reach out to agents because your film was just accepted into that fest.

Check filmmaker references (at least two!) on any sales agent who offers to take on your film. Ask them why they want to rep it and have them outline a sales and distribution plan for your particular film. Does it sound right to you? How many other films do they plan to rep during that film festival? Will they give your film enough attention or will they have so many other films that they will be distracted? Do they have a reputation for sticking with their filmmakers even if the film does not sell right away? Make sure you ask questions and consider the answers you get before making your final decision.

Once you have a sales agent involved, they will partner with you to build your film festival and marketing strategy, as discussed in Chapter 19 (*Marketing/Publicity*) and Chapter 20 (*Film Festivals*). The sales agent will need marketing materials and screeners to send out to distribution companies for consideration. The sales agent will follow up and stay in contact with the companies to work toward selling the film. If you do not find a sales agent, this task will fall solely to you—it's a big job but essential so you can find a buyer for your film.

International Sales

International sales are usually done on a country-by-country or regional basis. An international sales agent would look to sell different countries like France, Japan, Mexico, or Australia separately, or sometimes the project will be sold by region such as the United Kingdom/Ireland or Asia. For international sales agreements, find out if you have to pay for translation and subtitling—it will add to your deliverables costs.

Theatrical/Television Sales

Each country or region will allow you the opportunity to sell the film's theatrical (shown in theaters) and television rights. Depending on the marketplace and who is interested in buying which rights, you may not sell all the rights to all the territories and formats for your particular project. Many projects may not warrant a theatrical release but will do well for television or digital sales.

Television has different markets and windows for licenses. In the United States there is network television (NBC, ABC, CBS and Fox), public television (PBS), subscriber cable (HBO, Showtime, Cinemax, etc.) and cable television (IFC, Sundance, Bravo, A&E, National Geographic, etc.). You can sell to one market for a certain period of time and then do another sale to another market after that license period expires.

DVD/VOD/Digital Sales

This is the area of the business that is constantly changing. By the time this book has been published there will probably be several new ways to obtain and watch content. Right now DVD, Video On Demand (VOD), and Digital are the general ways we can watch. Digital includes free online, subscription, streaming, mobile, and lots more. Each project will probably dictate where best to sell and offer your project for viewing.

Deliverables

As discussed in Chapter 15, (*Post Production*), deliverables are the materials that must be delivered to a buyer when you sell the project. The contract for each sale will dictate the deliverables list and you need to scrutinize that part of any contract before you sign, so you know whether you can afford to produce them all for the buyers. A deliverables list can be found in the *Post Production* chapter. Remember to obtain E&O insurance if required (see Chapter 10, *Insurance*).

Self Distribution

Your options for self distribution are voluminous. As discussed earlier, you can use online websites to book your project into cinemas directly. You can hire a booker to contact independent cinemas across the United States to put together your own theatrical run. I would recommend that you do your research to find out if it will be financially viable to self distribute your project theatrically.

Some filmmakers sell their projects and other merchandise through DVD/VOD/digital downloads from their own website. Add a Shopping Cart feature to your website and either ship the physical purchases yourself or pay for a fulfillment company to do it for you. Other online entities can provide secure ways to allow downloads from your site as well.

Contacting and selling your project to subscription services like Netflix, Amazon, Hulu, and iTunes is another way to get your project seen by audiences. More options will continue to be created and evolve as technology allows.

Pick of the Week/Contests

Another way to get your film noticed and seen are various crowdfunding and/or independent film sites. So many of them have "Project of the Week/Month" or other contests to drive people to click, watch, and vote for new and interesting projects. By featuring your project, lots of people can watch and learn about your project; the attention can be most helpful. If you win one of these contests there may be a prize; at the very least you can announce it and add it to your press materials.

Future Distribution Models

It's hard to predict where the future lies regarding sales and distribution for independent projects. With technological "disruption" and ever-changing ways to create, watch, and sell content, there's no way to know exactly where evolution will lead the film industry. But that's what keeps it interesting to be a producer—you need to stay engaged and informed. So keep up to date on where things are headed and how best to proceed for your project.

RECAP

1. **Look for a sales agent who really understands and believes in your project. Check out references and discuss strategy for your film before signing up with one.**

2. **Usually you'll have one sales agent for domestic and another for international sales.**

3. **There are ever-evolving ways and media outlets for distribution so keep up to date on the industry news and trends.**

4. **Self distribution is a possibility for your project. Research your options to determine if you have the time and resources to undertake self distribution.**

5. **What will be the future distribution models? Let me know when you know!**

CHAPTER 22
WHAT'S NEXT?

WHAT COMES NEXT IN the world of independent producing is anyone's guess. But what has happened and is happening now is that the "barriers" to producing films are lower than they have ever been. Many more people can get their hands on a camera, some lights, and put together a cast and crew without much money. And that's great.

But just having access to the means of production doesn't make for a good project or one that is well produced. And that is the reason I wrote this book. Film producing is a craft, passed down from producer to producer. You learn by doing it—day after day, year after year.

In the past, you had to work your way up through the ranks to get the opportunity to produce a film. But now access is not much of a problem. You can do it, but can you do it *well*? Film festivals are flooded with applications all year long. But how many of those films are actually any good? Finding a brilliant script, hiring a talented director, and producing well is still the only way to make a great project. Though the means of production have changed, how to achieve

There is no libretto. We need wit and courage to make our way while our way is making us.

—*Tom Stoppard*, The Coast of Utopia

those goals hasn't changed. It's still a tremendous challenge, especially when you don't have all the resources you require.

Please use this book and the website *www.ProducerToProducer.com* to help you produce all your projects well. Enjoy the journey and have a great adventure on each and every one!

INDEX

A

The Academy of Motion Picture Arts and Sciences (AMPAS), 365
Acts of God, 218
Automated dialogue replacement (ADR), 310, 323
  looping, 324–325
AICP (Association of Independent Commercial Producers) awards, 385
American Federation of Television and Radio Artists (AFTRA), 111. *See also* SAG-AFTRA
American University's Center for Social Media, 202, 203, 344
Anaxagoras, Dave, 17
  advice of log lines, 17–18
  Animals and animal handlers, 274–275
Appearance release form, 152, 206
Archive materials, 78, 180, 181, 298, 341–346
  archive and research, 341–342
  archive libraries, 343
  archive researcher, 342
  archive usage and negotiation, 344–345
  cease and desist, 345–346
  fair use, 344
  license paperwork, 345
  national archives, 343–344
  steps to acquire and use, 342
  video and stills, 51
Art department returns, 278–279
Aspect ratio, 303
Assistant Director (AD), 52–53
  portrait of, 251–252
  safety responsibilities of, 269
Association of Film Commissioners International, 158, 180
Attaching an actor, 122–124
Attorney, 335, 344, 345, 346
Audio, 320–327
  adding sound effects, 324

automated dialogue replacement (ADR), 310, 323, 324–325
audio mix, 310–311
audio post production, 323
best sound on set, 321
building audio tracks/sound design, 323–324
Dolby Digital™, DTS™, or THX™, 326
Foley work, 306, 310, 323, 324
layback, 312, 326
music tracks, laying, 325
post production, 92–93
room tone, 322–323
sound editing, 310
sound mixing, 325–326
sound recording during principal photography, 73, 320–321
tech scouts, 321–322
wild sound, 323
Audio mix, 310–311
Audio tracks/sound design, building, 323–324
Audition/casting schedule, 124–125
Auto certificates, 221
Auto insurance, 213
Avid systems, 308

B

Background actors, 54, 126, 160
Best light transfer, 313
Best sound on set, 321
Binding Insurance policies, 219
Bit depth, 304
Blanket music rights agreement, 336
Blanket TV agreements, 336
Blanks, 282
Blogs, 4, 48, 115, 127, 138, 349, 358, 359, 360
Bomber, 127, 182, 333, 385
Brick, Richard, 262
Budget
  actualization, 105, 263, 288–289
  analysis, 298

locking, 104–105, 263
template, 290–297
Budgeting, 70–105
    breakdown, 66–67, 72–74
    cash flow, 103–104
    cast, 72–73
    catering/food costs, 73
    creating the estimated budget, 70–71
    creative fees, 90–91
    crew positions, 72, 73
    days to scout, 72
    days to shoot, 72
    detailed line items, 77–78
    equipment, 73
    equipment rental expenses, 88–89
    estimated, 19, 45, 53, 55, 74, 77, 263
    everything but the kitchen sink, 71
    film festivals, 74
    film production cost summary (*Sundae*), 94–102
    film stock, videotape stock and digital media, 89
    fringes, 77
    geography of, 75
    hair/makeup costs, 54, 55, 79, 85–86
    Included In proposal, 21, 28
    location expenses, 83–85
    locations, 73
    marketing and publicity, 74
    media/storage, 89
    miscellaneous, 74, 90
    music, 74
    overview, 69–70
    padding and contingency, 105
    post production, 73, 92–94
    pre-production/scouting expenses, 82–83
    props/art/picture vehicles, 73
    props/wardrobe/SFX, 85
    set construction labor expenses, 87–88
    set construction materials expenses, 88
    shooting ratio, 73, 90
    sound recording, 73
    spreadsheet mechanics, 74–75
    studio rental and expenses, 86
    sync sound, 73
    talent expenses, 91–92
    tax Incentives/credits, 106
    tax resale certificates 105–106
    top sheet, 75–76
    travel and transportation costs, 73
    working, 104–105
    See also Labor costs
Budgeting software, 71–72
    producer to producer budget template, 105–102
Burn In time code (BITC), 341

C

Call sheet, 136, 172, 271, 299
Callbacks, 126
Camera cars (process trailers), 279–280
Camera department expendables, 167
Camera sensor and dynamic range, 304
Camera test, 305
Cash flow schedule, 103
Cast contracts, 205, 298
Casting, 120–130
    attaching talent, 122–124
    auditions/casting sessions, 124–125
    background actors, 54, 126, 160
    breakdown sheet, 124
    casting director, hiring, 120–121
    extras, 126–127
    headshot, 124
    pay-or-play deal, 123
    schedule and backups, 127
    union paperwork, 127–130Casting sessions. *See* Audition/casting schedule
Cast insurance coverage, 201, 214, 268–269
Cease and desist, 337, 346–347
Certificate issuance, 220–221
Chain of command, 272–273
Clearance and Copyright, Michael Donaldson, 4
Clearing the rights, 329
Codec (coder-decoder), 303
Clones, 93
Collision damage waiver (CDW) fee, 82, 83
Color correct, 298, 305, 307, 312, 314, 326
    best light, 313
    digital intermediate (DI), 311–312

INDEX

film-to-digital, 313–314
one light or unsupervised, 313
supervised, 313
Color grading, 311–312
Color sampling, 304–305
Commercial general liability insurance, 185, 211
Community involvement, 113
Company moves, 64, 241, 249, 273–274
Comparison films, 19–20
documentary format, 20
narrative format, 19–20
Completion bond/guaranty, 147, 217–218
Confidentiality agreement 197
Confirm, 196
Consideration, 201
Contingency, 105
Co-op and condo boards, 186
Coots, J. Fred, 328–329
Copyright, 4–6
exclusive or non-exclusive, 5
law, 4, 202–203, 335, 337, 345
legal rights holder, 5, 337
own rights in perpetuity, 5
time duration for rights, 5
type of rights, 5
See also Rights
Cotter, Paul, 333
Cover set, 65, 239
Craft service, 73, 84–85, 103, 135, 160, 165, 171, 257, 258, 273
supplies list, 166
Cranes, 281
Creative fees, 90–91
Crew, hiring, 191–192
checking references, 195–196
crew positions, 191–192
finding talent, 193
hiring criteria, 193–194
most favored nation, 197
on hold/confirm or book/release, 196–197
paperwork, 197–198
salary negotiation, 197
watching demo reels, 194
Crew deal memo, 135, 158, 299
Crowdfunding, 117–118, 356–357

D

Dailies, 261
Daily production report, 260
Day-out-of-days schedule, 246–248
Deal memo, 197, 268
Dean, Carole, 115
Deductibles, 211
Deferred payment deals, 110–111
Deliverables, 50, 312, 276, 314–316, 373
Dennin, Sheila Curran, 385
Development, 1–51
checklist, 50–51
creating a proposal, 19–21
creating a pitch, 45–46
deliverables, 50
distribution plan, 47–48
documentary proposal example, 35–44
feedback on the script, 15
finding the Idea, 1–2
IMDb.com, 45
Interview with Benjamin Odell, 6–14
learning to say no, 2
log line, 16–18
marketing/publicity campaigns, 48
narrative proposal example, 22–34
presales, 48–49
producing a trailer, 46–47
rights of acquisition of script, 4–6
sales agents, 49
screenplay creation and revision, 6
screenwriting software, 15
script doctors, 16
studying scripts, 3
wrap up, 50
Writer's Guild of America (WGA), 16
Digital Imaging technician (DIT), 305
Digital intermediate (DI), 311–312
Digital sales, 372
Disability benefits law (DBL), 210
Disability insurance, 212–213
Distribution plan, 4, 20, 47–48, 371
Distribution/sales, 370–374
deliverables, 373
DVD/VOD/Digital sales, 372
future distribution models, 374
international sales, 372
pick of the week/contests, 373

sales agents, 49, 100–101, 347, 357, 361, 370–372
self distribution, 373
theatrical/television sales, 372
Documentary film proposal, 19–21
example, 35–44
Dolby/DTS licenses, 93, 311, 316, 326
Dolby/DTS-enabled theaters, 326
Domestic cable television network, 215. *See also* U.S. cable television rights
Donaldson, Michael, *Clearance and Copyright*, 4
Donations, 111–113
Dress code, 271
Drones, 280–281
DVD
rights, 109, 201
sales, 48, 372

E
Edge numbers, 314
Edit decision list (EDL), 306, 314
Editorial notes, 316–317
Egri, Lajos, 9
Element sheet creation, 225
Employer's liability coverage, 212, 215
Enemy of the production (EOP), 262–263
Equipment, 276–279
checking out, 277
damage control, 276–277
returns, 278–279
security against theft, 277–278
walkie-talkies, 278
Equipment rental
business, 149, 158
certificates, 220
expenses, 87–88, 103, 157, 263
Insurance coverage for, 222
Equity financing, 110
Equity investors, 110
Errors & omission (E&O) insurance, 215, 276, 336, 345
Estimated budget, creating, 70–71
spreadsheet mechanics, 74–75
E-Team, 35–44
Extra expense insurance coverage, 214
Extras/background actors, 54, 126, 160

F
Facebook, 348–349

Fair use, 202–203, 344
Family bereavement insurance coverage, 214
Faulty stock, camera, & processing insurance coverage, 213
FCP (Final Cut Pro), 308
Feature-length project, 47, 94, 128
Fee waivers and screening fees, 362–363
Field, Syd, 9
Film festivals, 361–369
fee waivers and screening fees, 362–363
film markets, 364–365
in or out of competition, 366
jury and audience awards, 366–367
Oscar eligibility, 365–366
other awards, 366
posters, postcards, and photos, 367–368
premieres, 365
strategy, 363–364
tech test, 368–369
technical issues at festivals, 368
what to expect, 367
Film festival rights, 5–6, 330
Filmmaking process
picking a format, 51, 70, 73, 302–305
Film markets, 364–365
Film production
green practices, 165
key crew positions to consider, 191–192
Film profit ROI reports, 370
Final checklist before deciding to produce the film, 50–51
Final Cut Pro (FCP), 308
Final Draft (screenplay software), 72
First day of principal photography
producer's to do list for the first day, 256–259
First position, 218
Fiscal sponsorship, 111–113
Foley work, 306, 310, 323, 324
Force majeure, 218
Foreign general liability, 216
Foreign package policy, 216
Foreign television rights, 49, 109
Foreign Workers' compensation, 216

INDEX

Foundation Center, 116
Frame rate, 303
Frame size, 302–303, 308
Fringes, 77–78
Funding, 108, 132–133
    community Involvement, 113
    creative labs, 116
    credit cards, 118–119
    crowdfunding, 117–118, 356–357
    deferred payment deals, 110–111
    donations and discounts, 111–115
    equity investors, 110
    find a mentor or executive producer, 116
    fiscal sponsorship, 111–113
    fundraising trailers, 116
    grants, 115–116
    in-kind donations, 112
    presales, 108–109
    sales agents, 109–110
    union signatory film agreements, 111
Fundraising trailers, 116
Future technology rights, 6

G

General liability insurance certificate, 185, 211
Gillespie, Haven, 328
Global events, 285
Green rooms, 155
Grip and lighting department expendables, 167
Gross production costs, 211–212

H

Hair/makeup costs, 54, 55, 79, 85–86
Headshot, 124
Health advisories, 285
Helicopters, 280
High definition frame size, 302, 308
Hiring
    casting director, 120–121
    personnel, 269–270
    publicist, 348, 359–360
    See also Casting; Crew, hiring
Hold/confirmation protocol, 156
Homeowner associations, 186

I

Idiot check, 189
IMDB.com, 45,121, 136, 357, 360

Independent Spirit Awards, 366
In-kind donations, 112
Instagram, 349
Insurance, 201, 210–221, 299
    Acts of God, 218
    audits, 221
    auto, 213
    binding policies, 219
    brokers, 219
    cast, 201, 214, 268–269
    certificate, 220–221
    claims, 221–222
    common policies, 211–217
    completion bond/guaranty, 217–218
    disability, 212–213
    employer's liability, 212, 215
    errors and omissions, 215, 276, 336, 345
    extra expense, 214
    family bereavement, 214
    faulty stock, camera and processing, 213
    force majeure, 219
    foreign package policy, 216
    general liability, 185, 211
    important things to know, 222
    need of insurance, 210–211, 222–223
    negative film production, 213
    other specialty coverage, 216–217
    production, 82, 83, 90, 134, 144, 159, 185, 210–211, 218–219, 222, 268, 271, 272, 275, 278, 280–284
    props, sets and wardrobe, 214
    for prop weapons, 283
    purchasing, 218–219
    statutory, 212
    third-party property damage, 214
    umbrella, 210–211, 214–215, 220
    union travel accident, 215–216
    watercraft, 217
    weather, 217
    worker's compensation, 211–212, 216
Investment particulars, narrative/documentary format, 20
Investor
    points, 110
    agreement, 204–205

J
Jibs, 281
Jury and audience awards, 366–367

K
Key artwork, 359–360
Keykode, 313–314

L
Labor costs, 72–73, 77–81
    labor rates, 79
    set construction, 87–88
Labor rules for minors, 126
Lackawanna Blues, 3
Lavaliere microphones, 322
Layback, 312, 326
Lee, Spike, 10
Legal, 199–209
    liability, 200–202
    list of agreements, 204–206
    never sign anything without proper legal advice, 207–208
    rights, 200
    See also Attorney; Copyright; Rights
Legal agreement lists, 204–206
    development agreement list, 204–205
    pre-production agreement list, 205
    production agreement list, 205–206
Legal concepts, 202–203
    fair use, 202–203
    most favored nation, 79–80, 197, 203
    pari passu, 110, 203
Legal corporate entities, 207
    corporation, 207
    limited liability company (LLC), 207
    limited partnership (LP), 207
Legal document, breakdown, 201–202
    contact information, 202
    fees, 201–202
    liability, 202
    limitations, 202
    parties, 201
    recourse, 202
    right to enter into agreement, 202
    rights, 201
    services, 201
    term, 201
Liability, 185
License paperwork, 345
License request for music, 331

Life rights, 5
Limited liability company (LLC), 207
Limited partnership (LP), 207
Location, 178–190
    back-up, 184
    certificate, 220
    co-ops and condos, 186
    create lists, 178–179
    day after the location shoot, 189
    green set protocols, 188–189
    idiot check, 189
    Insurance certificate, 185
    local film commissions checking for leads, 180–181
    location photo folders, 180
    negotiating the deal, 183–184
    paperwork, 184
    permits, 186–187
    police/fire/sheriff's departments, 187
    release form, 185
    run through with owner, 188
    scouting, 179, 181
    shoot-day protocol, 187–188
    tax incentive programs, 190
    tech scout, 162, 187
Location decisions, finalizing, 182–183
    location analysis, 270
    location permissions, 270–271
    location protection 271
    weather monitoring, 272
Location expenses, 83–85
Location release form, 185
Location scout, alternatives to hiring, 178–179
Locking the budget, 104–105, 263
Lock picture, 306, 309, 311, 331, 3342
Log line, 16
    creation, 17–18
Logo release form, 206
Look up table (LUT), 304
Looping, 323, 324
Loss run, 219

M
Makeup. *See* Hair/makeup costs
Man on Wire, 4, 53, 138, 157, 225
Marketing/publicity, 48, 347–360
    blogs, 349, 358, 359
    crowdfunding, 117–118, 356–357

INDEX

hire a publicist, 348, 359–360
IMDb.com, 357
key artwork, 359–360
press kit, 350–355
Producer of Marketing and Distribution (PMD), 348
production stills and publicity photos, 356
screeners, 357–358
social action campaigns (SAC), 358–359
social media, 348–349
website, 349–350
Marketing Insurance, 219
Marsh, James, 384
Master recording license, 328
McKee, Robert, 9
McKeel, John, 45
Meal penalties, 250
Media
   online, 48
   See also Social media
Minors, labor rules for, 126
Most favored nation (MFN), 334
Movie Magic Budgeting software, 72
Movie Magic Scheduling software, 72
Music, 328–339
   blanket TV agreements, 336
   cease and desist, 337
   copyright holder findings, 337
   creating soundtrack, 323–326
   E&O insurance, 336
   fair use, 335–336
   international rights, 329–330
   libraries and royalty free, 339
   license agreement, 206
   license request, 331
   most favored nation (MFN), 334
   music cue sheet, 336
   negotiating for rights, 333
   obtaining music rights, 328–329
   original composition, 338–339
   out of copyright or public domain, 335
   rights clearance person/company, 337–338
   rights needed, 329–330
   rights request letter format, 332
   supervisors, 339

Music cue sheet, 336
Music libraries and royalty free music, 339
Music rights
   clearance person/company, 337–338
   International, 329–330
   negotiating for, 333

N

Narrative film proposal, 19–21
   example—*Square Up and Send It*, 22–34
National archives, 343–344
National archives and records administration (NARA), 343–344
Negative film/videotape production insurance coverage, 213
1971, 53
Non-disclosure agreement (NDA), 197, 204
Non-union actors, 206, 216
North American sales rate, 371

O

Odell, Benjamin, 6
   interview, 6–14
One-light transfer, 313
On hold, 196
Online social networking. *See* Social media
Open call, 127
Option agreement, 204
Oscar eligibility, 365–366
Overhead cameras, 281
Overtime, 250

P

Padding and contingency, 105
Page counts, 62
Pari passu, 110, 203
Pay-or-play deal, 123
Permit certificate, 220
Personnel
   hiring, 269–270
   See also Casting; Crew, hiring
Petit, Philippe, *To Reach the Clouds*, 4
Petty cash, 289
   reconciling, 155
Picture vehicles, 55
Pitch creating, 45–46
Pixels, 302

Points, producer/Investor, 110
Portal to portal, 250
Posters, postcards, and photos, 359, 367–368
Post production, 73, 92–94, 301–319
    acquisition format, 308
    audio, 310, 312
    camera test, 305
    deliverables, 314–314
    editorial notes, 316–317
    film negative and match back, 313–314
    high definition and standard definition video, 308
    picking a format, 302–305
    post finishing, 312–313
    preplanning, 307
    put together the team, 306–307
    sample deliverables list, 315
    security for, 276–279
    supervisor, 313
    tech specs sheet, 305–306
    telecine/color correct/transfer, 313–314
    workflow, 301–302
    workflows example, 308–312
    work-in-progress screenings, 317–318
Pre-Production, 131
    Sundae production book, 139–142
Pre-Production countdown
    1 week before principal photography, 135, 165–170
    2 weeks before principal photography,135, 160–165
    3 weeks before principal photography, 135, 158–160
    4 weeks before principal photography, 134–135, 151–157
    5 weeks before principal photography, 134, 148–151
    6 weeks before principal photography, 134, 145–148
    7 weeks before principal photography, 134, 144–145
    8 weeks before principal photography, 133–134, 143–144
    12-9 weeks before principal photography, 133, 136–139
    final week countdown, 135–136, 170–172
Premium, 211
Pre-Production/scouting expenses, 82–83
Presales, 48–49, 108–109
Press kit, 350
    example, 351–355
Pre-visualization, 170, 254, 265
Principal photography
    first day of, 256–259
    sound recording during, 320–321
Process trailers, 279–280
Producer/director agreement, 205
Producer's guild of America (PGA), 165, 189
Production, 254–266
    budget actualization, 263
    camera test, 305
    cigars and fine chocolates, 264
    director's through–line, 265
    first day of principal photography, 256–259
    producer's to do list for the first day, 256–259
    high definition and standard definition video, 302–303
    night before your first day of principal photography, 254–256
    second day disasters, 261–262
    wrap checklist, 260–261
Production insurance, 82, 83, 90, 134, 144, 159, 185, 210–211, 218–219, 222, 268, 271, 272, 275, 278, 280–284
Production stills, 356
Production triangle, 131–132
Project information
    documentary format, 19
    narrative format, 19
Proposal creating, 19–21
    background/history of the project, 21
    biographies, 21
    budget and/or schedule, 21
    comparison films, 19–20
    documentary film proposal, example, 35–44
    investment particulars, 20
    legal disclaimer, 21
    narrative film proposal example, 22–34

INDEX

project information, 19
synopsis, 20–21
Props/wardrobe/SFX
    expenses, 85, 150, 153
    insurance coverage, 214
Prop weapons, 282–283
Protagonist, 17
ProTools, 310
Public domain (PD) music, 335
Publicist hiring, 348, 359–360
Publicity, 347. *See also* Marketing/publicity
Publicity photos, 356
Pull down/pull up, 303
Purchase orders, 289
Pyrotechnics, 283–284

R

Railroad tracks, 284
RAW files, 303–304
Reiss, Jon, 348
Release, 196
Remarketing, 219
Rewriting (revision process), 6
Rights, 4
    clearing, 329
    DVD, 109, 201
    exclusive/non-exclusive, 5
    film festival, 5–6
    foreign television, 49, 109
    future technology, 6
    Life, 5
    theatrical, 49, 110–111, 201, 206, 329, 345
    U.S. cable television. 48, 49, 109, 215, 329. 372
    worldwide, 5
    See also Copyright; Music; Music rights
Room tone, 322–323
Royalty free music, 339
Rush, George, 199, 204, 207

S

Safety, 267–285
    animals and animal handlers, 274–275
    equipment monitoring and protection, 276–279
    global safety Issues, 284–285
    location permissions and planning, 270–272
    on-set precautions and protocols, 272–275
    post-production security, 276
    preparing for safety in pre-production, 268–270
    pyrotechnics, 283–284
    safety for all, 267–268
    safety protocols for equipment and special conditions, 279–284
    speaking up, 275
Safety kits, 272
Safety meeting, 273
SAG (screen actors' guild), 111, 127
    safety hotline, 275
SAG-AFTRA, 72, 76, 94, 103, 111, 119, 127–129
    bond/escrow, 129, 134, 147
    contracts, 150, 151, 250, 275, 281, 298
    deferred payment contracts, 148
    union paperwork, 130–131, 133, 134, 143
SAG Indie, 111, 128
Sales agents, 49, 100–101, 347, 357, 361, 370–372
Scheduling, 224–253
    company move, 64, 249, 273, 274
    creating the shooting schedule, 224–225
    day-out-of-days schedule, 248
    each shoot day, 249
    element sheet creation, 225
    feed your crew every 6 hours, 249–251
    locking, 252
    meal penalties, 250
    meal time, 250
    overtime, 250
    portrait of an assistant director, 251
    principles, 239–242
    sample breakdown sheet, 226–238
    sample shooting stripboard, 245
    sample stripboard, 243
    script breakdown, 225
    shoot days, 249
    steps, 242
    stripboard, 242
    stripboard creation, 245

studio zone, 250
travel time, 250–251
turnaround time, 250
Screener, 341, 357–358
Screenwriting process
  advice of Benjamin Odell, 10–11
  getting feedback on the script, 15–16
  learning, 3–4
  table read or staged reading, 15
Screenwriting software, 15, 72
Script breakdown, 52–53
  action, 54
  analysis for *Sundae*, 64–66
  animals, 55
  breakdown details, 54–55
  breakdown for *Sundae* script, 63–64
  cast, 54, 62, 66
  day vs. night shooting, 65
  extras/background actors, 54, 62
  filling in breakdown sheet, 62–63
  hair/makeup, 54
  Int/ext and day/night, 62
  location, 54, 62, 64–65
  nuts and bolts, 53–54
  page count, 54, 62
  pages per day, 64
  props, 55, 62
  script title, 65
  shoot days, 77, 80–81
  stunts, 55, 62
  Sundae script, 56–61
  using the breakdown to adjust your script, 66–67
  vehicles, 55
  weather, 65
Script doctors, 16
Script supervisor, 81, 167, 240, 261, 309
Second day disasters, 261–262
Second unit photography, 256
Security and Exchange Commission (SEC), 20, 21, 110, 204
Seivers, Zach, 320
Selects, 313
Self distribution, 373
Set construction labor expenses, 86–87
Set construction materials expenses, 87
Shooting out an actor, 240
Shooting ratio, 73, 90

Sides, 125
Signatory, 128
SMPTE (Society of Motion Picture and Television Engineers), 314
Snyder, Blake, *Save the Cat!*, 9
Social media, 138, 348–349, 358
Software
  audio mixing, 310
  budgeting, 71–72
  scheduling, 72
  screenwriting, 15, 72
Sound effects, adding, 306, 309, 310, 324
Sound mixing, 325–326
Sound recording, during principal photography, 320–321
Sound recordist/production mixer, 321
Special effects (SFX), 53, 225, 240, 241
  expenses, 85
Specialty insurance coverage, 216–217
Spotting, 325
Square Up and Send It, 22–34
Staged reading, 15
Start paperwork, 197–198
Statutory Insurance, 212
Stone, Shelby, 3
Storyboards, 133, 136–137
Stripboard schedule, 242
Studio rental and expenses, 150, 156, 294
Studio zone, 250
Stunts, 55, 62, 281–283
Sundae
  breakdown analysis, 64–66
  breakdown sheet, 226–238
  budget analysis, 66, 298
  call sheets, 173–176
  cast availability, 66
  cast day-out-of-days for, 247–248
  cast list, 142
  chronological schedule, 243
  company move, 64
  crew list, 131–141
  day vs. night shooting, 65
  digital Intermediate, 102, 297
  director/creative fees, 100, 295
  editorial, 102, 297
  equipment & related expenses, 100, 295
  estimated budget, 94–102

INDEX

film production cost summary, 290–297
5-page screenplay, 56–61
locations, 64–65
location travel expenses, 98, 293
media/storage expenses, 100, 295
miscellaneous costs, 100, 102, 295, 297
music, 102, 297
pages per day, 64
post production expenses, 102, 297
post production sound, 102, 297
pre-production & wrap expenses, 98, 293
pre-production & wrap labor, 96, 291
press kit, 351–355
production book, 138–142
props related expenses, 98, 293
script analysis, 64–66
script breakdown, 52–55
set construction labor, 99, 294
set construction materials, 99, 294
shooting labor, 97, 292
shooting schedule analysis, 243–244
shooting stripboard, 245
stripboard, 243
studio rental expenses, 99, 294
talent & related expenses,101, 296
talent & related labor, 101, 296
titling/graphics/animation, 102, 297
weather contingency, 79
Supervised transfer, 313
Synchronization (sync) license, 328

T

Table read or staged reading, 15
Taft Hartley waiver, 128
Taft-Hartley Labor Act of 1947, 128
Talent fees, 91, 101, 296
Tax forms, 197–198
Tax incentives/credits, 106, 190
Tax resale certificates, 105–106
Tech scouts, 160–162, 187
Tech test, 368–369
Telecine, 89, 313
The Team, 385
The Winning Pitch, 45–46
Theatrical rights (domestic and foreign), 49, 110–111, 201, 206, 329, 345

Third-party property damage insurance coverage, 214
THX, 326
Time code, 314
Torte Bluma, 53, 181
Total running time (TRT), 90
Trailers (for cast and crew), 148, 169, 179, 183, 273
  process, 279–280
Trailer (film)
  fundraising, 116, 118
  producing, 46–47
  on website, 349
Transcoding, 303
Transfer, 312–314
  best light, 313
  edge numbers, 314
  film-to-digital, 73, 89, 313
  keykode, 314
  one light or unsupervised, 313
  supervised, 313
  time code, 314
Travel time, 250–251
Turnaround time, 250, 273–274
TV speakers, 325–326
Twitter, 349

U

Ultra high definition (UHD), 303
Umbrella Insurance, 210–211, 214–215, 220
Union contracts—crew and cast, 205
Union signatory film agreements, 111, 127–129
Union stewards, 273
Union travel accident insurance, 215–216
Unmanned Aerial Vehicles (UAVs) 280–281
Unsupervised transfer, 313
U.S. cable television rights, 48, 49, 109, 215, 329, 372

V

Vehicle identification number (VIN), 213
Vendor relationships, 149
Video on demand (VOD), 372
Volunteer lawyers for the arts (VLA), 208

W

Walkie-talkies, 278
Walking meal, 259

Wardrobe/costume, 85, 134, 150, 153, 167
Warranty, 215
Watercraft insurance, 217
Watermarks, 357–358
Weapons, 282–283
Weather contingency, 65
Weather insurance, 217
Weather monitoring, 272
Website, for marketing and publicity, 138, 349–350
    awards list, 350
    blogs, 138, 349, 358, 359
    home page, 349
    links, 350
    press kit, 349
    publicity photos, 349–350
    schedule, 350
    trailer, 349
Wild sound, 323
Wisconsin Death Trip, documentary, 2, 151, 181, 385
Workers' compensation insurance, 211–212, 216
Workflow, 301–302
    example, 308–312
Workflow test, 305
Working budget, 104
Work-In-program screenings, 317–318
Wrap, 258, 287
    actualized budget, 288–289
    budget analysis, 298
    checklist, 260–261
    deposit checks and credit card authorizations, 288
    film production cost summary, 290–297
    props related expenses, 288
    lost/missing/damaged, 288
    paperwork, 298–299
    party, 299
    rental return, 288
    wrapping out, some guidelines, 287–288
Wrap checklist, 260–261
Writer's contract, 204
Writers Guild of America (WGA), 16, 204
www.ProducerToProducer.com, 15, 53, 71, 72, 107, 112, 137, 152, 158, 190, 199, 218, 219, 240, 288, 289, 336, 343, 376

ABOUT THE AUTHOR

MAUREEN A. RYAN is a producer based in New York concentrating on narrative and documentary feature films. She is coproducer of James Marsh's *Man on Wire*, a documentary about Philippe Petit, the high wire artists who stunned the world when he walked between the World Trade Center towers in 1974. It won the 2009 Academy Award for Best Documentary and the 2009 BAFTA Award for Best British Film. Other awards include the Sundance Jury Prize and Audience Award for World Cinema documentary, the Critics Choice Award, the IDA Award, the National Board of Review, the NY Film Critics Award, the PGA Award and the L.A. Film Critics Award. Another documentary directed by Marsh and coproduced by Ryan, *Project NIM*, premiered at the 2011 Sundance Film Festival and won Best Director of World Cinema Documentary and was shortlisted for the Academy Award for Best Documentary that year. It screened theatrically in the United States and United Kingdom and premiered on HBO and the BBC.

Ryan is the production advisor on the first season of the Netflix series *Making a Murderer* by Moira Demos and Laura Ricciardi. She is co-executive producer of the television pilot titled *Stanistan* for USA Network/Universal Cable Production that filmed in Santa Fe, NM. She is the executive producer on *The Penny Black*, a nonfiction episodic series with a pilot episode already produced. She is also the re-creations producer for Johanna Hamilton's new feature documentary *1971*, which premiered at the 2014 Tribeca Film Festival and screened theatrically and on PBS. It won the Cinema Eye Spotlight Award and the IDA-ABC Video Source Award.

Her other re-creations credit is for Alex Gibney's feature documentary *Mea Maxima Culpa: Silence in the House of God*. The film had a U.S. theatrical run, screened on HBO, won the Peabody Award, the BFI

Grierson Award at the London Film Festival, and was shortlisted for the Academy Award for Best Documentary.

She is also a producer of the independent narrative film *Bomber* which premiered at the SXSW Film Festival, has won numerous film festival awards, and is distributed by Film Movement in the United States and Distribuzione Indipendente in Italy. Written, directed, and produced by Paul Cotter, it was shot in Brighton, UK, and Bad Zwischenahn, Germany. She produced a short film *Red Flag* that was written and directed by Sheila Curran Dennin. The film won awards at the Palm Springs International Shorts Fest, the Woods Hole Film Festival and the Taos Shortz Film Festival.

Ryan's other producing credits include *The Gates, Grey Gardens: From East Hampton to Broadway, The Team, The King, Torte Bluma, Last Hand Standing, Matchbox Circus Train,* and *Wisconsin Death Trip*. Additional awards include a Peabody award, three AICP awards, a Billboard award, a Freddie, a CMA award, an ACM award, 11 Addys, 5 Tellys, and the Paramount Studio Fellowship in Producing.

Ryan is the Chair and Associate Professor at Columbia University's Film Program. She holds an MFA (Film) from Columbia University's School of the Arts and a BA (Economics) from Boston College. Ryan has taught film seminars in various U.S. cities and internationally in Toronto, Canada; Amman, Jordan; Beijing, China; Brussels, Belgium; and Kinshasa, Congo (on a Fulbright grant). She is also the author of *Film & Video Budgets, 6th Edition*. The first edition of *Producer to Producer* has been translated into Chinese and Japanese. The companion website for this book is at *www.ProducerToProducer.com*.

For downloadable production templates
or to get in touch with Maureen Ryan, please go to
www.ProducerToProducer.com

For more resources, go to
www.mwp.com and click *Resources*

MICHAEL WIESE PRODUCTIONS

I N A DARK TIME, a light bringer came along, leading the curious and the frustrated to clarity and empowerment. It took the well-guarded secrets out of the hands of the few and made them available to all. It spread a spirit of openness and creative freedom, and built a storehouse of knowledge dedicated to the betterment of the arts.

The essence of Michael Wiese Productions (MWP) is empowering people who have the burning desire to express themselves creatively. We help them realize their dreams by putting the tools in their hands. We demystify the sometimes secretive worlds of screenwriting, directing, acting, producing, film financing, and other media crafts.

By doing so, we hope to bring forth a realization of 'conscious media,' which we define as being positively charged, emphasizing hope, and affirming positive values like trust, cooperation, self-empowerment, freedom, and love. Grounded in the deep roots of myth, it aims to be healing both for those who make the art and those who encounter it. It hopes to be transformative for people, opening doors to new possibilities and pulling back veils to reveal hidden worlds.

MWP has built a storehouse of knowledge unequaled in the world, for no other publisher has so many titles on the media arts. Please visit www.mwp.com, where you will find many free resources and a 25% discount on our books. Sign up and become part of the wider creative community!

MICHAEL WIESE, Co-Publisher
GERALDINE OVERTON, Co-Publisher

www.ingramcontent.com/pod-product-compliance
Lightning Source LLC
Chambersburg PA
CBHW081113160426
42814CB00035B/304